高校英语选修课系列教材

Translate

实用文体
翻译教程

主　编	宋红波　朱明炬
副主编	吴万伟　殷　燕　耿殿磊
编　者 （按姓氏笔画排序）	方庆华　吕　鸣　李金云　李敏慧　杨　锐 陈　英　陈佳媚　陈　涛　官德华　姚　刚

内容简介

本教程以文体学、翻译学相关理论为指导，系统分析科技文体、旅游文体、经贸文体、法律文体、新闻文体等常见的十种实用文体的英汉语言特点，通过大量的翻译实例，详细剖析各类文体的翻译原则、翻译方法和翻译技巧，旨在切实提高学生的实用文体翻译能力。本教程服务于高校的实用英语翻译教学，可作为非英语专业学生英汉互译的课程教材。

版权所有，侵权必究。举报：010-62782989，beiqinquan@tup.tsinghua.edu.cn。

图书在版编目（CIP）数据

实用文体翻译教程 / 宋红波，朱明炬主编.—北京：清华大学出版社，2016（2023.9重印）
（高校英语选修课系列教材）
ISBN 978-7-302-42434-5

Ⅰ. ①实… Ⅱ. ①宋… ②朱… Ⅲ. ①英语–翻译–高等学校–教材
Ⅳ. ①H315.9

中国版本图书馆CIP数据核字（2016）第306752号

责任编辑：曹诗悦
封面设计：平　原
责任校对：王凤芝
责任印制：宋　林

出版发行：清华大学出版社
网　　址：http://www.tup.com.cn，http://www.wqbook.com
地　　址：北京清华大学学研大厦A座　　邮　编：100084
社 总 机：010-83470000　　邮　购：010-62786544
投稿与读者服务：010-62776969，c-service@tup.tsinghua.edu.cn
质量反馈：010-62772015，zhiliang@tup.tsinghua.edu.cn

印 装 者：三河市龙大印装有限公司
经　　销：全国新华书店
开　　本：185mm×260mm　　印　张：23.25　　字　数：481千字
版　　次：2016年8月第1版　　印　次：2023年9月第9次印刷
定　　价：88.00元

产品编号：063537-05

前言

要做好翻译，两方面的知识通常必不可少：一是源语和目的语在语言、文化方面有哪些异同，翻译时如何处理；二是源语和目的语中都有哪些文体，各具有什么特点及如何翻译。

一般的大学英语教学主要教授"通用英语"（General English），关注语言知识的传授，同时介绍一些英语国家文化知识，对各类文体及文体翻译关注甚少。随着大学生英语入学水平的不断提高，仅仅教授通用英语已无法满足学生的学习需要。特别是，学生毕业后会接触各种类型的文体，没有相应的文体与翻译知识，要做好这些不同文体的翻译，简直不可想象。因此，很多高校开设了"文体与翻译""实用文体翻译"之类的拓展课程。

为了满足"实用文体翻译"等大学英语拓展课程的教学需要，我们这些奋战在大学英语教学第一线的高校教师合作编著了本教程。教程涵盖了包括科技文体、旅游文体、经贸文体、法律文体、新闻文体等在内的十种常见文体，从最基础的理论介绍入手，通过大量的实例，详细讲解这些文体的语言特征、翻译原则、翻译方法和翻译技巧。通过本教程的学习，学生能够基本具备各类实用文体翻译的能力。此外，在翻译实践过程中，很多学生都会遇到专有名词的翻译和出国留学文书的翻译，我们以附录形式专门讨论。

本教程的主要特点有以下三个方面。

一是教程涉及的文体多样，几乎覆盖了常见的非文学文体。考虑到对于实用文体的分类，学界还没有形成共识（甚至如何对文体进行分类，学界都有分歧），因此教程不为所谓的"科学分类"所囿，而是从学习者的现实需要出发，尽量将其日常学习、工作中经常会遇到的文体集于一书，内容非常实用。

二是教程的实践性很强。教程并没有过多地纠缠理论，而是主要通过实例来传授各类文体的翻译方法和技巧，引导学生通过模仿来学习，针对性强。

三是教程中的译例来源广泛。既有编著者自己亲手翻译的译文，也有来自各类书、刊、网站、数据库的译例，避免了译例来源单一带来的局限与不足。

本教程可供一学期的教学使用，总计需36~40学时。根据学生的英语水平及他们对各类文体的熟悉程度，每章教学可安排2~6学时。教师教学时应以学生为中心。例如在讲解文体的语言特点时，可让学生先分析、总结；在讲解译例时，可让学生先翻译，再针对译文展开讨论，教师适当点评。

本教程是集体心血的结晶，编著者的分工如下：朱明炬（第一章）、殷燕（第二章）、方庆华（第三章）、吕鸣（第四章）、杨锐（第五章）、陈英（第六章）、陈佳媚（第七章）、姚刚（第八章）、陈涛（第九章）、李金云（第十章）、李敏慧（第十一章）、吴万伟和官德华（附录）。吴万伟、殷燕、耿殿磊分别做了部分章节的审稿工作。全书的统稿、通审、校对等工作，由宋红波和朱明炬完成。

作为编者，我们深知一本教程的质量对于教学成功与否至关重要。因此，在编著过程中，我们尽心尽力，尽量让教程切合实际教学的需要。但由于编者水平有限，如果本教程使用者在教学过程中发现了任何问题，请一定与我们联系，以便我们改进。我们在此表示由衷的感谢！

编者

2016 年 1 月

目 录

前　言 i

第一章　概论 1
　　第一节　文体的概念 1
　　第二节　文体与翻译 5
　　第三节　实用文体的概念、分类和特点 13
　　第四节　实用文体的翻译 26

第二章　科技文体的翻译 38
　　第一节　科技文体的特点 38
　　第二节　科技文体的翻译原则和技巧 42
　　第三节　科技论文摘要的翻译 54

第三章　旅游文体的翻译 62
　　第一节　旅游文体的特点 62
　　第二节　旅游文体翻译中的常见问题 73
　　第三节　旅游文体的翻译原则 82
　　第四节　旅游文体的翻译技巧 86

第四章　经贸文体的翻译 ... 97

第一节　经贸文体的特点 ... 97

第二节　经贸文体的翻译原则和方法 ... 101

第三节　商务函电和单证单据的翻译 ... 107

第五章　法律文体的翻译 ... 116

第一节　法律语言与法律翻译 ... 116

第二节　法律文体的词汇特征及其翻译 ... 122

第三节　法律文体的句法特征及其翻译 ... 132

第四节　常见司法文书的翻译 ... 137

第六章　新闻文体的翻译 ... 150

第一节　新闻文体概论及其特点 ... 150

第二节　新闻文体的翻译原则和方法 ... 156

第七章　广告文体的翻译 ... 179

第一节　广告的功能和构成 ... 179

第二节　广告文体的语言特点及其翻译 ... 180

第三节　广告文体中的修辞与翻译 ... 185

第四节　广告文体的翻译方法 ... 188

第八章　会议文书的翻译 ... 196

第一节　会议文书的语言特点和翻译原则 ... 196

第二节　会议会务文书的翻译 ... 197

第三节　会议礼仪文书的翻译 ... 205

第四节　会议事务文书的翻译 ... 212

第五节　会议话语文书的翻译 ... 222

第九章　礼仪文书的翻译 228

第一节　礼仪文书的文体特点及翻译技巧 228
第二节　邀请函的翻译 231
第三节　请柬的翻译 236
第四节　名片的翻译 241
第五节　丧吊类文体的翻译 245

第十章　启事文书的翻译 255

第一节　启事文书的文体特征 255
第二节　启事文书的翻译原则与注意事项 258
第三节　常用启事文书的翻译 261

第十一章　公示语的翻译 282

第一节　公示语的定义和类型 282
第二节　公示语的语言特点 284
第三节　公示语翻译中存在的问题 288
第四节　公示语的翻译原则及方法 291
第五节　常用公示语规范翻译实例 294

附　　录 308

专有名词的翻译 308
出国留学文书翻译 328

参考答案 345

第一章 概论

"文体"一词,古已有之。汉贾谊的《新书·道术》中有"动有文体谓之礼,反礼为滥"等语;南朝钟嵘的《诗品》卷也有"宋澂士陶潜诗,其源出于应璩,又协左思风力,文体省净,殆无长语"等文字。但我们常说的"文体"到底指的是什么呢?为什么译者要关注文体呢?

第一节 文体的概念

"文体"一词由"文"和"体"两个汉字构成。根据许慎的《说文解字》:"'文',错画也。象交文。凡文之属皆从文。"吴东平认为:"'文'就是花纹之'纹'的古字"[1],因为汉字是古人对所观察的事物进行艺术简化演变而来的,而文字的笔画有横有竖,有交叉,有平行,就像纵横交错的花纹,所以"纹"被引申指"文字"的"文",后来又由"文字"引申为"文章""文献"。至于"体"字,本为"軆"[2],最初指人、动物的全身或身体的一部分,后来引申为物质存在的状态或形状。"文""体"两字合二为一,即指文章的类别、体裁、体制或风格。

文章像人。人有高矮、胖瘦、黑白、长幼之别,文章也有类别、体裁、体制、风格之异,表现出来就是文体上的不同。请看下面两段英文:

例1 The first snow came. How beautiful it was, falling so silently all day long, all night long, on the mountains, on the meadows, on the roofs of the living, on the graves of the dead! All white save the river, that marked its course by a winding black line across the landscape; and the leafless trees, that against the leaden sky now revealed more fully the wonderful beauty and intricacies of their branches. What silence, too, came with the snow, and what seclusion! Every sound was muffled, every noise changed to something soft and musical. No more tramping hoofs, no more rattling wheels! Only the chiming of sleigh-bells, beating as swift and merrily as the hearts of children.

---

1 吴东平.2006.汉字的故事.北京:新世界出版社.
2 古代"体"和"軆"是两个字:"体"是"劣",又指粗笨;"身体"的"体"本字是"軆",形声,从骨,今简化为"体"。

例 2 Solid form of water that crystallizes in the atmosphere and falls to the Earth, covering about 23 percent of the Earth's surface either permanently or temporarily. Snowflakes are formed by crystals of ice that generally have a hexagonal pattern. Snow cover has a significant effect on climate and on plant, animal, and human life. By increasing the reflection of solar radiation and interfering with the conduction of heat from the ground, it induces a cold climate. The low heat conduction protects small plants from the effects of the lowest winter temperatures; on the other hand, late disappearance of snow in the spring delays the growth of plants.

这两段英文的主题都是"雪"，但两段文字在用词、句式、修辞等方面都有很大的不同。

例 1 选自美国著名浪漫主义诗人亨利·沃兹沃斯·朗费罗（Henry Wadsworth Longfellow，1807–1882）的作品 *Kavanagh*。朗费罗的作品带有一种特别的音乐特质，虽然这里的选段不是诗歌，但读者分明可以感受到一种诗歌的美：初雪降临，一片静谧，白茫茫的大地上，唯有蜿蜒的河流，划出一道曲曲弯弯的黑线，雪橇的铃铛，正奏着和谐的乐声。为了描绘初雪降临的美，朗费罗在选词上狠下了一番功夫。在段落的前半部分，作者有意识地使用了不少单音节的词语，如 first、came、how、was、so、all、day、long、night、on、roofs、graves、dead 等，以描摹雪花的轻盈飞舞，避免多音节词读来产生的笨重的感觉。在后半部分，使用了 rattle、chime 这样的拟声词，与前面的静谧形成对比，更让人感觉到天地的安静。在句式上，陈述句和感叹句、长句和短句的交替使用，不仅描绘了景色，也传达了情感，还给行文增添了音乐般的节奏。特别值得称道的是，部分长句内逗号的超常规使用（如第二句竟有 6 个逗号），体现了作者的匠心：一个个小句，宛若一片片雪花，缓缓地从空中飘落，让人放松，让人沉醉。在修辞上，排比、明喻等手段的使用，则为文学作品中常见，为段落增色不少。

例 2 选自《简明不列颠百科全书》条目 Snow 下的内容。与前一段不同，这段英文无论是在选词还是在句式上，都质朴得多，没有使用任何表达感情的形容词，即便有也都是纯描述性的。所有的句子都是陈述句，也没有使用任何修辞手段。为了准确传递信息，编者还使用了部分科技语，如 crystallize、hexagonal pattern、solar radiation、conduction of heat 等，以严谨定义 snow 的含义。

文章与文章之间之所以会有文体上的区别，是因为不同的文章写作目的不同，面向的读者不同，反映的社会生活也不同，客观上要求文章的作者使用不同的语言。这一点很容易理解。写给父母的信和写给女朋友的信，当然得使用不同的语言；同样地，撰写科技论文和起草法律文书，也要使用不同的表达。另外，即使面向的是同样背景的读者，反映的是同样的社会生活，不同的作者因为个性不同，生活背景不同，受到的语言训练不同，也会使用不同的语言。这一点在作家身上表现得尤其突出，反映出来的就是作家的写作风格。

比如，同样都是描写长江，杜甫的《登高》这样写道："风急天高猿啸哀，渚清沙白鸟飞回。无边落木萧萧下，不尽长江滚滚来。万里悲秋常作客，百年多病独登台。艰难苦恨繁霜鬓，潦倒新停浊酒杯。"写景的同时充分抒发了自己的感伤情怀，传达了韶光易逝、壮志难酬的感怆，诗句沉郁悲凉，反映了人生的苦况。与之相比，苏轼在《念奴娇·赤壁怀古》中用的却是这样的词："大江东去，浪淘尽，千古风流人物。故垒西边，人道是，三国周郎赤壁。乱石穿空，惊涛拍岸，卷起千堆雪。江山如画，一时多少豪杰……"气象高远，意境开阔，格调豪壮，与杜甫的诗歌风格迥异。

语言学研究发现，语言有不同的变体（varieties）。总的说来，可以依语言的使用者和使用场合或领域的不同将语言变体进行归类。按语言的使用者进行分类，语言可分为不同的方言（dialect），一般包括地域方言（regional dialect）、时间方言（temporal dialect）和社会方言（social dialect）三种。而语言的使用场合或领域（即语域）有三个变量：语场（field）、语旨（tenor）和语式（mode）。

语场指的是话语涉及的主题内容。语场有两大类：专业性（technical）和非专业性（non-technical）。在专业性语场，人们使用的是各行各业的专用语言，如医学英语（Medical English）、计算机英语（Computer English）、工商管理英语（Business Administration English）、体育英语（Sports English）、旅游英语（Tourist English）等。非专业性语言主要指人们日常交际使用的语言，包括社交俗套话（social formulas）等。

语旨是指话语参与者之间的关系，涉及双方的地位（status）、接触（contact）和感情（affective involvement）等。语旨决定了交际双方所使用语言的正式程度、口气、态度等。

语式指的是话语交际的媒介，主要分口语形式与书面形式。口语是语言交际最主要的、最自然的媒介。与口语相比，书面语更加注意准确性、简洁性、雅致性。此外，口语可以借助重读、节奏、语调、音速等表达手段，书面语只能依靠传统的正字法，这就意味着作者在表达意义时必须考虑正字法系统。[3]

方言和语域理论为我们分析和研究文体提供了一个有价值的视角：赵本山的小品之所以广受欢迎，原因之一就是大量使用了东北方言中的元素，这些元素让亿万观众领略到了原汁原味的东北乡土气息；科技文体和法律文体之所以有很大不同，是因为两种文体使用的语场不同，前者关注的是科技信息，后者涉及的是法律法规；写给父母的信和写给女朋友的信需要使用不同的语言，是因为语旨有异；而正式文体和非正式文体的主要区别，就在于前者更多地使用书面语中常用的表达方式，后者则更多地使用口语中常用的表达方式。

除方言和语域理论外，语言的功能也是我们理解文体的一把钥匙。正如秦秀白所言，"社会交际的需要是文体存在的社会基础，语言成分在功能上的分化是文体存在的物质基础。"[4]

3　桂诗春.1988.应用语言学.长沙：湖南教育出版社.

4　秦秀白.1986.文体学概论.长沙：湖南教育出版社.

文体不同，其功能也会有所不同。比如科技文体，其主要功能是传递信息；而广告文体，其主要功能是劝说诱导。不同的功能，当然需要不一样的语言手段来实现。这就是为什么科技文体大多语言平实质朴，而广告语言则丰富多彩，极尽修饰煽情之能事。

英文中的 style 翻译成汉语，既可以译成"文体"，也可以译成"风格"。刘世生、朱瑞清认为："style 所含的内容有三层：①文体；②语域；③风格。文体指说话或写作的格调，它随时变化，由非正式到十分正式，看具体情景、对象、地点、语题等因素而定。语域指一个特定群体所用的特殊语言变体，这群体或者有共同的职业（如医生、律师），或者有共同的兴趣（如集邮者、足球爱好者），因而有其特定的语言变体。风格指特有的说话或写作方式，如莎士比亚的风格、弥尔顿的风格、18 世纪的风格、意识流风格，等等。"[5] 其实，在汉语中，不仅说话或写作的格调我们可以称之为文体——因此有所谓的"正式文体""非正式文体"，与语域有关的语言变体，我们也可以用"文体"来命名，如文学文体、新闻文体、广告文体等。

关于什么是 style，西方学者、作家曾给出了不少的定义，比如：The style is the man himself (George-Louis Leclerc de Buffon); Proper words in proper places, make the true definition of style (Jonathan Swift); To me style is just the outside of content, and content the inside of style, like the outside and the inside of the human body (Jean-Luc Godard); 等等。在这些定义中，穆卡诺夫斯基（Jan Mukařovský, 1891–1975）的"前景化说"（style as foregrounding）、穆卡诺夫斯基和斯皮泽（Leo Spitzer, 1887–1960）的"变异说"（style as deviation）以及恩奎斯特（Nils Erik Enkvist, 1925–2009）的"选择说"（style as the choice between alternative expressions）颇具启发意义。"前景化说"和"变异说"甚至构成了当代文体学研究的基础，前者提出文体即特定的语言成分在其他部分或背景的衬托下得到突出或者强调，后者将文体视为变异，即语言在常规的基础上产生的意义及形式的变化。

"前景化说"和"变异说"在本质上是一致的。"前景化说"中的"背景"就是"变异说"中的"语言常规"，"前景化说"中"得到突出或者强调的语言成分"就是"变异说"中的"意义及形式的变化"，而这些都是写作者有目的选择的结果。比如，我们常说英语科技文体中被动语态用得比较多，是英语科技文体的特色之一。显然，所谓"用得比较多"是相对而言的，可能是相对于文学英语而言，也可以是相对于日常英语而言，这里的文学英语或日常英语便构成了"语言常规"，也正是"前景化说"中的"背景"。

文体并不是建在空中的楼阁，一篇文章的文体特点归根结底表现在格式、词语（包括词语的发音）、标点、句子、修辞手段、篇章手段等的选择和使用上，因此对文体的分析，可以以方言和语域理论以及功能理论为指导，从上述这些方面进行。

5　刘世生、朱瑞清. 2006. 文体学概论. 北京：北京大学出版社.

第二节
文体与翻译

美国著名翻译家、翻译理论家尤金·奈达（Eugene A. Nida，1914–2011）在其与查尔斯·泰伯（Charles R. Taber，1928–2007）合著的《翻译的理论与实践》（*The Theory and Practice of Translation*）一书中给翻译下了这样的定义："翻译就是在译语中用最接近的、自然的对等语再现源语中的信息，这种对等首先是语义上的，其次还应是文体上的。（Translating consists in reproducing in the receptor language the closest natural equivalent of the source-language message, first in terms of meaning and secondly in terms of style.）"[6]

无独有偶，我国著名翻译家、翻译理论家刘重德（1914–2008）对文体也十分重视。早在1979年，他就提出了"信、达、切"翻译三原则，他指出："翻译工作者若想把自己的翻译做到尽善尽美，除掉要求能够保全原文意义与译文通顺易懂之外，还必须在切合原文风格和人物形象上狠下功夫。"[7]切合原文风格，事实上就是要求在译文中再现原文的文体特征。1992年，他又在"海峡两岸外国文学翻译研讨会"的发言中重申了"信、达、切"三原则，他说："参考……中外两家意见，取其精华，并结合个人翻译的体会，拟把翻译原则修订为'信、达、切'三字：信——信于内容；达——达如其分；切——切合风格。"

优秀的译文都充分再现了原文的文体特点。在这方面，王佐良（1916–1995）翻译的培根《论读书》可谓典范。请看培根的英语原文和王佐良的汉语译文。

例1

Of Studies

By Francis Bacon

Studies serve for delight, for ornament, and for ability. Their chief use for delight is in privateness and retiring; for ornament, is in discourse; and for ability, is in the judgement and disposition of business. For expert men can execute, and perhaps judge of particulars, one by one; but the general counsels, and the plots and marshalling of affairs, come best from those that are learned. To spend too much time in studies is sloth; to use them too much for ornament is affectation; to make judgement wholly by their rules is the humour of a scholar. They perfect nature, and are perfected by experience: for natural abilities are like natural plants, that need pruning by study; and studies themselves do give forth directions too much at large, except they be bounded

---

[6] Nida, Eugene A. & Taber, Charles R. 2004. *The Theory and Practice of Translation*. 上海：上海外语教育出版社.
[7] 刘重德. 1979. 试论翻译的原则. 湖南师院学报（哲学社会科学版），（1）：114–119.

in by experience. Crafty men contemn studies, simple men admire them, and wise men use them; for they teach not their own use; but that is a wisdom without them, and above them, won by observation. Read not to contradict and confute; nor to believe and take for granted; nor to find talk and discourse; but to weigh and consider. Some books are to be tasted, others to be swallowed, and some few to be chewed and digested; that is, some books are to be read only in parts; others to be read, but not curiously; and some few to be read wholly, and with diligence and attention. Some books also may be read by deputy, and extracts made of them by others; but that would be only in the less important arguments, and the meaner sort of books; else distilled books are like common distilled waters, flashy things.

Reading maketh a full man; conference a ready man; and writing an exact man. And therefore, if a man write little, he had need have a great memory; if he confer little, he had need have a present wit; and if he read little, he had need have much cunning, to seem to know that he doth not. Histories make men wise; poets witty; the mathematics subtle; natural philosophy deep; moral grave; logic and rhetoric able to contend. *Abeunt studia in mores*. Nay, there is no stond or impediment in the wit, but may be wrought out by fit studies: like as diseases of the body may have appropriate exercises. Bowling is good for the stone and reins; shooting for the lungs and breast; gentle walking for the stomach; riding for the head; and the like. So if a man's wit be wandering, let him study the mathematics; for in demonstrations, if his wit be called away never so little, he must begin again. If his wit be not apt to distinguish or find differences, let him study the schoolmen; for they are *cymini sectores*. If he be not apt to beat over matters, and to call up one thing to prove and illustrate another, let him study the lawyers' cases. So every defect of the mind may have a special receipt.

论 读 书

读书足以怡情，足以傅彩，足以长才。其怡情也，最见于独处幽居之时；其傅彩也，最见于高谈阔论之中；其长才也，最见于处世判事之际。练达之士虽能分别处理细事或一一判别枝节，然纵观统筹，全局策划，则舍好学深思者莫属。读书费时过多易惰，文采藻饰太盛则矫，全凭条文断事乃学究故态。读书补天然之不足，经验又补读书之不足，盖天生才干犹如自然花草，读书然后知如何修剪移接；而书中所示，如不以经验范之，则又大而无当。有一技之长者鄙读书，无知者羡读书，唯明智之士用读书，然书并不以用处告人，用书之智不在书中，而在书外，全凭观察得之。读书时不可存心诘难作者，不可尽信书上所言，亦不可只为寻章摘句，而应推敲细思。书有可浅尝者，有可吞食者，少数则须咀嚼消化。换言之，有只须读其部分者，有只须大体涉猎者，少数则须全读，读时须全神贯注，孜孜不倦。书亦可请人代读，取其所作摘要，但只限题材较次或价值不高者，否则书经提炼犹如水经蒸馏,淡而无味矣。

　　读书使人充实,讨论使人机智,笔记使人准确。因此不常做笔记者须记忆特强,不常讨论者须天生聪颖,不常读书者须欺世有术,始能无知而显有知。读史使人明智,读诗使人灵秀,数学使人周密,科学使人深刻,伦理学使人庄重,逻辑修辞之学使人善辩:凡有所学,皆成性格。人之才智但有滞碍,无不可读适当之书使之顺畅,一如身体百病,皆可借相宜之运动除之。滚球利睾肾,射箭利胸肺,漫步利肠胃,骑术利头脑,诸如此类。如智力不集中,可令读数学,盖演题须全神贯注,稍有分散即须重演;如不能辨异,可令读经院哲学,盖是辈皆吹毛求疵之人;如不善求同,不善以一物阐证另一物,可令读律师之案卷。如此头脑中凡有缺陷,皆有特药可医。

(王佐良 译)

培根的原文初次发表于 1597 年,语言文字简古、典雅。为了传达原文的文体风格,王译采用了浅近的汉语文言文体,有意识地使用了一些书卷气较浓的词语和表达方式,且词语的选择时刻照顾到与邻近词语的搭配和呼应,收到了很好的效果。这样的例子在译文中随处可见,如将 expert men 译为"练达之士",将 come best from 译为"舍……莫属",将 to find talk and discourse 译为"只为寻章摘句",将 a present wit 译为"天生聪颖"等,不仅准确地传达了原意,还再现了原文的语体风格。

原文的另一特点是用了很多排比和对仗,如:Crafty men contemn studies, simple men admire them, and wise men use them. Reading maketh a full man; conference a ready man; and writing an exact man. 这些排比节奏有力、气势不凡、语气坚定,而译文几乎全部保留了原文的排比、对仗句式,读起来朗朗上口。如前述两句,译文分别是"有一技之长者鄙读书,无知者羡读书,唯明智之士用读书"、"读书使人充实,讨论使人机智,笔记使人准确",都完美地再现了原文的文体风格。[8]

反之,即使译文忠实地传达了原文的意思,如果没有再现原文的文体风格,这样的译文也是失败的。请看下面三例:

例2 Our delegation attaches particular importance to the debate on the question of strengthening international security, which has been brought to the General Assembly for discussion on the initiative of our country.
根据我国的建议,加强国际安全问题已提交大会讨论,我国代表特别重视讨论这一问题。

原文是罗马尼亚驻联合国代表的发言,是典型的政论文体。翻译这类文体的句子时必须十分慎重,不能随意改变原文的结构关系,否则就会导致应该突出的没有突出,不需强调的反而得到了强调。本例的译文就犯了这样的错误,未能再现原文的文体特点;若大致

8　朱明炬、谢少华、吴万伟. 2007. 英汉名篇名译. 南京:译林出版社.

按照原句的词序改译成"我国代表团特别重视由我国向联合国大会提议的关于加强国际安全问题的讨论",则表达会更严谨、周密。[9]

例3 The DU-range universal indexing attachment is dispatched fully assembled in a packing case. When unpacking the equipment, the user ought to check the accessories against the packing list and make sure that the attachment has not been damaged during transportation; any defects thus found should be reported to the manufacturer and to forwarding agent. Belated claims shall not be entertained.

DU 系列万能分度附件是以完全装配好了的形式装在包装箱中运送的。用户在打开包装箱时,应按包装单逐一查清各种辅助设备,并弄清该附件在运输过程中是否受到损坏。应把由此而发现的短缺通知本厂和运输商。过期要求补货将不予承认。

原文是科技产品说明书,属科技文体,翻译时要求术语准确、行文简洁、表达清晰。本例的译文虽然将原文的意思表达出来了,但没能使用科技产品说明书的语言,比如"完全装配好了的形式""装在包装箱中运送""打开包装箱"等,有失专业。有鉴于此,不妨改译为:

DU 系列万能分度头以总装形式装箱交运。用户开箱时,应按装箱清单逐一清点各项辅助设备,查明运输过程中分度头有无损坏。如有缺损,应即通知本厂及运输商。过后要求补偿,概不受理。[10]

例4 After three championships with the Chicago Bulls, a second gold medal with the U.S. team at the 1992 Olympics, and all the accolades the game can bestow, Jordan felt his motivation slipping away.

在芝加哥公牛队打球得三次冠军,在美国队打球于 1992 年奥林匹克运动会获得第二枚金牌,并获得篮球所能给予的一切荣誉之后,乔丹说他打球的动力在消退。

本例译文并没有译错,也还通顺,但译者没有注意到体育报道的文体特点,特别是用词上的特征。建议改译成:"在加盟芝加哥公牛队连获三冠,入主美国队于 1992 年再获奥运金牌,并囊括篮球运动各项殊荣后,乔丹觉得自己打球的动力正日渐消退。"[11]

英汉翻译需要注意文体异同,汉英翻译时同样需要关注文体问题。请看下例:

例5 庐山初识,匆匆五十年矣。山城之聚,金陵之晤,犹历历在昨。别后音讯阔绝四十余年,诚属憾事。幸友谊犹存,两心相通。每遇客从远方来,道及夫人起居,更引起怀旧之情。近闻夫人健康如常,颇感欣慰。

Two score and ten years have elapsed since our acquaintance at Mt. Lushan. Our

---

9 陈登、谭琼琳.1997.英汉翻译实例评析.长沙:湖南大学出版社.
10 陈家麒.1985.语义明晰,文体贴切——科技资料翻译的要求.现代外语,(3):63.
11 李运兴.1998.英汉语篇翻译.北京:清华大学出版社.

gathering in Chongqing the Mountain City and our meeting in Nanjing the Stone City are still fresh in my mind as if they were occurrences only of yesterday. Much to our regret, we had been out of correspondence for forty odd years. Yet it is a comfort to us that we still retain friendship and mutual understanding. Every time a friend comes from afar and mentions your daily life, I cannot refrain from recalling our old associations. It is a supreme comfort to me when I am informed that you are as healthy as ever.

汉语原文出自 1988 年 5 月邓颖超致宋美龄的信的第一段。这封信表面看似私人函件，实则为关系海峡两岸的官方信函，因此使用了浅近的文言文，措辞严谨，用词字斟句酌，属标准的书卷体。为了传达原文严谨、典雅、庄重的文体特征，译者有意选用了英文中较正式的表达方式，像 two score and ten years、acquaintance、forty odd years、cannot refrain from recalling、it is a supreme comfort 等，收到良好效果。如果不考虑原文的文体特征，只是简单地按照字面意思译成如下的文字：

Fifty years have passed since I first got to know you at Mt. Lushan. It seems that our meetings in Chongqing and in Nanjing had taken place only the day before. I am really sorry that I haven't heard from you for more than forty years. Anyhow, our friendship is still there and we still understand each other. Whenever a guest from afar comes to see me and tells me about your everyday life, I cannot help recalling the days when we were together. And I am very pleased to hear that you are as healthy as you used to be.

虽然也传达了原文的意思，但原文典雅、庄重的韵味尽失，也不符合邓颖超的身份与口吻。

前文提到，文体指文章的类别、体裁、体制或风格，因此，再现原文的文体特征也必须从这些方面着手。当然，由于英、汉两种语言存在的差异，翻译时完全再现原文的文体特征通常是不可能的，在这一点上，正所谓"没有最好，只有更好"。

具体到翻译操作，首先，在宏观层面，要保证经翻译后，原文的类别和体裁不会发生变化。原文为小说，翻译后必须仍是小说，不能变成诗歌；原文是科技论文，翻译后仍应该是科技论文，不能变成科普文章；原文为议论文，不能改译成说明文。其次，在微观层面，要保证原文的语相[12]、语音、词汇、句子、篇章、修辞等特征在译文中得到最大程度的保留，如此才能确保原文的体制和风格在译文中得到最充分的再现。下面一一举例说明。

---

12 语相是语言学术语，指文本中用以表示意义的各种视觉符号或标记，如语篇的排版、标点、拼写、空格、缩进、段落结构、图画、图像以及诗歌中的长短行等。语言学研究发现，这些视觉符号或标记也反映了一定的文体意义，需要在译文中再现。

例6

```
l(a

le
af
fa
ll

s)
one
l

iness
```

孤（1
片
树
叶
落
地
了）
零
零……

原文是美国诗人卡明斯（e. e. cummings）的一首诗歌 *l(a*。卡明斯是美国现代实验派的杰出代表，他摒弃传统诗法的韵律和结构，在诗歌创作中融入现代抽象派绘画技巧，通过花样翻新的语相手段来传递信息和情感，以创造图像和语义的动态结合。比如该诗创造性地将 loneliness 和 a leaf falls 拆开写，下跨几行，精心模拟了树叶下落的过程，惟妙惟肖地描述了秋的肃杀和凄凉。同时，把 a leaf falls 包在单词 loneliness 之内，将 loneliness 的抽象概念和 a leaf falls 的具体意象关联起来，充分表达了孤独如一片落叶的意思。译文模仿原诗的语相，将部分汉字不规则斜排，以表现树叶下落时的飘零状，取得了一定的成功。

例7 此处不准抽烟！

Smoking is NOT allowed here.

原文中"不准"下面添加了着重号，为了译出强调语气，译文将 NOT 三个字母全部大写，收到了很好的效果。

例 8　The fair breeze blew, the white foam flew;
The furrow followed free.

(The Rime of the Ancient Mariner by Samuel Taylor Coleridge)

浪花纷飞，拂拂风吹，
舟迹随有如燕尾。

（朱湘 译）

英文原句中使用 f 音头韵来模拟柔风轻吹、浪花纷飞的声音，译文也有意识地使用辅音字母为 f 的汉字和词（"纷飞""拂拂""风"），原文的声音模拟在译文中得到了再现。

例 9

长 相 思

汴水流，
泗水流，
流到瓜洲古渡头，
吴山点点愁。

思悠悠，
恨悠悠，
恨到归时方始休，
月明人倚楼。

Long Longing

The Bian waters flow,
The Si waters flow,
Flow to the old ferry of Guachow.
The Woodland hills bow in sorrow.

My rues grow and grow,
My woes grow and grow,
Grow until comes back my yokefellow.
We lean on the rail in moonglow.

原诗押尾韵，译诗也押尾韵，且发音相似，再现了原诗的音韵美；重复 grow 这个单词，用 grow and grow 来译"悠悠"，是匠心独运，神来之笔。

例 10　Be ye faithful unto the end.

汝等应至死不渝。

原文古雅，不仅用了古旧词 ye 和 unto，而且句子结构也很正式。译文采用了"汝等"这样的古汉语词来翻译，较好地再现了原文古雅的文体色彩。

例 11 这小伙子干活真冲！

This young fellow does his work with vim and vigor.

"真冲"是口语体，因此翻译时相应地使用了口语词 vim，以再现原句的文体色彩。[13]

例 12 My sweet, clever, attractive, economical, sensible little girl, free at last.

我那性子又好、又聪明、又好看、又会当家、又识大体的女儿，这可自由了。

（吕叔湘 译）

译句几乎是顺着原句逐词直译的，完全再现了原句的结构，成功地传达了原句的形美；前长后短的句子结构安排，象征了说话人经过了很长时间的等待，终于看到女儿自由了，迫不及待与外人道的欣喜溢于言表。

例 13 The boy went out. They had eaten with no light on the table and the old man took off his trousers and went to bed in the dark. He rolled his trousers up to make a pillow, putting the newspaper inside them. He rolled himself in the blanket and slept on the other newspapers that covered the springs of the bed.

(*The Old Man and the Sea* by Ernest Hemingway)

孩子出去了。他俩吃饭的时候，桌上连个灯都没有。孩子走开以后，老头儿脱掉裤子，摸黑上了床。他把裤子卷成枕头，把那张旧报纸塞在里边，然后用军毯裹住身子，睡在铺在破床的弹簧上面的旧报纸上。

（海观 译）

众所周知，海明威的语言简洁明了、惜墨如金，有电报似的风格。译文也依此而行，尽量用短词短句来翻译，用词平易，句意清晰。原文除了 and 外没有使用任何其他的连接词，译文中起衔接功能的词也很少。原文和译文在文体风格上几乎对等。

例 14 若货物经中国商品检验局复检后发现质量与本合同规定不符，买方有权于货物抵达目的港后的 60 天内向卖方提出索赔。若经中国商品检验局复检发现货物重量与提单所示重量不符，买方有权于货物抵达目的港后的 60 天内向卖方提出短重索赔。

The Buyer shall have the right to claim against the Seller for compensation of losses within 60 days after arrival of the goods at the port of destination, should the quality of the goods be found not in conformity with the specifications stipulated in the Contracts after reinspection by the China Commodity Inspection Bureau (CCIB) and the Buyer shall have the right to claim against the Seller for compensation of shortweight within 60 days after arrival of the goods at the port of destination, should the weight of the goods be found not in conformity with that stipulated in the Bill of Lading after reinspection by the CCIB.

---

13 朱徽．2004．汉英翻译教程．重庆：重庆大学出版社．

原文是一份合同的节选。合同语言正式，逻辑严密，稍显繁复，但要将当事双方的责任权利表述得清楚明白。译文亦如此。原文的两个条件句，译成英语仍是条件句，由 should 来引导，这比用 if 要正式得多。抽象名词 compensation、arrival、reinspection、conformity 等的使用，也增加了译文的书面色彩，再现了原文的文体特点。

例15 所以吃饭时要有音乐，还不够，就有"佳人""丽人"之类来劝酒；……

Thus, there is music played at mealtimes, and what's more, there are "belles" and "sirens" and such who keep topping up their wine glasses.

原文中"佳人""丽人"两词都加上了引号，可见是委婉语，字面上说有美女相陪，其实暗指狎妓。英译百分之百保留了这种修辞格。[14]

总之，在译文中再现原文的文体特征，不仅有必要，操作上也是可能的。译文在多大程度上再现了原文的文体特征是决定译文质量的重要方面之一。

第三节 实用文体的概念、分类和特点

文体概念的提出暗示了各种不同类型文体的存在，而如何对这些文体分类一直是学界争论不休的话题。事实上，至今还没有令人满意的且为各方所接受的文体划分的方法，这是因为：文章本身兼有多种因素，往往出现跨类现象；各种文体相互渗透，相互影响，产生了不少边缘文体；长期形成的分类观念和习惯，尽管不够理想和科学，但已约定俗成；文体学的研究工作薄弱，缺乏创新意识；分类的标准不统一；等等。[15]

我们根据文体的性质、功能和形式特征，将文体大致分为文学文体和实用文体两大类。[16] 前者用语言塑造形象，反映社会生活，表达作者思想感情；后者反映客观真实对象，非虚构，不以韵律节奏的形式来表达内容，不以给人审美享受为旨归。

文学文体和实用文体在反映对象、社会功能、反映方式、成品形态等方面区别明显。在反映对象上，文学文体反映的是社会生活，即使是自然景物，也已经是"人化的自然"；实用文体不仅反映社会生活，也描写自然现象。在社会功能上，文学文体主要是寄托创作

---

14 郑雅丽. 2004. 英汉修辞格互译导引. 广州：暨南大学出版社.
15 李丰楷. 1994. 文体分类研究. 青岛师专学报，（2）：38.
16 这种对文体的划分，当然不是我们的发明。根据莫恒全《论文体分类及实用文章与文学作品的本质特征》一文所述：1917年起，陈独秀先后在《文学革命论》等著述中，将各种文章划分为"文学之文"和"应用之文"。1924年，叶圣陶的《作论论》将"普通文"与"文学"相提并论。后来，朱广贤在其《写作学概论》中把所有的文章划分为"文学作品门"和"实用文章门"两门，并由此建立了"两门—八类—多体"的三级次分类新体系。陈独秀的"应用之文"、叶圣陶的"普通文"和朱广贤的"实用文章门"，就是我们所说的"实用文体"。

主体的审美理想,丰富人们的精神生活,为人们提供精神享受;实用文体是实施社会行政管理职能和有序、有效地处理各行各业实际工作以及日常生活的有力工具。在反映方式上,文学文体以形象思维为主;实用文体以抽象思维为主。在成品形态上,文学文体往往需要丰富的审美想象,可以充分地虚构,具有非常鲜明的个性化内容;实用文体鲜少使用想象,不以凭空虚构代替事实,其情感不论多么强烈,也只限于对客观事实的爱憎评价,而不能在文中改变客观事物本身,一般带有相对稳定的模式性。[17]

实用文体涵盖了除文学文体之外的所有文体。实用文体可分成不同的子类。传统的分类方法将实用文体分成记叙文(消息、通讯、回忆录、传记、家史等)、说明文(科普说明文、辞书、教科书、产品说明书等)、议论文(政论、评论、序跋、杂文、学术论文等)和应用文(条据、规约、书信、公文等)四类。但这种划分存在一个问题:分类的标准不统一,前三类以表达方式为标准分类,而应用文则以社会功用为标准分类。

另一种分类方法按文章的写作目的和具体用途进行划分,将实用文体分成公文类、新闻类、外交类、科技类、财经类、司法类等子类。但文章的写作目的和具体用途举不胜举,按照这种分类方法,要想涵盖实用文体的所有子类几乎不可能。

考虑到本教程的性质和读者对象,我们基本上依据后一种分类方法,将实用文体中最常见的科技文体、旅游文体、经贸文体、法律文体、新闻文体、广告文体、会议文书等挑出来,逐一对其分析讲解。这样分类是因为这些文体相对来说比较常见,它们的翻译也最值得学习。

事实上,不论采用何种标准来对实用文体进行分类,同一类型的实用文体通常都拥有某些共同的特质。

第一,实用文体文本都是为了某个实用目的而撰写的。比如,学术论文的写作目的是传播学术信息,广告是为了诱导人们购买产品或服务,启事是为了告知大众事项,而商务合同是为了明确合同双方的责任权利,等等。

第二,实用文体文本面向的是真实的世界,其内容是真实的。即使由于科技水平的关系,科技论文中得出的结论将来可能会被证明是错误的,但这并不能改变其研究对象是客观世界这一事实。同样,即使广告文本中可能有夸大其词的成分,但其介绍的产品或服务是真实存在的,不是虚构的。

第三,同一类型的实用文体在体式上存在一定的规范,信息结构通常保持一致。比如,绝大多数英文商务信函都包括信头(Letter Head)、编号和日期(Reference and Date)、封内地址(Inside Address)、经办人(Attention)、称呼(Salutation)、事由(Subject)、正文(Body of the Letter)、结尾套语(Complimentary Close)、签名(Signature)等部分。又比如,绝大多数科技论文都包括标题(Title)、摘要(Abstract)、关键词(Key

---

17 王泽龙. 2013. 文体分类新探. 河南社会科学, (1): 92.

Words）、正文（Body）、参考文献（Bibliography 或 References）等部分。

第四，同一类型的实用文体在语言表达上通常具有某些共同的特点，也正是这些特点将不同类型的实用文体区分开来。比如，英语新闻的标题通常会省略冠词、代词、连系动词和助动词，多使用一般现在时，常用不定式代替将来时，多用介词、缩略词、复合名词、短小词和临时造词，等等。而法律英语的语言几乎无一例外地呈现规范、正式、庄重、严谨等特点；词汇方面则频繁使用中世纪英语、古英语和拉丁文词汇及常用词的非常用意义，大量使用法律术语、行话和套话，谨慎使用代词，很少使用程度副词如 very、rather、quite 等；表现在句法上，多使用长句、复杂句，等等。

虽然实用文体不以审美享受为目的，但这并不代表实用文体就不注重语言表达。事实上，有些实用文体文本非常有文采，只是相比其审美功能，实用文体的实用性更为突出，甚至其审美功能也是服务于实用目的的。请看下面两例：

例1 So long, chicken. Hello! Tofu. Tofu and a host of other products made from the mighty soybean are pushing aside meat, milk and even ice cream on grocery store shelves these days as scientists rave about the health benefits of soy.[18]

例2 Sensuously smooth. Mysteriously mellow. Gloriously golden. Who can resist the magic of Camus XO Cognac?

例1选自一篇分析豆腐营养的科技文章。在很多人眼里，科技文章大多严肃正经，但此段由于使用了 so long、hello、mighty、rave 这样一些词语，幽默风趣，文采斐然，使人对豆腐的兴趣油然而生。例2是一则白兰地酒的广告，头韵的使用令该广告语节奏分明，朗朗上口，有一种特别的音韵美；反问修辞手法的使用增强了该广告的诱导力。

总的说来，本教程讨论的十种实用文体中，广告文体和旅游文体最注重语言的表现力，语言的文学意味也最强。请看下面两例：

例3 BIG *in Japan*. BIG *in China*. BIG *on Asia*. With 45 years' experience in Japanese equities, Nikko AM was the first asset manager to be granted QFII status in China and continues to manage the largest, directly allocated investment quota.[19]

例4 They came, they saw—and they were conquered. The Romans arrived in this green valley nearly 2,000 years ago and, captivated by the miraculous stream of endless hot water, stayed for four centuries. The carefully restored remains of their tremendous bath and temple complex attract hundreds of thousands of visitors each year to what is still the social and historical heart of Bath. Fashionable Georgian England came to Bath to take the waters, and now bathers can once more experience a dip in the natural mineral water with the opening of a new spa, close to the old Roman Baths. There's

---

18 此例引自毛荣贵、张琦. 2005. 开卷有益：译文比读分析. 北京：中国对外翻译出版公司.
19 此例引自 *Financial Times*, 2007-08-27.

a lot more besides—stylish shops and restaurants, galleries and museums and a lively city with its historic past informing an exciting present.[20]

例 3 是日兴资产管理公司（Nikko AM）在 2007 年 8 月 27 日的《金融时报》上刊登的广告。广告一开头便用了三个排比的短语，而且短语中的单词或大写，或斜体，与其后的长句形成对比，夺人眼目。

例 4 是 *Pitkin City Guide: Bath* 中介绍巴斯（Bath）小城的一段话。首句便将凯撒大帝（Julius Caesar）著名的 *Veni, vidi, vici* (I came; I saw; I conquered) 改头换面，变成了 They came, they saw—and they were conquered，给人留下非常深刻的印象。

新闻文体以报道事件、记录社会、传播信息、反映时代为己任，有"硬新闻"（Hard News）和"软新闻"（Soft News）之分。前者关注报道的时效性，常采用所谓的"倒金字塔"（Inverted Pyramid）结构，将最重要的信息放在开头，称为"导语"；语言力求客观，用词简短，句子紧凑，多用扩展的简单句（extended simple sentences），信息密度大。例如：

例 5

Chile Volcano Calbuco Erupts Again[21]

Thu. Apr. 30, 2015 4:48pm UTC

SANTIAGO (Reuters)—Chilean volcano Calbuco, which erupted twice spectacularly last week, began erupting again on Thursday, sending a fresh cloud of ash and gas high into the sky, local TV pictures showed.

Calbuco spewed over 200 million tons of ash last week, coating nearby towns, wrecking the local salmon industry, and forcing the cancellation of flights as far as Buenos Aires, some 1,400 kilometers (870 miles) away.

The volcano had gone quiet, but geological officials had warned it was still unstable and could erupt again.

Calbuco, one of the most active along a chain of around 2,000 kilometers in Chile, is in the scenic Los Lagos region around 1,000 kilometers (620 miles) south of the capital, Santiago.

相比之下，软新闻的时效性略弱，更注重呈现事件的前因后果，可选择的叙述结构丰富多样，语言也更注重文采。请看下例：

20　此例引自 *Pitkin City Guide: Bath*. Hampshire: Pitkin Publishing Ltd.
21　此例引自 http://news.lycos.com/life/chile-volcano-calbuco-erupts-again-8c966601787d44665f3c4287db0d67a/.

例6

Graffiti, Pollution and Lack of Funds
Threaten Art Gallery on Berlin Wall[22]

By Allan Hall

Berlin is too broke to pay for the restoration of a crumbling section of its infamous wall that is one of the capital's biggest tourist magnets.

The famous East Side gallery—a stretch of avant-garde art painted on one of the last remaining stretches of the wall which divided the city for 28 years—is in danger of extinction due to a lack of political will combined with public apathy.

Pollution, bureaucracy, graffiti, the weather and a lackadaisical attitude among city dwellers mean the art could vanish along with most other symbols of a divided Germany.

Located among the banks of the Spree River near the city's main eastern rail station, the best-known wall remnant and its artwork have fallen on hard times.

Created in 1990 in celebration of the wall's collapse, the gallery features works by an international group of artists who expressed their reactions to the November 9, 1989 event through painting. The works cover a half-mile long section of the wall that has come to be known as the East Side Gallery.

But the artistic efforts are in danger of disappearing beneath graffiti or fading from years of exposure to Berlin's weather. The famous kiss mural, for example, depicting Soviet President Leonid Brezhnev and East Germany leader Erich Honecker with locked lips in a socialist smacker is pockmarked and cracked.

The area around mirrors the decline of the artworks. The strip of land facing the other, graffiti-strewn, side of the wall has become a home to derelicts and drug addicts. A murder victim was stumbled upon in a clean-up project several years ago.

Some 118 artists from 24 countries used the wall—the "anti-fascist protection barrier" in the argot of the socialist rulers of the German Democratic Republic—as a canvas upon which to paint their farewell to the regime which erected it back in 1961. It is now up there with the Brandenburg Gate and the Holocaust Memorial as a must-see icon for tourists to the city.

But restoring its fading glory seems an impossible task. To repair the crumbling wall would necessitate the destruction of the pictures. They would subsequently be repainted by the same artists who said they are willing to do it. The total cost of the renovation project is estimated at more than $2.2 million—not a huge civic sum, but Berlin is broke to the tune of billions.

---

22 此例引自 *The Independent*, 2007-08-18.

With kindergartens being closed, swimming pools shut, fountains turned off and roads left potholes, a project that city fathers believe is backed by only a few intellectuals does not feature high on the political agenda. A recent survey by the *Tagesspiegel* newspaper suggested only 27 per cent of locals are in favour of the renovation.

But Kani Alavi, co-founder and president of the Artists' Initiative East Side Gallery says it's a small price to pay for the upkeep of a crucial part of Berlin's history. "The gallery serves as a document," he said, "and we and the city authorities have to be prepared to protect the history of Berlin."

So far the city government is willing to pay for the technical restoration of the wall but not the repainting.

Joerg Flaehmig, who works for the city's planning authorities, says the renovation work cannot commence until the project has been financed in its entirety.

"We are still trying to secure the money for the repainting, but we're not yet sure where it will come from. We're currently still trying to ascertain which funding pot we can tap into to cover the costs," he said.

But four of the artists have already died and the paintings grow shabbier by the day. Those who have pledged to preserve the East Side gallery are going cap-in-hand to corporations asking for their financial support.

"I wish the authorities would stop dragging their feet," Mr. Alvi said, "We must maintain the Wall for future generations, to bring the terrible history alive."

科技文体以客观规范、简洁准确、用词严谨、语气庄重为主要特点，常使用大量的科技术语。根据语场、语旨、语式的不同，方梦之将科技文体分成专用科技文体和普通科技文体两种[23]。专用科技文体的例子如：

例7 The problem of aerodynamic improvement of dust collecting systems and equipment in the production of refractories is closely associated with the toxicological effect of dust on the human organism and with the state of the technosphere. Rather severe medical, social, and technological situations arise that unavoidably acquire an economic resonance. Dust generated in the production of refractories may be the cause for the appearance not only of pneumoconiosis, but also of other diseases of the respiratory system, skin, and mucous membrane, including dust bronchitis, bronchial asthma, pneumonia, lesions to the mucous membrane of the nose and nasopharynx, conjunctivitis, and skin lesions, such as desquamation, coarsening, acne, furunculosis, and sometimes eczema and dermatitis.[24]

---

23 方梦之. 2008. 科技翻译教程. 上海：上海外语教育出版社.

24 此例引自 Krasovitskii, Y. V. & E. V. Arkhangel'skaya. 2013. Medico-ecological Monitoring and Toxicology of Dust in the Production of Refractories. *Refractories and Industrial Ceramics*, (3): 254.

普通科技文体的例子如：

例8 The human body, over the years of its existence, has learned to survive many immune challenges presented by nature and by civilisation. The baby, although vulnerable to disease and infection, is well protected by the mother, and the slow introduction to new environments allows the time for immunity to all common diseases of the local environment to build up. However, modern life has now imposed its own problems. Not only does Man travel more, and risk exposure to new diseases to which immune defences have not been developed, but additionally the survival age in most populations is rising fast. Older people are therefore more vulnerable in the population to these new diseases, whether brought into their own country by travellers or encountered by ageing globe-trotters. Fortunately, communications improve every day, and the movement of diseases round the world can be monitored so that drugs can be prescribed to help meet the challenges.[25]

经贸文体涵盖的范围很广。理论上，所有与商业活动有关的文本都可以算是经贸文体，如商务信函、商务合同、企业介绍、产品说明等。经贸文体的各子类也呈现出不同的文体特征：如商务信函要求"7C"，即完整（completeness）、清晰（clearness）、具体（concreteness）、简洁（conciseness）、正确（correctness）、礼貌（courtesy）和体谅（consideration）；而商务合同则带有法律文体的特点，要求准确严密、正式庄重、用词专业，常用固定的格式与表达方式，句子较长且内部结构复杂等。下面是商务信函的例子：

例9

Dear Mr. Barlow,[26]

During my February visit to Taipei, I spoke to Mr. Jack Huang, who later sent information on your company. After careful review of your operations and manpower, my organization believes that your company is ideal for serving our Asian market needs. To this effect, we'd like to know further your terms and conditions as related to the services that we would be requiring from you.

We are interested in the importation of used motorbikes from Taiwan—no more than five years old with good bodies and perfect working engines. We'd require from FETS the services of sourcing and QC adhering to the above specifications and guaranteeing the bikes' condition before shipment.

We eagerly await your reply.

Yours faithfully,

John Davis

---

25 此例引自 Marion D. Kendall. 2002. *Dying to Live: How Our Bodies Fight Disease*. 上海：上海外语教育出版社.
26 此例引自庄锡宗. 2008. 商务实战英语书信实例. 台北：希伯伦股份有限公司.

Managing Director
BARA ROSE LTD.

下面一例为商务合同文本：

例10

VEHICLE SALES AGREEMENT[27]

THIS VEHICLE SALES AGREEMENT is made this _____ day of ___, 20___, by and among _____ of _____ (hereinafter known as "Seller") and _____, of _____ (hereinafter known as "Buyer"). Buyer and Seller shall collectively be known herein as "the Parties".

BACKGROUND

WHEREAS, Seller desires to sell the vehicle described below, known herein as the "Acquired Vehicle", under the terms and conditions set forth below;

WHEREAS, Buyer desires to purchase the Acquired Vehicle offered for sale by Seller under the terms and conditions set forth below; and, therefore,

TERMS AND CONDITIONS

IN CONSIDERATION of the mutual promises and other valuable consideration exchanged by the Parties as set forth herein, the Parties, intending to be legally bound, hereby agree as follows:

A. Description of Acquired Vehicle.
1. Make: _____
2. Model: _____
3. Body Type: _____
4. Body Color: _____
5. Year: _____
6. Miles: _____
7. Vehicle Identification Number ("VIN"): _____

B. Consideration.

1. Purchase Price. The total purchase price to be paid by Buyer to Seller for the Acquired Vehicle is _____ dollars ($_____) (U.S.) (hereinafter "Purchase Price") consisting of the following components:

  i. Down-payment: $_____ (Due to Seller on or before execution of this agreement.)

  ii. Payment Due at Delivery of Vehicle to Buyer: $_____

The "down-payment" and "payment due at delivery" are to be made by Buyer to

---

27　此例引自 http://www.donnyspi.com/images/vsa.pdf。

Seller in cash, by certified check, or through another instrument acceptable to Seller. Buyer must receive permission in advance from Seller for use of a non-certified check in payment of the Purchase Price.

C. Delivery of Acquired Vehicle and Conveyance of Title.

1. <u>Delivery of Acquired Vehicle</u>. Seller shall deliver the Acquired Vehicle, and Buyer shall take possession of same, at Seller's premises (either in person or through a third party) on or before _____ ("Delivery Date"). If delivery is to be made at a date after the execution of this contract, it is Seller's duty to ensure that the Acquired Vehicle is delivered in the same condition as when last inspected by the Buyer (or, if no Buyer inspection, the execution date of this agreement). It is Buyer's duty, either in person or through a third party, to appear at Seller's premises during standard business hours on or before the Delivery Date to remove the Acquired Vehicle from Seller's premises. However, if Buyer fails to appear at Seller's premises on or before the Delivery Date to accept possession of the Acquired Vehicle, then risk of loss passes to the Buyer on the Delivery Date.

2. <u>Conveyance of Title</u>. Seller shall convey title to Buyer upon delivery of the vehicle to Buyer. Seller agrees and covenants to execute all documents presented by Buyer which are necessary to finalize transfer of title and registration upon the Acquired Vehicle to Buyer.

D. Representations, Warranties, and Disclosures.

1. <u>Warranties</u>.

This vehicle is sold "AS IS", and Seller does not in any way, expressly or impliedly, give any warranties to Buyer. Seller expressly disclaims any implied warranties of merchantability or of fitness for a particular purpose.

2. <u>Odometer Declaration</u>. Seller hereby states that the odometer in the Acquired Vehicle now reads _____ miles and to the best of Seller's knowledge it reflects the actual mileage of the vehicle described herein.

3. <u>Buyer Representation</u>. The individual signing this agreement on behalf of Buyer hereby represents to Seller that he or she has the power and authority to do so on behalf of Buyer.

E. Buyer's Responsibility—Insurance and Tags. Buyer acknowledges that unless prohibited by applicable law, any insurance coverage, license, tags, plates or registration maintained by Seller on the Acquired Vehicle shall be canceled upon delivery of the Acquired Vehicle to, and the acceptance of, by Buyer.

F. Continuation of Representations and Warranties. All representations and warranties contained in this Agreement (if any) shall continue in full force and effect after execution of this agreement. If either party later learns that a warranty or representation that it made is untrue, it is under a duty to promptly disclose this information to the other party in writing. No representation or warranty contained herein shall be deemed to have been waived or impaired by any investigation made by or knowledge of the other party to this Agreement.

G. Indemnification of Attorneys Fees and Out-of-pocket Costs. Should any party materially breach this agreement (including representations and warranties made to the other side), the non-breaching party shall be indemnified by the breaching party for its reasonable attorneys fees and out-of-pocket costs which in any way relate to, or were precipitated by, the breach of this contract (including the breach of representations or warranties). This provision shall not limit in any way the remedies either party may have otherwise possessed in law or equity relative to a breach of this contract. The term "out-of-pocket costs", as used in this contract, shall not include lost profits.

H. Integration. This Agreement, including the attachments mentioned in the body as incorporated by reference, sets forth the entire agreement between the Parties with regard to the subject matter hereof. All prior agreements, representations and warranties, express or implied, oral or written, with respect to the subject matter hereof, are hereby superseded by this agreement. This is an integrated agreement.

I. Severability. In the event any provision of this Agreement is deemed to be void, invalid, or unenforceable, that provision shall be severed from the remainder of this Agreement so as not to cause the invalidity or unenforceability of the remainder of this Agreement. All remaining provisions of this Agreement shall then continue in full force and effect. If any provision shall be deemed invalid due to its scope or breadth, such provision shall be deemed valid to the extent of the scope and breadth permitted by law.

J. Modification. Except as otherwise provided in this document, this agreement may be modified, superseded, or voided <u>only</u> upon the written and signed agreement of the Parties. Further, the physical destruction or loss of this document shall not be construed as a modification or termination of the agreement contained herein.

K. Acknowledgements. Each party acknowledges that he or she has had an adequate opportunity to read and study this Agreement, to consider it, to consult with attorneys if he or she has so desired.

L. Exclusive Jurisdiction for Suit in Case of Breach. The Parties, by entering into this agreement, submit to jurisdiction in _____ for adjudication of any disputes and/or claims between the parties under this agreement. Furthermore, the parties hereby agree that the courts of _____ shall have **exclusive** jurisdiction over any disputes between the parties relative to this agreement, whether said disputes sound in contract, tort, or other areas of the law.

M. State Law. This Agreement shall be interpreted under, and governed by, the laws of the state of _____.

IN WITNESS WHEREOF and acknowledging acceptance and agreement of the foregoing, Seller and Buyer affix their signatures hereto.

SELLER   **BUYER**

_____   _____

Dated: _____ _____, 20 _____   Dated: _____ _____, 20 _____

法律文体在本书所列的十种文体中最正式。在语言上，用词庄重规范，多用古语、外来词，大量使用命令词和情态动词；句式方面，多使用完整句，通常不使用省略句，长句多，短句少，句子内部逻辑关系紧密。例如：

例11 Where a data controller cannot comply with the request without disclosing information relating to another individual who can be identified from that information, he is not obliged to comply with the request unless (a) the other individual has consented to the disclosure of the information to the person making the request, or (b) it is reasonable in all the circumstances to comply with the request without the consent of the other individual.[28]

会议文书、礼仪文书、启事文书的共同特点是都服务于非常具体的目的，大多有固定的格式。三者相比，会议文书的语言更正式，而礼仪文书和启事文书语言可以很正式，也可以很口语化，取决于文书发出者和接受者之间的关系。请看下面三例：

例12

Call for Papers

2009 International Symposium on ESP (English for Specific Purposes) and Its Teaching

Organizer: Wuhan University of Science and Technology

Co-organizers: Fooyin University (Taiwan), Taiwan ESP Association

Dates: October 24–25, 2009

Venue: Conference Hall, Wuhan University of Science and Technology, Wuhan, China

Theme: *Various Purposes, Varied Approaches: ESP and Its Teaching in the 21st Century*

Papers relevant to ESP are also welcome.

1. The conference will be conducted and published in English. Abstracts are invited for 30-minute presentations (including 10 minutes for questions and answers).
2. Abstracts should be about 300 words and include a list of appropriate keywords.
3. Abstract submission: Abstracts should be submitted as attachment to

---

28 此例引自 *Data Protection Act 1998*. http://www.legislation.gov.uk/ukpga/1998/29/section/7.

espconference@wust.edu.cn. Acceptable file format is MS Word (.doc).

4. **Deadline for abstract submission:** July 10, 2009
   Abstract acceptance notification: July 15, 2009
   Final paper due: August 20, 2009
5. **Conference formats:** keynote speech, paper presentation, panel discussion
6. **Keynote speakers:**

(1) **Ken Hyland:** Professor of Education in the School of Culture, Language and Communication and Head of the Centre for Professional and Academic Literacy at the Institute of Education, University of London. His areas of interest include: academic and professional literacy; English in higher education; writing in a second language; scientific discourse; genre analysis; and learning and teaching of English. He has published over 120 articles and 11 books. Recent publications include *Disciplinary Discourses* (Longman, 2000/University of Michigan Press, 2004), *Teaching and Researching Writing* (Longman, 2002), *Second Language Writing* (CUP, 2003), *Genre and Second Language Writers* (University of Michigan Press, 2004), *Metadiscourse* (Continuum, 2005), *English for Academic Purposes* (Routledge, 2006) and *Feedback on Second Language Writing* (Edited with Fiona Hyland, CUP, 2006). He is co-editor of the *Journal of English for Academic Purposes* (with Liz Hamp-Lyons).

(2) **Vitali Ashkinazi:** Associate Professor in the Foreign Language Department of Saint Petersburg State University of Refrigeration and Food Technology, Russia, and managing editor of online journal of *ESP World*.

(3) **Thomas Orr:** Professor and Director of Center for Language Research in the School of Computer Science and Engineering, University of Aizu, Japan. He has taught English for more than 20 years in the United States and Japan, and his research has been published by IEEE, Wiley-InterScience, Halldin, Rodopi, Blackwell, TESOL, JALT, JACET, etc.

7. **Registration:** Participants are expected to register for the Symposium before September 10, 2009. Online registration is available at http://www.espconfernce.wust.edu.cn. Registration fee for Chinese participants is 800 RMB; and for overseas participants, 150 US dollars. Registration fee includes all costs except accommodation during the symposium and travelling before and after the Symposium. A 2-day cultural visit (October 26–27, 2009) to the Three Gorges on the Yangtze River will be arranged, which has already been covered by the registration fee. For any further information regarding registration, please contact Mr. Bright Chu of the Organizing Committee at espconference@wust.edu.cn.

Contact Information:

TEL: 86-27-6886 ****, 86-1580 **** *** FAX: 86-27-6889 ****

Organizing Committee for 2009 International
Symposium on ESP and Its Teaching

例 13

Dear Mr. and Mrs. Jefferson,

  Thank you very much for the invitation to dinner next Thursday. Renata and I are very happy to accept and look forward to seeing you at 8:30.

Yours sincerely,
Domineco Piazza

例 14

Lost Dog

  I am a 9-month-old **Australian Shepherd** who goes by the name of **TUCKER**. I am blonde in colour and my two front paws are white and I have a docked tail. I am about 45–50 lbs and have been missing since Saturday, May 2, 2015. I was last seen in the Crystal Beach Area. If you have seen me or found me please contact my owners

Stacy & Terry at 613-799-8888

公示语比较特殊。语言大多直截了当、简明扼要，短的可能只有一个词，如 DANGER，长的一般也不超过一段；多用祈使句，时态上只用现在时；为了吸引人注意，常使用大写形式。请看例子：

例 15 EXIT For Emergency Use Only

例 16 CAUTION BEWARE OF VEHICLES

例 17 WARNING

  Lock it

  or

  lose it!

  Always lock your car

  Close all windows

  Take valuables with you

  or keep them out of sight

第四节
实用文体的翻译

实用文体是人们传播信息、进行人际交往、维持正常生活秩序等活动的重要手段。随着科技进步和社会发展，人与人之间的关系越来越密切，交往越来越频繁。自然地，实用文体在我们工作、生活中的地位也越来越重要。另外，全球化和信息化时代的到来促进了中国和其他国家在政治、经济、文化、科技等方面的交流，实用文体翻译的重要性也愈加凸显。实用文体翻译已经远远超过文学翻译，成为当今翻译活动的主流。

实用文体与文学文体有很大区别，实用文体翻译和文学翻译在侧重点、翻译原则和翻译方法上也有很大差异。

首先，文学文体的主要功能在于表情（emotive function）和娱乐（recreational function），而为了实现表情和娱乐的功能，在文学翻译中，忠实于原文本的内容和忠实于原文本的形式同样重要。所以，文学翻译多以原文为指归，追求的是如何再现原文的美学特征。相比之下，实用文体主要有信息功能（informative function）、人际功能（interpersonal function）、行事功能（performative function）、寒暄功能（phatic function）或元语言功能（metalingual function），其中又以信息功能为主。所以，实用文体翻译通常关注的是如何在译文中传递原文的信息。至于原文的形式，在翻译时当然也要顾及，但不是考虑的重点。

其次，与文学文体相比，实用文体的目的性和指向性更加明确，更加具体。有不少学者提出，实用文体翻译当以汉斯·威密尔（Hans Vermeer）、克里丝汀·诺德（Christiane Nord）等人提出的"翻译目的论"（Skopos theory）为指导。该理论认为，翻译是一种有目的的行为活动，译者需根据客户或委托人的要求，结合翻译目的和译文读者的特殊情况，从原作所提供的多源信息中进行选择性的翻译；翻译所要达到的目的，决定了翻译的整个过程。[29]也就是说，为了实现翻译的目的，考虑到译文读者在文化心理和美学需求上不同于原文读者的情况，译者可以发挥自己的主观能动性，对原文的形式作一定程度的改变，特殊情况下甚至可以部分地改变原文的内容。

用"翻译目的论"来指导实用文体翻译确有其合理性。与文学文体不同，实用文体的主要特征就在其实用性。因此，判断实用文体翻译成功与否的首要标准应该是翻译的目的是否达到。如果翻译目的没有达到，不论译文在内容上和形式上多么忠实于原文，也没有多大的价值。这一点很好理解。比如，广告文本旨在推动某种产品或服务销售的增长，如果广告文本的译文不能发挥这样的功用，那么译还不如不译。

---

29 Nord, Christiane. 2001. *Translating as a Purposeful Activity: Functionalist Approaches Explained*. 上海：上海外语教育出版社．

翻译实用文体可以采用的方法也很多，包括直译、意译、改译、编译、摘译、创译等。下面将分别举例说明。

例1

Request for Leave of Absence[30]

Dear Mr. Brooks,

Paul was not at school this morning as he had an appointment at the dentist. He will be absent again next Tuesday morning as he has another appointment then.

请 假 条

尊敬的布鲁克斯先生：

保罗今天上午不在学校，因他与牙科医生约好了。下周二上午他还要缺席，因那时还有一次预约。

译文几乎是照着原文直译出来的，只是在小句内部略有词序上的调整。译文忠实、通顺，全面地传递了原文的信息。

例2

专业技术资格证书

本证书由湖北省职称改革工作领导小组办公室批准颁发。它表明持证人通过相关专业高级评审委员会评审，具备相应的专业技术职务任职资格水平。

Certificate of Professional Qualifications

This Certificate, awarded by the Office of Hubei Provincial Commission on Professional Title Reform Work, indicates that the bearer has passed the evaluation of Senior Professional Title Evaluation Committee and is qualified for the corresponding professional or technical position.

原文两个句子，被译成了一个复合句，但译文的词序基本依照原文安排，可谓直译中有意译，以直译为主。

例3

Laughing Kookaburra

By William Eastman

The Laughing Kookaburra is one of the commonest and best known of all Australia's birds.

The raven-sized male and female Laughing Kookaburra look very much alike, but close observation shows two distinct differences. First, the male bears a bright blue rump patch, in contrast to the female's brown one. Secondly, the patch over the eye

---

30 此例引自井升华、井俊. 2007. 内容英语：单据·证件·证明类. 北京：外语教学与研究出版社.（原文和译文均有修改）

is white on the male and buff-coloured on the hen. Young kookaburras appear to be similar to their mothers.

  Without a doubt the most distinctive thing about the Laughing Kookaburra is his laugh. Most often the laugh is uttered in a sunrise or sunset serenade. Usually, it is a danger or territory defence call. The laugh may be uttered by a bird sitting alone and may or may not be answered by another lone bird. The laugh may become a chorus of two lone birds. At other times, one to four birds may utter the sound singly or in chorus in the same tree or side by side on the same limb.

  The call itself almost suggests insanity in sound. It consists of two parts—though not always. It begins with a rattle, gurgle or chuckle through a closed beak. Then the call changes into a laugh. With the mouth open and the beak pointed skyward, a long series of "Ha Ha Ha Huh, Ho Ha Huhs" comes forth in an almost deafening sound. At the conclusion of most calls are long, drawn-out rasping gurgles.

笑　鸟

  笑鸟是澳大利亚鸟类中最常见、最有名的一种。

  笑鸟和渡鸦一样大，雄的和雌的长得很相像。但是仔细观察，就会发现两个明显的区别。首先，在靠近尾巴的地方，雄鸟披着天蓝色的羽毛，与雌鸟的棕色羽毛截然不同。其次，眼睛上边，雄鸟是一片白，雌鸟却是浅黄色。幼鸟的相貌，看来随母亲。

  笑鸟最突出的特点当然是它的笑声。它多在早晚发笑，像是唱黎明曲或黄昏歌。这笑声通常是一种信号，表示危险将要到来，或者需要奋起保卫自己的领地。有时一只孤鸟发出笑声，另一只孤鸟也许响应，也许不响应。这笑声也许是两只孤鸟的合唱曲。有时一两只或三四只笑鸟同栖一棵树上，或并列在一根树枝上，它们也许各自发出笑声，也许来一段大合唱。

  笑鸟的叫声听起来似乎是一种疯狂的声音。这叫声包括两部分，但也并不总是如此。开始的时候，闭着嘴，发出咯咯或吭吭或咕噜咕噜的声音。接着叫声变为笑声。这时，张口仰天，反复发出"哈哈哈呼，多哈呼"的声音，简直能把人的耳朵震聋。在笑声结束的时候，往往还要拖上一阵沙哑的咯咯声。

（庄绎传 译）

  原文是一篇科普文章，语言质朴平实，但翻译起来却并不容易。为了准确地传递原文信息同时又不至于读来佶屈聱牙，译者采用了直译意译相结合的翻译策略。比如，译 raven-sized 为"笑鸟和渡鸟一样大"，the male bears a bright blue rump patch 为"在靠近尾巴的地方，雄鸟披着天蓝色的羽毛"，Most often the laugh is uttered in a sunrise or sunset serenade 为"它多在早晚发笑，像是在唱黎明曲或黄昏歌"，Usually, it is a danger or territory defence call 为"这笑声通常是一种信号，表示危险将要到来，或者需要奋起保卫自己的领地"等，都体现了译者的灵活变通。

例4

各位长辈：大家晚上好！

今天是我十岁生日宴会。在这里我只想说两个字：感谢！

首先感谢我的爸爸妈妈，是他们给了我生命，让我来到这个美好的世界。他们不仅给我创造了优越的学习环境，而且还为我创造了美好的生活，同时还辛勤地哺育我成长，给了我一个温暖的家。

然后感谢我的爷爷奶奶、外公和外婆，是他们精心呵护我长大，给我喂奶、洗澡，教我走路、说话，给我买玩具，给我讲故事，让我每天幸福、快乐。在和外公外婆一起生活的两年多时间里，他们给我留下了美好的回忆，这些美好回忆是我今后成长最珍贵的财富。

最后还要感谢在座的所有爷爷、奶奶、叔叔、阿姨，是你们的关心和爱护使我的童年多了一份自然和洒脱，使我对未来的学习有着更美好的憧憬，使我有了一份自信：那就是用优异的学习成绩来回报所有亲人的关心和厚爱。

请您们放心吧！我一定学好本领，做一个勤奋、好学、上进的人，做一个有作为的真正的男子汉！

请大家举杯，祝长辈们身体健康，万事如意！

祝小朋友们和我一样幸福、快乐！

干杯！

Dear elders and distinguished guests,

Good evening!

Today is my 10th birthday. What I want to say here is nothing but "Thank you all!"

First, I want to thank my mom and my daddy. You gave me life; you brought me into this world; you provide me with excellent learning environment; you give me a happy family. Under your protection and love, I have been growing healthily.

Next, I want to thank my grandmas and grandpas. Since I was a baby, you have been looking after me: you fed me when I was hungry; you bathed me when I needed a bath; you taught me to walk and talk; you bought me toys; you told me stories; you made me happy and joyful every day. In the two years when I lived with my maternal grandparents, I have got some of the best memories. These memories will remain my most precious treasure.

Last, I want to thank all the grannies, uncles, and aunts present. Your love and care gave me a grace to be admired, a great hope for the future, and a confidence in myself. I promise you here that I will study hard to pay you back with high grades.

Trust me, dear all! I will do what I am expected to do, studying hard and striving to make progress day by day. I will grow into a real man!

Now, please raise your glasses and let us drink to the health and happiness of all the elders and guests present.

May all my little friends happy and joyful!

Cheers!

原文是一篇演讲稿，是为一个男孩的生日宴会准备的。男孩的父母希望能将演讲稿译成英文，以便男孩能在宴会上用英文对所有宾客宣读。翻译这样的演讲稿，不一定非要字字忠实于原文，关键是要译出原文中的真情，同时兼顾英文演讲文体特点，让演讲稿读起来地道自然。为此，译者在翻译时对原文做了不少改动。比如，原文中只有"各位长辈"这样的称呼语，译文中添加了distinguished guests，以便包括所有出席宴会的宾客；原文用第三人称称呼出席宴会的爸爸妈妈、爷爷奶奶和外公外婆，译文将其改成了第二人称，变成了男孩直接向这些人表示感谢，符合英文演讲的习惯；译文有意采用了排比句式，不仅可以充分地表达演讲者深深的感激之情，也符合典型的英文演讲的文体特征。译者所做的这些改动，严格说来已经不是意译了，而是改译，但改译的幅度并不是很大，效果也是很明显的。

例5

新疆维吾尔自治区副主席：新疆稳定大局是可控的有保证的 [31]

新华网北京6月12日电（记者王希）新疆维吾尔自治区副主席史大刚12日说，新疆稳定大局是可控的、有保证的。"可以负责任地跟大家说，大家可以很放心地到新疆去。"史大刚说。

史大刚在此前国新办举行的新闻发布会上回答相关提问时表示，社会稳定与经济发展两者相辅相成、缺一不可，只有抓好社会稳定才能保证经济快速发展，通过经济快速发展反过来促进社会稳定。

他介绍，第一次中央新疆工作座谈会自2010年召开以来，天山南北发生了令人振奋的历史性变化。新疆国民生产总值从2009年的4277.1亿元提高到2013年的8510亿元，年均增长11.5%，增速由2009年的全国第30位跃升到2013年的第6位；城乡居民收入连续四年增速居全国前列，其中城镇居民人均可支配收入由2009年的12 258元增加到2013年的19 982元，农民人均纯收入由2009年的3883元增加到2013年的7394元，超过西部地区平均水平；旅游人数2013年达到了5206万人次，比2009年翻了一番多。

此外，新疆自2010年以来连续五年实施"民生建设年"活动，近三年自治区财政用于民生的支出占公共财政总支出的70%以上，年均增长29.7%，累计支出4829亿元，长期积累的住房、就业、教育、社会保障、水电路气等突出问题正在逐步得到解决，使各族群众享受到了改革发展的成果。

31　此例引自 http://www.chinadaily.com.cn/china/2014-06/12/content_17583650.htm.

史大刚表示，当前和今后一个时期，我们将以贯彻落实第二次中央新疆工作座谈会精神为契机，围绕社会稳定和长治久安的总目标，以推进新疆治理体系和治理能力现代化为引领，以经济发展和民生改善为基础，以促进民族团结、遏制宗教极端思想蔓延为重点，坚持依法治疆、团结稳疆、长期建疆，努力建设团结和谐、繁荣富裕、文明进步、安居乐业的社会主义新疆。

Stability in Xinjiang "Controllable and Guaranteed": Official

BEIJING, June 12 (Xinhua)—Stability in northwest China's Xinjiang Uygur Autonomous Region is "controllable and guaranteed," a local official said on Thursday.

Shi Dagang, deputy governor of the region, said at a press conference in Beijing that people can be reassured about traveling in Xinjiang, and that incidents of violence are very rare and isolated cases.

The remarks came two weeks after the second central work conference on Xinjiang, held in the wake of a series of bloody terrorist attacks in the region, including one in an open air market in the regional capital Urumqi that left 39 people dead and 94 injured on May 22.

At the central work conference, President Xi Jinping stressed that a priority of good governance is to improve livelihood so that people from all ethnic groups feel taken care of by the Party and state.

In a follow-up move, China's top economic planning body announced last week that it will work to implement a variety of support policies in employment, education and poverty reduction in the region.

According to Shi, in the past three years, public expenditures on livelihood projects, which added up to 482.9 billion yuan (78.5 billion U.S. dollars), accounted for more than 70 percent of the regional government's total public spending.

Chronic issues in housing, employment, education, social security and infrastructure are being solved, he added, noting that social stability and economic development are both indispensable and can reinforce each other.

Also at Thursday's press conference, authorities confirmed that the fourth China-Eurasia Expo will run from September 1 to 6 in Urumqi, with a focus on the construction of the Silk Road Economic Belt.

During the Expo, countries including Turkey, Belarus, Malaysia, India and Germany will put on events to boost investment and trade.

A textile-themed exhibition as well as a farm produce and food exhibition will also be held to help boost regional employment and promote Xinjiang's agricultural sector.

原文是一篇新闻报道，面向的是国内读者。要将其译成英语，让英语读者喜闻乐见，就必须研究英语读者的信息需求和文化心理，对原文的内容有增有删，删去不感兴趣的内容，补充必要的背景知识。对比原文和译文，发现译文删去了如下内容：

（记者王希）
国新办举行的
他介绍，第一次中央新疆工作座谈会……比2009年翻了一番多。
此外，新疆自2010年以来连续五年实施"民生建设年"活动
年均增长29.7%
使各族群众享受到了改革发展的成果
史大纲表示，……努力建设团结和谐、繁荣富裕、文明进步、安居乐业的社会主义新疆。

译文增加了下述内容：

northwest China's
in Beijing
and that incidents of violence are very rare and isolated cases
The remarks came two weeks after… that left 39 people dead and 94 injured on May 22.
At the central work conference, … feel taken care of by the Party and state.
In a follow-up move, China's … education and poverty reduction in the region.
(78.5 billion U.S. dollars)
Also at Thursday's press conference, authorities confirmed that… to help boost regional employment and promote Xinjiang's agricultural sector.

仔细分析发现，译文中的这些增删是非常必要的。比如，英语读者不一定知道新疆在中国的什么地方，译文增加 northwest China's，读者心中就有概念了；原文的第三段包含了太多读者不一定有兴趣的数据，原文的最后一段若直接翻译不符合英语新闻报道的文体特点，因此翻译时将其删去，是明智而正确的。只有这样，才能实现翻译的目的。不过，这种大规模的增删，已经不是前面所说的以改动细节为区别性特征的改译了，应该归到编译之下。

例6

Sunlight Chandeliers

The lofty departure lounge of the Manchester airport in England is bathed in reflected sunlight from dawn to dusk with natural full-spectrum illumination that's easier on the eyes than artificial light. Four 20-foot-long crystal chandeliers recently were covered from electric bulbs to solar power in a $200,000 project.

Called Lightron, the system was developed by Bomin Solar in Lorrach, Germany.

For each chandelier, there's a suntracking heliostat on the airport roof. This bounces the light through a glass-domed opening via a fixed-angled mirror. The concentrated beam shines vertically down the hollow chandelier onto an internal array of small prisms and mirrors called a sparkle tube, which diffuses the sunlight sideways onto the surrounding glass elements.

The heliostats are controlled by a custom computer that is programmed until the year 2500, says Bomin marketing manager Klaus Klompenhouwer. "Here daylight has the energy equivalent of around two kilowatts," he says. "You'd need eight kilowatts of artificial light for the same effect. But energy conservation is not generally billed as a major factor because you need electricity for the tracking motors and computer. The big thing is that we bring sunlight indoors—where there's normally none—and provide this light without heat. Special mirrored glass that filters out infrared radiation does the trick.

For night operation, Klompenhouwer explains, each chandelier has four kilowatts of integrated floodlight that can't match sunlight for brightness. The artificial lights are switched on and off automatically by the computer. Easy maintenance is an advantage of the converted chandeliers because there's no need to clean or replace numerous electric bulbs, a difficult and time-consuming job.

Lightron installations in Germany have added brilliance to a BMW showroom in Munich, the atrium lobby of a Frankfurt bank, and a shopping mall in Darmstadt. The largest facility is a mammoth solar lighting system at the Stuttgart airport, which has 48 tracking heliostats, 96 fixed mirrors, and 144 floor-based reflectors.

While it has no immediate plans to bring the system to the U.S. housing market, Bomin Solar now is targeting American businesses—and not just windowless inner offices. "Summer sun through big windows heats the room," says Klompenhouwer. "So you turn up the air conditioner and perhaps put down the shade and switch on the lights. You're wasting energy. With our system, you have light without heat for a big saving."

阳光枝形吊灯

设在德国洛拉黑的博明太阳能公司开发了一种叫莱特隆的照明系统，该系统用计算机控制的定日镜跟踪太阳，定日镜反射的阳光，经过一个固定角度的反射镜，穿过屋顶上的拱形玻璃窗口，沿中空的枝形吊灯垂直向下照射，照到吊灯内由许多小的棱镜和反射镜组成的闪光管上，闪光管把阳光散射到周围的玻璃元件上。由于采用了特制的反射镜玻璃滤掉了红外辐射，所以该系统在将阳光引入室内的同时，还不产生热。至于夜间照明，该系统的每个枝形吊灯都有四千瓦的组合泛光灯。

莱特隆照明系统不需要清扫和更换大量的灯泡，因此容易维修。该系统已被安装在英国曼彻斯特机场的候机室、德国宝马汽车公司在慕尼黑的展厅等地点,但尚未进入美国住房建筑市场,虽然博明公司有进入美国市场的打算。

原文是一篇科技报道。译文没有选择全译,而是拣选原文中的重要信息进行翻译,然后重新组合成一篇较短的汉语科技报道,以满足读者只关心原报道中关键信息的需求,这种翻译方法称为摘译。摘译的优缺点都很明显:优点是经过译者的挑译,读者可以在较短的时间内迅速掌握原文中的关键信息,而缺点则是读者无法通过译文了解原文的全貌。此外,摘译过程中译者必须甄别信息重要与否,译者对信息的判断和评价决定了摘译的质量。虽然如此,作为一种翻译方法,摘译在实用文体翻译中自有其不可替代的作用。

例 7　功课终于做完了!真累啊!如果有一瓶乐百氏奶⋯⋯
A Robust a day makes me work, rest and play.

原文是曾风靡全国的乐百氏奶的广告语。译者在将其译成英文时,几乎完全脱离原文,仿拟英文中著名的谚语 An apple a day keeps the doctor away,创造性地将其译成 A Robust a day makes me work, rest and play,为英语读者所喜闻乐见,取得了不俗的广告效果。这种翻译方法,可称之为创译。

总之,根据翻译目的,实用文体的翻译可以采用多种多样的方法。一般说来,在翻译一篇实用文本时,首先需要在全译和变译中做选择。所谓全译,指的是基本按照原文的信息结构将原文内容完完整整地翻译出来。所谓变译,"是译者据特定条件下特定读者的特殊需求,采用增、减、编、述、缩、并、改等变通手段摄取原作有关内容的翻译活动"。[32]

如果译者决定全译,则有直译、意译两种方法。一般说来,由于英、汉两种语言的差别太大,完全直译的情况很少见,大多数情况都是既有直译,又有意译。总的原则是,如果直译能使译文通顺畅达,则直译,反之则意译。常玉田在讨论商务翻译时给出的经验可以作为参考,"局部可以直译,整体需要意译;短句可以直译,长句需要意译;事实应当直译,观点最好意译;陈述应当直译,意象大多意译。"[33]

如果译者决定变译,同样需要根据具体情况选择具体的翻译方法。采用改译、编译,大多是因为原语读者和译语读者在信息需求、文化心理、美学趣味上有区别,译者需要对原文进行适当的加工,以满足译语读者的信息、文化、美学需求。选择摘译的方法是因为译语读者关心的只是原文中的关键信息,没有兴趣或时间阅读原文的全译。至于创译,则主要为广告文体翻译所用。

互联网的快速发展给翻译工作者带来了诸多便利。今天,越来越多的实用文体译者利用网上资源辅助翻译。互联网给译者带来的便利主要表现在以下几个方面:

---

32 黄忠廉. 2002. 变译理论. 北京:中国对外翻译出版公司.
33 常玉田. 2011. 直译当先,意译方成圆——兼谈商务英译汉的特点. 中国翻译,(4):91.

第一,诸多网上在线词典为译者查找相关词语的意思提供了极大的方便。网上词典类型多样,英汉互译经常用到的英语词典、汉语词典、英汉双语词典、英语搭配词典、英语同义词词典等,都可以很容易地通过搜索引擎找到。这里简单介绍几个常用的在线词典:[34]

The Free Dictionary (http://www.thefreedictionary.com/):号称"世界上最全的词典",英文界面,可以查找英语单词或词组的英文释义、同义词或词组、中文释义,及包括西班牙语、德语、法语、意大利语等多个语种在内的词语的英文释义。

OneLook (http://www.onelook.com/):集成几十部英语权威词典,英文界面。只要将英语单词或词组输进搜索框,就会显示几十部词典的超链接,从而查找到该词或词组的释义。同时,该网站还提供单词的词源信息。

爱词霸 (http://www.iciba.com/):提供英语单词或词组的英/汉语释义、例句、同义词、反义词等,也提供汉语词语的汉语释义和英语译法。

海词 (http://dict.cn/):提供英语词语的英汉释义、例句及译文、常见句型、常用短语、词汇搭配、词义辨析、词源解说、近/反义词、经典引文及多个语种词汇的汉语释义等。

句酷 (http://www.jukuu.com/index.php):可检索中、日、英三种语言的词语的例句和对应的英语、日语译文。

有道词典 (http://dict.youdao.com/):功能同"海词"类似。

ozdic 英语搭配词典 (http://www.ozdic.com/collocation-dictionary/):给出可与某个英语单词搭配的其他词语。

汉典 (http://www.zdic.net/):提供汉语字典、汉语词典、成语词典等的查询功能,可以查询到某个汉字在《康熙字典》和《说文解字》中的释义,及其英文对应词或解释。

第二,网上的在线百科为译者了解某一学科的知识提供了便利。实用文体翻译通常涉及某一具体学科,而绝大多数译者不可能了解自己翻译的文本所涉及的每一个学科,因此需要在翻译前或翻译中恶补学科知识,了解某个特定学科术语或概念的准确含义。这时,在线百科就能发挥巨大的作用。译者经常用到的在线百科包括:

《大英百科全书》在线版:http://www.britannica.com/

维基百科英文版:http://en.wikipedia.com

百度百科:http://baike.baidu.com/

搜狗百科:http://baike.sogou.com/

需要提醒的是,与《大英百科全书》相比,维基百科、百度百科和搜狗百科条目的编者是众多的网民,因此提供的信息不一定权威。不过,我们可以利用其他网上资源进行复核,以便了解这些条目内容的准确性。相比较而言,维基百科的条目内容要比百度百科、

---

[34] 需要说明的是,网上信息变动很快,编者无法保证这里给出的网站地址将永远有效。

搜狗百科更可靠。

第三，网上海量的、免费的平行文本（parallel text）和可比文本（comparable text）为译者翻译实用文体提供了最实用的指导。所谓平行文本，指的是相对应于源语文本的译语文本；所谓可比文本，指在相似情境中产生的包含相似信息、发挥相似功能的另一种语言的文本。平行文本和可比文本在文体上与要翻译的文本同属一类，因此研究这两种文本能够给译者翻译带来很多启发。

第四，网上的众多翻译论坛为实用文体的译者提供了一个相互交流、分享翻译经验的园地。这些翻译论坛大多免费，只要注册就可以进入论坛参加讨论，即使不是会员，在有的论坛也可以浏览帖子。与传统的翻译论坛相比，网上论坛全年无休，成员背景多样，藏龙卧虎。加入这些论坛，不仅可以免费学习别人的翻译经验，下载翻译参考资料，还可以在遇到翻译难题时咨询有经验的译者，可谓好处多多。

练习一

一、回答下列问题。

1. 什么叫文体？研究文体对于翻译工作者来说有什么意义？
2. 实用文体与文学文体相比有什么特点？
3. 实用文体翻译应该遵循什么原则？为什么？
4. 实用文体有哪些常用的翻译方法？分别适用于什么情况？

二、分析下列两个文本的文体特点。

1.
> The Seller hereby warrants and represents to the Purchaser that: (a) The Seller owns and has good and marketable title to the property being conveyed herein, free and clear of any pledges, liens, judgments, encumbrances, security interests, claims or contract rights, and further promises and covenants to refrain from so encumbering same from the date of execution of this agreement until closing; (b) No approval or consent of any third person is required to effect the sale; (c) The execution and performance of this agreement will not violate any agreements to which the Seller is a party or any federal, state or local laws, rules or regulations; (d) The Seller's representations, warranties and agreements shall be true and complete as of the date hereof and as of the closing and shall survive the closing and the transactions contemplated by this agreement.

2.

Message for Apology

Dear Liz,

  Just a short note to apologize about the noise and upset.

  I can assure you it won't happen again. We're very sorry.

Rob & Marisa

三、通过互联网查找三到五篇下面文本的可比较文本,分析这些可比较文本的文体特点,并在此基础上,将此文本译成英文。

普通高等学校毕业证书

  学生王大伟,男,1992年6月1日生,于2010年9月至2014年6月在本校外国语学院英语专业四年制本科学习,修完教学计划规定的全部课程,成绩合格,准予毕业。

校长:孔建益
校名:武汉科技大学
2014年6月30日

证书编号:201414118023

第二章 科技文体的翻译

科技文体是人们从事科学技术活动的过程中所形成的一种独立文体形式，涵盖科技论文、研究报告、技术标准、科技产品指南、科技著作、科普读物等多种类型，涉及自然科学和工程技术各个方面。本章首先简述英语科技文体的特点，其次介绍科技文体的翻译原则、翻译策略、翻译特点，最后介绍科技新词的翻译以及科技论文摘要的翻译。

第一节 科技文体的特点

科技文体不同于文学文体，具有自身的特点和规律。为了准确地描述客观世界，科技文体在语言形式上尽可能地简洁准确，在语义表达上明晰连贯，在语言使用上客观规范。与之相比，文学语言用于构建鲜明的文学形象，反映的是经过作家加工了的客观世界，常常借助音韵和节奏、语调和句式、思想和情感等手段来塑造独特的人物、环境和情节，在语言使用上洒脱自如，有时甚至违背常规的语法定式，以突显语言的风格和人物的鲜活。[1]

科技语言与日常语言也有很大不同。在表达同一内容时，科技语言和日常语言的行文和表述方式是不同的。比如，日常生活中妈妈教孩子什么是食盐时可能会说："盐是我们做饭时用来调味的东西。"但在科普读物中，同样的意思往往会这样表述："食盐是家庭烹饪时常用的调味料。"可见科技文体强调用词严谨、语气庄重。请看下表中的两段英文，通过逐句比较，可以清楚地认识科技语言和日常语言在词汇、语法等方面的差异。

---

1 王卫平、潘丽蓉.2009.英语科技文献的语言特点与翻译.上海：上海交通大学出版社.

表 2-1　科技英语与日常英语比较

Graves' Ophthalmopathy(格雷夫斯眼病)[2]	
English for Science and Technology	English for General Purposes
Graves' ophthalmopathy usually occurs in association with hyperthyroidism（甲状腺机能亢进）. Only a small percentage of Graves' ophthalmopathy patients have no excessive production of thyroid（甲状腺）. Its occasional occurrence in the absence of thyroid disease suggests, however, that it may be a separate autoimmune（自身免疫的）disorder.	People usually get sick with eye disease, known as Graves' Disease, when their body produces too much thyroid. But not every patient is the same. A small number of patients produce too little thyroid. So people may, sometimes, get this disease because they have a problem with their immune system.

　　上面两段英文都是介绍格雷夫斯眼病，分别以科技英语和日常英语撰写。左栏属于科技英语，表述客观，行文简练，句式严整，用词正式，专业术语多，名词性短语多，句中主要信息前置，通过主语传递主要信息；而右栏文本用日常英语撰写，表述主观，用词通俗易懂，句式简洁明白，表达方式直观。

　　可见，同样的内容，科技文体的行文和日常英语的表述方式有很大差异。正因为此，科技文体的翻译也不同于其他文体的翻译。在翻译科技文体文本时，译文除了需要准确和通顺外，还要得体，保持原文严谨周密、准确简练、逻辑性强的行文风格。下面进一步分析科技文体的特点，为探讨科技文体的翻译策略和技巧打下基础。

一、使用专门的科学术语

　　科技文体传递科学技术信息与事实，要求概念明确无误，以体现科学、准确、严谨的特征，这需要借助科技术语来实现。因此，与其他类型的文体相比，科技文体在词汇层面上表现出的典型特征就是大量科技术语的使用。如在表 2-1 的例子中，Graves' ophthalmopathy（格雷夫斯眼病）、hyperthyroidism（甲状腺机能亢进）、thyroid（甲状腺）和 autoimmune（自我免疫的）等，都是医学专业术语。

二、使用非人称句

　　在表 2-1 中，左栏文本共三个句子，句子主语分别是 Graves' ophthalmopathy、a small percentage of Graves' ophthalmopathy patients 和 its occasional occurrence。右栏文本共四句，句子主语分别是 people、every patient、patients 和 people。两者的差异非常明显：科技文体中，句子多为正式的非人称句（impersonal formal style），即用无生命的名词作主语；日常英语中，句子多采用有生命的人作主语。一般来说，科技人员着眼于对客观事物和规律的准确描述，

---

[2]　此例引自 Wall, J. R. et al. 1981. Graves' Ophthalmopathy. *Canadian Medical Association Journal*, 124(7): 855–862, 866.

在很多情况下，涉及人的字眼是不必要的，[3]而非人称句突出客观事物本身，使表达不掺杂作者的主观感情而显得更加客观。因此，科技文章往往采用非人称句。当然，人称句在科技文章中也会出现，只是占的比例很小。

三、使用被动语态

被动结构的大量使用是科技英语在句子层面最为显著的特征。据统计，在英语科技文章中，使用被动句的频率比其他各类非科技文章要高得多，科技文献中大概有三分之一的动词需用被动语态的形式。这是因为科技文章侧重叙事推理，强调客观准确，其叙述的对象往往是事物、现象或过程，强调的是所叙述的事物本身，而非科技活动主体，第一、二人称若使用过多，会给读者造成主观臆断的印象。请看下例：

例1　Once the mold has been made, it must be prepared for the molten metal to be poured. The surface of the mold cavity is first lubricated to facilitate the removal of the casting. Then, the cores are positioned and the mold halves are closed and securely clamped together.[4]

此例由三句组成，七个动词都为被动形式。这样的句式既显得陈述客观，又可将主要信息前置，放在主位（Theme）的位置，利于突出主题或关键词。这也是英语科技文本广泛使用被动语态的主要原因之一。

四、使用名词化结构

《当代英语语法》（*A Grammar of Contemporary English*）在论述科技英语时指出，大量使用名词化结构（nominalization）是科技英语的特点之一。因为科技文体强调存在的事实，而非某一行为动作，所以科技英语文本广泛使用表示动作或状态的抽象名词或起名词作用的动名词。如在表2-1的科技文本中，如果把各句中表动作或状态的抽象名词（即名词化结构）换成动词来表达，则会变成下列各组的b句：

- a. Graves' ophthalmopathy usually occurs in association with hyperthyroidism.
  b. Graves' ophthalmopathy usually associates with hyperthyroidism.
- a. Only a small percentage of Graves' ophthalmopathy patients have no excessive production of thyroid.
  b. Only a few Graves' ophthalmopathy patients produce no more thyroid than necessary.
- a. Its occasional occurrence in the absence of thyroid disease...
  b. Occasionally, people's getting sick with this type of eye disease has nothing to do with thyroid...

3　严俊仁. 2004. 汉英科技翻译. 北京：国防工业出版社.
4　此例引自 http://www.custompartnet.com/wu/SandCasting.

相比之下，a 句表达概念更加准确、严密，语气正式，突出了存在的事实；而 b 句动作性很强，表达较口语化，这种句式适合用来描述动作行为而非存在的事实。

五、使用非谓语动词

非谓语动词在句子中起名词、形容词或副词的作用，动词的非谓语形式有分词和动词不定式两种形式。非谓语动词可以代替关系从句，使语言精练，因此，在科技英语中，往往使用分词短语代替定语从句或状语从句，使用不定式短语代替各种从句。

1. 使用分词短语代替定语从句或状语从句

过去分词结构可代替包含被动词的关系从句，例如：

例2 图 1 中用框图表示的电源是一个单相开关逆变器。[5]

a. The power supply, which is shown in block-diagram in Fig. 1, is a single-phase switch-mode inverter.

b. The power supply shown in block-diagram in Fig. 1 is a single-phase switch-mode inverter.

现在分词结构可代替使用主动语态的关系从句，例如：

例3 已经在汽车领域中接替人类工作的机器人开始出现在其他行业中，只是使用程度低一些。[6]

a. Robots that already take over human tasks in the automotive field are beginning to be seen, although to a lesser degree, in other industries as well.

b. Robots already taking over human tasks in the automotive field are beginning to be seen, although to a lesser degree, in other industries as well.

2. 使用不定式短语代替关系从句

关系从句可用较短的不定式短语来代替，例如：

例4 使高级语言及编程程序标准化的努力，近年来受到很大关注。[7]

a. Efforts that are used to standardize high-level languages and compilers have received much attention in recent years.

b. Efforts to standardize high-level languages and compilers have received much attention in recent years.

比较译法 a 和译法 b，译法 b 中由于使用了不定式短语代替关系从句而更为精简。

5　此例引自朱永强、尹忠东. 2007. 电力专业英语阅读与翻译. 北京：中国水利水电出版社.
6　此例引自盛楠等. 2010. 实用科技英语教程. 2 版. 北京：人民邮电出版社.
7　此例引自李心广. 2010. 新编计算机英语教程. 北京：人民邮电出版社.

六、使用结构复杂的长句

为了完整、准确地表达事物间的内在联系，科技文体常常使用长句来解释科学现象或科技名词和术语。例如：

例5 月球完全是一个毫无生气的世界，是一片多山的不毛之地。在酷热的白昼，太阳向它倾泻着无情的烈焰，而漫长的严寒却远远不是我们在地球上所能体验到的。[8]

The moon is a world ① <u>that</u> is completely and utterly dead, a sterile mountainous waste on ② <u>which</u> during the heat of the day the sun blazed down with relentless fury, but ③ <u>where</u> during the long night the cold is so intense ④ <u>that</u> it far surpasses anything ever experienced on the earth.

此例采用合译法，将原文的两个句子合译成一个复杂的英文长句，含有四个关系句：①是由关系代词 that 引导的定语从句，修饰 a world；②是介词 on + 关系代词 which 引导的定语从句，修饰 a world 的同位语 a sterile mountainous waste；③是关系副词 where 引导的定语从句，也修饰 a sterile mountainous waste；④是 so... that 句型的结果状语从句。

第二节
科技文体的翻译原则和技巧

科学的根本任务在于认识事物和现象的本质，揭示其运动规律，并将这些知识用于生产实践。科学家主要进行分析、归纳、推理、论证等思维活动，科学的语言自然具有专业性、抽象性、概括性、精确性、严密性、紧凑性、逻辑性等特点，因此科技文体的翻译应遵循专业、客观、精确、简洁四大原则。在科技翻译中，译文用语要规范，要具有专业性和学术性；译文表达要真实客观、严谨准确；译文用词要精练，要用最少的词句表达最多的信息。

一、专业性

科技文体专业性强，大量使用专业名词和科技术语。所谓科技术语，是指在科技语言中有着精确和单一意义的词，这种词即使出现在口语中，也会让人感到它们属于某一专业领域。在科技文体中，无论是概念的解释还是原理的阐述，都要使用准确的术语和严谨恰当的措辞，不能含混不清或模棱两可，更不能出现错误。作为科技文体的翻译者，不但要有丰富的专业知识，还必须具备娴熟的双语专业词汇转换能力。例如：shoulder 一词，常用意思是"肩膀或肩负、承担"，但在土木工程文献中常译作"路肩"；surface finish 在

---

[8] 此例引自 Jones, S. H. S. 1959. *Life on Other Worlds*. London: Scientific Book Club.

冶金专业文献中应该译作"表面光洁度"。译者一定要有敏感的专业意识和厚实的专业基础，才能有效地排除科技翻译上的疑难。如果不能准确地把握术语的专业性，译文就会让读者不知所云。如果要翻译某个行业的科技资料，译者一定要事先熟悉基本的专业术语，本着严谨的态度，查阅相关专业资料、词典或百科全书，切忌望文生义。例如，在科技文献中，bearing 可能会被译作"轴承"、machine 译作"切削或机械加工"、tolerance 译作"公差"、dog's ears 译作"轧件表面上的疤痕"，等等。

通常，科技术语可采用以下三种译法：

1. 意译

在翻译科技术语时，应尽可能采用意译，以准确译出原词所表达的科学概念。例如：

- liquid-crystal 液晶
- horsepower 马力
- data stream 数据流
- 活性表面 active surface
- 压扁试验 squeezing test
- 长征二号 F 运载火箭 Long March 2F rocket

2. 音译

音译是指根据原词的发音译成目的语中读音与原词大致相同的词。一般来说，在科技术语初次译入目的语时，由于还未形成广为接受的规范译名，可能会直接音译，等到时机成熟时，有些音译词又渐渐会被意译词所取代，不过也有少量的音译词保留下来。例如：

- sonar 声呐
- karst 喀斯特（地形）
- hertz 赫兹（频率单位）
- 天宫一号 Tiangong-1
- 神舟八号 Shenzhou-8
- 阴阳 [中医] Yin Yang

音译逐渐被意译取代的词，如 penicillin 先音译为"盘尼西林"，后被意译"青霉素"取而代之；E-mail 初译为"伊妹儿"，后来其意译"电子邮件"逐渐普及；vitamin 原音译为"维他命"，今天大多使用"维生素"。

3. "形+意"或"音+意"结合译法

这种翻译方法是保留原术语或词的一部分音译或不译，而另一部分意译。例如：

- T-steel T 型钢；丁型钢
- X-ray X 射线
- B-2 bomber B-2 轰炸机

- ZR 关系　Z-R relationship
- X 标杠理论　X-Bar Theory
- 锯齿扫查　Zigzag scan

　　科技术语的翻译，选词用字必须是规范的技术词语，既不能用日常词语代替科技词语，也不能舍弃约定俗成的规范技术词语不用，随意创造"技术新词"。通常翻译科技术语时需注意以下四点：

　　（1）科技术语的译名应注意规范化和统一化，凡约定俗成的译名，不宜随意更动。

　　科技名词作为知识传播与科技交流的载体与工具，促进科技和文化发展。人们经过长期实践而认可的科技术语，不宜轻易改动，否则会造成新的混乱，影响各方的交流。《科学时报》就曾专门刊登过文章，讨论海峡两岸因术语不统一影响到合作交流："海峡两岸本是同祖同根，同文同语，然而，50 多年的骨肉分离已经影响到术语的使用和交流，在两岸经贸、文化、学术交流中，因术语不同而影响理解的'梗阻现象'也越来越频繁。据媒体报道，2005 年春节海峡两岸包机，飞行员与地面指挥塔台的对话，就存在名词术语的沟通障碍。结果为了确保安全，两岸包机飞行员与对方地面指挥塔台的对话只得用英语术语来沟通。"[9]

　　译名不统一必然造成交流双方沟通困难，因此，科技术语译名的规范化和统一化是译者必须遵循的首要原则。Myocardial Infarction 是译成"心肌梗塞"，还是"心肌梗死"？Arrhythmia 是译成"心率不齐"，还是"心律不齐"？译者应以约定俗成为指导性原则。也许上述两个名称比较常见，这点文字上的细微差别似乎无关紧要。但是，如果涉及不常见或根本没见过的术语，例如抗寄生虫药物 Albendazole 一词，有的译为"阿苯达唑"，有的则译成"丙硫咪唑"，若不加以规范统一，则可能导致病人误以为是两种不同的药而过量服用的危险。又如大气科学中的 nowcast 一词，业内已经采纳了最能代表其内涵的"临近预报"为其规范译名，就应该淘汰"现时预报""现场预报""即时预报"和"短时预报"等其他译名。

　　（2）在同一篇文章或同一本书中，专业术语的译名必须全篇统一，否则会影响译语读者对译文的理解。

　　下面一例，ergonomics 一词在该篇文章的汉译中没有使用统一的译名，因而读起来令人费解。

例1　Ergonomics is a complex science—a mix of biology, psychology, engineering and design, that studies the interaction and relationship between humans and the surrounding. The place where the importance of ergonomics is most commonly

---

9　李晓明. 2008. 术语不统一带来混乱，科技名词期待规范与创新. (2008-02-28) [2015-03-14]. http://www.chinanews.com/gn/news/2008/02-28/1176273.shtml.

articulated is in the office. We may have what we call an <u>ergonomic</u> chair. We may have an <u>ergonomic</u> keyboard or an <u>ergonomic</u> mouse. Like most people who sit at a desk with a computer all day, you've probably got a sore back, throbbing knees, aching wrists, and eyestrain. Sound about right? Then you need to familiarize yourself with <u>ergonomics</u>.[10]

<u>人机工程学</u>是一门融合了生物学、心理学和工程设计的复杂科学，主要研究人和环境的相互作用关系。办公室是最能体现<u>工效学</u>重要性的场所：有<u>人体工学</u>椅子、有<u>人体工学</u>键盘或<u>人体工学</u>鼠标。和大多数整天坐在办公桌电脑前的人一样，你可能感到背痛，膝盖阵痛，手腕疼痛以及眼睛疲劳。听起来确实如此？那么你就有必要了解一下什么是<u>人类功效学</u>。

此例译文中，术语 ergonomics 在同一段中被译成四种不同的译名，分别是"人机工程学""工效学""人体工学"和"人类功效学"。译名不统一不仅会误导读者，更会造成理解上的困难，必须避免。

（3）科技新词的译名要能正确表达出事物的真实含义，要尽量译出原词的确切含义，必要时可辅以音译。

例如，vital signs 不能简单地字对字地翻译成"重要的"（vital）+"符号"（signs）="重要符号"，而应该译出该词本身的含义"生命体征"。又如，dustoff 不能译成"尘土"（dust）+"离开"（off）="尘土离开"，而应译成"战地救护直升机"。该词因战地救护直升机起飞和降落时扬起尘土而得名，译名体现了事物的真实含义。此外，有些科技新词如 Internet，如果类比 international 译成"国际的"的译法，Internet 则会被译成"网际"。但"网际"太过抽象，显然不适合用来指称一件事物，似乎更适合描述一种状态，所以在这种情况下应该另辟蹊径，直译 net 并辅之以 Inter 的音译，最终译成"因特网"——词的重心落在"网"字上，词义是"一种网络"，确切含义一目了然。再如 gene bank 一词，gene 已有现成的音译名，所以顺理成章地译成"基因库"。

（4）注意同一术语在不同的专业领域会有不同的译法。

有些科技术语虽然在某一专业只有一个词义，但是在其他专业中又有其他词义，译者在翻译时要认真考究，按其不同的含义分别定名，对号入座，不要张冠李戴。比如，plasma 一词，物理学将其定名为"等离子体"，而医学则将其定名为"血浆"。又如 series 一词，在化学上译作"系"，在地质学上译作"统、段"，在数学上译作"级数"，在电学上译作"串联"，而在动物学上又译作"列、组"等。[11]

10　此例引自 http://3y.uu456.com/bp-fbd40220sq0102020740qc1c-1.html.
11　程若春、李宏志. 1994. 浅谈科技英语术语的翻译. 上海科技翻译，（4）：7–9.

二、客观性

科技文献以客观世界的万事万物为研究对象，反映的是事物发展的客观规律，因此，客观性是科技文体的重要特征。这里的客观性包含两层含义：一是内容上的客观；二是表达形式上的客观。首先，译文的内容必须客观，必须反映事物发展的客观规律，不能添油加醋。译文是否符合知识的客观性，是我们判断译文对错的首要标准。其次，译者所采用的语言表达形式必须客观。在汉译英时，译者可以采用"非人称句和被动语态"的句型和语态手段来实现译文语言上的客观。

非人称句和被动语态避免了采用第一、二人称或施事者为主语而造成的主观色彩，使句子意思表达清晰、结构简洁、客观性强。请看译例：

例2 我们的体温是靠消耗血液中的糖分来维持的。

　　a. We keep our body warm by consuming sugar in the blood.（日常英语）

　　b. Our normal body temperature is maintained by the consumption of sugar in the blood.（科技英语）

　　c. The maintenance of our normal body temperature is achieved by the consumption of sugar in the blood.（科技英语）

译文 a 用第一人称作句子主语，使叙事者置身其中，显得比较主观；此外，叙述的语气是一种个人观点的表达，不够客观。相比之下，译文 b 和 c 使用非人称句和被动语态，既突出了关键信息 maintenance of our normal body temperature，又表达了一种客观事实。译文 a 与译文 b、c 的不同在于 idea 和 fact 的区别：译文 a 表达的是 an idea，译文 b 和 c 陈述的是 a fact，后两种译法比第一种译法更正式、更庄重。请再看一例：

例3 为了连接金属部件，常用机用螺钉、固定螺丝钉和内六角螺栓。机用螺钉常用螺丝刀来固定。[12]

　　a. People frequently use machine screws, set screws and cap screws to fasten metallic elements. They usually apply machine screws with a screwdriver.

　　b. For fastening metallic elements, machine screws, set screws and cap screws are frequently used. Machine screws are usually applied with a screwdriver.

比较两种译法，译文 a 采用主动语态，分别用 people 和 they 作主语，使译文带上主观色彩，而这一点在科技翻译中应该尽量避免。而译文 b 采用非人称句且使用被动语态，两个主语都指向客观事物，体现了很强的客观性。

科技英语中有 1/3 的句子是被动句，而汉语中被动语态使用的频率要小得多，所以在汉译含被动语态的句子时，要注意汉语的表达习惯，不必拘泥于两种语言形式上的对应。通常可作如下处理：

12　此例引自黄丽文．2010．汉英科技翻译客观性研究．现代商贸工业，(16)：282-283．

1. 译成主动句：若原文中已含有施动者，就将其译成主语；若原文中没有施动者，则根据上下文补充一个主语，或增加"大家""人们"等泛指性主语。

例4 Water can be changed from a liquid into a solid.[13]
　　a. 水能被从液体变成固体。
　　b. 水能从液体变成固体。

译文 a 将此句译成汉语的被动句，不符合汉语表达习惯，读起来别扭。译文 b 将此句译成汉语的主动句"水能从液体变成固体"，通顺流畅得多。再看一例：

例5 Captured underwater noise was transmitted directly from the hydro-phone to operator's ear-phones.[14]
　　a. 被捕捉到的水下噪声直接被水中听音器传递到操作员的耳机中。
　　b. 水中听音器将捕捉到的水下噪声直接传递到操作员的耳机中。

主动句译文 b 较之被动句译文 a 更通顺，更符合汉语表达习惯。

2. 译成无主句：当不愿、没有必要或不可以说出施动者时，则采用无主句来表示。

例6 A gas may be defined as a substance which remains homogeneous.[15]
　　a. 人们可以把气体定义为一种始终处于均匀状态的物质。
　　b. 所谓气体就是一种始终处于均匀状态的物质。

译文 a 补充泛指主语"人们"，使读者觉得气体可以有好几种定义，既可以这样定义，也可以那样定义，明显不如译文 b 的无主句表达客观。

3. 译成被动句：需要特别突出被动者或特别强调被动动作时，可译成汉语的被动句。

例7 The substance which gives up hydrogen is said to be oxidized and the one which accepts the hydrogen is said to be reduced.[16]
　　放出氢的物质被称为氧化了的物质，而接受氢的物质被称为还原了的物质。

英语原文突出 the substance which gives up hydrogen，翻译时仍然把原文强调的信息放在主位的位置上，译成"放出氢的物质"，将整个句子译成汉语的被动句，以突出英语原文的意图。

总之，客观性是科技文献的重要特征之一，是科技英语翻译的要求，译者应该从内容和表达形式上满足这种要求。

13　此例引自 http://www.hjenglish.com/new/p209350/.

14　此例引自 http://game.ali213.net/thread-2557717-1-1.html.

15　此例引自 http://www.0771fanyi.com/news/20120402388.htm.

16　此例引自武力等. 2000. 科技英汉与汉英翻译教程. 西安：西北工业大学出版社.

三、准确性

科技文体的非文学性决定了科技翻译应遵守"准确为主、平实为体"的基本原则。准确性是科技语言的灵魂。科技文体翻译的准确性是指译文要忠实于原文,要语意确切、论证周详,以保持原文与译文所表达的意义一致。要做到准确翻译科技文本,在表达上必须注意以下三个方面。

(一)规范性

科技文体讲究语言规范,译文也必须用符合科技文体规范的语言来表达。请看译例:

例8 The instrument is used to <u>determine</u> how fully the batteries are charged.[17]

    a. 这种仪表用来<u>确定</u>电瓶充电的程度。

    b. 这种仪表用来<u>测定</u>电瓶充电的程度。

译文 a 将 determine 一词译作"确定"不符合专业规范,而译文 b 将其译为"测定",才是准确的表达。

例9 All bodies consist of molecules and <u>these</u> of atoms.[18]

    a. 所有的物体都由分子和原子所组成。

    b. 所有的物体都是由分子组成,而分子又由原子组成。

原文是一个并列句,为了避免重复,第二个 of 前省略了谓语动词 consist,并用 these 指代 molecules。译文 a 没有正确理解原句,也忽略了分子和原子之间的关系,漏译了 these of atoms 中的指示代词 these,所以不准确。译文 b 则忠实地再现了原文的内容,表达准确。

汉译英也存在同样的情况,例如:

例10 如果不适当地处理,锅炉及机动车排出的废气就会造成城市空气污染。[19]

    a. Exhaust from boilers and vehicles causes air pollution in cities, unless it is properly treated.

    b. Exhaust from boilers and vehicles, unless properly treated, causes air pollution in cities.

译文 a 中 unless it is properly treated 放在句末,容易引起歧义,让读者误解为修饰"空气污染",而实际上该成分是修饰 exhaust 的。译文 b 采用非谓语动词形式插在句中,修饰 exhaust,表意精准,避免了可能的误解。

---

17 此例引自 http://dict.hjenglish.com/w/instruments.

18 李亚舒等. 2000. 科技翻译论著新萃. 北京: 气象出版社.

19 于建平. 2001. 科技论文汉译英中若干问题分析. 中国翻译, (1): 32–34.

（二）逻辑性

科技文章概念明确，逻辑严密，表述经得起推敲。译者必须用符合逻辑的语言传达出原作者的意图和思想。因此，译者不仅要考虑句中的各种语法关系，更要注意各概念之间的逻辑关系。请看译例：

例11 A seed consists of an embryo, a supply of food and one or more seed coats surrounding the young plant and its food supply.[20]
　　a. 种子含有胚、胚乳和一层或几层包在幼苗和它的胚乳外面的种皮。
　　b. 种子含有胚、胚乳和一层或几层包在胚和胚乳外面的种皮。

分析原句各成分之间的内在逻辑，seed 包括 an embryo, a supply of food 和 one or more seed coats，并且 seed coats 是裹在 young plant 和 food supply 外面的一层或几层种皮。young plant 前有定冠词 the 特指前面提到过的事物。根据各成分之间的关系，可以判断 the young plant 和 an embryo 指的应是同一事物"胚"，译文 a 把 the young plant 译为"幼苗"是误译，语言表达上突然出现第四样事物，与前文内容逻辑上产生冲突。译文 b 才是正确的译法。

同样的情况也存在于科技文本的汉译英中，例如：

例12 大小备件都应分类储存。[21]
　　a. Large and small spare parts should be classified and stored.
　　b. The spare parts, large or small, should be categorized in the storehouse.

原文中隐含的逻辑关系是："所有备件，无论大小，都应该分类储存。"译文 a 没有体现这种隐含的逻辑关系，而是把"大小"译成定语，变成了"大的和小的备件应该分类并储存"，而把"非大非小或中等大小"的备件排除在外，曲解了原文的含义。译文 b 才准确表达了原意。

（三）使用长句

科技论文表达科学理论、原理、规律以及各事物之间错综复杂的关系，而很多时候复杂的科学思维无法使用简单句来表达，所以语法结构复杂的长句便较多地应用在科技英语当中。科技英语长句通常结构复杂，修饰成分相互套嵌，语序错综，在翻译时有一定难度。为了使译文逻辑严密、层次分明，译者需要对英语长句进行解构，然后根据叙述层次和顺序重组。就翻译方法而言，可以分为顺序法、逆序法、分译法和重组法四种。

1. 顺序法

所谓顺序法，是指译文基本保留原文的语法结构，在语序上不作较大变动。当英语长

20　此例引自田传茂、许明武等. 2003. 生命科学（科技英语阅读系列）. 武汉：华中科技大学出版社.
21　此例引自郄春生. 2008. 汉英科技翻译中隐含逻辑关系的表达. 中国科技翻译，（4）：5–9.

句的叙述和逻辑顺序与汉语相近时，可以按照英语的原文顺序逐次翻译，但要注意定语从句和被动语态的处理。长句汉译英的处理原则相同。例如：

例13 Many man-made substances are replacing certain natural materials because either the quantity of the natural products cannot meet our ever-increasing requirement, or more often, because the physical properties of the synthetic substances, which is the common name for man-made materials, have been chosen, and even emphasized so that it would be of the greatest use in the field in which it is to be applied.[22]

许多人造材料正在取代某些天然材料，这或者是因为天然产品的数量不能满足人类不断增长的需求，或者更多的是因为合成材料（各种人造材料的统称）的物理特性被选中，甚至被突出，以便它在拟用领域能发挥最大的作用。

例14 交流机不受这种限制，唯一的要求是相对移动，而且由于固定电枢和旋转磁场有很多优点，这种安排是所有容量超过几千伏安的同步机的标准做法。[23]

No such limitation is placed on an alternating-current machine; here the only requirement is relative motion, and since a stationary armature and a rotating field system have numerous advantages, this arrangement is standard practice for all synchronous machines rated above a few kilovolt-amperes.

2. 逆序法

当英语长句的表达和逻辑顺序与汉语习惯不相同甚至完全相反时，一般用逆序法翻译：从原文的后面译起，按汉语习惯逆着英语原文的顺序进行翻译。例如：

例15 Aluminum remained unknown until the nineteenth century, because nowhere in nature is it found free, owing to its always being combined with other elements, most commonly with oxygen, for which it has a strong affinity.[24]

铝总是和其他元素结合在一起，最常见的是和氧结合在一起，因为铝对氧有很强的亲和力，因此，在自然界任何地方都找不到处于游离状态的铝，所以铝直到十九世纪才为人所知。

例16 各种机器零件无论多么脏，形状多么不规则，用超声波处理后，就可以被洗得干干净净，甚至干净得像新零件一样。[25]

Various machine parts can be washed very clean and will be as clean as new ones when they are treated by ultrasonic, no matter how dirty and irregularly shaped they may be.

3. 分译法

有时英语长句中主语或主句与修饰词的关系并不十分密切，翻译时可以依汉语多用短

22　此例引自毛荣贵. 2002. 新世纪大学英汉翻译教程. 上海：上海交通大学出版社.
23　此例引自王爱君等. 2004. 科技英语阅读与翻译实用教程. 北京：新时代出版社.
24　此例引自熊海虹. 2010. 高等学校研究生英语综合教程（下）. 北京：外语教学与研究出版社.
25　此例引自王振国. 2008. 新英汉翻译教程. 北京：高等教育出版社.

句的习惯，把长句的从句或短语分译成几个单句，再依据单句之间的逻辑关系重新组织。例如：

例17 Odd though it sounds, cosmic inflation is a scientifically plausible consequence of some respected ideas in elementary-particle physics, and many astrophysicists have been convinced for the better part of a decade that it is true. [26]

宇宙膨胀学说虽然听似奇特，但它是基本粒子物理学中一些公认理论的科学合理的推论。许多天体物理学家过去十年来都认为这一论说是正确的。

例18 一个结构受到的载荷可以分为静载和动载两类。静载包括该结构各部分的重量。动载则是由于人和可移动设备等的重量而引起的载荷。[27]

The loads a structure is subjected to are divided into dead loads, which include the weights of all the parts of the structure, and live loads, which are due to the weights of people, movable equipment, etc.

4. 重组法

当上述几种译法都无法流畅地表达原文的句意时，为了使译文流畅且更符合汉语叙事习惯，在厘清长句结构、弄懂长句原意的基础上，彻底摆脱原文语序和句子形式，在翻译时对句子进行重新组合。例如：

例19 With the advent of the space shuttle, it will be possible to put an orbiting solar power plant in stationary orbit 24,000 miles from the earth that would collect solar energy almost continuously and convert this energy either directly to electricity via photovoltaic cells or indirectly with flat plate or focused collectors that would boil a carrying medium to produce steam that would drive a turbine that then in turn would generate electricity. [28]

随着航天飞机的出现，将一个沿轨道运行的太阳能发电站送到离地球24 000英里的定常轨道上去将成为可能。太阳能发电站几乎不间断地收集太阳能，并用光电池将太阳能直接转换成电能，或者用平板集热器或聚焦集热器将太阳能转换成电能，即集热器使热传导体汽化，驱动涡轮机发电。

例20 低温学的过冷作用将液态氦及某些气体变成"超流体"，将某些金属变成"超导体"，使它们没有电阻，从而在很多方面改变世界面貌。[29]

The super-cooling effects of the cryogenics which convert liquid helium and other gases into "superfluids" and metals into "superconductors", making them non-resistant to electricity, could change the world in a number of ways.

26　此例引自张磊.2013.红宝书·考研英语10年真题.7版.西安：西北大学出版社.
27　此例引自王爱君等.2004.科技英语阅读与翻译实用教程.北京：新时代出版社.
28　此例引自何宏.2011.电气信息类科技英语教程.北京：机械工业出版社.
29　此例引自王爱君等.2004.科技英语阅读与翻译实用教程.北京：新时代出版社.

四、简洁性

用简洁的语言表达精确的内容是科技文体的特点。鉴于汉、英表达上的差别,在翻译科技英语的过程中,不能受英语语言形式的制约,必须根据汉语表达习惯进行精简,避免结构臃肿。试看下面两例:

例21 A typical foliage leaf of a plant belonging to the dicotyledons is composed of two principal parts: blade and petiole.[30]

 a. 一片属于双子叶植物科的典型的营养叶由叶片和叶柄这两个主要部分组成。

 b. 双子叶植物典型的营养叶由两个主要部分组成:叶片和叶柄。

译文 a 的表达太拘泥于原语形式,明显受英语形合语言的影响,句子冗长,句意不清晰。译文 b 将"一片属于双子叶植物科的典型的营养叶"换成"双子叶植物典型的营养叶"后,显得简洁,更具科技语言风格。

例22 It is a common property of any matter that is expanded when it is heated and it contracts when cooled.[31]

 a. 任何物质,如果遇到热,它就会膨胀,如果遇到冷,它就会收缩,这是共性。

 b. 热胀冷缩是所有物质的共性。

译文 b 省略了不必要的词,并做了语序调整,符合汉语特点,明显比译文 a 简洁。

在汉英科技翻译过程中,可以使用名词化结构、非谓语结构、with 引导的伴随状语和介词短语等手段使译文简洁。

(一)使用名词化结构

名词化结构主要由"动词名词化 +of+ 普通名词"构成。该结构可以代替句子传递等值的信息,使逻辑关系更明确,表达更严密。使用名词化结构,可增加词句负载信息的容量。叶斯帕森曾说过,"名词化是表达科学思想的一种工具,用在政论文体或科技文体中具有庄重感和严肃感,更能体现哲理性和科学性。"[32] 请看下例:

例23 阿基米德最先发现固体排水的原理。[33]

 a. Archimedes first discovered the principle that water is displaced by solid bodies.

 b. Archimedes first discovered the principle of displacement of water by solid bodies.

译文 b 使用了名词化结构 displacement of water,代替译文 a 中的同位语从句 that water is displaced,一方面简化了句子,另一方面强调了 displacement 这一事实。请看另一例:

---

30 此例引自 http://cfl.cqupt.edu.cn/itet/jiaoxueneirong/kechengneirong/2011-03-22/182_2.html.
31 此例引自刘文俊.1994.科技英语翻译也讲究"雅".中国科技翻译,(3):10–15.
32 孔令翠.2002.实用英汉翻译.成都:四川大学出版社.
33 此例引自 http://www.iciba.com/fyjg.

例24 添加或者去除热量可以改变物体的状态。[34]

    a. If we <u>add or remove</u> heat, the state of matter may change.

    b. The <u>addition or removal</u> of heat may change the state of matter.

译文 a 和译文 b 意思基本一样，不同之处在于：译文 b 为简单句，译文 a 为复杂句；译文 b 使用名词化结构，译文 a 使用主动语态的从句；译文 b 主语为物，译文 a 中从句的主语为人；译文 b 的信息焦点在名词化结构上，译文 a 的信息焦点在分句的动宾结构上。从句子结构来看，译文 b 要比译文 a 简洁；从表达方式看，译文 b 要比译文 a 客观。总之，译文 b 更符合科技文体的风格。

（二）使用非谓语结构

科技英语行文简练、结构紧凑，往往会采用分词短语、分词独立结构或不定式短语来代替各类从句。例如：

例25 热量从地球辐射出来，使得气流上升。[35]

    a. <u>When it is radiating</u> from the earth, heat causes air currents to rise.

    b. <u>Radiating from</u> the earth, heat causes/forces air currents to rise.

（三）使用 with 引导的伴随状语

例如：

例26 大多数金属都是良导体，而银是最好的导电金属。[36]

    a. Most metals are good conductors, <u>and silver is the best of the metals that conduct electricity</u>.

    b. Most metals are good conductors, <u>with silver being the best</u>.

（四）使用介词短语

例如：

例27 蓄热储能材料的选择应有效降低热耗。[37]

    a. Materials <u>which are used for heat storage and accumulation</u> are chosen so as to effectively reduce heat loss.

    b. Materials <u>for heat storage and accumulation</u> are chosen so as to effectively reduce heat loss.

从以上各类译例可以看出，将中文的科技文章翻译成英文，可以通过各种策略使译文更加简洁。

---

34 此例引自林红. 2008. 论科技英语名词化结构的语用翻译. 外国语言文学研究，（2）：6–11.

35 同上。

36 同上。

37 同上。

第三节
科技论文摘要的翻译

一、科技论文摘要及其特点

摘要（Abstract）是论文内容的高度浓缩。作为学术论文的重要组成部分，论文摘要提供给读者的信息包括论文的主要概念和讨论的主要问题。论文摘要一方面有助于编辑人员判断该论文是否有录用的价值；另一方面也有助于读者决定是否有必要进一步细读全文。通常，好的论文摘要在内容和形式上具有以下特点：

（一）内容完整性

摘要可以看作是一篇结构完整、内容具体的"微论文"，它可以独立于论文而存在，所以是完整的、独立的、能充分说明论文内容的简短陈述。读者即使不阅读全文也能对论文的主要信息有较全面的了解。

（二）语言经济性

论文摘要篇幅短小。学术论文摘要的长度一般为正文字数的2%—3%，国际标准化组织建议不少于250词，不超过500词。摘要过短无法涵盖论文内容，太长则不能突出重点。针对这一点，美国的 *The Engineering Index* 就要求：摘要中应取消或减少背景信息；不出现本学科领域的常识性内容，只叙述新情况、新内容；不涉及未来计划；不加进文章内容以外的解释和评论，尤其是不自我评价，以提高语言的使用效能。此外，摘要不宜加入公式、图、表以及非公用的符号，内容要求简明扼要，一般包括该项研究的目的、背景、对象、方法、结果、结论以及结论的适应范围等。

在我国，已发表学术论文的摘要能否被 SCI、EI 这些主要的国际检索所收录，已成为衡量文章水平和价值的重要尺度。因此，如何译出精练达意、语言规范的英文摘要越来越受到广大学者、科技工作者和期刊编辑的重视。作为科技翻译的一个重要组成部分，学术论文摘要的翻译一要做到"信"，忠实于原文；二要符合学术论文摘要的语言使用规范。

二、科技论文摘要翻译技巧

（一）常用动词的互译

中、英文学术论文摘要写作都会使用一些较为固定的谓语动词，在翻译时，可以直接使用英、汉谓语动词对等词。以下为科技论文摘要中常见的英汉谓语动词：

汉语	英语
是	to be
描述	to present；to describe
介绍	to introduce
分析	to analyze
讨论；论述	to discuss
重点讨论	to focus on; to concentrate on
研究；探讨	to study; to investigate; to explore; to examine
说明	to explain
运用；使用	to apply; to use
计算	to calculate; to compute
阐明；举例说明	to clarify; to illustrate
表明	to indicate; to suggest
表示；显示	to show; to demonstrate
考虑	to consider; to take... into consideration
证明	to prove
结果发现	to find; to conclude
概述；总结	to summarize; to sum up
提出	to suggest; to put forward; to propose

（二）程式化句子的互译

在翻译论文摘要时，除了常用的谓语动词可以直接对应转换外，一些惯用的句子也可以对应转换。无论是中文还是英文科技论文的摘要，都会使用一些固定的表达方式，形成许多程式化的句子，翻译时，可以直接套用对应的程式化句式。

1. 论文摘要开头句开门见山、点明主题，其常见英汉对应句式如：

- 本文简要介绍了……
  This paper gives a brief introduction to...
- 本文详细描述了……的研究
  This article describes a detailed study of...
- 本文讨论了……
  This paper discusses...
- 本文介绍了一种新的……方法
  In this paper, a new method is described for...
- 本文对……进行了分析
  In this paper, an analysis of... was carried out...

2. 用来进一步概述文章具体内容的常用句式，例如：

- 本研究拟……
  The aim of this study is to...
- 本研究以……为理论基础
  Our study of... is based on...
- 本研究拟对……进行分析和对比
  This research sets out to analyze and compare...
- 本研究结论与……进行对比
  Comparison of our results with...

3. 用来总结全文或提出建议的常用句式，例如：

- 研究得出结论……
  It concludes that...
- 研究结果表明……
  The result shows that...
- 研究发现……
  It finds that...
- 本研究建议……；本研究提出……
  This research suggests (proposes) that...

（三）时态的处理

英语科技论文的摘要所用的时态变化相对简单。一般过去时主要用于对研究和实验的具体陈述，一般现在时主要用于介绍研究目的、内容、结论等客观事实，两者使用广泛。不过，由于中、英文在表达习惯上存在一定差异，所以在互译过程中要注意区分实验和事实，并进行相应的时态转换。请看下面两例翻译的时态转换：

例1 ① This experiment <u>was performed</u> to determine the factors that positively influence enzyme reaction rates in cellular activities since some enzymes seem to be more effective than others. ② Catecholase enzyme activity <u>was measured</u> through its absorption rate in a spectrophotometer, using light with a wavelength of 540 nm. ③ We <u>compared</u> the absorbance rates in samples with varying enzyme concentrations and a constant pH of 7, and with samples with constant enzyme concentration and varying pH levels. ④ The samples with the highest enzyme concentration <u>had</u> the greatest absorption rate of 95 percent compared to the sample with the lowest concentration and an absorption rate of 24 percent. ⑤ This <u>suggests</u> that a higher concentration of enzymes <u>leads to</u> a greater product production rate. ⑥ The samples with a pH between 6 and 8 <u>had</u> the greatest absorption rate of 70 percent compared to an absorption rate of 15 percent with a pH of 4; ⑦ this suggests that Catecholase is most effective in a neutral pH ranging from 6 to 8.[38]

①某些酶似乎比其他一些酶在细胞活动中活性更强，所以<u>进行该项实验以测定细胞活动中积极影响酶反应速度的因素</u>。②本项实验<u>使用</u>波长为 540 纳米的光，通过分光光度计<u>测量</u>儿茶酚酶的吸收率进而<u>测定</u>其活性。③我们把具有不同酶浓度和恒定 pH7 值样品的吸收率和具有恒定酶浓度和不同 pH 值样品的吸收率<u>进行了比较</u>。④酶浓度最高的样品吸收率最大（高达 95%），与此相比，酶浓度最低的样品吸收率最小（仅为 24%）。⑤<u>这表明</u>，酶的浓度越高，产品生产率就越大。⑥pH 值在 6 和 8 之间的样品吸收率最大（为 70%），与此相比，pH 值为 4 的样品吸收率仅为 15%。⑦<u>这一点表明</u>儿茶酚酶在中等 pH 值范围内（介于 6 和 8 之间）活性最大。

原文共 7 句。句子①、②、③、④、⑥是对研究和实验的具体陈述，所以时态为一般过去时；句子⑤、⑦介绍研究结论，是对客观规律和事实的陈述，所以采用一般现在时。而在汉语译文中，由于汉语没有屈折变化，根据表达习惯，除了句③用了语气助词"了"，其他句子均没有加"了"。

例 2 ①旋转超声端面铣削（RUFM）工艺方法是一种高效的脆性材料加工方法，本文提出将其<u>应用于</u>光学玻璃的平面加工。②通过对压痕断裂力学理论、脆性材料的材料去除特性和金刚石磨粒运动学原理的分析，<u>建立了脆性材料 RUFM 去除模型</u>。③在此基础上，<u>开展了</u> RUFM 和 K9 钻石铣加工光学玻璃的对比试验。④扫描电子显微镜（SEM）观察两种加工方式的表面形貌<u>显示</u>：与传统的 K9 钻石铣加工方法相比，RUFM 以较小的碎屑完成材料去除，具有较小的径向裂纹和侧向裂纹尺寸。⑤亚表面损伤磁流变抛光斑点检测的结果<u>表明</u>：RUFM 可以更有效地降低光学玻璃加工亚表面损伤深度。⑥理论和试验研究<u>表明</u>，RUFM 工艺方法是光学玻璃等脆性材料的有效加工方法。[39]

① Rotary ultrasonic face milling (RUFM), an effective processing method for brittle materials, <u>was introduced</u> into flat surface machining of optical glass. ② A material removal model <u>was presented</u> for RUFM based on the analysis of the indentation fracture mechanics theory, the material removal characteristics of brittle materials and the kinematics and dynamics of diamond grits. ③ And the surface properties given by RUFM and diamond milling of K9 glass <u>were compared</u>. ④ The surface topographies observed by a scanning electron microscopy (SEM) <u>show</u> that the sizes of radial cracks, lateral cracks and chipping with RUFM <u>are</u> smaller than with traditional processing. ⑤ Subsurface damage observations of optical glass <u>show</u> that RUFM more effectively <u>reduces</u> the subsurface damage depth than traditional processing as determined by

---

38 原文引自 http://writing2.richmond.edu/training/project/biology/abslit.html.
39 张承龙等. 2012. 光学玻璃旋转超声端面铣削表面特性. 清华大学学报,（11）: 1616–1621.

the magnetorheological finishing spots test method. ⑥ This theoretical and experimental research shows that RUFM provides effective processing method for brittle materials such as optical glass.

此例原文前 3 句①、②、③是对研究和实验的具体陈述，④、⑤、⑥介绍研究结论，是对客观规律和事实的陈述。因此，翻译成英语时，①、②、③用一般过去时，后 3 句采用一般现在时。

（四）人称代词与语态翻译的处理

GB/T 6447–1986《文摘编写规则》（2008）规定：中文摘要"要用第三人称的写法"；应采用"对……进行了研究"、"报告了……现状"、"进行了……调查"等记述方法；标明文献的性质和文献主题。对国内科技期刊"投稿/稿约要求"进行调查，不难发现绝大多数期刊对中文摘要在人称代词与语态的使用方面做了具体要求，如使用第三人称、不得使用被动句等。中文期刊所附的英文摘要基本上是从中文摘要翻译过来的，这就要求译者必须根据英文摘要的具体特点进行得体的转换。根据陆元雯[40] 2009 年对数学、物理、农业和医学四个学科的 12 种期刊（其中美国期刊 7 种、英国期刊 4 种、德国期刊 1 种）中的 1562 篇英文科技论文摘要的语料统计分析结果，科技论文英文摘要中极少使用第一人称单数 I、第二人称 you、第三人称 he 和 she；较少使用人称代词的宾格；提倡使用第三人称单数 it 作主语用于被动语态、系表结构和"it +主动态动词+宾语"结构，第三人称复数 they 主要出现在"they +主动态动词+宾语"结构中；主动语态中可用第一人称复数 we 作主语。如果从话语功能的角度来概括英文摘要中人称代词的使用，那就是：在叙述研究内容、研究过程和研究方法时，可用 we 作主语，用主动语态；表达研究结果和结论时，主要用 it 作主语；指代前文出现过的名词主要用 they。在摘要的英、汉互译过程中，应考虑中、英摘要各自对人称以及语态的使用要求。请看下例：

例3 ①高速大吨位起重机大量用于制造业、港口运输业和建筑业，目前是以人工操作为主，自动化程度低。②为了有效解决实现起重机自动化的关键技术问题，建立了回转塔式起重机实验台，用于研究起重机动力学和控制策略的有效性。③回转塔式起重机实验台由回转机构和变幅机构组成，模拟回转塔式起重机的变幅运动和回转运动。④本文确定了回转塔式起重机实验台的总体结构方案以及变幅运动和回转运动的传动方案。⑤研究结果表明这一实验台的建立对实现起重机自动化，提高工作效率、安全性、可靠性有着重要的意义和价值。[41]

① High-speed and big-tonnage cranes are widely used in manufacturing, harbor transportation and construction, but most of the cranes are operated manually with low

---

40 陆元雯. 2009. 基于语料库的科技论文英文摘要的人称代词与语态研究. 中国科技期刊研究，（6）：1167–1170.
41 此例引自 http://sites.sdjzu.edu.cn/jwc/Upfiles/200762130844.doc.

automatization. ② To cope with the key technical problems and realize the automation, we set up an experimental system for rotary tower cranes so that the validity of crane dynamics and proposed control strategies could be experimented. ③ The experimental system consists of a rotary mechanism and a luffing mechanism and is used for the simulation of luffing motion and rotating motion of rotary tower cranes. ④ We designed not only the overall scheme for the frame of this system, but also the scheme for transmission of luffing motion and rotating motion. ⑤ It is concluded that the erection of this system is valuable and significant for the crane in its automatization, efficiency, safety and reliability.

为方便对比分析，我们将上例中文摘要和英文摘要中谓语部分进行对比，如下所示：

（原语）中文摘要	（译语）英文摘要
①……大量用于……以人工操作为主。②为了……建立了……③……由……组成，模拟……④本文确定了……方案。⑤研究结果发现……	① ... are widely used... but... are operated... ② To cope with... we set up... ③ ... consists of... and is used for... ④ We designed... ⑤ It is concluded...

中文摘要共 5 句，均采用第三人称视角，句子主语分别是"起重机、（无人称）、实验台、本文、研究结果"，使用的基本上都是主动语态。相比较而言，英文摘要较少使用主动语态。具体分析：句①、③是对客观规律和事实的陈述，所以译成被动语态且使用一般现在时；句②、④叙述研究内容、研究过程和研究方法，可用 we 作主语，译成主动语态并且使用一般过去式；句⑤表达研究结果和结论，用 it 作主语，译成被动语态，使用一般现在时。由于两种语言在论文摘要的组句谋篇上方式不同，所以在翻译过程中必须针对不同的情况作相应的处理。

练习二

一、将下列句子译成中文。

1. Rapid cooling from above the critical temperature results in hard structure, whereas very slow cooling produces the opposite effect.
2. Since this chemical separation of the carbon component occurs entirely in the solid state, the resulting structure is a fine mechanical mixture of ferrite（铁素体）and cementite（渗碳体）.
3. Material is fed into a heated barrel, mixed, and forced into a mold cavity（模腔）where it cools and hardens to the configuration of the mold cavity.

4. Spark（电火花）machining finds many applications in the repairing and modifications of hardened cavities and cores.
5. The spark is localized and metal is progressively removed in small quantities over a period of time.

二、将下列句子译成英文。

1. 数据库有三种主要类型：统计、文献目录和资料全文。
2. 大多数金属密度相对较高，尤其是与聚合物相比较而言。
3. 冶金学是涉及金属从矿石提炼到最后产物的物理学、化学和工程学总称。
4. 钢可以通过硬化来抵抗切削和磨损，也可以通过软化以允许机械加工。
5. 因为石油深埋地下，所以单靠研究地表还不能确定有无石油储量。

三、将下面的科技短文译成中文。

Hardening

Hardening is the process of heating a piece of steel to a temperature within or above its critical range and then cooling it rapidly. If the carbon content of the steel is known, the proper temperature to which the steel should be heated may be obtained by reference to the iron-iron carbide phase diagram. However, if the composition of the steel is unknown, a little preliminary experimentation may be necessary to determine the range.

A good procedure to follow is to heat-quench a number of small specimens of the steel at various temperatures and observe the result, either by hardness testing or by microscopic examination. When the correct temperature is obtained, there will be a marked change in hardness and other properties. In any heat-treating operation the rate of heating is important. Heat flows from the exterior to the interior of steel at a definite rate. If the steel is heated too fast, the outside becomes hotter than the interior and uniform structure cannot be obtained. If a piece is irregular in shape, a slow rate is all the more essential to eliminate warping and cracking. The heavier the section, the longer must be the heating time to achieve uniform results. Even after the correct temperature has been reached, the piece should be held at that temperature for a sufficient period of time to permit its thickest section to attain a uniform temperature.

四、将下面的科技短文译成英文。

自然能量

自然界的能量有许多不同的形式，热能就是一种形式的能量。热能有许多来自太阳。森林大火也可以产生热能,甚至一只老鼠温暖的身体也可以产生少许的热能。光是能量的另一种形式,也来自太阳和星星。一些动物甚至植物也可以产生少量的光能。无线电波和紫外线也是能量形式。此外,电能也是一种能量形式。

有关能量的一些事情很难理解。能量不断地从一种形式转变为另一种形式,就像一位化装艺术家一样。当你自认为了解它的时候,它突然变成了另一种完全不同的形式。但是有一点是肯定的:能量永远不会消失,同样,它也不会无端地产生。过去,人们认为能量和物质是两种完全不同的东西。现在我们知道,能量和物质是可以相互转换的。微量的物质可以转换为令人难以置信的巨大核能。太阳利用氢氦反应制造核能,随着物质转化为能量,其质量日复一日在减小。

五、翻译下列论文摘要。

1. 英译汉

Abstract: Foamed metals are widely used as engineering materials. A simplified structural failure model（失效模型）was developed for these reticulated porous metals with high porosity（高孔率网状泡沫金属）to investigate failure modes of the corresponding porous components under bending loads, covering the tensile rupture, the shearing fracture and the yield of the porous body pore struts. The systemic mathematic relationships were derived for pore strut failures（孔棱失效）due to bending loads on these porous components（弯矩载荷作用）, including the mathematic relationships between the nominal bending moment（名义弯矩）and porosity（孔率）for these porous components under bending loads resulting in the strut failure, as well as the condition expressions corresponding to various failure modes. The analytical results indicate that the tensile rupture（拉断破坏）tends to occur on the pore struts for brittle porous bodies and the shearing fracture（剪切断裂）may occur on the pore struts for ductile porous bodies when the corresponding porous components are subject to bending loads.

2. 汉译英

摘要: 对油膜轴承进行计算时,空化模型（cavitation model）的选择是决定计算精度的重要因素之一。目前常用的润滑油空化模型一般基于实验得到的油膜压力分布而提出,而该文结合油膜轴承润滑油空化的机理提出了一种新的基于空气溶解度的空化模型。使用该模型对某径向轴承进行计算流体力学（computational fluid dynamics / CFD）计算,在不同的偏心率下的计算结果均与实验值吻合,计算精度与 Half-Sommerfeld 空化边界条件相比有显著的提高,并且该模型具有很好的算法稳定性。

第三章 旅游文体的翻译

旅游业被誉为"无烟产业"和"永远的朝阳产业"。随着世界经济的发展和全球化的日益加深，跨国旅游已经成为丰富人们精神生活和促进当地经济发展的一种重要手段。跨国旅游离不开翻译，跨国旅游的重要性也决定了旅游翻译的重要性。

旅游文本的涉及面很广。就其内容而言，旅游文本包括旅游标识语（告示标牌）、导游词、旅游广告、旅游宣传册、旅游指南、旅游景点介绍、旅游合同、旅游地图、旅行见闻等。本章主要探讨以景点介绍为主的旅游文本的语言特点及其翻译。

第一节 旅游文体的特点

旅游文体翻译是一种跨语言、跨社会、跨时空、跨文化、跨心理、跨宗教的交际活动，属于应用翻译（applied translation）或实用翻译（practical translation）。同其他实用文体的翻译一样，旅游文本翻译应以传递信息为主要目的，且要注重信息的传递效果。译者要注意旅游文本本身的语言特点，包括用词、语法、句式结构、修辞等方面。译者还要注意两种语言背后的文化在旅游文本中的体现以及翻译时采取的策略，针对不同的情况，采用不同的翻译技巧。

一、旅游文本的用词特点

（一）中英文旅游文本用词的共同特点

旅游文本起着旅游宣传的作用，其主要目的就是要让游客读懂、看懂相关信息，从中获取关于自然、地理、文化、风俗等方面的知识。旅游文本的用词要符合旅游文体的功能特点，实现旅游宣传的目的。中英文旅游文本在用词方面有一定的共同特点，譬如都会使用一些描述性很强的词汇，较多使用形容词的比较级和最高级，使用专门词汇、专有名词、甚至是外来词语，使用第二人称代词等。

1. 使用描述性很强的词汇

在介绍宣传景点时，旅游文本中都会使用一些描述性很强的形容词或动词，以渲染所介绍的景点之美，说服读者来旅游。请看以下几个例子。

例1 北京作为世界旅游名城，有着极为丰富的旅游资源：雄伟壮丽的天安门，金碧辉煌、气象万千的故宫，气势宏伟的万里长城，湖光山色、曲栏回廊的颐和园，建筑精巧、独具艺术风格的天坛，烟波浩渺、黛色风光的北海公园，以及建筑宏大的明代帝王陵寝——十三陵……这些举世无双、驰名中外的古代建筑，历来是旅游者的竞游之地。

例2 Although relatively small compared to the park's other geothermal areas, Midway Geyser Basin is home to some impressive hot springs, including Grand Prismatic Spring, Yellowstone's largest single hot spring and the world's third largest hot spring. This enormous pool is not only huge, but colorful, too, as rising steam reflects the colors of the rainbow in an impressive display.

例1中"雄伟壮丽、金碧辉煌、气象万千、气势宏伟、湖光山色、曲栏回廊、建筑精巧、烟波浩渺、黛色风光"等词置于不同的景点之前，极具描述性，凸显了北京多个著名景点的不同特色，起到很好的宣传效果。例2中 impressive、enormous、huge、colorful、rising 等形容词生动勾勒出 Midway Geyser Basin 令人流连忘返的绮丽风光。

2. 较多使用形容词的比较级和最高级

旅游文本，尤其是英文旅游文本，常常会使用一些有积极意义的、令人愉快的形容词的比较级或最高级，以突出所介绍的旅游景点优于其他同类旅游景点，从而启发读者做出"不二"的选择。

例3 故宫的宫殿建筑是中国现存最大、最完整的古建筑群，总面积达72万多平方米，有殿宇宫室9999间半，被称为"殿宇之海"，气魄宏伟，极为壮观。现在故宫收藏有大量古代艺术珍品，据统计共达 1 052 653 件，占中国文物总数的1/6，是中国收藏文物最丰富的博物馆，也是世界著名的古代文化艺术博物馆，其中很多文物是绝无仅有的无价国宝。

例4 Acidity in the steam is responsible for the surface rock in this area breaking into clay. Clay and steam pushing through the rock have created the most popular attraction in the basin, the Fountain Paint Pots, which are Yellowstone's most easily accessible large group of mud pots.

例3中"最大""最完整""最丰富"等形容词最高级的使用，足以体现出故宫的气势和地位，让人心向往之。例4中 the most popular 及 the most easily accessible 的使用，使读者更倾向于选择 the Fountain Paint Pots 作为旅游目的地。

3. 使用专门术语、专有名词和外来词语

在谈到旅游文本的词汇特点时，伍峰等[1]指出，旅游词汇涉及文化、经济、政治、宗教、地理、历史、民俗、休闲与娱乐等，有时会使用某一领域的专门术语。例如，pyramidal steep（锥形屋顶）、tope/stupas（佛塔）、karst topography（喀斯特地貌）分别属于建筑术语、宗教术语和地理术语，但它们都曾被用于旅游文本中。

有的旅游文本涉及特定文化，还会使用相关的专有名词，如人名、地名等。苏迪（Sudi Causeway）、西子（Xishi）、杜甫草堂（Du Fu Cottage）、昭君墓（Zhaojun's Tomb）、Big Ben in London（伦敦大本钟）、Cape of Good Hope（好望角）等就是很好的例子。

旅游文本甚至会使用外来词语。外来词的使用一方面可以加强与旅游者（说这种语言的旅游者）之间的互动，使旅游者有身份上的认同；另一方面可以使旅游者在心理上产生一种自豪感。另外，其他国家或民族的旅游者还会感受到一种异国情调。[2]

例5 Camden Town is the London smorgasbord par excellence.

例5中的par excellence是法语，意思是"卓越超群的"，让游客感受到一种异国的风情。

4. 使用第二人称代词

第二人称代词有时并不特指某个人，而是一种泛指；用在旅游文本中会拉近与读者的距离，产生一种亲近感。

例6 在杭州，你可以饱览西湖的秀色，也不妨漫步街头闹市，品尝一下杭州的名菜点心，还可以购上几样名特土产。

例7 当你步入沟中，便可见林中碧海澹荡生辉，瀑布舒洒碧玉。一到金秋，满山枫叶绛红。盛夏，湖山幽翠。仲春，树绿花艳……

例8 You can view this large terrace and its colorful springs from several vantage points. To your left, follow the boardwalk to an overlook of New Blue Spring. One of the best examples of the area's dynamic character, New Blue Spring shifts activity frequently and can become active or inactive several times in one year.

例9 Calcite Springs Overlook provides you with a unique glimpse of a rock formation that looks like a manmade stone "railing" or fence. It's beautiful and is situated across the Yellowstone River, far below you.

以上四例中，第二人称代词"你"或you的使用，有效地拉近了与读者的距离，使人"身临其中"，起到很好的宣传和推介旅游景点的作用。

（二）中英文旅游文本用词的不同特点

汉英民族有着不同的文化背景、价值观念和思维方式，因此在语言的选择和使用上也

---

1 伍峰等. 2008. 应用文体翻译：理论与实践. 杭州：浙江大学出版社.
2 丁大刚. 2011. 旅游英语的语言特点与翻译. 上海：上海交通大学出版社.

不尽相同。英语旅游文本在选词上注意简洁明快,表达直接、通俗,重在传递景点的地理环境、服务设施、优势与不足等方面的信息,信息准确、丰富、实用。相比之下,汉民族在介绍旅游景点时,大多使用描述性语言,言辞华丽,文笔优美,用词凝练、含蓄,而且大量使用四字结构,以增强语气和语势,增加语言的感染力,达到"情景交融"的效果。[3]

例10 云台山以山称奇,以水叫绝,因林冠幽,以史诲人。这里四季分明,景色各异。春来冰雪消融,万物复苏,小溪流水,山花烂漫,是春游赏花、放松休闲的好去处;夏日郁郁葱葱的原始次生林,丰富独特的飞瀑流泉,造就了云台山奇特壮观、如诗如画的山水景观,更是令人向往的旅游避暑胜地;秋季来临,层林尽染,红叶似火,登高山之巅,观云台秋色,插茱萸,赏红叶,遥寄情怀;冬季到来,大自然又把云台山装扮得银装素裹,冰清玉洁,但见群山莽莽苍苍,雄浑奇劲,不到东北就可以领略到壮美苍茫的北国风光。

例10中的中文景点介绍大量使用四字结构的词语,言辞华丽,文笔优美,富有感染力,给读者留下极美的感受。

例11 As you'll discover during your travels in the Yellowstone region, this part of the country contains a wealth of natural wonders, outdoor adventures, historic sights, friendly towns and more. It's a unique slice of the American landscape with nearly limitless options for a fun-filled vacation. You can drive a scenic byway or go on a covered wagon ride. Or get your adrenaline pumping by paddling a stretch of pristine whitewater, going rock climbing, or ziplining down from a mountain peak. Visit a museum or take in a rodeo. Spend a day fishing some of the best trout waters in the country, see wild horses running free.

例11主要介绍美国黄石公园的景致,措辞简洁质朴,逻辑严谨,语言通俗易懂,亲切而真实地描述了黄石公园的各种景色,体现了英语旅游文本的基本特点。

二、旅游文本的句法特点

(一)中英文旅游文本在句法上的共同特点

中英文旅游文本在句法上存在一些相同之处。譬如,都会使用祈使句,旨在给读者一些旅游方面的建议;使用问句,意在启发读者,激起读者的热情。

1. 使用祈使句

旅游文本属于呼唤类文本,一般号召读者采取行动,享受某一旅游服务或游览某一旅游景点,因此中英文旅游文本中都会使用祈使句来号召、敦促旅游者旅行。请看下列例句:

例12 泰国以其独特的佛教文化和迷人的热带风情闻名世界,椰林下的斑驳古迹诉说

---

[3] 汪翠兰. 2006. 河南旅游英语翻译的跨文化审视. 中国科技翻译, (11): 40–43.

着一场场远古的爱恋。让心灵放一次假,去享受空气中清醇浓厚的茶香,耳边曼妙的音乐,街上郁郁葱葱的树木,和煦迷人的东南亚阳光。体验"慢生活",享受好心情,放慢脚步,让心灵一起去度个蜜月吧!

例13 In southwestern Idaho, pay a visit to Bruneau Dunes State Park, where you can see the continent's tallest single sand dune rising more than 470 feet above the desert floor. You can also enjoy a number of recreational opportunities.

例14 To explore Mesa Verde Country is to travel back through time. Step into a room and smell centuries old soot. Look out the window, and appreciate the same views the original architects enjoyed.

以上例子均使用祈使句,起到了号召和呼唤的作用,促使读者到该旅游景点畅游一番。

2. 使用疑问句

疑问句的功用主要是提出问题,启发读者思考。旅游文本中经常使用疑问句,目的在于加强语气,引起读者的注意,从而发挥旅游文本的宣传、号召作用。

例15 避暑,你还有什么好犹豫的呢?这里将是你出行最好的选择!那红红的石英砂岩,在太阳底下泛着红红的光,那摇曳的松树,为你遮阳!

例16 那挺拔在山峰上的松树,总是绿的,绿得让人怀疑:这是秋天吗?

例17 Throughout Mesa Verde Country questions abound—who were these people? How did they build such magnificent homes? Why did they leave? Curiosity bubbles forth as purely as canyon waters, fed by the immediacy—the accessibility—of this culture.

例15、例16中的疑问句实际是反问句,答案不言自明。例17中多个特殊疑问句的使用,生动而具体地展现出读者的好奇。这些疑问句就像对话,读起来令人备感亲切,拉近了旅游文本与读者的心理距离,起到了很好的宣传、感召作用。

(二)中英文旅游文本在句法上的不同特点

由于中英文属于不同的语系,在句法上有着各自的特征,这种特征的不同也反映在中英文旅游文本上:英文旅游文本多使用短句,而中文旅游文本多使用对偶平行的并列结构,读起来朗朗上口,富于节奏感;英文旅游文本会使用句子片段,而中文旅游文本会用无主句;英文旅游文本较多使用现在时和被动语态,句子结构紧凑,逻辑关系清晰,而中文旅游文本多引用诗词、对联等来突出所介绍景点的历史价值和美学价值。[4]

1. 英文旅游文本多使用短句,中文旅游文本多使用并列结构

短句短促有力,通俗易懂,用在旅游文本中可以更好地发挥其广告宣传作用。英语句子重句法结构,绝大多数句子为主谓结构。英文旅游文本中,简短的主谓结构句子随处可见。

例18 Sheridan's history is captured in its museums. King's Museum presents the largest

---

[4] 彭萍. 2010. 实用旅游英语翻译. 北京:对外经济贸易大学出版社.

collection of saddles and leather tools. Trail End State Historic Site features the region's rich ranching heritage. Bradford Brinton Memorial & Museum details the cultured past of a gentleman rancher.

例19 Located in the Grand Canyon of the Yellowstone, Lower Falls plunges 308 feet into the Yellowstone River. In some places, the walls of the canyon are 1,200 feet tall. Upper Falls, just upstream of Lower Falls, cascades 109 feet into the canyon. There are numerous vantage points for both waterfalls.

以上两个例句都使用了短句，读来朗朗上口，会吸引更多的游客，更好地发挥旅游文本传递信息的作用。

旅游文本作为一种宣传材料，应具有美感功能，这样才能起到感召和呼唤的作用。中文旅游文本多用逗号将若干对偶平行的小句连在一起，结构优美，朗朗上口，同时将所介绍的景点描写得细致入微，惟妙惟肖，令人心生向往之感。

例20 黄山云海，特别奇绝。黄山秀峰叠峙，危崖突兀，幽壑纵横。气流在山峦间穿行，上行下跌，环流活跃。漫天的云雾和层积云，随风飘移，时而上升，时而下坠，时而回旋，时而舒展，构成了一幅奇特的千变万化的云海大观。

例20介绍黄山的美景，对偶平行小句的使用增加了句子的结构美，描写生动，令人无限向往。

2. 英文旅游文本使用句子片段，中文旅游文本使用无主句

有时，英文旅游文本会使用一些句子片段，意在提供信息的同时加强宣传语气。

例21 The Grand Canyon, a great way to vacation!
例22 Easy to get to. Great deals. And, oh, the snow!

例21虽是句子片段，但远比陈述句 The Grand Canyon is a great way to vacation! 富有表现力。例22虽然没有完整的句子结构，但传递的信息丰富，重点突出，语气更强烈。oh, the snow! 寥寥三个字，让人联想万千，回味无穷，有一种"一切尽在不言中的"美妙意境。

汉语强调意义，不太强调句子结构，许多句子没有主语，但意思是明确的。[5]正因为如此，中文旅游文本会使用一些无主句。无主句表达客观，语气公正，有时表示某种建议。使用无主句可以暗示所宣传的旅游项目适合所有读者，突出读者的中心地位，激发他们的旅游热情。

例23 探海松在天都峰顶。经过天桥，可望见一棵古松悬在危崖上，即为探海松。
例24 登西峰极目远眺，四周群山起伏，云霞四披，周野屏开，黄渭曲流，置身其中若入仙乡神府，万种俗念，一扫而空。

例23中的"经过天桥，可望见……"没有主语，但语气客观，突显信息真实可信。

---

[5] 陈宏薇. 1996. 新实用汉译英教程. 武汉：湖北教育出版社.

例 24 中"登西峰极目远眺……"是无主句,但无形中却给读者提供了建议,令读者产生跃跃欲试的念头。

3. 英文旅游文本较多使用现在时和被动语态

英文的语法呈外显性(overtness),体现在句法上则是时态、语态及语气均有明确的符号标记。汉语的语法呈隐含性(covertness),时态、语态及语气往往没有明显的符号标记。因此,与中文旅游文本相比,英文旅游文本在句法上有明显的不同,具体表现为较多使用现在时和被动语态,如例 25、例 26。

例 25 Grand Teton National Park preserves a spectacular landscape rich with majestic mountains, pristine lakes and extraordinary wildlife. The abrupt vertical rise of the jagged Teton Mountains contrasts with the horizontal sage-covered valley and glacial lakes at their base, creating world-renowned scenery that attracts nearly four million visitors per year.

例 26 Shoshone Canyon is framed by Rattlesnake Mountain to the north and Cedar Mountain to the south. The north and south forks of the Shoshone River are divided by Sheep Mountain, and Carter Mountain is prominent on the southern skyline.

4. 英文旅游文本句子结构紧凑,逻辑关系清晰

汉语的句法重意合(parataxis),而英语的句法重形合(hypotaxis)。因此,汉语句子意连形不连,句子之间的意义关系隐含其中,即使是长句,虽有脉络与气韵,但标记不明显;英语句子以形连表意连,表关系的关联词语如关系代词、关系副词都起着重要的纽带作用,主从关系、并列关系、因果关系、让步关系、条件关系等十分明确。正因为如此,英文旅游文本在句子上体现出明显的特点:结构紧凑,逻辑关系清晰。

例 27 There are countless ways to experience the wonder of Victoria Falls: by hot air balloon, helicopter, even on the back of an elephant. But if you're the type that prefers to keep your feet on the ground, a hike through the falls should do you nicely. Just be sure to bring your rain gear because a constant mist soaks everything in sight.

例 28 从老虎嘴俯瞰五花海的全貌,俨然是一只羽毛丰满的开屏孔雀。阳光一照,海子更为迷离恍惚,绚丽多姿,一片光怪陆离,使人进入了童话境地。一湖千变万化的锦绣,叫人痴迷沉醉。通过清澈的水面,可见湖底有泉水上涌,令人眼花缭乱。山风徐来,各种色彩相互渗透、镶嵌、错杂、浸染,五花海便充满了生命,活跃、跳动起来。

例 28 文采浓郁,具有散文风格。行文如流水,描写亦虚亦实,充满诗情画意,让人浮想联翩,心神向往。但是,与例 27 英文表述相比,例 28 的中文句子结构不够紧凑,逻辑关系不明显。

5. 中文旅游文本较多引用诗词、对联或其他古典文体,句式工整

古典诗词简洁洗练、含蓄优美、抑扬顿挫，寥寥数行，却给读者提供了一个广阔的想象空间，令人回味无穷。中文旅游文本倾向突出旅游资源的人文特色，常常使用诗词、楹联等对景点进行颂扬衬托，突出中文旅游文本句式工整的特点。

例29 望客松在玉屏峰至莲花沟的途中。松干粗矮，树皮黝黑，树冠密集而倾斜，姿态苍劲优美，因其挺立高崖，似登高眺望游客，故名"望客松"。有《相见欢·望客松》词咏之："千年久立高岩，笑颜堆。待客情深乍见，又分开。留难住，欢声去，几时回？望眼欲穿挥泪，盼重来。"

例30 汉阳月湖畔古琴台是后人为纪念俞伯牙和钟子期而建造的。史载"伯牙鼓琴，钟子期听之，曰'善哉乎鼓琴，魏巍乎若大山'。少选之间，而志在流水，钟子期曰'善哉乎鼓琴，汤汤若流水'。"于是伯牙子期结为至交，约定第二年中秋明月清风时再会。钟子期死，伯牙破琴绝弦，终身不复鼓琴，以为世无足复为鼓琴者。为此有对联曰："一曲高山一曲流水，千载传佳话。几分明月几分清风，回时邀游人。"

例29中的古诗词，突出描写了景点的美妙之处，点睛之笔，增加了文本的感召力。例30中引用的对联高度概括了"高山流水觅知音"这一历史典故，句式对仗。读者在领略胜地风光的同时，对其人文背景知识也有了更多的了解。

三、旅游文本的修辞特点

为了使语言表达更具吸引力，让读者获得更多的美感，从而激发他们游览的兴趣，旅游文本经常使用多种修辞手法。由于中英文语言文化背景下审美心理存在明显差异，中文文本往往引经据典，以期给人以美的享受，而英文文本则直扣主题，很少穿插与主题无关的内容；中文重修辞华美，为借景抒情而运用各种修辞手法，而英文重客观描述，文风质朴，逻辑严谨，[6] 所以中英文旅游文本中修辞手法的使用频率有很大差异。当然，英文旅游文本并不是完全摒弃修辞手法，事实上，由于各民族的思维和语言之间有共通点，所以中英文旅游文本中具有某些共同的修辞手法。下面详述中英文旅游文本中常用的修辞手法。

（一）比喻

比喻就是"打比方"，也叫譬喻，通过事物之间的相似点把某一事物比作另一事物，从而把抽象的事物变得具体，把深奥的道理变得浅显。比喻包括明喻、暗喻和借喻等。旅游文本中的比喻可以使被描写事物的形状或景色更加生动形象、新鲜有趣，给读者（潜在的旅游者）留下深刻的印象。

例31 争艳池位于四川省阿坝州南坪县南部，发育于黄龙沟的左侧，计有彩池五百多个，是黄龙沟内规模最大的彩池群。池堤金甲银鳞，流光溢彩，缤纷耀眼。池态有

---

6 张光明、陈葵阳、李雪红、黄世平．2009．实用文体翻译．合肥：中国科学技术大学出版社．

的形若荷花，有的状如莲叶，有的小可藏袖，有的大若亩田，形状殊异，参差错落。

例32 Dragon's Mouth Spring is this area's most popular feature. This is a spring that fills a cave in the side of a hill. The gases that rise to the surface cause the water to splash back and forth against the three cave walls. This splashing of water resembles a tongue lashing out, and gives the spring the name.

例31中的"形若荷花""状如莲叶""大若亩田"等比喻直观地将争艳池中形状各异的彩池展现在读者的面前。例32中 resembles a tongue lashing out 也是明喻，形象地解释了"龙口喷泉"名字的由来。

（二）拟人

拟人，就是根据想象把物当作人来叙述或描写，使"物"具有人一样的言行、神态、思想和感情。运用拟人的修辞方法，可以使抽象的事物具体化，使无生命的事物活跃起来，增强语言的形象性和生动性。旅游文本中拟人手法的使用可以使读者对所介绍的景点产生鲜明的印象，引起共鸣。

例33 树正群海大小海子19个，逶迤相衔长达5公里，高差100余米，构成梯状湖群。海水湛蓝，色泽鲜艳，风流倜傥，十分壮观。灰黄色的钙华湖堤，精巧别致，长满了柳、柏、松、杉。上部海子的水翻越湖堤，从树丛中溢出，激起白色的水花，在青翠中跳跳蹦蹦，穿梭奔窜。水流顺堤跌宕，形成幅幅水帘，婀娜多姿，婉约变幻。整个群海，层次分明，那绿中套蓝的色彩，童话般的天真自然。

例34 One of Montana's most stunning scenic drives is the Going-to-the-Sun Road in Glacier National Park. It crosses the Continental Divide at 6,646-foot-high Logan Pass, and passes through glacial lakes and cedar forests in the alpine tundra. Scenic viewpoints line the road.

例33中，海水"风流倜傥"、水花"跳跳蹦蹦，穿梭奔窜"、水帘"婀娜多姿，婉约变幻"，拟人修辞手法的运用使原本静态的景点富有动态感和生命感，拉近了与读者的距离，起到很好的宣传作用。例34中的 crosses 和 passes through 也是拟人的手法，把原本没有生命的景点描写得栩栩如生，容易引起读者的共鸣。

（三）夸张

所谓夸张，就是在表述中故意言过其实，或夸大事实，或缩小事实，目的在于给读者留下深刻的印象。一般说来，旅游文本中的夸张均为"夸大其实"，用于渲染宣传的语气。[7] 比较英汉旅游材料可以看出，中文旅游文本多用夸张来突出所描写的景点，而英文旅游文本只是在有些情况下用到夸张的修辞手法。

---

7 彭萍.2010.实用旅游英语翻译.北京：对外经济贸易大学出版社.

例35 雪花飞上了千条巨壑，飞上了万座峰岗，千峰万壑接受了冰雪的洗礼，变成了一个晶莹剔透的冰雪世界——古人形容说："一夜寒风起，万树银花开"，雪后的黄山，银装素裹，玉树琼枝，满目琼楼玉宇，观之如痴如醉。

例36 The greater Yellowstone landscape is dotted with guest ranches, and you're sure to find one that suits your style and budget, and where you'll enjoy friendly hospitality in a gorgeous setting with limitless fun outdoor activities to choose from.

例35介绍雪后的黄山。"沟壑众多"是黄山的一大特点，为了突出该特点，例35用了夸张的手法，借助"千条巨壑""万座峰岗""千峰万壑"等词语，不仅传达了黄山"峰多壑多"的特点，还渲染了黄山的磅礴气势。例36的夸张体现在limitless一词中，展现了美国黄石公园的风景美、人文美以及各种户外运动带来的无穷乐趣，令读者充满遐想。

（四）反复

反复是指重复使用某一词、某一短语、某一句等用以强调和突出文字，加强表达的语气和感情，加深读者的印象。在旅游文本中使用反复的修辞手法可以加强宣传的语气，给读者留下深刻的印象。

例37 漓江，是中国锦绣河山的一颗明珠，是桂林风光的精华，是桂林风光的灵魂，是桂林风光的精髓。

例38 There's a place where time travel isn't make-believe, where you can trace the very footstep of history. There is a place where the past and the present walk hand-in-hand. Come and reflect in this place, in a land called Colorado.

"是桂林风光的……"这一结构在例37中重复使用了三次，增加了气势，强调了漓江在桂林风光中首屈一指的地位。例38中重复使用"There's a place where..."的句式，不仅增加了句子的结构美，也突出体现了美国科罗拉多州"历史与现代交融，给人带来无限思考"的特点。

（五）设问和反问

设问和反问主要通过提问及作答或不作答的方式激发读者去思索、体会，真正目的在于突出所要表达的内容和观点，引起读者的注意。中英文旅游文本都会使用设问的修辞手法，旨在突出所介绍的景点，吸引读者的注意，从而起到宣传作用。

例39 无数滑鼠一起畅游，是要暗示现代人类成了科技的奴隶吗？百搭的中国传统桃花图案，又传达了怎样的社会现象？到澳门塔石艺文馆看看就自有分晓。

例40 Do you want to eat like the Yellowstone region's early explorers did? Sign up for an Old West cookout.

上面两个例子用了或设问、或反问的方式，激发读者去思索、去联想，甚至去行动。

（六）对仗

对仗也叫对偶，即用语法结构相似、音节数目相等的一对句子来表达相对立或者对称的意思。汉语讲究对仗，这是汉语的审美意识所决定的。汉语旅游文本也常常用到对仗，有很好的宣传效果，如下例：

例 41 黄山松千姿百态，或耸立挺拔，似擎天巨人；或翠枝舒展，如流水行云；或虬根盘结，如苍龙凌波；或矫健威武，如猛虎归山——迎客松、送客松、陪客松，让人备感亲切；竖琴松、连理松、探海松、让人浮想联翩……

（七）倒装

倒装是英语特有的语言现象，分为语法倒装和修辞倒装两种。这里讲的倒装指修辞倒装，即为了句子的平衡美或是为了突出某一部分信息而将主语和谓语的语序颠倒。

例 42 Throughout the desert are 2000-year-old rock art sites and other cultural and spiritual sites.

例 43 Six miles west of Cody is Buffalo Bill Reservoir in Buffalo Bill State Park, named for Colonel William "Buffalo Bill" Cody.

例 42 的主语 2000-year-old rock art sites and other cultural and spiritual sites 相对谓语 are throughout the desert 而言太长，如果放在句首，会给人"头重脚轻"的感觉。倒装之后，句子具有平衡美。例 43 的主语 Buffalo Bill Reservoir in Buffalo Bill State Park, named for Colonel William "Buffalo Bill" Cody 因为太长被置于句尾，采用倒装的修辞手法，不仅保持了句子的平衡，也突出了旅游文本的主题信息。

四、旅游文本的语篇特点

语篇由句子组成，是连贯而完整的较大的语言交际单位。语篇超越句子的范畴，具备特定语境中的交际功能。旅游语篇的最终目的是通过对旅游景点和景区的细致描写，增强语篇的感染力，给读者（潜在的旅游者）提供丰富的信息，带来美的享受，并使其产生游览欲望。因此，旅游语篇同时具有信息功能和呼唤诱导功能。信息功能指为旅游者提供丰富的旅游资讯，传达旅游景点的形象信息，让旅游者感受到人文和自然之美；呼唤或诱导功能指语篇发出呼唤或诱导性信息，并产生明显的"语后效应"（perlocutionary force），直接刺激旅游者的参观欲望。

杨敏等学者曾经进行过英汉旅游篇章的跨文化对比分析，结果显示英美旅游语篇重在景点地理环境、服务设施、优势与不足等方面的信息传递，而风光景色的描述则着笔不多；汉语旅游语篇往往更加突出旅游资源的社会身份特征，如社会影响、历史沿革、发展业绩等，突出风光景色和人文特色，甚至占用很多篇幅来引用史书、文学作品及诗歌等对景点进行颂扬和描述。请看以下两例：

例44 青岛是中国优秀旅游城市。青岛独特的地理位置和历史背景使其自20世纪20年代就成为著名的观光旅游城市和疗养避暑胜地。青岛风光秀丽，气候宜人。蜿蜒连绵的前海海滨，起伏多姿的海上山峦，红瓦绿树的城市风景，浓缩近现代历史文化的名人故居，具有典型欧陆风格的多国建筑，构成了一道中西合璧的山、海、城交融的海滨风景线，是旅游观光、度假休闲、商务会展的最佳目的地。青岛市区，西部为"红瓦绿树、碧海蓝天"的老风貌保护区，东部为现代化建筑风貌区，新老两区相融相映，形成了"海上都市、欧亚风情"的城市特点。

例45 Exeter is an important commercial center for the South West, and successfully combines the advantages of a modern city with the charm of one with a long and colorful history. Aspects of this history are easily seen in the medieval Cathedral, the Guildhall and the Quay, which is now a popular waterfront venue. Exeter has a population of around 100,000 and has all the shops and cultural and recreational facilities you would expect to find in a thriving university town. Some of the best countryside in Britain is very close to Exeter. The Dartmoor National Park is to the west, and Exmoor, which also has spectacular scenery, is to the north. The coastal town of Exmouth, with its sandy beaches, is about nine miles away.

例44是关于中国旅游城市青岛的介绍，例45是关于英国西南部城市艾克赛特（Exeter）的介绍。从以上两例可以看出，英、汉旅游语篇中都融入了信息功能、呼唤或诱导功能。在呼唤或诱导功能上，两种语篇的内在目的相同，都是为了吸引读者前去观光。英、汉旅游语篇实现信息功能的方式有明显的差异：例44对景物的描写着墨较多，用词凝练、含蓄，音韵很美，景物刻画不求明细，讲究"情景交融"，追求一种意象的朦胧之美。例45却不同，在描写景物时客观具体，重理性，重写实，重形象而非意象，追求一种流畅自然之美。可见，英文旅游语篇主要发挥提供资讯的功能，突出信息传递的客观性和科学性；中文旅游语篇不仅介绍旅游地的地理环境，更突出其社会影响、历史地位及人文特色等。[8]

第二节
旅游文体翻译中的常见问题

随着中国对外开放的深化和国内游、出境游的蓬勃发展，旅游翻译变得日益频繁和重要。旅游翻译的目的，在于向外国游客介绍国内景点或向国内游客介绍国外景点，传递相关信息，吸引游客游览。如何才能将纷繁复杂的旅游资料译成清楚明了、准确地道的目标

8　康宁. 2005. 从语篇功能看汉语旅游语篇的翻译. 中国翻译，（3）：86–87.

语，让目标游客直接获取信息，以更好地了解旅游地的自然风光和人文、历史知识呢？翻译界的学者给出了种种建议。但是，旅游翻译依然存在诸多问题。[9]

一、汉英旅游文本翻译中的问题

（一）拼写错误

产生拼写错误主要是因为校对不够仔细。表面看来，这类错误并非翻译水平不够所致，显得无关紧要。但是，这类错误容易引起外国游客的误解，甚至让他们感到一头雾水，莫名其妙。这样一来，旅游文本的宣传效用就会大打折扣，严重的错误还会贻笑大方。

例1 蜀中胜景窦团山欢迎您。
Welcome to the Famous Senic Sport of Bashu Doutuan Mountain.

译文中 Senic 的正确拼写为 Scenic，Sport 的正确拼写为 Spot。

（二）用词不准

中英文中的很多词都存在一词多义的情况，在不同语境中有不同的含义；在翻译时，两者并不能简单地一一对应，翻译过程中也不可简单地照搬词义。因此，作为译者必须吃透原文，根据具体的语境选用合适的词语。如果望文生义，只按简单的字面意思对应翻译，就很难做到忠实，反倒容易引起误解，造成不良影响。

例2 ……不断有外国友人来杭，到20世纪，一百多个国家和地区的元首、政要、学者、商贾、平民都纷至沓来。[10]
Ever since then, up to the end of 20th century, statesmen and heads of over 100 countries, businessmen, scholars and all kinds of people visited Hangzhou.

且不论译文中时态、冠词等方面的语法错误，我们只看"平民"一词的翻译。"平民"者，平常百姓也，怎么会是 all kinds of people？是否也包括了前面提到的元首、政要、学者等？更遗憾的是，译文把原本限定"元首、政要、学者、商贾、平民"的"一百多个国家和地区"翻译成只限定"元首、政要"的定语，和原文意思相悖。建议将译文改为："From then on up to the end of the 20th century, people from more than 100 countries or regions have visited Hangzhou, including heads of state, statesmen, scholars, business people and ordinary tourists."

中国有 56 个民族，许多旅游景点带有独特的民族特色和地方特色，在宣传时，旅游文本会出现"独特的民族风情"等字眼。据了解，不少旅游资料把"独特的民族风情"翻译成 foreign amorous feelings。诚然，在《汉英词典》里，"风情"有 amorous feelings 这一译法。但是"风情"意思很多，《汉英词典》给出了至少五种译法：① information

---

9 文军、邓春、辜涛. 2002. 信息与可接受度的统一——对当前旅游翻译的一项调查与分析. 中国科技翻译，（1）：49–52.

10 此例引自刘建明. 2001. 旅游资料汉译英典型错误评析. 中国科技翻译，（3）：1–4.

about wind direction, wind-force, etc. ② bearing; demeanor ③ feelings ④ amorous feelings; flirtatious expressions ⑤ local conditions and customs。"民族风情"应该指民族风俗，而不是风情万种之"风情"，所以应该采用第五种译法。"独特的民族风情"应译为 unique customs of the local people。否则，误译 foreign amorous feelings 会给读者或游客以误导。

（三）语法错误

译文语言符合语法规则是合格翻译的最低要求。然而遗憾的是，不少旅游景点的英文译文中，语法错误比比皆是，其中很多错误属简单的语法错误，不可原谅。

例3 1997年被联合国教科文组织列为世界文化遗产。

In 1997, it is put on the list of the World's Culture Heritage by the UNESCO.

"被列为世界文化遗产"发生在1997年，应该用过去时态；文化遗产中的"文化"应该用 culture 的形容词形式 cultural，而且应该有 site 一词。建议将译文改为：In 1997 it was listed as a World Cultural Heritage Site by UNESCO.

例4 一年一度的西湖国际友好马拉松比赛，如今已举办第十届，它已成为杭州金秋的一项传统赛事。

Annual International West Lake Friendship Marathon will be witnessing its 10 anniversary and it has become the conventional festival for the golden autumn event of Hangzhou.

译文把基数词和序数词混为一谈，而且"国际"和"西湖"两个修饰词的先后次序也颠倒了。正确译文应为：The annual West Lake International Friendship Marathon has become a regular event in the golden autumn of Hangzhou, and will be celebrating its 10th anniversary this year.

冠词为英语所特有，汉语中没有这一类词，所以许多英语学习者往往很难做到正确使用冠词，常常该用冠词的地方不用，不该用的地方反而乱用。例如，"泸沽湖"被译为 LuGu Lake，忽略了在前面加定冠词 the；"南京路"被译为 the Nanjing Road，误用了定冠词 the。

（四）句子逻辑关系混乱

汉语句子松散，不讲究严密的逻辑关系。将旅游文本译为英文时，如果译者不对句子的逻辑关系进行梳理和研究，仅仅进行简单的字码转换，译出的句子往往让人不知所云。

例5 杭州市总面积16 596平方公里，人口603.22万，其中市区面积683平方公里，常住人口166.73万。

The municipality of Hangzhou covers a total area of 16,596 square kilometers with a population of 6.03 million, of which the city proper covers 683 square kilometers with a population of 1.66 million.

原文中的"其中"被翻译为 of which，引导定语从句，容易引起歧义：which 究竟指面积还是指人口？为了避免逻辑混乱，此处改用并列句来翻译更为准确：The municipality of Hangzhou covers a total area of 16,596 square kilometers with a population of 6.03 million, whereas the city proper covers 683 square kilometers with a population of 1.66 million.

再如，在介绍"大慈岩"时，"远望如琼楼仙阁"被译为 Looking from afar is like Heaven Pavilion，这是典型的字对字翻译的例子，逻辑关系混乱。首先，"远望"并不是句子的主语；其次，"远望"的是人而不是其他，"如琼楼仙阁"的是"大慈岩"而不是"远望"。理清原文的逻辑关系后，译文需改为：Seen from afar, it looks like a heavenly pavilion.

又如，在介绍"严子陵钓台"时，"严子陵钓台"被译为 Yan Ziling Angling Terrace——a famous hermit in East Han Dynasty, loving angling here. 究竟 Yan Ziling 是 famous hermit，还是 Angling Terrace 是 famous hermit？逻辑混乱。如果译文改为 The Yan Ziling Angling Terrace——Yan Ziling, a famous hermit in the Eastern Han Dynasty, used to angle here，就不会有误解了。

（五）传递冗余的信息

如前所述，汉语旅游文本喜欢引用古诗词、谚语、名人名言等来增加所介绍景点的美感和特色，还常常用到对仗。这些对中国游客来说是享受，但对于外国游客而言，却是信息过量、实用性不强，因为他们需要的是能传递景点地理环境、服务设施、优势与不足等方面信息的旅游资料，而不是陌生的诗词歌赋及典故，或是浓墨重彩的描写。但是，在旅游翻译实践中，常常会有生搬硬译的情况，导致大量冗余的信息阻断了译文的连贯性，大大影响了阅读理解的效果。

例6 境内怪峰林立，溶洞群布，古木参天，珍禽竞翅，山泉潺潺，云雾缭绕。

There are countless strange peaks, clusters of limestone caves, ancient trees as high as the sky, rare and precious birds, flowing mountain springs and clouds like mists floating above you.

原文极尽描述之能事，采用了夸张、拟人、排比等修辞手法，注重辞藻的华丽，用字工整对仗。译文过于拘泥原文，有重复冗余之嫌，如 countless 和 clusters、rare 和 precious 重复，as high as the sky 冗余，like mists floating above you 既没有美感又不太好理解，属于"中式英语"。

例7 华清池内有一贵妃池，相传是杨贵妃当年沐浴的地方。唐代名诗人白居易的《长恨歌》中有"春寒赐浴华清池，温泉水滑洗凝脂"的诗句。[11]

---

11 此例引自陈刚. 2009. 旅游英汉互译教程. 上海：上海外语教育出版社.

76

Inside the Huachingchih Spring, there is a bathing pool called Kueifeichih which is said to have been the bathing place of Yang Kueifei. The famous poet Po Chu-i of the Tang Dynasty wrote "The Ballad of Endless Woe" which contains the following verses:
It was in the chilly springtime
They bathed in Huaching Lake.
And in the tepid waters
They crusted winter slack.

原文引用唐代诗人白居易的诗句以衬托所介绍景点的历史意义以及池水的清澈，但直译这一诗句反倒让英文读者感到迷惑，信息冗余。

（六）中式英语

翻译汉语旅游文本时，译者由于受汉语的干扰和影响，在翻译的过程中易按照汉语规则和习惯造出不合规范或不合英语文化习惯的英语表达方式，这些表达对于译语读者来说不可理解或不可接受，属于中式英语。

例8 地下游览惊险刺激。[12]

The underground voyage is full of danger and risk.

译文中的 danger and risk 显然是受中国思维的影响，但对于英文读者而言，就令人望而却步了。此处"惊险"不妨译为 adventure。

例9 ……是集山水、人文、古代、现代为一体的综合性公园。[13]

It is a comprehensive park with hills and waters, centuries of ancient and modern times concentrated.

"人文、古代、现代为一体"被译为 centuries of ancient and modern times concentrated，显然是中式英语，而且"人文"的意思没有完全译出来，comprehensive 显得多余。如果译为 It is a park with hills and waters as well as human landscape in ancient and modern styles，意思更加清楚，结构更加合理，表达也更地道。

例10 （该地区）是成都近郊不可多得的休闲、度假、避暑、登山的好去处。

Hence the area is a nice place for pleasure searchers, holiday-makers, mountain-climbers and those who want to be away from the summer heat.

例11 ……令人神往，令人流连。

You will be chanted by all these as to forget about home.

以上两例均摘自"西岭雪山风景名胜区简介"。相比较而言，英文读者在具体的上下

---

12 此例引自文军、邓春、辜涛. 2002. 信息与可接受度的统一——对当前旅游翻译的一项调查与分析. 中国科技翻译，（1）：49–52.

13 同上。

文中能推测出例 10、例 11 译文的大概意思，但其表达依然是中式英语，不地道，不能带来美感或起到宣传作用。以上两例的译文不妨分别修改为：

- Hence the area is a nice place for tourists to relax, spend holidays, climb mountains and enjoy a cool summer.
- You will be too enchanted to leave.

例 12 北京的腿，西安的嘴，桂林的山和水。

Beijing's leg, Xi'an's mouth, and Guilin's mountain and water.

原文的意思是：北京名胜之多，走也走不完；西安古迹之盛，道也道不完；而桂林则是山水环绕之地，其美丽也不需用言语来表达。译者生搬硬译，翻译出的译文让缺乏中国文化背景知识的外国读者或游客感到不知所云。不妨采用增译的方法，把原文的意思补充完整，让外国游客一目了然。译文改为：In Beijing, there are so many places to see that the tourist guide has to walk a lot; in Xi'an, there are so many histories to tell that he has to talk a lot; in Guilin, he doesn't have to talk or walk a lot because the beautiful mountains and rivers are attractive enough for the travelers themselves to see and enjoy.

（七）文化误译

旅游景点简介中常常包含许多文化因素，如著名历史人物、典故、趣闻轶事、俗语等，传递了原语文化所特有的事物、人物和概念。如何翻译旅游文本中包含的文化因素是译者遇到的最头疼的问题之一。[14] 在汉英旅游文本翻译中，常常会出现文化误译的现象。

例 13 阴阳界

the boundary between dark and bright

例 14 遵守游览秩序，坚持五讲四美。

Observe the tourist order and insist on the "Five Particulars" and "Four Beauties".

例 15 上有天堂，下有苏杭。

There is a heaven above and Suzhou and Hangzhou on the earth.

"阴阳界""五讲四美""上有天堂，下有苏杭"等词语带有浓厚的中国文化色彩，译文没有真正把握其中的文化内涵，只是找到对应词，进行简单的直译，结果让译文读者感到一头雾水。这种误译僵硬、笨拙，往往带来适得其反的效果。

考虑到译文的可接受性问题，对这类表达可采取意译为主的翻译方法，其译文不妨改为：

- the boundary between the living and the dead
- Observe the tourist order and keep good manners.

---

14 汪宝荣. 2005. 旅游文化的英译：归化与异化以绍兴著名景点为例. 中国科技翻译，(1)：13–17.

- The beautiful scenery makes Suzhou and Hangzhou a paradise on earth.

（八）景点名称翻译前后不一致

改革开放以来，我国与世界其他地区的交流广泛而深入，世界各国来华人士也与日俱增。在全国各大旅游景点中，有关旅游信息的汉英双语标识已经随处可见，这为外国游客提供了很多便利。但遗憾的是，有些景点的译名存在着前后不一致的问题，令人感到疑惑。

例16 雨花石博物馆

Rain Flower Stone Museum	（北门导游图上的译文）
Yuhua Pebbles Museum	（群雕前导游图上的译文）
The Museum of Yuhua Stones	（景区功能分布图上的译文）
Rain Flower Pebbles Museum	（景点指示牌上的译文）

在同一景点"雨花台烈士陵园"的四个不同指示牌上，"雨花石博物馆"竟然有四种不同的翻译，让人备感疑惑。雨花石的"石"到底该用哪个词呢？汉语对雨花石的解释是：一种光洁的小卵石，有美丽的色彩和花纹，可供观赏，主要产于南京雨花台一带。pebble 一词的意思是：small stone made smooth and round by the action of water，译为"小圆石，卵石"。从外形来看，这个比较合适。但是雨花石的形状除了圆的，还有其他形状的。而且，pebble 一般总是和 beach 出现在一起，或者说总是和水相关的，用在此处不太合适。stone 的英文解释可以总结为：石头的总称，除了表示一般的石头之外，还可以表示珍贵的石头，即 precious stone。因此，应该用 stone 更合适些。此外，"雨花"要不要翻译出来呢？可以不译。但是 Yuhua Stones 放在 Museum 之后好像不符合地名的常用表达方式，直接译为 Yuhua Stone Museum 更简明。

二、英汉旅游文本翻译中的问题

与汉英旅游翻译相比，英汉旅游翻译虽然相对容易，但依然存在不少问题，主要涉及以下三方面：

（一）生搬硬译，令人费解

中文译者在英汉旅游文本翻译上可能更感觉得心应手。但是，这并不意味着英汉翻译很简单，有时对照翻译行得通，但忽视中英文各自语言特点的盲目对照就会使译文显得别扭，甚至令人费解。

例17 If all this isn't enough, and you want something quirkier, why not come in January for the annual ice canoe race, when five-man/woman teams haul canoes across the ice floes?

如果这还不够，且您想来点新奇，那为什么不等到五人一队的赛手划着船穿过浮冰的一月来观看一年一度的冰上船赛？

表面上看，译文既保留了原文的句式，又照顾到汉语把定语放在所修饰词之前的习惯，但整个译文从逻辑上及可读性上都显得别扭、拗口，属于生搬硬译。不如将 why not... 改译为祈使句，采用断句的方法将原文翻译为："如果这不够刺激，想来点新奇，那就到一月来观看一年一度的冰上船赛吧，届时五人一队的赛手将划着船穿过浮冰。"

例18 In addition to the comfortable buses provided by our company all other means of transport, belonging to the reliable Swiss transport system, can be used.

除被我公司提供的舒适汽车外，其他属于可靠的瑞士运输系统的其他运输方式都可以被使用。

译文从语态上过于拘泥于原文，将过去分词 provided、谓语动词 can be used 均直译为被动语态，显得晦涩；此外，belonging to the reliable Swiss transport system 译成定语显得冗长拖沓，不如译为并列短语。译文可以修改为："除我公司提供的舒适巴士，还可乘坐其他交通工具，这些交通工具均属于瑞士安全可靠的交通系统。"

（二）译文平淡，缺少"汉"味

英文旅游文本重在传递有关景点的地理环境、服务设施、优势与不足等方面的信息，极具实用性。将其翻译成汉语时，如果不注意汉语旅游文本重描写、重修辞、语言鲜活等特点，译文很容易归于直白、平淡，缺乏想象力，其宣传、感召的力度会大打折扣。

例19 The fanciful names at Arches National Park like Fiery Furnace, Three Gossips, Marching Men, Dark Angles, etc. do justice to the otherworldly rock formations they denote.[15]

石拱门国家公园内那些奇怪的景点名称如"熔炉""三怨妇""行进者""黑天使"等与超凡脱俗的山石形象正好吻合且名副其实。

译文忠实地传达了原文的意思，但语言平淡无奇，缺乏想象力，没有体现出汉语旅游文本的特色。在充分把握原文意思的基础上，译文如果能兼顾使用四字成语及合适的修辞手法，效果会更好。原文不妨改译为："石拱门国家公园内各景点的名称可谓五花八门、极富创意。'火炉烈焰''三婆姨''行进者''黑天使'等用来形容那些形状怪异的山石可谓恰如其分、惟妙惟肖。"修改后的译文表达更形象，更具美感。

（三）专有名词翻译混乱

旅游文本中常常会出现一些专有名词，如地名、机构名称等。有些译者在处理这些专有名词时比较随意，如在汉语译文中直接保留英文单词，或是对照英文发音随意给出相应的汉语等。译者没有留意该专有名词是否在汉语里已有约定俗成的表达，也没有考虑该译文是否有效传递了原文的信息及含义，对专有名词的翻译很不规范。

---

15 丁大刚．2008.旅游英语的语言特点与翻译．上海：上海交通大学出版社．

例20 One of the places that the MGBahn network takes visitors is right into the UNESCO World Heritage Swiss Alps Jungfrau-Aletsch, which was named as the first Natural Heritage site in the Alps by the UNESCO World Heritage Committee in 2001. The Aletsch Glacier—at 22 kilometers the longest anywhere in the Alps—is the centerpiece of the whole area.

MGBahn铁路网带游客进入的游览胜地之一是联合国教科文组织世界遗产瑞士阿尔卑斯山的Jungfrau-Aletsch，该地区于2001年由联合国教科文组织世界遗产委员会命名为阿尔卑斯山区的首个自然遗产。长达22公里的Aletsch冰河是阿尔卑斯山区最长的冰河，也是整个地区的中心。

UNESCO译为"联合国教科文组织"，Alps译为"阿尔卑斯山(区)"，这是公认的译文，但MGBahn、Jungfrau-Aletsch、Aletsch以英文的形式保留在译文中，让中国读者感到陌生。事实上，在互联网上均能查到这些英文名称的中文译文，分别为"马特宏圣哥达铁路公司"、"少女峰——阿莱奇地区"、"阿莱奇"。

例21 Thomas Cook ranks high as travel specialists and tour operators inbound/outbound. Our services range from arranging well-planned itineraries for groups/individuals/business executives to issuing traveler's checks acceptable world-wide, freighting cargo and other allied travel activities.

托马斯库克是一流的出入境旅行专家和旅游经营公司。我们为团体、个人和商业管理人士提供各类服务，从精心安排旅游日程，到签发全球通用的旅行支票、货物运输及其他有关的联运旅游服务。

Thomas Cook有两种译法：对业内人士来说，译为"通济隆"即可；对非业内人士来说，可以采取增词法，译为"通济隆旅游公司"。但译者根据发音将Thomas Cook翻译为"托马斯库克"则不是规范的译文。

例22 The well-known Rushmore National Monument in the United States is erected on the Rushmore Peak, 1,829 meters above sea level, of the Black Hills in the south-east of South Dakota. It is a group of huge stone statues of four American presidents, George Washington, Thomas Jefferson, Abraham Lincoln and Theodore Roosevelt.[16]

美国著名的拉什莫尔国家纪念碑位于南达科他州西南一座海拔1829米的布莱克山拉什莫尔峰顶。这座纪念碑由雕刻在岩石上的乔治·华盛顿、托马斯·杰斐逊、亚伯拉罕·林肯以及西奥多·罗斯福四位美国总统的巨型头像组成。

译文将Rushmore音译为"拉什莫尔"，因此Rushmore National Monument的译文是"拉什莫尔国家纪念碑"。这对中国游客而言，既难读也难记，反而其俗称"总统山"更为人熟知。所以，Rushmore National Monument不妨就译为"总统山"，或是用"音译+增词"

---

16 此例引自 http://www.xzbu.com/9/view-6487709.htm。

法，译为"拉什莫尔国家纪念碑（俗称总统山）"，这样翻译有更好的宣传效果。译者翻译四位总统的名字时，采用中国读者耳熟能详的译名，便于理解。

从上面例子可以看出，翻译英文专有名词并非想象的那么简单，在译文中保留英文单词绝不是一个好的选择，而音译专有名词也并不总是管用。比较妥当的方法是：首先查阅资料看是否已经有译名，如果有，则沿用已有译名，如果没有，则根据专有名词的构成进行翻译，该音译时音译，该意译时意译。

第三节 旅游文体的翻译原则

旅游文体翻译属于实用翻译，是一种目的性很强的交际活动，理论上应以功能目的论为指导。本节将介绍旅游文本的功能及目的，兼顾中英文旅游文本的用词、句法、修辞以及语篇特点，从功能翻译理论和翻译目的理论的视角探讨旅游文体的翻译原则。

一、旅游文本的功能和目的

旅游文本是一种应用文体，是介绍和宣传旅游景点和旅游目的地、提供旅游指南和介绍游览行程等的书面资料。旅游文本旨在让普通游客读懂、看懂相关信息，帮助其从中获取自然、地理、文化、风俗等方面的知识。所以大多数旅游文本包含丰富的信息，极具信息功能。旅游文本还具有呼唤功能，即"唤起读者前往旅游目的地"。旅游文本是一种"信息型、呼唤型文体，或者信息—呼唤复合型文体，以描述见长，与异国情调、民俗文化不可分离"[17]。换言之，"旅游资料是一种对外宣传资料，其主导功能在于吸引游客，激发他们对风景名胜的兴趣。这种诱导性功能的实现，必须以提供足够的信息为前提"[18]。所以，旅游文本具有诱导功能。

旅游文本体现了两个主要功能——信息功能、呼唤或诱导功能，信息功能是前提，而呼唤或诱导功能是其最终目的。

二、旅游文体的翻译原则

旅游文本翻译是为开展旅游活动、促进旅游业发展所进行的一种跨语言、跨社会、跨时空、跨文化、跨心理的交际活动，属于应用翻译（applied translation）或实用翻译（practical translation）。[19] 旅游文本翻译应以传递信息（实现其信息功能）为主要目的，

---

17 伍峰、何庆机.2008.应用文体翻译：理论与实践.杭州：浙江大学出版社.
18 孟庆升.2009.新编实用汉英翻译教程.沈阳：辽宁大学出版社.
19 丁大刚.2011.旅游英语的语言特点与翻译.上海：上海交通大学出版社.

又要注重信息的传递效果（实现其呼唤功能或诱导功能）。从翻译策略来看，基本上应以"归化"为导向，以目的语读者为中心（TL reader-centered）。同时，还要充分考虑到中英文旅游文本在用词、句法、修辞、语篇等方面的异同点，确保信息的准确传达。因此，旅游文本有如下几个翻译原则：

（一）以实现旅游文本的功能为目的

实现旅游文本的功能是旅游文本翻译的主要目的。美国著名翻译家尤金·奈达（Eugene Nida）提出的"动态对等"和"功能对等"的翻译理论对旅游文本的翻译有很好的借鉴作用。

"功能对等原则"的前身是"动态对等原则"，基于"动态对等"基础上的翻译要求译者关注的并不是源语信息和译语信息的逐一对应关系，而是一种动态关系，即译语接受者和译语信息之间的关系应该与源语接受者和原文信息之间的关系基本相同。就此而言，翻译必须达到四个标准：（1）达意；（2）传神；（3）措辞顺畅自然；（4）读者反应类似。所以，译者在翻译过程中应该注意原文的意义和精神，而非拘泥于原文的语言结构或寻求形式对应。奈达认为，采用动态翻译的译者可能比采用直译的译者更忠实于原文，因为前者可以更全面、更充分地理解原文的意义。

在20世纪80年代，奈达对"动态对等"加以修正，将其改为"功能对等"。他认为"动态对等"过于强调"译文与原文在内容上的一致优于形式上的一致"有失偏颇，或会令人产生误解；而"功能"二字把翻译视为一种交际形式，着重于翻译的内容和结果，比"动态"更为合理。

旅游文本翻译要确保交际成功，就必须保证原文信息在译文中充分传递，并且要实现原文的功能。有学者指出："旅游资料的功能是通过对景点的介绍、宣传，扩展人们的知识，激发人们旅游、参观的兴趣。因此，旅游文本翻译的最终目的就是通过信息来吸引读者。"[20] 所以，旅游文本翻译要实现吸引游客、传递文化信息的目的。

综上所述，翻译旅游文本首先要考虑到旅游文本的功能和目的，在忠实地传达原文实质性信息（如景点名称、交通、食宿、游览路线等信息）的基础上，注重旅游文本的宣传、广告效应，以使译文吸引更多的目的语读者前来游览观光。

（二）以目的语读者为中心

德国翻译功能学派学者弗米尔（Hans J. Vermeer）从人类行为理论的视角来审视和研究翻译活动，认为翻译具有明确的目的性和意图性，是一种在译者的作用下以原文文本为基础的跨文化人类交际活动。弗米尔的"翻译目的论"（Skopos Theory）将翻译视为一种人际间的互动活动，涉及译文发起者、译者、原文作者、译文读者和译文文本的使用者等。

---

20 顾维勇. 2005. 实用文体翻译. 北京：国际工业出版社.

翻译活动的发起者确定翻译目的并规定翻译要求（Translation Brief），其中包括：（1）文本功能；（2）译语文本的接受者；（3）接受文本的时代及地点；（4）传播文本的媒介；（5）生产或接受文本的动机等。弗米尔认为译文接受者对于翻译过程起着重要的作用，因此任何有关译文接受者的信息对于译者来说都很重要。

旅游文本的译文必须在功能上与原文一致，但又要符合目的语的体裁规范，达到与目标读者交际的目的，因此，旅游文本翻译必须以目的语读者为中心。旅游文本的翻译通常要满足客户的要求，译者需要在牢记目标读者期望的情况下对原文进行调整或改写。译文实际上就是在目的文化和目的语言中传达原文信息。

例1 绍兴鲁迅纪念馆成立于1953年，为建国后浙江省最早建立的纪念性人物博物馆。[21]

Established in 1953, the museum is the earliest construction in Zhejiang in memory of personalities.

"纪念性人物博物馆"是中国特有的概念，可对应英文中的 memorial hall，如林肯纪念堂的英文名称是 Lincoln Memorial Hall。译文加入解释性信息 in memory of personalities 来进行补充说明，却带来误解：其一，in memory of 后面应接 Lu Xun；其二，personalities 一般特指娱乐界或体育界名人，与鲁迅的身份和形象不符。因此，原译文可改为：Lu Xun Museum in Shaoxing, erected in 1953, is the first memorial hall ever constructed in Zhejiang province.

（三）考虑中英文旅游文本的语言特点及文化差异

汉英民族有不同的文化背景、价值观念和思维方式，因此汉英旅游文本在语言文体特色和风格上也不尽相同。英语旅游文本大多句式严整，行文注重逻辑性，用词简洁。相比之下，汉语旅游文本大多言辞华丽、用词含蓄；表达上多使用四言排比和对偶平行结构，以求行文工整、声律对仗，达到言、行、意皆美。

英美旅游语篇重在对景点地理环境、服务设施、优势与不足等方面的信息传递，而风光景色的描述则着笔不多；汉语旅游语篇往往更加突出旅游资源的社会身份特征，如社会影响、历史沿革、发展业绩等，突出风光景色和人文特色，甚至着重引用史书、文学作品及诗歌对景点进行颂扬和描述。

翻译旅游文本时，译者要考虑两种语言之间的文化差异和审美差异，以目的语读者为中心，以实现原旅游文本的功能为目的，在两种语言之间进行恰当的转换。

例2 The Grand Canyon has several weather environments. The top is often much different from the bottom. On some winter day, for example, you may find cold winds and snow

---

21　汪宝荣. 2005. 旅游文化的英译：归化与异化——以绍兴著名景点为例. 中国科技翻译，（1）：13–17.

at the top. But at the bottom, you may find warm winds and flowers.

大峡谷地区有好几种气候环境。谷顶和谷底的气候通常大相径庭。冬季来临时，谷顶可能寒风呼啸、遍布积雪，谷底却暖风拂面、鲜花盛开。

原文用词平实，描述简洁、直观。译文多用四字词语，言辞华丽，符合汉语读者的审美情趣。显然，译文的成功之处在于充分考虑到中英文旅游文本的用词特点，实现了双语的巧妙转换。

例3 Since 1872, Yellowstone National Park was founded, there have been more than 60 million tourists who come here. Visitors from all over, all kinds. The feeling is naturally rich and varied: there is pleasant praise, there is fear, or surprised sighs, there is awe of meditation, there are thrills to stimulate fear, there are pairs of natural power and quiet insight, as well as bittersweet experiences...

自从1872年黄石公园建成以来，已有六千多万人来此观光。游人来自五湖四海，形形色色，所获得的感受自然也就丰富多彩，各不相同：有赏心悦目的赞美，有敬畏或惊诧的感叹，有肃然起敬的沉思，有惊险恐惧的刺激，有对大自然威力的沉静领悟，还有悲喜交加的经历……

原文用词朴实，句子简短，逻辑关系清晰，通俗易懂，有利于宣传。译文用词凝练，多用四字成语和并列结构，句式齐整，读起来朗朗上口，富于节奏感，使目的语读者对黄石公园充满了遐想，起到了很好的宣传作用。

例4 苏州园林体现的却是所谓的"诗意的栖居"，"诗意"不只是小桥流水、茂林修竹、奇石假山、画栋雕梁……，也不只是所谓借景的艺术，而是体现着存在的根本意义，是关系到人要活在一个什么样的世界上——这个是必须要搞清楚的中国认识。高速公路、水泥楼房、玻璃、钢筋、塑料、汽油固然不错，可以加快我们的生活速度，但在加速改造之后的这一切的尽头是什么，是新的失眠纪录还是苏州园林？是伊甸园还是万物死亡的荒野？是"明月松间照，清泉石上流"，还是沙尘暴和污水池？现代人被现代化的过程所迷惑，但人生的意义在于安心。没有心的人我就不说了，那些从中国文化继承了心和存在感的人们，你们的心要安在何处？

The classical gardens of Suzhou demonstrate the concept of poetic dwelling. The poetry refers not only to little bridges and flowing streams, bushy trees and slim bamboos, grotesque rockeries and ornate buildings, nor simply to the arts of "borrowed views", but also indicates the fundamental meaning of human existence and what kind of world men want to live in. Modernists may be seduced by the process of modernization, but the real meaning of human life lies in ease of heat.

原文作者由苏州园林想到中国式"诗意的栖息"，从而引发对现代化的"弊"的思考并提出"有心"的人心安在何处的问题。原文中画线部分为主观思考，对于以传递信息为主的旅游文本来说，超出了目的语读者的审美期待。考虑到中英文旅游文本的不同特点，译者采用简化法，删去了原文思考的问题，侧重于表达"小桥流水""茂林修竹""奇石假山""画栋雕梁"等具有中国园林特色的意象。简化后的译文表达简洁，信息集中，语境效果强。

涉及中文旅游材料中的文化处理要遵循两个原则，即"中国文化为基准，以译文读者为导向"[22]。也就是说，在宣传中国文化的同时，要不拘泥于原文，本着向读者传达信息的目的进行翻译。

因此，在翻译旅游文本时，应根据具体的文化现象灵活地处理译文，在尽可能保存原文信息的情况下满足译文读者的文化需求和审美预期，从而达到宣传目的。

（四）灵活选用翻译技巧

旅游翻译是为旅游业服务的，以旅游者为导向。因此，翻译技巧的运用必须与旅游业紧密结合。要考虑旅游者、市场、经济效益等诸多因素，讲究职业道德和规范。在进行具体翻译操作时，译者要基于旅游文本的功能和目的，针对不同的情况灵活选用翻译技巧。这对译者来说，是要求，也是挑战。译者需要在分析诸如翻译目的、语篇类型、译文读者的认知环境和期待视野等多方面的社会文化因素的基础上，进行两种文字的转换。对译者而言，加强和巩固双语能力是准确灵活运用各种翻译技巧的前提。

第四节
旅游文体的翻译技巧

由于旅游翻译的实用性和特殊性，在翻译技巧和手法的使用上往往不拘一格。下面介绍旅游文本英汉互译中常用的翻译技巧。

一、选词

选词（Diction），即理解原文词义，然后在翻译表达中择取单词。英汉两种语言中都存在一词多词性、一词多词义的现象，因此不仅要根据词性来确定词义，而且还要依据上下文来选择词义，再选用相应的译文表达。选词时，还要注意两种语言在组词造句方面的差异以及词与词之间的逻辑关系。

例1 Crisscrossed by ferries and carpeted with yachts on weekends, Sydney Harbor is both the city playground and a major port. Its multiple sandstone headlands, dramatic

---

22 孟庆升．2009．新编实用汉英翻译教程．沈阳：辽宁大学出版社．

cliffs, rocky islands and stunning bays and beaches make it one of the most beautiful stretches of water in the world, and offer a close-up of Aussie beach culture at its best.
悉尼港是悉尼市的游乐场所和主要港口，周末无数的渡船和游艇穿梭于此。它多样的砂岩岬角、引人注目的悬崖峭壁、多岩石的岛屿、美丽的海湾和海滩使它成为世界上最美丽的连绵水域，淋漓尽致地展现了澳大利亚的海滨文化。

原文中 crisscrossed by 和 carpeted with 是过去分词，分别表达"被纵横交错于，被交叉往返"和"被完全覆盖，被铺上一层"的意思，描述了悉尼港上众多渡船和游艇交叉往返、纵横交错的画面。译者用"无数的"和"穿梭"两词，巧妙地传达了原文表达的意思。原文中 stretch 指"伸展，延伸"，与 water 用在一起，表示"水域宽广"；译文选用"连绵水域"一词，译得恰到好处。at its best 表示"最好、最佳"的意思，offer a close-up 指"给特写"，相应的译文"淋漓尽致"和"展现"两词再现了原文的风姿，体现译者选词之精妙。

例2 黄山自古云成海，云流动在千峰万壑之中，浩瀚天际，壮丽非凡。峰尖浮海，犹如孤屿，时隐时现，似见未见，瞬息万变，气象万千。变幻莫测的云海与朝霞、落日相映，色彩斑斓，壮美瑰丽。
The clouds float over the mountain and among its peaks and gullies like a sea in which the peaks from time to time appear and disappear, often in the twinkling of a moment, like isolated small islands. The cloud sea is even more splendid at sunrise and sunset.

原文行文华丽，讲究对仗，渲染情感；译文表达精细，描述直观，选词精准、传神，成功地再现了原文的意境。"云海""孤屿""隐""现""瞬息"等被译为 cloud sea、isolated small islands、disappear、appear、in the twinkling of a moment，不仅达意，而且传神。"千峰万壑"用了夸张的手法，表达"峰壑很多"的意思，是典型的汉语表述方式；译文没有使用夸张的修辞手法，仅用 peaks 和 gullies 两词来表达原文的意思，虽然不华丽，但也写实、具体，选词准确。最后一句中的"变幻莫测""色彩斑斓""壮美瑰丽"为典型的汉语四字词语，辞藻华丽，重在写意。译文 The cloud sea is even more splendid at sunrise and sunset，选词简练，但意思丰富，令人充满遐想。

二、增译

增译（Amplification）是指在翻译中，根据原文语义、语法、修辞等方面的需要，在不改变原文语义信息的前提下，在译文中适当添加原文没有的字眼，使译文既忠实地传达原文的内容和风格，又符合译入语的表达习惯。

例3 Towers, domes, balanced rocks, and arches have been formed over millions of years of weathering and erosion, and the process continues, constantly reshaping this fantastical rock garden.[23]

---

23 此例引自罗选民. 2011. 新英汉翻译教程. 北京：清华大学出版社.

岁月沧桑，风化雨蚀，造就了这里奇特的山体风貌：满山"巨塔"高耸，"穹丘"浑圆，"不倒翁"摇摆欲坠，"大拱门"凌空而立，奇形怪状，浑然天成。大自然造物不尽，还在不断创造新的神奇。

"奇特的山体风貌""满山""高耸""浑圆""摇摆欲坠""凌空而立""奇形怪状""浑然天成"等是基于原文信息而增译的部分，便于国内游客了解美国石拱门国家公园的风貌。同时，译者在遣词造句上也兼顾了汉语的行文风格，将英语简约的表达化作汉语读者喜闻乐见的形式。译文言辞华丽，句式齐整，更具感召力。

例4 林边有一个洞，叫鬼谷洞，传说孙膑的师傅鬼谷子曾经在这里修炼。[24]
Near the forest is the Guigu Cave which is said to be the very place where Guiguzi, the legendary hero as well as the master of Sun Bin, cultivated himself according to Buddhist doctrine.

译文用 the legendary hero 来补充说明孙膑师傅"鬼谷子"的身份；增加了 according to Buddhist doctrine 来帮助读者理解原文中"修炼"的确切含义。这两处增译更有利于英文读者理解原文的信息。

例5 On the road leading from central Europe to Adriatic coast lies a small Slovenian town of Postojna. Its subterranean world holds some of Europe's most magnificent underground galleries. Time loses all meanings in the formation of these underground wonders. The drip stone-stalactites, columns, pillars and translucent curtains, conjure up unforgettable image.
从中欧通往雅德里亚海岸的路上有一座斯洛文尼亚小城，叫作波斯托伊那。这座小城的地下藏着欧洲一些最为神奇的美术馆，这些地下奇迹蔚为壮观，历史悠久，置身其中，可以欣赏到钟乳石、石柱、透明的石帘，可谓形象千姿百态，令人流连忘返。

对照原文和译文，我们不难发现，"蔚为壮观""置身其中，可以欣赏到""可谓""千姿百态"等属于增译的部分，是对原文意思的补充和发挥。这种补充迎合了中文读者的审美诉求和思维习惯。

三、加注

由于英汉文化存在许多差异，某些文化词语在目标语中没有对等词，形成了词义上的空缺。在这种情况下，英汉互译时常常要采用加注法（Annotation）来弥补空缺，便于读者理解。

例6 六奇阁位于黄石寨上。
Six Wonders Pavilion (which refers to six wonders of Zhangjiajie: namely the wonders

---
[24] 此例引自赖少华. 2005. 旅游资料中的文化翻译. 广西教育学院学报，（3）：127–129.

of the mountains, the waters, the clouds, the rocks, the trees and the variety of rare animals) is located in Yellow Stone Village.

"六奇"指的是张家界"山奇、水奇、云奇、石奇、植物奇以及动物奇"。译文中对六奇的加注说明让外国读者更加清楚地了解"六奇"的具体内容，有效传达了旅游信息。

例7 佛跳墙

Fo Tiao Qiang or Buddha-Jump-Over-the-Wall (Steamed Abalone with Shark's Fin and Fish Maw: Fujian's Number One special dish, carefully prepared with shark's fin, abalone and more than 20 other ingredients. The dish is so tempting that even a Buddhist monk will jump over the wall for it.)

对来华游览的外国人来说，一项必不可少的内容就是品尝和享受中国的美味佳肴。但中国烹调方式繁多，命名方式多样，这就给菜名的翻译增加了难度。例7就是典型的例子。

"佛跳墙"不论是翻译成Fo Tiao Qiang还是Buddha-Jump-Over-the-Wall，都会让外国读者感到茫然，因为译文没有给出任何相关的信息，如食材、烹调方法等，其表达的意思也与美食毫不相关。译者采用"音译+直译+加注"的翻译方法，既保留了菜名的生动形象，又向外国读者说明了该菜名的由来，展示了丰富文化，唤起了游客的好奇心，起到很好的宣传作用。

例8 Carnival is a four-day celebration before the start of Ash Wednesday which is the beginning of Christian Lent. The idea behind Carnival is to enjoy life to the fullest by feasting, drinking, and dancing before the fasting period.

圣灰星期三（大斋节的第一天，复活节前的第七个星期三，该日有用灰抹额以示忏悔之俗）标志着基督教大斋节的开始。嘉年华在圣灰星期三之前举行，有连续四天的庆祝活动。人们举行嘉年华的初衷是，在斋戒期之前大吃大喝，尽情跳舞，好好享受生活。

不少中国人对基督教习俗知之甚少，因此，有必要对"圣灰星期三"进行加注说明，让中国游客了解基督文化，从而更好地融入旅游地的节庆活动中。

四、省略

省略（Omission）是指出于语法、意义、修辞、文化等方面的需要，翻译时适当删减词语，并尽可能做到"减词不减意"。在英汉翻译中，采用省略法往往是出于语法、意义的需要；在汉英翻译中，采用省略法通常是出于意义、修辞、文化等方面的需要。

例9 You're not permitted to bring your own food to the park; you can only consume the fast food sold on the premises.

不允许自带食物进入园中，只能在里面的快餐店用餐。

例10 The local meteorological statistics show that March brings more rain than any other month.

当地的气象统计资料表明，三月份降雨量最多。

例9译文省略了对代词you和your的翻译，因为无主句更符合汉语旅游文本的表达。例10省略了any other month的翻译，"最"实际上已译出any other month的意思，简洁直观。

例11 境内怪峰林立，溶洞群布，古木参天，珍禽竞翅，山泉潺潺，云雾缭绕。

Inside are clusters of strange peaks, limestone caves, rare birds as well as the towering big trees with spring babbling on the way and mists weathering the mountain tops.

原文中"林立"和"群布"同义，"古木参天"中的"参天"是虚义，"珍禽竞翅"中"竞翅"也是虚义。译文中省略了虚指的部分，用clusters表达"林立""群布"之意，简洁不重复；并采用英文特有的倒装结构，地道的表达让游客感受到句子的结构美。

例12 唐刘禹锡赞九华山"奇峰一见惊魂魄"，宋王安石誉为"楚越千万山，雄奇此山兼"，素有"东南第一山"之称。

Many famous ancient poets wrote poems to praise the stunning and spectacular beauty of Mount Jiuhua; it is thus known as the First Mountain in the Southeast.

译文省略了原文中"刘禹锡"和"王安石"两位诗人的名字和诗句，但留下了旅游者需要的主要信息，易于被游客接受。

五、词性转换

词性转换（Conversion）是常见的翻译技巧。旅游文本翻译过程中，由于两种语言在语法和表达习惯上的差异，有时必须改变某些词语的词性才能有效地传达出原文的意思。汉语句式中，动词的使用频率大大超过英语，因此，要使译文符合目的语的习惯表达，就需将汉语中的很多动词转换为名词、形容词、介词、副词等，或是将英语中的很多名词、形容词、介词、副词等转换为动词。除动词转换之外，英汉互译也涉及其他词性的转换。

例13 湖水泛着涟漪，四周山林茂密，点缀着楼台亭阁，西湖是我国最有名的旅游景点之一。

With ripples on the water's surface and thickly-wooded hills dotted by exquisite pavilions on its four sides, the West Lake is one of China's best-known scenic spots.

例14 宽阔的水帘拍石，声似万马奔腾、巨雷轰鸣，惊心动魄，数里之外可闻。

Here the large body of water comes plunging down on the rocks below, creating a thundering, soul-stirring boom that can be heard for miles around, like the noise of thousands of horses in stampede.

例13中动词"泛着"被译为介词短语with... on...，主谓结构"山林茂密"被译为名词短语thickly-wooded hills，动词"点缀"被译为过去分词dotted。例14中动词词组"巨雷轰鸣""惊心动魄"分别被译为形容词 thundering 和 soul-stirring。这种处理使译文符合译入语的表达习惯，符合读者的审美期待。

例15 Rough, black rocks of lava jut out of the water along parts of the coastline. In some places, cliffs rise almost straight from the water's edge. Along the gentle sloping land areas to the southeast are beaches of yellow, white and black sands.

部分海岸层岩叠嶂，熔岩乌黑，悬崖峭壁破水而出。而有的地方，则坡度平缓，沙滩连绵，黄沙似金，白沙似银，黑沙如铅，一路向东南延展，煞是好看。[25]

原文 rocks 为复数形式，被译者演绎为主谓结构"层岩叠嶂"，词组 black rocks of lava 又被译者译为主谓结构"熔岩乌黑"，意思一目了然；介词短语 along... to... 被译为动词词组"一路向……延展"；sands 用复数形式，指"许多沙滩"，被译为主谓结构"沙滩连绵"，翻译传神；形容词 yellow, white and black 被转化为主谓结构"黄沙似金，白沙似银，黑沙如铅"，形象生动。考虑到汉语多用动词和四字词语的特点，译者不仅改变了词性，而且用了六个四字词语，使译文构成排比结构，具有气势，突显美感，颇为地道。

六、语态转换

在旅游文本翻译中，语态转换（Voice Shifting）是常用的技巧。英语中被动语态用得较多，而汉语中被动语态的使用则相对较少。因此，英译汉时被动语态常常要转化为主动语态，而汉译英时，汉语中的主动语态根据表达习惯也经常转换为被动语态。

例16 A fascinating city between sea and sky, like Venus rising from the waves, Venice welcomes tourists from the five continents drawn to her by the charm of her water and pellucid light, free from all dust and cooled by the sea breeze. She also offers the intellectual pleasures to be derived from her masterpiece which mark the meeting of East and West.[26]

威尼斯水城海天相连，景色宜人，宛如碧波中涌现的维纳斯，吸引着五大洲的游客。她水色旖旎，波光澄澈，清风拂面而来，荡去你心中的不快与烦恼。而城中那些集东西方艺术之大成的杰作，更给人以精神上的享受。

原文中过去分词短语 drawn to her by 表被动，译者将其被动的意思融入 welcomes 一词中，用了主动结构"吸引着"，符合汉语表达习惯；过去分词短语 cooled by the sea breeze 译为主动结构"清风拂面而来"，be derived from 译为主动结构"给……"，译文流畅、地道。

例17 Arriving at St. Peter's Square, the visitor is immediately impressed by the size of the memorable square facing St. Peter's, surrounded by the magnificent four-row

---

25　此例引自胡惺春. 2013. 功能目的论关照下的景点文本英汉对译策略. 武汉商业服务学院学报，（2）：71–74.
26　顾维勇. 2005. 实用文体翻译. 北京：国际工业出版社.

colonnade masterpiece of Gian Lorenzo Bernini. Only when one gets inside the basilica, slowly climbing up the sweeping three flights of steps designed by Bernini, one will be truly amazed by the size and splendor of the largest church in the world, the symbol of Christianity, extending over a total of about 22,000 square meters.

置身于圣彼得广场，映入眼帘的是由杰安·劳伦佐·贝尼尼设计的四根壮丽精美的柱廊环绕中的圣彼得教堂。对面的纪念广场规模宏大，吸引着来自世界各地的游人。只有当你亲自置身于教堂之中，沿着贝尼尼设计的三段弯弯曲曲的楼梯拾阶而上的时候，才会真正被世界上最大教堂的宏伟壮丽所震撼，大教堂占地 22 000 平方米，是基督教的象征。

原文的被动结构 is immediately impressed by 被译为主动结构"映入眼帘的是"，是典型的汉语表达；过去分词短语 surrounded by、designed by Bernini 分别被译为主动结构"环绕中""贝尼尼设计的"。译者将被动结构转换为主动结构是基于汉语少用被动语态的特点，但并不是所有的被动语态都必须转化为主动语态，如原文的被动结构 be truly amazed by... 被译为"被……所震撼"，译文自然。

例18 明代寺毁，清康熙九年（1670 年）由笑宗和尚发起重建，形成了现在一塔、五殿、十六院的建筑群，占地 120 亩，用 400 多根石柱支撑，殿堂寺院，规模宏大，雄伟壮丽，门窗檐拱雕刻精美，佛像观音，栩栩如生。

The temple was destroyed by war in the Ming dynasty (1368–1644) and its reconstruction was started by monk Xiaozong in 1670 during the Qing dynasty. This new temple is actually an architectural complex of one pagoda, five halls and sixteen courtyards, covering a total area of about 8 hectares (20 acres). Supported by over 400 stone pillars, the temple buildings boast a grand and magnificent structure. Their doors, windows, eaves and arches are exquisitely carved and the statues of Buddha and Guanyin (Goddess of Mercy) are true to life.

在汉英翻译中，根据需要，主动结构常常被译为被动结构。例 18 中，"寺毁"译为被动结构 the temple was destroyed by war，by war 是译者结合历史背景知识补译的，传达信息准确、完整。主动结构"发起重建""用 400 多根石柱支撑""雕刻精美"分别译为被动结构 its reconstruction was started by、supported by over 400 stone pillars、are exquisitely carved，体现了英语常用被动语态的特点，符合目标语读者的语言习惯。

七、拆分

拆分（Division）也是英汉互译中用到的重要技巧之一。英语旅游文本大多使用简短句以使行文简单易懂，但有时也会出现较复杂的长句。汉语旅游文本大多由多个短句构成，每个句子又可以包含多个并列结构的短句。在英汉互译过程中，有时需要将一个长句拆分成两个或两个以上的短句。

例19 The sky reflected in the water turned the Seine into a lovely shade of blue which trembled in the hazy sunshine filtering through leafy branches of the trees lining the river's edge.

天空映照在水面上,给塞纳河染上了一层怡人的蓝色;朦胧的阳光透过两岸枝繁叶茂的树木,照得河水碧波荡漾。

原文是典型的英语长句,通过过去分词、定语从句、现在分词形成鲜明的逻辑关系。翻译时,可以根据原文的逻辑关系把长句拆分成几个部分:① The sky reflected in the water / ② turned the Seine into a lovely shade of blue / ③ which trembled in the hazy sunshine / ④ filtering through leafy branches of the trees / ⑤ lining the river's edge。然后再依次把每个部分的意思译出:①天空映照在水面上 /②把塞纳河染成了漂亮的蓝色 /③(塞纳河)在朦胧的阳光的照耀下碧波荡漾 /④(阳光)透过枝繁叶茂的树木 /⑤(树木)排列在河的两岸。最后根据汉语的表达习惯添加适当的词语并调整语序,获得译文。[27]

英译汉常使用拆分法,而在汉译英时也会遇到由几个并列短句构成的长句。译者可以根据需要,将汉语长句拆分为英语的小句。

例20 青岛坐落在山东半岛南部,依山临海,天姿秀美,气候凉爽,人称"东方瑞士"。白天,青岛宛如镶嵌在黄海边的绿宝石。夜里,则像一只在大海中摆动的摇篮。难怪许多人乐意来这里疗养。

Qingdao, known as the "Switzerland of the Orient", is situated on the southern tip of Shandong Peninsula. Wedged between hills and waters, the city is endowed with beautiful scenery and a delightful climate. By day, she looks like a green gem inlaid in the coastline of the Yellow Sea and, at night, a cradle rocking upon the sea waves. No wonder so many people come to seek rest and relaxation.

原文中第一句概写了青岛的地理位置、自然景观和佳名美誉。英译时如果处理为一个长句,不仅信息过载,语言形式也会显得臃肿不堪。将此句一分为二,先介绍佳名美誉和地理位置,再描写自然景观,译文显得逻辑清楚,主次分明,让外国游客一目了然。[28]

八、重组

重组(Restructuring & Reorganizing)是指在英汉互译时,为了使译文流畅,更符合目的语的表达习惯,在理清句子结构、句间逻辑关系和把握整体意思的基础上,摆脱原文的语序和句子形式,对其进行重新组合。

例21 在四川西部有一美妙去处,它背依岷山,主峰雪宝顶,树木苍翠,花香袭人,鸟语婉转,流水潺潺。它就是松潘县的黄龙。

---

27 丁大刚. 2011. 旅游英语的语言特点与翻译. 上海:上海交通大学出版社.
28 陈刚. 2009. 旅游英汉互译教程. 上海:上海外语教育出版社.

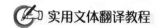

One of Sichuan's scenic spots is Huanglong (Yellow Dragon), which is located in Songpan County against Xuebao, the main peak of the Minshan Mountain. The green forest is endowed with fragrant flowers, bubbling streams and chirping birds.

原文第一句介绍黄龙的地理位置及美妙的景色，第二句点题，给出主题信息。将主题信息置后是汉语的典型表达方式，而英语主题信息往往出现在段首。译者据此对内容进行了重组和调整。译文第一句点题，同时介绍黄龙的地理位置；第二句主要介绍黄龙的美妙景色，条理清楚，符合英语读者的审美情趣。

例22 当你步入沟中，便可见林中碧海淡荡生辉，瀑布舒洒碧玉。一到金秋，满山枫叶绛红。盛夏，湖山幽翠。仲春，树绿花艳……四时都呈现出它的天然原始，宁静幽深。

Mystic lakes and sparking waterfalls captivate your eyes as you enter the ravine. The trees are in their greenest in spring when intensified by colorful flowers. In summer, warm tints spread over the hills and lake lands. As summer merges into autumn, the maple trees turn fiery red. Splashing color through the thick forest hills...Tranquility pervades primitive Jiuzhaigou throughout the year.

例22介绍的是九寨沟的风景，原文在描述其四季不同的美景时，采取的是"秋—夏—春"的顺序。译者翻译时，对原文进行了重组，按照四季更替的自然顺序"春—夏—秋"来重组原文内容，增强了译文的可读性。

例23 Here in New Hampshire there are many opportunities to find a peaceful spot hidden among the lush forests of tall evergreens and hard-woods or next to a rambling or pictorial lake. [29]

新罕布什尔州森林茂密，树木坚实高大，葱绿长青，湖水蜿蜒而流，湖泊风景如画，好多地方都是幽然寂静的好去处。

重构后的译文符合汉语景色描写的用语习惯，体现了汉语旅游文本的文体特点。如果句子结构不做调整，直译为"这儿，在新罕布什尔州，有很多机会在茂密的高高的长青树林中或阔叶树林里，或在潺潺的小溪旁，或在风景如画的湖边，找到一个安静的地方"，虽然在信息上忠实于原文，但平淡无奇，没有美感，难以吸引游客，不能很好地实现旅游文本的呼唤和感召功能。

29　此例引自 http://blog.sina.com.cn/s/blog_4981930801000983.html.

练习三

一、将下列句子译成英文。

1. (张家界国家森林公园)境内群峰拔地而起,如巨笋傲指苍穹;金鞭溪夹岸断岩绝壁,野藤古树,好一派原始风采;溪水如条条彩带铺展于千山万壑之间。在黄狮寨顶观山,气势磅礴、千罗万象,让人叹为观止。
2. 崂山,林木苍翠,繁花似锦,到处生机盎然,春天绿芽红花,夏天浓荫蔽日,秋天遍谷金黄,严冬则玉树琼花。其中,更不乏古树名木。景区内,古树名木有近300株,50%以上为国家一类保护植物,著名的有银杏、柏树等。
3. "烟水苍茫月色迷,渔舟晚泊栈桥西。乘凉每至黄昏后,人依栏杆水拍堤。"这是古人赞美青岛海滨的诗句。青岛是一座风光秀丽的海滨城市,夏无酷暑,冬无严寒。西起胶州湾入海处的团岛,东至崂山风景区的下清宫,绵延80多华里的海滨组成了一幅绚丽多姿的长轴画卷。
4. 故宫是中国现存最好、最完整的古代建筑群。占地面积达72万平方米,建筑面积约15万平方米。由大小数十个院落组成,房屋九千多间……
5. 张家界国家森林公园以峰称奇,以谷显幽,以林见秀。春天山花烂漫,花香扑鼻;夏天凉风习习,最宜避暑;秋日红叶遍山,山果挂枝;冬天银装素裹,满山雪白。

二、将下列句子译成中文。

1. Located in southwestern South Dakota, Badlands National Park consists of 224,000 acres of sharply eroded buttes, pinnacles and spires blended with the largest, protected mixed grass prairie in the United States. Established as Badlands National Monument in 1939, the area was redesignated "National Park" in 1978. Over 11,000 years of human history pale to the ages old paleontological resources, Badlands National Park contains the world's richest Oligocene epoch fossil beds, dating 23 to 35 million years old.
2. Sitting in the north of the Pacific Ocean, the string of Hawaii islands has some of the most beautiful beaches on earth. With pure white sands lined with green cliffs, in summer the sea is great for surfing, swimming and diving. The mild climate, green trees and charming flowers offer beauty and harmony to tourists all year round.
3. Built from 7,000 tons of iron and soaring 300 meters in the Parisian sky, the Eiffel Tower is the greatest engineering feat of the 19th century. It is considered by many to be the most

beautiful structure of the world and is the number one tourist destination of Paris.
4. A wealth of variety awaits the visitor to Virginia, from the Chesapeake Bay, the largest and most biologically productive estuary in North America, to the Blue Ridge, one of the world's oldest mountain ranges.
5. City of Diverse Cultures, The Garden City, The Fun City, City for the Arts and Gateway City—these are some of the names given to Singapore to show visitors what this exciting destination can offer to visitors who want to indulge their senses on a holiday as well as those who have a wish to stay in Singapore.

第四章 经贸文体的翻译

从纯粹的经济学角度来看，从具有法律效力的政策法规、商业合同、协议、单证等，到有关经济的理论研究及有关经贸的报刊报道或评述性文章，甚至商业信函、广告宣传，均属经贸文本的范畴。[1] 而从文体形式看，经贸文体包括公文体（如商业信函）、广告体（如商务广告）、论说体（如经济贸易评论）、契约体（如商务合同、协议）、应用体（如招商通告、请柬和说明书）等。[2]

由此可见，内容宽泛、形式多样是经贸文体的典型特征。一般而言，针对不同的文体形式，宜采用不同的翻译方法和标准。但由于经贸文体涉及面广，与其他文体的特点也多有重合，很难在一章中清楚、全面地介绍其文体的各种形式和翻译方法。因此，本章仅探讨与日常经贸活动直接相关的、涉及具体经贸往来的文体，主要包括商务函电、银证单据、外贸单证等，并试图从语言特色、翻译原则和翻译方法等方面逐一介绍。

第一节 经贸文体的特点

一、一词多义

大部分经贸英语词汇仍是日常词汇。但在经贸语境中，许多常见词汇被赋予了新的含义，通常为经贸语境所独有。因此，如不能正确掌握词汇的特有含义，将造成理解障碍。

例1 a. Behaviorism <u>claims</u> that consciousness is neither a definite nor a usable concept.
b. <u>Claims</u>, if any, one of the original policies which have been issued in two original(s) together with the relevant documents shall be surrendered to the company.

此例中，a 句为一般语境，claim 在此的含义为"声称"；而在经贸语境下，b 句中的 claim 指"索赔"。

---

1 刘振前、黄德新. 2001. 经贸英语翻译与写作（上册）. 济南：山东教育出版社.
2 马会娟. 2005. 论商务文本翻译标准的多元化. 中国翻译，（5）：81–84.

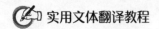

例2 All credits must stipulate an expiry date for presentation of documents for payment, acceptance or negotiation.

这是一个典型的经贸语句。句中的四个词汇在经贸语境下被赋予新的含义。下表为这四个单词在一般语境和经贸语境下的词义区别。

	一般语境意义	经贸语境意义
credit	信誉；信用；声望；学分	信用证
document	公文；文件；文献	单据
acceptance	接受；接纳	承兑
negotiation	谈判；协商	议付

由此可见，只有熟练掌握经贸专业词汇的含义，才能成功理解译文，顺利完成翻译。

二、用词正式

经贸文体行文正式，信息量大，内容准确严密，因此常用正式词汇及名词化结构。

（一）正式词汇

试比较下列例句：

例3 a. The committee was not prepared to use its discretion and grant special dispensation.
b. The committee was not prepared to use its discretion and give special dispensation.

例4 a. Please inform us of any changes of address.
b. Please tell us any changes of address.

以上两例中，a句都使用了相对正式的词语，而b句使用了日常词语。相比之下，a句语气更加正式严谨，b句口语化色彩较重。

试分别比较下列左右两栏词汇的特点：

acquaint	be familiar with
amend	change, correct
assist	help
cease to do	stop doing
commence	begin/start
constitute	include
effect	make
grant	give
in accordance with	according to
inform	tell

initiate	begin
miscellaneous	other matters
purchase	buy
require	ask
terminate	end

（二）名词化结构

名词化（nomination）通常是将动词、形容词转化为名词，一般可分成两类：（1）直接转化：即同一单词可以用作动词、形容词，又可以用作名词，但名词为其抽象化含义，如：increase、drop、prestige 等。（2）增加名词后缀，如：pay-payment、grow-growth、effective-effectiveness 等。名词化结构的特点是表述客观正式，内容准确周密，信息量大但又相对简洁。例如：

例5 a. In the event of the seller's failure in effecting shipment upon the arrival of the buyer's vessel at the shipping port…

b. If the seller fails to effect shipment upon the arrival of the buyer's vessel at the shipping port…

例6 a. After the date of effectiveness of the contract, the customer shall…

b. After the contract is effective, the customer shall…

以上两例 a 句和 b 句意思基本相同。从句式结构看，a 句使用名词化结构，为简单句，b 句为从句，相比而言 a 句更加简洁；从表达方式来看，a 句中的 failure、effectiveness 表现出一种客观存在，更符合经贸文体正式严谨的风格。

三、缩略词出现频率较高

缩略词构词简单，表达准确，形式固定，可用简练的方式表达复杂的内容。相比其他文体，缩略词在经贸文体中所占比例更高。经贸英语中的缩略词主要有以下几种类型：

（一）专门术语

专门术语与日常词汇相对，特指某一专业领域中独有的表达。在长期经贸活动中，许多专门术语逐渐形成了固定的缩略形式，通常采用首字母缩略和半缩略（截取词汇的某一部分进行简化）的方式。例如：经贸文本中常见的 B/L (bill of lading) 提单、CIF (cost insurance and freight) 到岸价格、FOB (free on board) 离岸价格、L/C (letter of credit) 信用证、MAWB (Master Air Way bill) 航空总运单、T/T (telegraphic transfer) 电汇、VAT (Value Added Tax) 增值税等，都属于首字母缩略词；ad valorem freight 从价运费、Container No. 集装箱号、Customs Ves. # 海关编号、S/O No. (shipping order) 装货单号、Inv. 发票等，则是典型的半缩略形式。

（二）专有名词

专有名词的缩略多见于组织机构、公司名称、地名和国家名等。如：

APEC	Asia-Pacific Economic Cooperation	亚太经合组织
AT&T	American Telephone & Telegraph	美国电话电报公司
EU	European Union	欧盟
IMF	International Monetary Fund	国际货币基金组织
OPEC	Organization of Petroleum Exporting Countries	石油输出国组织
WTO	World Trade Organization	世界贸易组织

（三）度量单位

经贸英语中的度量单位，常以小写字母的缩略形式出现。如：

Cu.m.	Cubic meter	立方米
Gal.	Gallon	加仑
In.	Inch	英寸
Kw.	Kilowatt	千瓦
lb.	Pound	磅
Sq.ft.	Square foot	平方英尺

需注意的是，以上各类缩略词都有其固定的缩略形式和对应含义，在翻译中也要严格遵循其固定表达，做到准确、规范。

四、句子结构相对复杂

经贸文体常带有法律效力，为了能准确、严谨地传递信息，常会出现结构复杂、语义严谨的长句。所谓英语长句，即除了主、谓、宾（表）等主要成分外，句中往往还有各种修饰成分（如从句、短语或独立主格等），其定语或状语可以一环套一环，修饰中另有修饰或限定，形成了峰回路转、错综复杂的长句结构。[3]

英语长句动词较少，词序灵活，语法关系复杂但脉络清楚。在理解此类长句时，首先要区分句子中的主干结构，找出句中的各种修饰、连接成分（如谓语结构、非谓语结构、介词短语、从句的引导词），最后分析从句及短语的功能。

例7 A credit by its nature is a separate transaction from the sale or other contract on which it may be based and the bank is in no way concerned with or bound by such contract, even if any reference whatsoever to it is included in the credit.

此句采用并列结构，用 and 连接前后半句，主语分别为 credit 和 bank；全句有两个从句，分别为 on which 引导的定语从句，修饰 the sale or other contract 和 even if 引导的表示假设

---

[3] 宋天赐. 2008. 翻译新概念英汉互译实用教程. 5版. 北京：国防工业出版社.

的状语从句。两个从句中都出现了代词 it,分别指代 credit 和 bank,理解时需注意理清指代关系。

五、文体格式相对固定

为了清楚、准确地传递经贸活动的信息,经贸文本形成了一些固定的表达以及格式化的语言。这是经贸文体区别于其他文体的一个明显特征。[4] 例如:

例 8 It is not applicable to guarantee, such as pledge, charge, etc. or any other legal use. Duplicate of this certificate is invalid.

不能用于质押、抵押等担保用途,也不具备其他法律效用,且副本无效。

例 9 Any modification and alteration to the content of this certificate all make the certificate invalid.

对本证明书的任何内容的修改、涂改均使本证明书无效。

例 10 The Assured shall settle the premium immediately after receiving the Debit Note. Bank fees or charges on premium remittance shall be borne by the payer.

被保险人须在收到保费通知书后立即付清全额保费;保费汇寄过程中发生的银行收费和/或其他费用应由保费支付人负担。

例 11 ... warranted that no known or reported loss of or damage to the Subject Matter insured on or before the confirmation date of this quotation.

截至被保险人确认日和/或保单生效日无损失记录。

以上各例中的中英文表述都比较固定,经常见于各类单据、单证及具有法律效力的文件中。

第二节
经贸文体的翻译原则和方法

经贸文本涉及经贸双方的经济利益,其中任何信息有纰漏都可能产生意想不到的后果,所以准确、规范是翻译时需要遵循的主要原则。换言之,译文用语要准确严谨,译文表达要符合经贸交流的规约和习惯。

一、准确性

准确性原则是指正确理解原文,然后用目的语准确、贴切地表达出来,使译语读者获

---

[4] 丁棣. 1996. 外贸英语语体功能及翻译刍议. 中国翻译,(1): 17-18.

得与原文内容相等的信息，即信息等值。[5]要做到信息等值，译者首先要能正确把握原文词句的确切含义，并利用各种翻译方法，使用恰当的词语、明确的指代，清楚地将原文信息传达给译文读者。

（一）词语的翻译

1. 准确翻译词义

译者需要积累一定的专业术语和专业词汇，根据语境选取合适的词义，并对原词进行适当的转译或推理。例如：

例1 公司应保有产品责任险、第三方责任险和其他有关险种，以保护公司、其雇员、代理人及其他有关方不会成为索赔对象。
The Company shall maintain product liability insurance, third party liability insurance and other relevant insurance coverage in order to protect the Company, its employees, agents and other appropriate parties from claims.

翻译此句时必须知道"产品责任险""第三方责任险"等专业术语的英译法。

例2 a. Enclosed is our new Quotation No. _____ in lieu of the previous one.
b. Many rural women have changed from concerning themselves only with household affairs to state affairs and quotations of markets, from believing in fate to science and themselves.

经贸英语涉及不同领域，行业不同，某些专业词汇的意义可能发生变化。quotation 在经贸英语中可理解为"报价，（股市、市场）行情"。在 a 句中，根据语境应理解为"报价"，即例句可译为："随附我公司第 ___ 号新的报价单以替代前发的报价单"。而在 b 句中，quotations of markets 应理解为"市场行情"，即例句可译为："不少农家女由只关心家庭琐事转向关心国家大事，关心市场行情；由相信命运转向相信科学、相信自己。"

例3 This column shows the borrower's exposure to changes in international interest rates.

exposure 常指"暴露"，但在此句中，如译为"暴露"则会令读者不知所云。此处应为"处于……的影响之下"，这里可具体理解为处于国际汇率变化的影响之下。故该句可译为："这栏表示借款者受到了国际利率变化的影响。"

2. 缩略语的翻译方法

诸多学者对经贸英语缩略语的翻译方法进行过讨论，一般认为分如下几种：（1）音译。音译是指根据英语发音直接转换翻译。比如：OPEC 欧佩克、NASDAQ 纳斯达克等。（2）意译。意译是直接将原文含义译出。如：CPI 消费者物价指数、GDP 国民生产总值等；（3）零翻译（不译）。零翻译是指直接将原文缩略语用于目的语。随着

---

[5] 姜荷梅. 2011. 商务英语的汉译原则. 上海翻译，（1）：29-32.

对外交流的增加，零翻译法已经十分普遍，常见于商品名称、公司名和商标名的翻译。如：IPAD、IBM、AT&T、SKII等。[6]

需注意的是，经贸英语中大部分缩略语，尤其是术语类缩略语都有约定俗成的翻译方法，因此在翻译时需注意准确对应，不能随意更改、创编。

（二）长句的翻译

经贸英语文体中的长句较多，习惯使用各种修饰限定成分，偏好使用名词或名词结构。而汉语句子相对简短，讲究节奏，偏好使用动词。翻译时，通常要做适当的调整，使语言通顺流畅，合乎英汉语言各自的表达习惯。长句翻译方法通常包括顺序法、逆序法、分序法以及综合法。

1. 顺序法

顺序法是指在翻译时，译者不做语序上的调整，使用与原文相同的语序或表达方式进行翻译。

例4 In order to make economic development agreements more attractive to investors, some developing countries have attempted to strengthen the security of such agreements, specifying that the agreements will be governed by "general principles of law recognized by civilized nations"—a set of legal principles or rules shared by the world's major legal systems.

例4一句由一个目的状语、一个主句、一个伴随性状语从句组成。其中从句中用破折号进一步解释说明了"总的法律原则"。整个句子共有四层含义：①为了使协议更具吸引力；②发展中国家试图提高协议安全性；③规定这些协议受"总的法律原则"约束；④这些原则由世界几个主要法律体系所共有的一套原则和规范组成。上述含义的表达顺序与汉语完全一致。因此，可以用顺序法进行组合，译为："为了使经济开发协议对投资者更具吸引力，有些发展中国家试图提高协议的安全性，规定这些协议受'文明国家公认的总的法律原则'的约束，这些原则由世界几个主要法律体系所共有的一套原则和规范组成。"

例5 The investor shall, within 45 days after the invalidation of the official approval and with the examination and approval of foreign exchange bureau, purchase and exchange the RMB to foreign currency and remit it out of China.

上例主句谓语动词连用，表明了动作发生的先后顺序，两个伴随性状语用作插入语，起修饰限定作用。整句逻辑关系与汉语一致，因此可译为："投资者应在批准失效之日起45日内，经外汇局核准后将结汇所得人民币资金购汇并汇出境外。"

---

[6] 余富林. 2000. 外贸英语缩略语的特点及翻译. 中国科技翻译，（5）：25–29. 柯发春. 2008. 证券英语缩略语及其翻译. 中国科技翻译，（5）：30–32.

2. 逆序法

逆序法是指在翻译时，按照与原文相反的语序或表达方式进行翻译。采用逆序法主要是因为英汉语在表达习惯上有差异，因此，在翻译时有时需调整语序以符合译文读者的表达习惯。

例6 In order to recover under this insurance the Assured must have an insurable interest in the subject-matter insured at the time of the loss.

此句结构并不复杂，可分为三部分理解：①为了获得本保险单项下的赔偿；②被保险人必须对保险标的物具有可保利益；③在发生损失时。在英语中，修饰限定词常位于被修饰语之后，而汉语习惯将其置于被修饰语之前。因此，③需放在句首。再看①、②的逻辑关系，虽然 in order to 引导的是目的状语，但此句中应理解为满足了②这个条件，才能达到①的目的。因此，在理清主句和目的状语之间逻辑关系的情况下，此句宜采用逆序法进行翻译，即："在发生损失时，被保险人必须对保险标的物具有可保利益，才能获得本保险单项下的赔偿。"

3. 拆分法

英语长句多修饰成分，且层层叠加。汉语句子简短，多用动词。在翻译时，需理清句子成分，明确修饰对象，将长句拆成短句。

例7 Consequently, the undertaking of a bank to pay, accept and pay draft or to fulfill any other obligation under the credit is not subject to claims or defenses by the applicant resulting from his relationships with the Issuing Bank or the Beneficiary.

此句中的名词化结构、动词连用和对名词的修饰限定使全句信息量大而又紧凑严谨。其中主语采用名词化结构，也是全句翻译的重点。主语中心词应该是 obligation，那么在译为汉语时，可将 undertaking 还原为动词词义，即"做出……承诺"，并将主语部分拆分翻译。全句可译为："因此，一家银行做出的付款、承兑和支付汇票或履行信用证项下的其他义务的承诺，不受申请人与开证行或与受益人之间的关系而提出的索赔或抗辩的约束。"

例8 Not only is the amount in excess of the maximum sum the bank can loan any individual legally, but it is absolutely without endorsement or security.

此句的翻译重点在后半句。absolutely 对 without... or 进行了强调，在翻译时将其进行拆分，使用"既……又"句型能更好地突出语气。可译为："不仅数目超过了银行发放私人贷款的最高限额，而且既无担保，又无抵押。"

4. 综合法

当单用上述几种译法无法准确清楚地表达原文句意时，在正确理解长句结构和句意的基础上，可以综合上述一至两种翻译方法，使译文流畅且符合读者的表达习惯。

例9 Collection means the handling by banks of documents as defined in sub-Article 2(b), in accordance with instructions received, in order to obtain payment and/or acceptance, or deliver documents against payment and/or against acceptance, or deliver documents on other terms and conditions.

上例为 Collection 的定义和描述。整句可分如下层次理解：①主句关系清楚，可直接译为："托收是指……"；②宾语部分较复杂，需理清结构，the handling by banks of documents 为英语长句中常见的名词化结构，强调银行处理单据的行为；而翻译时可直接按照汉语习惯用动词译出，即"银行处理单据"；③ as defined in sub-Article 2(b) 为 documents 的定语，汉语定语通常前置，可直接用"的"字句译出，即："下述第（2）款所界定的单据"；④ in accordance with instructions received 为伴随性状语，对 the handling 起修饰限定作用，按照汉语逻辑关系，修饰词一般放在被修饰部分之前；⑤ in order to 引导目的状语，按汉语的逻辑关系，一般行动在前，目的在后，因此这一部分可置于句子最后。综上，此句可译为："托收是指银行依据所收到的指示，处理下述第（2）款所界定的单据，以便取得付款及/或承兑；或付款交单及/或承兑交单；或按照其他条款和条件交付单据。"

（三）价格、时间、数量等相关表达

经贸文本中数字出现的频率较高，通常涉及价格、时间、数量等。翻译时，译者务必注意相关表达方式，以免误译。例如：

例10 从今以后，我们将以布朗公司的名义继续营业，特此奉告。

此例中的"从今以后"不能译为 after，因为 after 语义模糊，可指某日之后的任意一天。在英语正式文体中，"从今以后"需用 on and after... 表示，意为从公告发布之日起。此例可译为：We inform you that, on and after this date, our business will be carried on in the name of Brown & Co.

例11 Your reply must reach here on or before May 15th.

此例中的 on or before 对时间进行了限定。翻译时也需准确译出，即："贵方答复务必于 5 月 15 日或之前寄达我方。"

二、规范性

经贸译文的内容和格式要严整规范，符合国际贸易惯例，且必须准确使用专业术语。在翻译具有法律效力的经贸文本时尤其需严谨规范，以防出现法律纠纷。

例12 如受保人于保单生效日前已染上后天免疫能力缺乏症（HIV）将不会获得赔偿。

We shall not pay any benefits for sickness if the covered person was infected with any Human Immunodeficiency Virus (HIV) prior to the policy effective date.

例13 所保货物，如发生保险单项下可能引起索赔的损失或损坏，应立即通知本公司下述代理人查勘。

In the event of loss or damage which may result in a claim under this policy, immediate notice must be given to the company's agents as mentioned hereunder.

此处两例选用了 prior to、hereunder 等具有法律语言风格的词汇，而不用常见单词 before、under this，对于 HIV 也采用了全称来表述，均体现了文本的正式、规范、严谨。

为保证译文的规范性，可采取的具体翻译方法有套译法和增译法两种。

（一）套译法

套译法即套用目的语中约定俗成的现有表达方式。

例14 We hereby certify that up to ×××××× (DD/MM/YYYY) Mr./Mrs./Ms. ××× has deposit accounts with this Bank as follows:

兹证明×××先生/女士截至××××××（年/月/日）在我行存款如下：

例15 This certificate of deposit becomes valid on and after the issuing date and remains valid until the expiry date.

本存款证明开出后，在截止日期前有效。

例16 The insurance on the materials, machinery and equipment allocated to the Insured Vessel prior to application for insurance attaches from the day of inception of insurance specified in the Schedule to the Policy.

在投保前已分配至船上的物资和机械设备，自保险单中列明的保险起期日开始时生效。

事实上，hereby certify that、becomes valid on and after the issuing date and remains valid until the expiry date、attaches from the day of inception of insurance specified in the Schedule to the Policy 等，都是英语银证保险单据中常见的表达，汉英翻译时可尽量套用。

（二）增译法

增译法是为了使译文更清楚而加入原文中没有出现的词句，或是将原文的隐藏含义更明确地表达出来。对于需要明确指代的地方，宁可重复、繁琐，也不能错译、漏译。

例17 A credit is irrevocable even if there is no indication to that effect.

信用证是不可撤销的，即使信用证中对此未作指示也是如此。

例18 Altogether, exports are looking up.

总的说来，出口贸易在好转。

第三节
商务函电和单证单据的翻译

一、商务函电

（一）概念及其语言特点

商务函电是指在日常的商务活动中用来进行商务沟通的各类信函及文书。相对于普通信函，商务信函用语正式礼貌、格式固定、句子信息量大、内容简明扼要。

例1
China National Cereals, Oils and Foodstuffs Imp & Exp Corp.
8 Jianguomen Nei Dajie
Beijing 100005, China
Telephone: 86-10-6526-8888
Fax: 86-10-6527-6028
E-mail: carl@cofco.com.cn

15th November, 2015

Our Ref.
Your Ref.

556 Eastcheap
London, E.C.3, England
<u>Attention: Import Dept.</u>

Dear Sirs,

Subject: Aquatic Products

We thank you for your enquiry of 5 November.

In compliance with your request, we are sending you herewith a copy of our illustrated catalogue and a quotation sheet for your reference.

All prices are subject to our confirmation for our aquatic products that have been selling well this season. Therefore, we would suggest that you advise us by a fax in case of interest.

We await your early favorable reply.

Yours truly,
Sig.
(Manager)
China National Cereals, Oils and Foodstuffs Imp & Exp Corp.

Enclosures

cc our Shanghai Branch Office

P.S. We require payment by L/C for a total value not exceeding USD50,000.

例2

尊敬的王林经理：

听闻贵公司欲将亚麻制品投向巴林市场。本公司担任多家厂家的独家代理，专营精制棉织品，包括各种家用亚麻制品，行销中东。与贵公司向有业务联系，互利互作。贵公司纺织部亦十分了解有关业务合作之情况。

特来此函，盼能成为贵公司独家代理，促销在巴林市场的货品。上述建议，烦请早日赐复，以便进一步联系合作。

此致，

敬礼！

亚捷公司经理
李森
2015 年 11 月 20 日

由以上两例可以总结出商务信函的语言特点如下：

1. 英语商务信函中较多使用陈述句。

英文商务信函多用陈述句，如例 1 中：We are sending you herewith a copy of our illustrated catalogue and a quotation sheet for your reference. We await your early favorable reply. 而中文商务信函中多使用祈使句，如例 2 中："盼能成为贵公司独家代理"、"烦请早日赐复"。

2. 英文信函中较多使用情态动词。

如例 1We would suggest that you advise us by a fax in case of interest 句中 would 的使用，或者 We should be grateful if you would help us with your suggestion 句中 should 的使用。而在中文商务信函中，常用"盼……"、"希望……"、"可否……"、"烦请……"等句型。

3. 英文商务信函结构相对复杂，但模式固定。

结构主要包括信头（Heading）、信内地址（Inside Address）、日期（Date）、信函编号（Our Ref./Your Ref.）、收函方（Recipient）、具体收信人（Attention Line）、称呼（Salutation）、事由标题（Caption/Subject）、正文（Body）、结束语 / 函尾套语（Complimentary Close）、发信人姓名（Signature & Printed Name）、发信人职务（Position）、附件（Enclosures）、抄送（Copy to/cc）、附言（Postscript/P.S.）。相较而言，中文商务信函结构略为简单，主要包括标题、收函方、正文、结束套语、发函人、发函时间。

（二）翻译原则及方法

翻译商务函电时，必须准确理解各种专业词汇、固定表达，并按照相应格式，用符合中英文表达习惯的方式进行翻译。具体翻译原则有以下几点：

1. 措辞应尽量正式礼貌

商务函电的发出方和接收方之间是商务伙伴关系，比较正式，因此商务函电的措辞也应正式礼貌。

例3 We would be most grateful if you could put this matter right immediately.
如蒙贵方马上纠正此事，我们将不胜感激。

例4 Kindly confirm receipt of this order.
敬请来函确认承接此批订货。

此处两例译文中的"如蒙""贵方""不胜感激""敬请"都是礼貌的表达。此外，商务函电英译汉常用到的礼貌用语还有"请""烦请""贵公司""收悉""见谅"等。同理，商务函电汉译英时也应尽量使用礼貌的表达，如 please、appreciate、be grateful 及情态动词等。事实上，不少英汉商务函电中的礼节性表达都互有对应，熟悉这些对应表达将使翻译工作事半功倍。这些表达具体可分为开篇套语、结束套语、其他常用语三类，举例如下：

1）开篇套语：

We are in receipt of your letter. / We acknowledge receipt of your letter. /We admit receipt of your letter. 来函获悉。

We are pleased to inform you... / Notice is hereby given that... 特此告知。

In reply to your letter of... / Regarding your letter of... / Referring to your letter of... 兹回复贵方来函……

Thank you for... / We are glad (pleased) to... / We are grateful (obliged) for... 感谢……／深表感谢……

2）结束套语：

We regret to... / We are very sorry to... 非常遗憾……

We would appreciate it if you would... / I would be grateful if you could... 如蒙……甚为感激。

We would like to apologize for... 对……谨表歉意

3）其他常用语：

If / Should you have any queries/ enquiries... 如有疑问／如欲查询……

Please do not hesitate to contact (somebody). 请随时与（某人）联系。

We would appreciate /should be obliged for an early reply. 如蒙早日赐复，不胜感激。

Enclosed we hand you... / Enclosed please find... / We are enclosing... 随函附上……

Your kind reply will greatly oblige us. / Your (prompt) reply would be appreciated. / Looking forward to your positive (favorable/affirmative) reply. 敬请回复 / 盼复。

2. 注意简洁

商业信函的目的是传递信息、相互沟通，而这又必须建立在目的语读者认同目的语文本的基础上。换言之，商业信函的翻译必须以目的语读者为中心。因此，翻译时可在深入理解原文的基础上，进行适当删减或改译，以实现功能上的对等。具体而言，可采用如下方法：

1）简化套语

例5 我行是中国国际化和多元化程度最高的银行，在中国内地、港澳地区及29个国家为客户提供全面的金融服务。
Our bank provides a broad range of financial products and services to customers, corporations and institutions across the Chinese mainland, Hong Kong, Macao and 29 countries.

此例中，译文对原文进行了删减，去掉了中式色彩较浓的措辞，在表意上更加简洁，更加符合目的语读者的表达习惯。

2）删除冗余信息

例6 我厂能生产大衣、西服、时装、衬衣、毛衣等不同类型服装用的上千个花色品种的纽扣，产品规格齐全、品种繁多、设计新颖。
We can produce various types of buttons in thousands of designs for coats, suits, fashions, shirts and sweaters.

原文中的"规格齐全、品种繁多"与"不同类型服装用的上千个花色品种"语义反复，语气得到加强。如果谋求译文在形式上与原文一致，必然导致英文译文结构臃肿。

总之，作为经贸活动中传递信息和洽谈业务的主要手段之一，商务函电有其自身的语言特色。翻译商务函电时，只有充分了解中英文函电语言使用上的差异，熟练掌握翻译原则和技巧，才能译出令人满意的译文。

二、外贸单证单据

（一）银证保险单据

银证保险单据泛指银行、证券和保险机构出具、使用的支付结算凭证或相关文件及随附证明等。银证保险单据通常具备一定的法律效力，语言正式、严谨。

例7

保险单序号：PICC No 000575511

PICC 中国人民保险公司 河北省分公司
The People's Insurance Company of China, Hebei Branch
总公司设于北京　　一九四九年创立
Head Office in Beijing　　Established in 1949

货物运输保险单
CARGO TRANSPORTATION INSURANCE POLICY
发票号 (INVOICE NO) 00-02822　　保单号次
合同号 (CONTRACT NO) QFG2002-1　(POLICY NO.) PYCA200213030100000137
信用证号 (L/C NO) LCE6200200005
被保险人：
Insured　CHINA YAOHUA GLASS GROUP CORPORATION

中国人民保险公司（以下简称本公司）根据被保险人的要求，由被保险人向本公司缴付约定的保险费，按照本保险单承保险别和背面所载条款与下列条款承保下述货物运输保险，特立本保险单。

THIS POLICY OF INSURANCE WITNESSES THAT THE PEOPLE'S INSURANCE COMPANY OF CHINA (HEREINAFTER CALLED "THE COMPANY") AT THE REQUEST OF THE INSURED AND IN CONSIDERATION OF THE AGREED PREMIUM PAID TO THE COMPANY BY THE INSURED, UNDERTAKES TO INSURE THE UNDERMENTIONED GOODS IN TRANSPORTATION SUBJECT TO THE CONDITIONS OF THIS POLICY AS PER THE CLAUSES PRINTED OVERLEAF AND OTHER SPECIAL CLAUSES ATTACHED HEREON.

标记 MARKS & NOS	包装及数量 QUANTITY	保险货物项目 DESCRIPTION OF GOODS	保险金额 AMOUNT INSURED
N/M	散装 10 000 吨 IN BULK	SODA ASH DENSE	USD 901,620.00

总保险金额：
TOTAL AMOUNT INSURED: US DOLLARS NINE HUNDRED AND ONE THOUSAND SIX HUNDRED AND TWENTY ONLY
保费：
PREMIUM:　CHARGED　　DATE OF COMMENCEMENT:　03/19/2002　 PER CONVEYANCE: GREAT IMMENSITY
　自　　　　　　　　经　　　　　　　至
FROM　OREGON, USA　VIA　　　　　　TO　QINHUANGDAO
承保险别：
CONDITIONS:

COVERING ALL RISKS AS PER OCEAN MARINE CARGO CLAUSES (1/1/1981) OF THE PEOPLE'S INSURANCE COMPANY OF CHINA. (W/W CLAUSES IS INCLUDED)

所保货物，如发生保险单项下可能引起索赔的损失或损坏，应立即通知本公司下述代理人查勘，如有索赔，应向本公司提交保单正本（本保险单共有 两 份正本）及有关文件，如一份正本已用于索赔，其余正本自动失效。
IN THE EVENT OF LOSS OR DAMAGE WHICH MAY RESULT IN A CLAIM UNDER THIS POLICY, IMMEDIATE NOTICE MUST BE GIVEN TO THE COMPANY'S AGENT AS MENTIONED HEREUNDER. CLAIMS IF ANY ONE OF THE ORIGINAL POLICY WHICH HAS BEEN ISSUED IN TWO ORIGINAL(S) TOGETHER WITH THE RELEVENT DOCUMENTS SHALL BE SURRENDERED TO THE COMPANY IF ONE OF THE ORIGINAL POLICY HAS BEEN ACCOMPLISHED THE OTHERS TO BE VOID.

中国人民保险公司秦皇岛市开发区支公司
TEL: 0335-8051480/8051058
TELEX:
CABLE:
FAX: 0335-8051597

例8

中国银行
BANK OF CHINA

个 人 存 款 证 明
PERSONAL CERTIFICATE OF DEPOSIT

号　　码 No:
开立日期 Date:

兹证明 _____ 先生/女士（有效身份证件名称：_____ 证件号码：_____）
自 ___ 年 ___ 月 ___ 日到 ___ 年 ___ 月 ___ 日在我行存款如下：
　　　We hereby certify that from ____ (DD/MM/YYYY) to _____ (DD/MM/YYYY) Mr./Ms._____
(type of valid identification _____ ID No. _____) has deposit accounts with the bank as follows:

存款账号 Deposit Accounts No.	存款种类 Type of Deposit	币种/金额 Currency / Amount	存入日 Deposit Date

中国银行股份有限公司　　　行（盖章）
Bank of China Limited　　　Branch (Seal)

通过以上两例的分析，银证保险单据的语言特点可归纳为：句子结构相对复杂；名词的出现频率较高；代词的使用相当慎重。如例7保单中的句子非常正式，全篇均为复杂句，并使用了非常正式的词语，如 hereinafter、as per、overleaf 等。此外，使用抽象名词和不使用代词也是另一比较突出的语言特征。

（二）外贸单证

外贸单证指对外经贸活动中涉及的单据、文件和证书，这些材料通常用以处理国际货物的支付、运输、保险、商检、结汇等。常见的外贸单证大致可分为资金单据、商业单据、货运单据、保险单据以及其他单证，包括汇票、支票、信用证、发票、提单、运单、原产地证明等。本节只在翻译层面对外贸单证略作介绍。

外贸单证是一种典型的"信息型"文本，表现为"告之"或"规定"功能，具有法律约束力。英文外贸单证的语言特点如下：

1. 大量名词连用

这方面的例子比较常见，比如：cargo insurance（货物运输保险）、cash and delivery（付款交货、货到付款）、certificate of quantity（货物数量证明书）、accepting bank（承兑银行）、accepting house（承兑行）、net weight（净重）、air waybill（航空运单）、gross weight（毛重）、packing list（装箱单）、total packages（合计件数）、ocean vessel（船名）、return commission（回佣）、cost and freight（成本加运费价）、telegraphic transfer（电汇）、document against payment（付款交单）、document against acceptance（承兑交单）、certificate of origin（一般原产地证）、customs liquidation（清关）等。

2. 大量使用正式词汇

外贸单证具有法律约束力，文本正式，格式规范。单证中经常出现相当正式的古旧词，如：hereafter（此后）、hereof（在本文件中）、hereinafter（在下文中）、thereon（其上）、thereto（就其）、therewith（对此）、whereof（关于那事）等。

3. 近义词或同义词连用

为了保证文本的准确、严谨，在具有法律效力的经贸文本如单证、协议或合同中，常见近义词或同义词连用现象，这些词语连用回避了可能出现的歧义。比如：terms and conditions（条款）、losses and damages（损失）、controversies and difference（争端）、methods and procedures（途径）、on and after（自，起）等。

经贸文体翻译作为加强我国和其他各国之间国际贸易和国际交流的桥梁，对我国的对外经济贸易发展起着重要作用。相较于其他文体，经贸文体形式多样，在实际翻译活动中，要求对贸易各方之间的关系有足够的把握并具备一定的经贸专业经验和知识，掌握相应文本的特点和翻译方法，这样才能保证翻译质量，更好地达到沟通互惠的目的。

练习四

一、将下列句子译成英文。

1. 本公司成立于1999年7月1日，为大型国有企业，是由中央直接管理的国家授权投资机构和资产经营主体。
2. 随函附上一整套有关此批货物的货运单据，敬请查收。
3. 本证明为一联正本（盖章有效），其复印件或影印等对外无证明效力。
4. 客户在本行的所有业务均须本人亲自办理，本行可能要求客户出示本人身份证明文件，如未能出示，本行将拒绝为客户办理任何业务。
5. 被保险人与本公司之间的一切有关保险的争议，应通过友好协商解决。如果协商无法达成协议，可申请仲裁机构仲裁或向法院提出诉讼。

二、将下列句子译成中文。

1. We'd be greatly appreciated if you would send us your latest catalog.
2. Please keep the memo carefully. Part of unused RMB can be reconverted into foreign currency within twenty four months with your passport and the memo presented.
3. The Certificate of Deposit cannot be taken as an instrument of guarantee or collateral issued by the bank. It only proves that the depositor has deposit with the bank in a fixed term and the deposit stated on the Certificate cannot be withdrawn or transferred within the valid period of the Certificate.

4. Management fees will be deducted from customer's account monthly starting from the fourth month after the account opening date, no matter such account has been used or not.
5. All shipping documents to be sent direct to the opening office by registered airmail in two lots.

三、将下面的商务信函译成中文。

Dr. Simon Smith
1221 Tennessee Blvd
Murfreesboro, TN 37130

Dear Dr. Smith:

Thank you for your letter of 20 March. I have given much thought to the equipment we need in the Art Education Department. We need to purchase several new computers and programs to learn about graphic designing. Attached is a list of needed computer-related equipment and a floor plan sketch after the installation of the new equipment.

Sincerely,

Jane Doe,
Art Teacher
janeannedoe@email.com

Enclosures:
Equipment Proposal
Floor Plan

四、将下面的单据条款译成英文。

　　银行对任何单据的形式、充分性、准确性、内容真实性、虚假性或法律效力，或对单据中规定或添加的一般或特殊条件，概不负责；银行对任何单据所代表的货物、服务或其他履约行为的描述、数量、重量、品质、状况、包装、交付、价值或其存在与否，或对发货人、承运人、货运代理人、收货人、货物的保险人或其他任何人的诚信与否，作为或不作为、清偿能力、履约或资信状况，也概不负责。

第五章 法律文体的翻译

第一节 法律语言与法律翻译

一、法律语言

法律文体指在立法和司法等活动中形成和使用的具有法律专业特点的各种话语文本，包括法律、法规、条例、规章、协定、判决、裁定、合同、章程、契约等。法律文体使用的语言即法律语言，它与我们日常使用的语言有很大不同。

法律语言与生俱来便具有精英性特征，属于抽象层次的话语，是法律人垄断的专利。尤其是法律英语，伴随普通法的产生和沿革，法律英语词语的词义以及法律文本的语法结构都逐渐发生了质的升华，最终使得法律英语成为英美法系国家百姓心目中的"外语"。[1] 正因如此，才有人说：法律语言太难，理解和翻译它等于遭罪，由此翻译出的译文也让读者遭罪。法律语言是一种"专门技术语言"，包括了许多法律专业术语和法律概念，其中的奥秘绝非一般人可以轻易破解，只有谙晓外语和母语法律知识的"法律人"才可真正做到"法人法语"。

德博拉·曹（Deborah Cao）认为法律语言主要具有规范性（normative nature）、行为性（performative nature）、技术性（technical nature）和不确定性（indeterminative nature）四大特征。这些特征主要通过词汇、句法、语用及语体显现，由此使得法律语言成为可识别的一种语言体系。[2]

法律的基本功能就是指导人的行为，规范人与人之间的关系。表现为命令、定义、强制执行某种约定、关系或程序，维持社会共同遵守的行为模式。自然地，实现这些法律功能的法律语言就表现为规定性、命令性及祈使性。法律语言是一种规范性语言，它的主要功能就是规范社会中人与人之间的行为。

与法律语言的规范性密切相关的是法律语言的行为性。法律依靠语言来实现其法律功

---

[1] 宋雷. 2006. 法律翻译理解之哲理. 四川外语学院学报,（1）: 96–100.
[2] Deborah Cao. 2008. *Translating Law*. 上海：上海外语教育出版社.

能。约翰·朗肖·奥斯汀（John Langshaw Austin）和约翰·罗杰斯·塞尔（John Rogers Searle）认为语言的重要功能就是以言行事。如果在法庭上法官说"你有罪"或者"你将被判处服刑1年"，那么你的生活就会被改变。法律语言的这种行为性正是法律实现其规范人的行为、陈述义务、发出禁令和允许的一种手段。

法律语言是一种独特的技术性语言。法律语言的独特性在于，它以法律体系和特定的法律制度的存在为前提。法律语言的技术性还体现在其词法、句法上。法律术语只有在特定的法律体制和法律制度的语境下才有意义。

法律语言还具有不确定性，主要表现在两个方面：一是语言本身存在模糊性，这种模糊性无处不在，这种不确定性根深蒂固，无法根除；二是法律概念的模糊性导致了法律语言的模糊性。尽管法律本身要求准确、严谨，但法律语言的不确定性是无法避免的，它可以是语言内的，也可以是不同语言间的。这种不确定性给法律翻译带来了挑战。

二、法律翻译与法律文化

法律文化具有独特的含义，是指特定社会中植根于历史和文化的法律价值和观念。张法连（2009）认为法律文化与法律制度既有联系又有区别。法律文化可分为内行法律文化与外行法律文化、官方法律文化与民间法律文化、主流法律文化与非主流法律文化、本土法律文化与外来法律文化以及传统法律文化与现代法律文化。[3] 在当代中国法治进程中，法律文化与法律制度之间以及不同法律文化之间存在冲突，我们应采取新的路径整合这些冲突。美国学者劳伦斯·弗里德曼（Lawrence Friedman）在《法律文化与社会发展》一文中最先提出并界定了法律文化的含义。他认为，法律文化是指"与法律体系密切关联的价值与态度，这种价值与态度决定法律体系在整个社会文化中的地位"。弗里德曼后来对法律文化的含义有一些变通的表述，如"法律文化是关于法律体系的公共认知"、"法律文化是一般文化的组成部分"。

法律语言是法律文化的重要构件，法律文化又是法律语言存在的背景条件。法律语言同民族共同语一样，在本质上是一个民族的价值系统，它体现着民族法律文化的特点，规范着法律文化的深层结构。[4]

在进行法律翻译时，必须理解蕴含在法律语言中的法律文化。这点显而易见。比如：一个不具备法律文化背景知识的人在翻译句子 He may earn merit good time for extraordinary behavior and industrial good time for participation in the prison industries 时，很难将句中的 good time 理解为"减刑"，也很难区分有关 WTO 的 *Multilateral Trade Agreement*（《多边贸易条约》）和 *Plurilateral Trade Agreement*（《复边贸易条约》）之间的差异。

---

3 张法连. 2009. 法律英语翻译中的文化因素探析. 中国翻译，（6）：48–51.
4 尹延安. 2007. 英、汉法律语言中法律文化特征对比浅析. 安徽农业大学学报，（5）：90–93.

马莉（2010）认为，在法律术语翻译中要特别注意法律文化的缺省，特别是以下几方面的文化缺省：[5]

（一）法律体系

法律体系，又称部门法体系，是指一个国家现行的全部法律按照一定的结构和层次组织起来的统一整体。一国法律体系有其深刻的政治、经济以及文化根源，很少和他国的法律体系雷同，即使是基于相同法系的国家之间的法律体系也是如此。

法律体系不同，很容易造成一国法律术语在另一国语言中的文化缺省。例如：英国财产法律制度中有 tenancy in common 和 joint tenancy 两词，《英汉法律词典》分别将其翻译为"共有租赁"和"共同租借权"。但了解英国财产制度和独特的信托制度的专业人士会发现，这种翻译容易引起误解。tenancy in common 指的是共有人对共有财产享有可加确定的份额，共有人死亡后，其份额可转至其合法继承者手中；而 joint tenancy 指的是合有财产，是一个不可分割的整体，当其中一合有人死亡后，其权利转移给生存的其他合有人，而不是其继承者，直至该权利转到最后的生存者为止。因此，tenancy in common 译为"共有租赁"、joint tenancy 译为"合有租赁"似乎更为合适。再比如：highest penalty 直译成中文为"极刑"。但如果了解了美国的刑罚制度，就会发现这样翻译会引起歧义。在中国，"极刑"的意义即为"死刑"（death penalty）。但美国大部分州已经取消了死刑，所以在美国"极刑"并不是"死刑"的意思，因此，翻译成"最高刑罚"更为准确。

中国一些独有的法律制度在英美国家并不存在，翻译时应注意准确表达。如在中国法律语言中"劳动教养"（indoctrination through labor）、"人民调解"（people's mediation）两词是专门的法律术语，有着独特的含义。而在英美法律制度中根本不存在类似的法律制度，因此其法律语言中也就没有对应的法律术语。我国的人民陪审员制度与美国的陪审制度均称为"陪审"，但是由于两大法系的渊源、文化历史传统等因素的差异，两者虽然名称相同但有实质差异。法律英语中的 juror 专指英美国家的陪审员，中国的陪审员最好译成 judicial assessor 以示含义不同。

正是这种法律体系差异以及部门法之间的差异，增加了法律词汇翻译的难度。虽然有些学者认为法律术语中的一词多义现象造成了理解的困难，也有损法制的尊严与统一，但我们有时必须面对法律现象的无限性与语言符号的相对有限性之间的矛盾，通过具体的语境确定某一词汇的确切含义。

（二）法律概念

法律概念的特定性是造成法律语言翻译中文化缺省的原因之一。在语码转换过程中，对法律概念在不同法律文化背景下的理解差之毫厘，则谬之千里。法律翻译必须再现原文

5　马莉. 2010. 法律术语翻译中的文化缺省. 中国科技术语，（5）：33–36.

严格的法律含义和定义域，防止解释不一。对文化缺省现象需通过各种翻译技巧来增加或补充解释。翻译时，须将细微的差别具体化，使表述更加准确。例如：deposition 是英美诉讼法上所特有的制度，指双方当事人在审判前（pre-trial）互相询问对方或其证人作为采证（discovery）。因为是在审判前，又是在庭外进行，如果直译为"录取证词"或"采证"都不够准确。陈忠诚教授建议译为"（庭外采取的）证词或供词的笔录"较为妥当。

司法制度的差异对法律概念及其翻译的影响，可以用 verdict 一词的翻译为例加以阐述。英美法系诉讼制度中以陪审团制度（Jury）最负盛名。刑事案件的裁定由陪审团做出，法官只是庭审的组织者和裁定的宣读者，很难左右案件的最终判决。我国虽然原则性地制定了陪审员介入诉讼的相关立法，但尚未确立陪审团制度。因此，我国大陆法域中不存在 verdict 一词的相应语境。根据 *Oxford Dictionary of Law* 和 *Black's Law Dictionary*，"verdict"一词首先指陪审团依据案件事实的认定或判决（jury's finding），在没有陪审员的裁判（a non-jury trial）时，指法官对某一案件的粗略判定以及验尸官的调查结果。而我国，最终做出裁判主要取决于审理法官的判断，因此，中文的"判决"翻译为 judgment 更为恰当。

（三）文化语境

法律制度的共性与语言的普遍性为法律语篇的可译性提供了基础，而各种语言的特殊性及本土性又使法律语言翻译在不同文化语境下面临文化缺省的问题，因此探索法律术语文化语境及其具体的补偿方法，对实现法律文本特殊的社会功能和实用价值至关重要。就英汉对应词语而言，一种文化寓意在一种语言中存在，而在另一种语言中则完全不存在，这种情况在英汉法律翻译中经常出现。例如：英语的 bench 和汉语的"长凳"算是对应词语。英国法庭最初习惯性地在庭上随意设置一排长凳，用作法官（judge）或治安官（magistrate）的席位，于是 bench 一词便逐渐被赋予了"法官席位""法庭""裁判庭""法官""议员席位" 等与法律密切相关的语义，相关的术语也就随之而出现，如 the Upper Bench（英国 12 世纪共和政体时期的高等法院）、the full bench（全席法庭，指法院所有法官出席组成的法庭）、bench warrant（法官签发的拘捕令，拘捕的多是藐视法庭命令的人）、Queen's Bench（英国高等法院的女王座分院）、King's Bench（英国高等法院的王座分院），而 He is on the bench 也表示"他是一位治安法官"（He is a magistrate.）。但汉语的"长凳"则完全没有这种特殊的法律文化寓意。法律的文化语境反映了不同国家的社会制度、传统文化及特定的历史原因，只有认识语言表象背后的文化内涵，才能达到法律翻译的忠实性要求。

（四）民族心理

翻译法律文本时，译者可能会忽略源语文化独特的民族心理，以译者自己的文化现实为基础进行"归化"翻译，造成译文读者对原文的错误理解。例如：国内一些参考书将

cross-examination 译成"盘问""盘诘"或"反复询问",可以说都是译者根据自己的中国法律背景想当然的翻译。按照英美法系的审判制度,起诉方和被告方均可要求法院传唤证人出庭作证,在庭上先由要求传证人的一方向证人提问,然后再由对方向证人提问,也就是起诉方讯问被告方的证人或被告方讯问起诉方的证人,这就是 cross-examination,可译为"交叉讯问"。

语言反映文化并受文化制约。法律文化因素影响制约着法律翻译。要做好法律翻译,平时应勤于积累语言,加强对母语和有关法律文化知识的学习。只有重视研究英汉两种语言和中西法律文化的特点,并准确地理解和把握有关的法学知识,才能准确、有效地进行法律翻译。

三、法律翻译的原则

有关翻译的基本原则,众说纷纭,如严复提倡"信达雅",林语堂提出"忠实、通顺、美",傅雷则强调"重神似不重形似"。法律翻译不同于普通翻译,两者在必须遵守的原则上有很大的不同。李克兴(2010)[6]、熊德米(2011)[7]、宋雷(2007)[8]等人对此有专门论述,具体可归纳如下:

(一)语义原则

法律语言以"精准"著称,以"因循守旧"为特征。在法律语言的理解、阐释或翻译过程中,语义原则是优先原则。译者应确认源语作者的本意与法律原文本中词语的明确含义,优先从原文本所使用的词语本身去寻找文本的意蕴,强调严格按照字面意思进行理解和翻译。在确定语义的过程中,译者应当按照同一语言共同体中一般成员所理解的词语的含义去理解原文本。译者应尽量阻却非法律人的意识观念和思维模式,杜绝曲解法条中的词义:如将刑法规定中的"缓刑"理解为"缓期执行",把"假释"曲解为"假释放",将 civil prisoner 误认为是"民事罪犯",将 final judgment 错当成"终审判决"。

再比如,在英文中,domicile 与 habitual residence 都可译成"住所"或"住处",但在法律上,它们的含义完全不同。domicile 是"住所地",即户籍所在地。法人的住所地为法人的主要营业或办事机构所在地。所以有些词典将 domicile 译作"户籍"。而 habitual residence 是指"经常居住地",它不一定是一个人的户籍所在地。法律文本的翻译稍有差错或语义含混不清,都可能在经济上、政治上造成极大损失,招致严重的后果。

(二)专业性原则

法律翻译的专业性原则主要体现在对译者、翻译过程和翻译产品的规定三个方面。对

---

6 李克兴.2010.论法律文本的静态对等翻译.外语教学与研究,(1):59–65.
7 熊德米、熊姝丹.2011.法律翻译的特殊原则.西南政法大学学报,(4):128–135.
8 宋雷.2007.从"翻译法律"到"法律翻译".四川外语学院学报,(9):106–111.

法律翻译者而言，在翻译过程中，译者有义务查阅和掌握所译材料的相关法律知识，一丝不苟地传达原文的一切法律信息，做到不"旁参己见"。法律翻译产品应当接受专业检验，包括法律信息传达的准确性和法律专业语言形式的法律性。显然，法律翻译涉及法律文本的词句和法律篇章等，只是法律专业问题的一个方面，更重要的是要接受公权机关及其他社会成员的专业性检验。确保将一种法律语言翻译成另一种法律语言，而不是翻译成另一种语言。以下例子可以看出专业性原则的重要性：

原文	非法律专业译文	法律专业术语
access right	通行权	（父母对子女的）探视权
apparent agency	明确的代理	表见代理
case of first impression	未发生过的案件	无先例案件
construction of law	法律构建	法律解释
derivative acquisition	派生获得（所有权的）	继受取得
indeterminate sentence	不特定刑罚	不定期刑
law reports	法律报告（普通法）	判例汇编
overlapping of laws	法律的重叠	法规竞合
prize law	奖惩法则	捕获法
res judicata	已判决的事件	既判力原则
security measures	保安措施（诉讼）	保全措施
separation of powers	权力的分开	三权分立
servient owner	从属所有人	供役地所有人

（三）等效性原则

法律翻译和文学翻译所强调的等效性原则的重要区别在于，后者关注译文读者的美学感受，前者关注的却是法律语言的具体影响力，即译文法律语言应具有与原文法律语言相同的"语力"（language power）。

法律翻译涉及不同法律文化，有时很难在目的语中找到完全等效的词语，因此，法律翻译寻求的不是词语的完全对应，而是在法律文化体系的框架内寻找近似词语，不仅得到译文法律语言的认同，而且达到与原文相同的法律效果，在意识形态上取得等效性。例如，现行中国法律体系中的"城管""劳动教养""人民陪审""地票交易"等法律语言的翻译，应能让完全不同法系的西方读者感受到原始文本的法律含义。

然而，在法律翻译过程中，常会有一些词无法找到确切的译法，很难实现法律信息的等效传译。如英美法里的 equity charter（物许状）、lay judge（非职业法官）等，为英美法系中所独有，汉语法律中根本没有类似的表达，其相应的汉语译法能否在汉语读者（甚至是专业读者）中产生相同的法律效果，难以估计。同样，在中华法系的当代法律语言中，也有许多西方法律文化所没有的表达，如"联产承包责任制""协警""保安"等。这些中国特色的法律语言被翻译成英文之后，也难以在英美读者中产生等值的法律效果。

（四）准确性原则

法律语言的准确性指"语义与所反映的客观事物（现象）完全相符，不仅是正确的，而且是准确的、精密的；不仅准确地反映事物（现象）的主要特点，而且准确地反映事物（现象）的一般特点"。准确性（精确性）可以说是法律文本的灵魂，因为一词之差导致官司的例子并不鲜见。美国阿肯色州的一起遗产纠纷案，其争论主要就是围绕遗嘱中所使用的 between 一词。这份遗嘱中有这样一个句子：The remainders of the testator's property should be divided equally between all of our nephews and nieces on my wife's side and my niece. 立遗嘱人妻子一方的外甥及外甥女共有 22 人。上述遗嘱到底是立遗嘱人遗产的一半归其妻一方的 22 个外甥及外甥女，另一半归其自己的侄女，还是将遗产在双方外甥、外甥女、侄女之间平均分配呢？最后法官裁定为前者，其理由是"只有表示'在两者之间'或'在两方之间'，才用'between'，如按后一种理解，即在 23 人中平均分配，就必须用'among'"。可见准确性对法律文本的重要性。

第二节
法律文体的词汇特征及其翻译

一、常用词及其特有法律意义的翻译

法律专业词语是法律专业文本构建的基本要素，包括一般法律词语和法律专业术语。一般法律词语指法律文本的本族语读者基本能结合法律语境从字面上解读，并能按照词语所表达的意思行事的语言单位。这类词语在任何法律语言中都占主要成分，体现了法律作为"天下之程式的"宗旨。但正是这类词语会给跨语言的读者和译者造成不少障碍。例如，consummate/consummation 在一般语境中的意思是 complete/completion，通常翻译成"完成""结束""完结"等，但在法律语境尤其是刑法中，其基本含义为"达到犯罪目的、完成犯罪行为"，如 consummate crime or offender、consummation of fornication，严谨的法律翻译应为"既遂罪/既遂犯"和"奸淫既遂"，如果译成"完成犯罪/犯罪结束"或"强奸完毕"，与严谨的法律翻译大异其趣。再如，英文的 enterprise crime 通常被误译成"企业犯罪"，事实上该词相当于 organized crime，准确翻译应为"有组织的犯罪"；

injunction 不是词典上给出的"禁令""命令",而是英美法院系统所签发的"强制令"或"法院强制令"。

英美法中有许多由普通单词组成的词组或搭配,但它们与其普通的字面含义相去甚远,译者必须具备相关的法律专业知识,了解这些词组或搭配在法律语境中的意义,否则将无法正确理解和翻译。如 Baby Act 不能理解为"婴儿法",而应是"规定未成年不承担某些责任的法律",此处的 baby 等同 minor,应做"未成年人"解。

以下列举一些英语常见单词在日常生活和法律语言中的不同意义:

英语单词	日常意义	法律意义
adverse	相反的	非法的
aggravation	加重	处死刑的加重情节
alienation	疏远	转让
battery	电池	伤害、人身攻击
brief	简短的、简洁的	案情说明书(并非一定简明)
condemn	谴责	判刑、定罪
construction	建设	(法律)解释
declaration	声明、宣言	申诉书
deed	行为	文据、契约证书
execution	执行	签订
exhibit	展出	物证
hear	听见	听审
immunity	免疫力	豁免权
leave	离开	休庭
motion	运动	动议
practice	练习、实践	诉讼程序、诉讼实务
prejudice	偏见	损害、侵害
prize	奖赏或奖金	捕获
proceed	进行	起诉
report	报告	揭发
service	服务	送达
strike	打击、袭击	删除
satisfaction	满意	清偿、补偿
subject matter	主题	标的物
sentence	句子	判决

vacation	假期		休庭期
warrant	保证		拘捕令

二、法律语言中古旧词的翻译

法律英语词汇中还保留着一些古旧词，常见的主要是由 here、there、where 和介词合成的单词，如：

hereby 由此、以此、特此	hereinafter 在下文
herein 其中、在此处	hereinbefore 在上文
hereof 至此、由此	heretofore 直到此时
hereto 至此、关于这个	hereinabove 在上文
hereunder 在下面	hereunto 于是
therein 其中	thereafter 此后、据此
therefore 因此	herefrom 由此、从那里
thereof 由此、因此	thereto 在那里
thereon 关于那、在其上	whereof 关于那个
wherein 在那方面	whereby 靠那个

这类词中的 here 应理解为 this，there 应理解为 that，where 应理解为 which。所以，hereof=of this，hereon=on this，thereof=of that，thereto=to that，whereby=by which。这些词的使用可避免关键词语的重复，准确严密。此外，法律文献中出现频率较高的古旧词还有：aforementioned（上述的）、aforesaid（如前所述）、thence（从那时起）、thenceforth（其后；从那时起）、whosoever（不管是谁）等。

例1 依照《中外合资经营企业法》批准在中国境内设立的中外合资经营企业（以下简称合营企业）是中国的法人，受中国法律的管辖和保护。

Chinese foreign equity joint ventures (<u>hereinafter</u> referred to as joint ventures) established within Chinese territory upon approval in accordance with the *Law on Chinese Foreign Equity Joint Ventures* are Chinese legal persons, who shall be governed and protected by Chinese law.

例2 A contract shall be an agreement <u>whereby</u> the parties establish, change or terminate their civil relationship. Lawfully established contracts shall be protected by law.

合同是当事人之间设立、变更、终止民事关系的协议。依法成立的合同，受法律保护。

例3 Neither Party <u>hereto</u> shall assign this Agreement or any of its rights and interests <u>hereunder</u> without the other Party's prior written consent.

未经另一方事先书面同意，本协议的任何一方不得转让本协议或协议下规定的任何权利和利益。

三、法律语言中拉丁语的翻译

拉丁语从公元 597 年传入英国起就已渗入到英语中，到了 14、15 世纪，大量拉丁语词汇直接或间接进入古英语，但主要是法学等专业领域。在当代法律英语中，用拉丁语词汇表达的法律术语更是不在少数。例如：

ad hoc 专门地	corpus delicti 犯罪事实
de facto 事实上的	ex parte 单方面的 / 片面的
guardian ad litem 法定监护人	inter alia 除了别的因素以外
in esse 实在的	in re 关于
ipso facto 因以下事实	mens rea 犯罪企图
nolle prosequi 撤诉	per se 自身
pro rata 按比例	prima facie 表面的、初步的
res judicata 已判决的事件、既判案件	res inter alios 与本案无关的
sine die 无限期	versus 对、诉

四、其他法律术语的翻译

历史上法国人曾统治英国，那一时期，法语成为英国的官方语言，在宫廷、法院和学校中广泛使用。仅在 1250—1400 年，就有大约 10 000 个法语词汇进入英语中，其中 75%一直沿用至今。法律英语中的法语词汇可以分为两类：一类已经与英语同化，成为法律英语词汇的组成部分；另一类未被同化，仍保留了法语形式，在当今的法律文件中还常常用到，如：feme sole（独身女子 / 未婚女子）、feme covert（已婚女子）、estoppel（禁止翻供 / 不容反悔）、lashes（长期不行使权利 / 对行使权利的懈怠）、quash（撤销）、fait accompli（既成事实）、voir dire（预备询问 / 预先审核）等。这类术语语义稳定，没有引申意义，文体效果突出，在一定意义上更富有权威性。

法律英语文体正式，大量使用专业性的法律语言，包括法律术语及行话。法律术语或行话是指用来准确表达特有的法律概念且具有特定意义的专业词汇。如 certiorari，意思是"上级法院向下级法院发出的调取案卷进行复审的令状"，又如 tort（侵权行为）、alibi（不在犯罪现场）等。这些术语语义精练、规范严谨，符合法律英语严肃的文体特征。这些词语都有特定的确切含义和适用范围，不能随意引申，不能被其他词汇所取代，具有极强的专业性和行业特征。比如"某人去世了"，律师在起草法律文件时不会用 dead 而往往用行话 deceased。

下面是一些常见的英文法律词汇及其汉译：

affidavit 宣誓书	homicide 杀人
custody 拘留	prosecute 起诉

testimony 证词	orbiter 仲裁人
veto 否决	alias 化名、别名
alibi 不在犯罪现场	legal 合法的
minor 未成年人	appeal 上诉
mediator 调停者	declaration 申诉
notary 公证人	per capita 人均
pro forma 形式上的	force majeure 不可抗力

法律英语中还有许多 -ed 和 -ee 型名词，例如：

the deceased 死者、继承人	the accused 被告人
the insured 受保人	the escapee 逃跑者
the acquittee 被宣告无罪的人	the arrestee 被逮捕的人
the nominee 指定人	the assignee 代理人
the pledgee 质权人	the obligee 权利人
the devisee 继承人	the lessee 承租人

例 4 第二百四十八条，承租人应当按照约定支付租金。
Article 248, the lessee shall pay the rent as contracted.

例 5 被继承人的子女先于被继承人死亡的，应由其晚辈直系亲属代为继承。
In case the children of the deceased die prior to the deceased, the junior lineal kinship of the deceased shall take succession by subrogation.

五、法律语言中情态动词的翻译

法律英语中情态动词使用频繁，使用频率最高的情态动词依次是 shall、may、must 和 should。

（一）shall 和 may 在法律英语中的含义

Collins Cobuild English Dictionary 对 shall 和 may 的用法有如下解释：

shall: 4. You use *shall* to indicate that something must happen, usually because of a rule or law. You use *shall not* to indicate that something must not happen.

may: 7. You use *may* to indicate that someone is allowed to do something or has the choice of doing something, usually because of a rule or law. You use *may not* to indicate that someone is not allowed to do something.

法律文书中，shall 表示强制性义务和规定，该词的使用充分体现了法律文件的权威性与强制性，在汉语中可翻译为"必须"或"应"；它的否定式 shall not 则应翻译成"不得"或"不应"。may 则表示根据法律条文规定，允许其"可以做……"；may not 表示剥夺其权力，可以翻译为"无权做……"。

试比较 shall 和 may 在下面几例中的翻译：

例6 A person shall be liable for using a domain name under subparagraph (A) only if that person is the domain name registrant or that registrant's authorized licensee.

只有域名注册者或该注册者授权的被许可人才应对（A）目规定之下的域名使用行为承担责任。（即域名注册者或该注册者授权的被许可人有义务必须为其使用行为承担法律责任）

例7 The effect of provisions of this Act may be varied by agreement, except as otherwise provided in this Act…

本法条文的效力可以通过协议变更，除非本法另有规定……（此条文的效力当然也可不变更，并不具有强制性，而具有可选性）

如果句子本身语气中就已体现出其强制力，shall 有时可不译出来，如：

例8 Everyone shall have the right to life and to inviolability of his person. The liberty of the individual shall be inviolable.

每个人都（应）有生存的权利，并且这种权利神圣不可侵犯。每个人的自由不（应）受侵犯。

（二）shall 与 should、must、will 的比较

在汉语法律文书中，"必须"一词出现的频率相当高。汉译英时，很多人会根据字面意思将其翻译成 must，或将"应当"和"必须"混为一谈，导致错译。

shall 意为 command or duty，但在非正式文体或口语中，常为 must、should 或 have to 所取代。will 无论在语气上还是在强制力方面都要比 shall 弱，应译为"将""愿""要"。现将这几个情态动词在法律英语中的用法总结如下：

shall 表示强制性义务和规定，具有法律约束力，语气最强；

must 用于非正式文体或口语中，不具法律约束力，语气强；

should 表示一般道义上的义务，不具有法律约束力，语气弱；

will 表示表态或下决心或一般将来时，不具法律约束力，语气最弱。

法律翻译是一项极其严肃的工作，容不得半点差错，否则就有可能造成不必要的法律纠纷。我国某些法律的英译本出现很多将含有强制含义的"必须"翻译成 should 的情况，例如：

例9 合格投资者必须遵守中国的法律法规和其他有关规定。

QFII should comply with laws, regulations and other relevant rules in China. （如果该投资者不遵守我国的法律，是否仍允许其继续在境内进行证券投资？）

例10 托管人必须将其自有的资产和受托管理的资产严格分开。

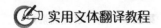

A custodian should strictly separate its own assets from those under its custody. （原文用了"必须"和"严格"两个词来显示此规定的强制性，应用 shall。）

除了常被误用为 should 外，还出现了在不该用 shall 的地方错用 shall 的情况，如：

例 11 The persons entitled to bring up a child shall decide whether it shall receive religious instruction.

这里的 the persons entitled to bring up a child 是权利人而非义务人，他们有权决定孩子是否应接受宗教指导，并非有义务，因此不能用 shall。要特别注意，在一个主动语态的句子中，当主语是权利人也就是被赋予某项权利时，不能使用 shall，如 shall have the right to、shall enjoy the right of 等。因此，例 11 应改为：The persons entitled to bring up a child will have the right to decide whether it will receive religious instruction.

六、美国与英国法律英语词汇的差别

自美国独立以后，美国英语逐渐形成了自己的特点，因此英美两国在法律语言上存在一些差异。具体表现在以下几个方面：

（一）语汇空缺

语汇空缺（lexical gaps）是指由于民族、地域、历史、政治等因素，一种语言的某些词汇在另一地域的另一种语言里找不到对应的词。英国的司法体系是以王权为基础发展完善的，而美国的司法体系是在以议会为中心的基础上形成的联邦与各州的两级司法体系，加之各自的法律文化传统不同，因而不可避免地出现了法律词汇空缺现象。一些美国法律英语词汇，在英国法律英语中却不存在，如 assembly（议会）、assemblyman（议员）、president（总统）、Congress（国会）、Senator（参议员）、lynch（私刑）等；而一些英国法律英语词汇，在美国法律英语中却不存在，如 the House of Lords（上院）、Court of Common Pleas（民诉法院）、Court of King's Bench（王室法院）、Privy Council（枢密院）、Suitor（审判）、Governor（总督）、Chancellor（大法官）等。

（二）词汇的拼写差异

美国法律英语词汇较简化，这是美国英语区别于英国英语的主要特征。这种简化现象表现为：其一，读音与拼写同时变化，如：copper（英）和 cop（美）；其二，只有拼写变化，没有读音变化，如：honour（英）和 honor（美）。常见的拼写不同的英国英语与美国英语法律词汇列举如下：

英国英语	美国英语	中文释义
accepter	acceptor	承兑人
acknowledgement	acknowledgment	债务承认人

cheque	check	支票
copper	cop	警察
defence	defense	被告，辩护律师
offence	offense	罪过，犯法
draught	draft	草稿，草案
practice	practice	诉讼业务
judgement	judgment	裁定，判决
programme	program	程序

（三）词汇的语义差异

英美法律词汇的语义差异主要表现在同一概念在英国英语和美国英语中使用不同的词汇来表达，或同一词语在英国和美国英语语境下有不同含义。

1. 同一概念，英国和美国英语中用不同的词汇表达。如：

中文释义	英国英语	美国英语
慈善信托	charitable trust	charitable corporation
大监狱	penitentiary	large prison
执法官	law man	policeman
流氓	hoodlum	gangster
有限责任公司	Ltd.	Inc.
律师费	barrister's fee	contingent fee

2. 同一词汇，英国和美国英语语境下各有不同的解释。如：

英语词汇	英国英语语境	美国英语语境
bylaw	地方法规	公司章程
Senate	上院	参议院
parliamentarian	议会议员	国会法规专家
marshal	海事法院执行法官	法院执行法官
lieutenant	副总督	副州长
counselor	参赞	顾问咨询律师
turnover	营业额	（资金、货物）周转金

七、汉语法律词汇的英译

汉语词义灵活多变，但法律表达必须严谨。汉语法律文本英译时，若按字面意思进行翻译，常会造成英语读者理解困难。例如，我国通常将"醉驾"译成 drunk driving，含义模糊甚至存在严重歧义，可借鉴英语里意义完全相同的表达，如美国 *Penal Code* 中将"醉驾"表述为 drive in intoxication，加拿大 *Penal Code* 用 drive in an alcoholic state 来描述。再如法律谚语"公为法之本，正为法之器"，其中的"器"字颇让译者头疼。其实，此言与张之洞所说的"中学为体、西学为用"如出一辙。句中"器"，实际等同于"用"，所以此句话可以理解为"公正乃立法之根本，正义让法律得以顺利执行"，由此可译为：Fairness is key to law while justice is key to practice of law. 现代法律汉语中还有一些专门的法律术语需要译者格外留意，现归纳为以下几种类型：

（一）法律、法规名称的翻译

汉语中，法律、法规的典型名称是"××法"（条例、实施条例、暂行条例、实施细则、实施办法）。英文中，表示法律的词有 law、statute、legislation、act、code 等。在美国的立法中，即便法律名称再长，一般都是用 Act 这个词，而且是放在法律名称的最后。legislation 和 statute 这两个词都不用在法律的名称中，两者指的是"立法"和"制定法"。前者强调的是通过立法机关制定的法律，包括行政法规；而后者强调的是制定法，与判例法或者普通法相对照。code 指的是法典，"某一法律部门经过系统编纂而形成的比较集中的独立的法律文件"，如美国的 *Internal Revenue Code*、瑞士的 *The Civil Code* 等。我国目前还没有一部法典，因此，我国的法律也就不适合用 code 这个词。我国的"××法"翻译成英文时，一般都直接用 Law 来表示。在我国官方出版的法规汇编中，法规中的名称"条例"一般都用复数，例如：《中华人民共和国律师暂行条例》、《行政复议条例》分别译为 *Interim Regulations of the People's Republic of China on Lawyers* 和 *Regulations on Administrative Reconsideration*。"行政法规"一般译为 administrative regulations。

下面列出常见的法律法规名称的英译：

法律法规	英译
法	Law
条例	Regulations
规定	Provisions
办法	Measures; Procedures
实施细则	Implementing Rules; Rules for the Implementation of...
决定	Decision
暂行规定	Interim Provisions; Provisional Regulations
试行规定	Provisions for Trial Implementation
管理规定	Provisions for the Administration of...

续表

法律法规	英译
试行办法	Trial Measures
通知	Notice; Circular
意见	Opinions
纲要	Outline
文件	Document
目录	Catalogue

（二）判例名称的翻译

我国的判例名称和西方的判例名称在形式上存在很大差别。我国的判例名称一般包括一方或者双方当事人的名字以及案件的性质，而西方国家的判例名称一般只包括双方当事人的名字及时间。请看例子：

例12 高淳县民政局诉王昌胜、吕芳、天安保险江苏分公司交通事故损害赔偿纠纷案（英译：Case of the Compensation on Personal Injury by Traffic Accident Gaochun County Civil Administration Bureau v. Wang Changsheng, Lv Fang & Tian'an Insurance Jiangsu Branch）

例13 长治市华茂副食品有限公司与长治市杰昌房地产开发有限公司合作开发房地产合同纠纷案（英译：Case of Dispute over Contract of Jointly Developing Real Estate: Huamao Non-Staple Food Co. Ltd., Changzhi City v. Jiechang Real Estate Development Co. Ltd., Changzhi City）

例14 Dred Scott v. Sandford (1857)

例15 U.S. v. Nixon (1974)

（三）法律条款的翻译

汉语法律法规中的结构一般为"编""章""节""条""款""项""目"。

《美国联邦宪法》总共有7个article，每个article下面设若干个section。例如Article 1下面共有8个section。有的section只有一段，有的有若干段。section由若干paragraph和subparagraph组成。

《美国法典》可以说是世界上最复杂的立法，其结构从上到下依次为：Title > Subtitle > Chapter > Subchapter > Part > Subpart > Section。《美国法典》共有50个title，各包含一个主题，有的title甚至就是一部法典，比如第26个title实际上就是美国的《税收法典》。section相当于我国立法中的"条"，由若干paragraph组成。paragraph相当于"款"，有的paragraph还可能包括若干个subparagraphs，相当于我国立法中的"项"。subparagraph

下面还可能有"目"。美国立法中对于编排体例中条、款、项、目没有明确的法律规定，而是怎么合适，怎么安排，所用的词也不完全一致。因此，译者在翻译美国的法律文章时，所用的中文表述也不一致。比如，《统一商法典》中的 articles 是关于信用证的，有人就将它译为"信用证篇"。即便是借用我国的立法体例，也没有所谓的"篇"，而只有"编"。但"编"下面还设"章"和"节"，然后才是"条"和"款"。但是美国《统一商法典》的 article 下面只有 section，即"条"。这里的 article 到底该如何翻译，值得推敲。综上所述，我国立法的编排体例中所用的"编 > 章 > 节 > 条 > 款 > 项 > 目"不妨可以译为：Part > Chapter > Section > Article > Paragraph > Item > Subitem。[9]

（四）部委名称的翻译

汉英法律翻译中常涉及有中国特色的术语，如中央及地方各委员会、部、办公厅、局、办公室等，这些词都有特定的英译，列表如下：

机关名称	英译
委员会（中央）	Commission
委员会（地方）	Committee
部	Ministry
办公厅（中央）	General Office
总局、局	General Administration; Administration; Bureau; Office
总署	General Administration; Administration
办公室	Office
司、厅	Department

第三节
法律文体的句法特征及其翻译

为了保证表述的严谨准确，法律英语文本会牺牲简洁明了和可读性，多用结构紧密、说理完整的长句，常常使用并列结构和复杂的同位语成分。据专家统计，在英美普通法法系的法律文件中，句子的平均长度约为 271 个单词。相比之下，中文法律文本结构较简练，省略大量句子成分。此外，中文法律的条款还会用某个词或词组充当多个动词的主语，形成一个主语引导下的一系列动词短语结构，既体现了中文法律语言的简洁，又符合汉语意合的语言特点。

9　金朝武 . 2009. 论汉英法律翻译中的形式对等问题 . 中国翻译，（2）：62–67.

一、法律英语句法特征及翻译

法律英语句子结构复杂，多使用复合长句，如条件句、定语从句等，逻辑关系明晰。

例1 After a civil act has been determined to be null and void or has been rescinded, the party who acquired property as a result of the act shall return it to the party who suffered a loss.

民事行为被确认为无效或者被撤销后，当事人因该行为取得的财产，应当返还给受损失的一方。

原句中由 who 引导的两个限制性定语从句分别修饰两个 the party，分别说明有过错方和受损失方，从而清楚地规定了有过错方对受损失方应承担的责任。

例2 Whoever selling deliberately a commodity whose registered trademark is falsely used, which constitutes a crime, in addition to making compensation for the losses suffered by the party whose right has been infringed, shall be investigated for the criminal responsibility according to the law.

销售明知是假冒注册商标的商品，构成犯罪的，除赔偿被侵权人的损失外，依法追究刑事责任。

原句中由关系代词 whose 引导的两个限制性定语从句分别修饰和限定名词 a commodity 和 the party；关系代词 which 引导的非限制性定语从句，修饰前面所指的内容，形成了复杂的句子结构。

例3 An enterprise as legal person shall terminate for any of the following reasons: (1) If it is dissolved by law; (2) if it is disbanded; (3) if it is declared bankrupt in accordance with the law; or (4) for other reasons.

企业法人由于下列原因之一终止：（1）依法被撤销；（2）解散；（3）依法宣告破产；或（4）其他原因。

原句使用了多个并列从句，这在其他英语文体中是不常见的，因为英语句型通常要求结构富于变化，使用相同的句子结构会使文章平淡、沉闷和臃肿，但这样的结构和用法在法律英语中却很常见。

此外，法律英语中使用大量的被动语态，这些带有被动语态的句子相当于汉语中带有"被、让、由"等表被动意义的词的句子或主动句、无主句以及"是……的"判断句，这也是法律英语句型结构的一大特色。[10]

例4 It shall be unlawful for any person engaged in commerce, in the course of such commerce, to pay or grant, or to receive or accept, anything of value as a commission, brokerage, or other compensation, or any allowance or discount in lieu thereof except

---

10 吴彬. 2007. 论法律英语的句法特征. 华中农业大学学报（社会科学版），（5）：167–171.

for services rendered in connection with the sale or purchase of goods, wares, or merchandise, either to the other party to such transaction or to an agent, representative, or other intermediary therein where such intermediary is acting in fact for or in behalf or is subject to the direct or indirect control of any party to such transaction other than the person by whom such compensation is so granted or paid.

此句的原译是:"商人在交易过程中,支付、准许、收取或接受佣金、回扣或作为替代的任何补贴或折扣都是非法的。但与商品购销合同有关的提供给另一方当事人或代理机构、代表人或其他中间机构的劳务除外。中间机构指事实上、或代表或服从于交易一方的直接或间接控制,而不是受准许支付回扣或支付回扣一方控制。"

根据原句的语法结构,这是由主句和复杂的介宾结构组成的长句,在介宾结构中有两个层次不同的后置定语分别修饰 services 和 intermediary。句中,it 是形式主语,真正的主语是不定式结构,句子的主干是:"It shall be unlawful for any person... , to pay or grant, or to receive or accept anything of value...",即"任何人……支付、准许、收取、接受任何有价值的东西……都是非法的",后面的 except for 结构带出的是假定条件及可为行为。因此,整个句子可改译为:"商人在其商业过程中,支付、准许、收取、接受佣金、回扣或其他补偿,或作为替代的任何补贴或折扣是非法的。但对同商品购销相关的,提供给另一方当事人或代理机构、或代表人、或其他中间机构的劳务除外。这里的其他中间机构是事实上、或代表或服从于该交易一方的直接、间接控制,而不是受准许支付回扣或支付回扣一方所控制。"

逻辑性是立法与司法公正性的内在要求。大部分法律英语文本都包含四个成分:情况、条件、法律主体以及法律行为。而中国法律规范的逻辑结构一般包括三要素:假定、处理、制裁(法律后果)。在语言层面上,中外法律规范在选词、造句、立篇过程中,逻辑标准无不得到充分、准确的印证。翻译时,准确的概念、判断和推理源于准确地理解这些概念之间的逻辑关系。根据英美国家的法律法规,可以把法律英语的句法结构特点大体归纳为:多以条件句为主构成长句,逻辑连接词 and 和 or 在句中发挥重要的逻辑衔接作用,其他的修饰限定成分起到进一步明确具体细节内容的作用。注重译文的内在逻辑性特别是形式逻辑在法律英语翻译中非常重要。

例6 Article 113 If either party fails to perform its obligations under the contract or does not perform its obligations as contracted and thus causes losses to the other party, the amount of compensation for the loss shall be equivalent to the loss actually caused by the breach of contract and shall include the profit obtainable after the performance of the contract, but shall not exceed the sum of the loss that might be caused by a breach of contract and has been anticipated or ought to be anticipated by the breaching party in the making of the contract.

这则由近百个单词构成的法律条文由一个条件句、连接词 or 和 and 构成的并列形式以及其他修饰限定成分构成,周密严谨,意义明确清晰。应将其译为:"第 113 条 当事人一方不履行合同义务或者履行合同义务不符合约定,给对方造成损失的,损失赔偿额应当相当于因违约所造成的损失,包括合同履行后可以获得的利益,但不得超过违反合同时预见到或者应当预见到的因违反合同可能造成的损失。"[11]

二、法律汉语句法结构及翻译

出于严谨的需要,法律汉语常会出现盘根错节的复句和被动句。"的"字句的翻译也是法律汉语英译的一个难点。

(一)"的"字结构的翻译

法律汉语中结构助词"的"(不包括置于名词之前作定语的"的"字结构)字使用频率极高,特别是在立法中占了绝对比例。究其原因,"的"字结构在法律语言中较大的概括性,可以概括同一个范畴,具有表示人或事的"类"和"举要"性质。此外,还经常呈现出一种贬义色彩,这种"的"字结构有时只包孕着一个词组,有时包孕着一个简单句,有时却包孕着复句。例如:

例7 为了犯罪,准备工具、制造条件的,是犯罪预备。
Preparation for a crime refers to the preparation of the instruments or the creation of the conditions for a crime.

本例中的"的"字结构带有贬义色彩,是"犯罪预备"规定的"系指",包孕的是两个并列名词短语。

例8 有下列情形之一的,合同无效。
A contract is invalid under any of the following circumstances: ...

本例中的"的"字结构是"合同无效"的情形分述,即"合同无效"包括几种规定情形,翻译成由 under 构成的介词短语,达到了包举无遗的效果。

例9 要约以非对话方式做出的,承诺应当在合理期限内到达。
If an offer is not made orally, the acceptance shall reach the offer or within a reasonable period of time.

此例中的"的"字结构为法律规定的条件,这种"的"字结构包孕着由 if 引导的条件状语从句,通常译成 If A... , B shall... 的形式。

(二)状语的位置

法律语言句子的复杂不仅源于冗长的从句,而且源于句子内部层层叠叠、环环相扣的

---

11 马艳姿、李永芳. 2009. 语法整合及立法英语翻译的法哲学阐释. 南华大学学报(社会科学版),(2):106–110.

修饰语。法律汉语英译时,为了使语义清楚、不产生歧义,往往不追求形式上的优美而更注重内在的逻辑关系,故将状语放在比较特别的地方。例如:

例10 在犯罪过程中,自动放弃犯罪或者自动有效地防止犯罪结果发生的,是犯罪中止。
Discontinuation of a crime refers to a case where, in the course of committing a crime, the offender voluntarily discontinues the crime or voluntarily and effectively prevents the consequences of the crime from occurring.

例11 承诺应当以通知的方式做出,但根据交易的习惯或者要约表明可以通过作为作出承诺的除外。
An acceptance shall be made in form of a notice, unless, in light of trade practices or as indicated by the offer, the offeree may indicate the assent by performing an act.

以上两例译文中,均将作状语的介词短语放在关联词 where 和 unless 与从句主语之间,清楚地表明它们只是修饰状语从句的谓语。[12]

(三)语句成分的安排

法律汉语与法律英语的差别会给翻译过程中语句成分的安排造成困难。中国法律法规的翻译有时会出现语句杂乱问题,例如:

例12 未经审批管理机关批准,擅自转让探矿权、采矿权的,由登记管理机关责令改正,没收违法所得,处10万元以下的罚款;情节严重的,由原发证机关吊销勘查许可证、采矿许可证。
Whoever without authorization, transfers exploration rights or mining rights without approval of the examining and approving agency, shall be ordered to make amends by the registration agency, have confiscated its illegal gains and be imposed a fine of not more than 100,000 yuan; the circumstances are serious, the original licensing agency shall revoke the exploration license or mining license.

此处译文不仅存在语法问题,而且拘泥于原文的句式,不符合法律英语的表达习惯。

众所周知,英语是线性结构的语言,主谓宾泾渭分明,时体、数格、性别、语态等语法形式标记明显,构成了"形合"的有型标记。汉语则是非线性语法结构的语言,主谓关系淡漠,重文章的整体意义,轻时体、数格、语态等有形标记;对文本的理解,主要依靠文本构造者和接受者之间长期形成的"共识"。英汉法律翻译时,译者必须超越两种语言的表层结构,回归本族语地道的表达方式。例如:

例13 If under the customs of any trade, the weight of any goods in bulk inserted in a contract of carriage is a weight ascertained or accepted by a third party other than a shipper or a carrier and the fact that the weight is so ascertained or accepted is stated in the contract

---

12 许凤娇. 2002. 我国法律英语翻译选词和择句中的几个问题. 湖南省政法管理干部学院学报,(12): 151–155.

of carriage, then:

(1) the contract of carriage is not prima facie evidence against a carrier of the receipt of goods of that weight and

(2) the accuracy of that weight at the time of shipment shall not be deemed to have been guaranteed by a shipper.

如果根据贸易惯例，运输合同中记载的散装货物的重量是托运人或承运人以外的第三人所确认或接受的重量，并且经此确认或接受的重量已记载于运输合同上，那么：

（1）该运输合同不是承运人按此重量接收货物的初步证据；且

（2）装船时货物重量的准确性不应视为已得到托运人的保证。

原文是一个常见而典型的"预设—处理"型法律英语长句，环环相扣，前后关联，逻辑严密。类似的长句在法律英语中较为常见，是翻译中的难点。上述译文做出了一定的努力，但由于亦步亦趋地将原文句法照搬到了译文里（如使用了"如果……，那么……"、"且……"等句型），译文读来不够通顺；若去掉译文中的"如果""那么""且"之类的形态化词语，既可传达原文的意义，又符合汉语读者的句法审美习惯。[13]

第四节 常见司法文书的翻译

司法文书是法律行为的具体表达，是公、检、法等司法机关和诉讼机关、当事人及其代理人依据法定程序在诉讼活动中或与诉讼有关的非诉讼活动中，依据事实，使用法律法规所制作并使用或提交的具有法律效力、法律意义或法律价值的各类文书的总称。

作为应用文体的一种，司法文书的体裁、样式和结构相对稳定，格式规范，叙述清楚，说理充分透彻，论证于法有据，用语规范得体。李克兴、张新红（2006）认为翻译司法文书时应注意以下几点：（1）要透彻理解原文；（2）要注意表达形式，原则上"客随主便"，译文顺应原文，不打乱原文的句、段及总体安排，保持原文的格式；（3）译文用词应严格遵守一致性原则；（4）要注意法律术语翻译的准确性。[14] 本节主要依据这四个原则提供常见司法文书及其翻译范本。

一、一般授权委托书

在法律英语中，Power of Attorney 和 Proxy 均可用来表示授权的委托书，区别在于

---

13 熊德米、熊姝丹. 2011. 法律翻译的特殊原则. 西南政法大学学报，（4）：128–135.
14 李克兴、张新红. 2006. 法律文本与法律翻译. 北京：中国对外翻译出版公司.

Power of Attorney 所指的被委托人应为律师，即具有律师身份；而 Proxy 则无此种要求，即被委托人一般不需具备律师身份。

例1

GENERAL POWER OF ATTORNEY

I, ××, of ××, hereby appoint ××, of ××, as my attorney in fact to act in my capacity to do every act that I may legally do through an attorney in fact. This power shall be in full force and effect on the date below written and shall remain in full force and effect until ×× or unless specifically extended or rescinded earlier by either party.

Dated
STATE OF
COUNTY OF

一般授权委托书

我，××（姓名），××（地址等），在此指定××（姓名），××（地址或律师事务所名称等），为我的律师，以我的身份履行一切实践中我通过律师所能从事的合法行为。本权利在以下载明日期全权生效并一直持续到×× 或持续到双方当事人规定的延展期或提前撤销期。

日期：××

（签名处）

州名和县名：××

例2

委 托 书

兹有我，××（姓名），为××（公司名称及性质），以下署名股东，在此任命和指定××（姓名）为我的事实和合法授权代理人，为我和以我的名义、职位和身份，在上述公司于××（日期）召开的或就此延期召开的股东大会上作为我的代理人对与会前合法提交大会讨论的任何事项进行表决，且为我和以我的名义，在大会上全权履行我的职责；在此我撤销此前所作的任何其他授权委托。

于20××年××月××日签字盖章，特此为证。

签名：

PROXY

BE IT KNOWN, that I, ××, the undersigned Shareholder of ××, a ×× corporation, hereby constitute and appoint ×× as my true and lawful attorney and agent for me and in my name, place and stead, to vote as my proxy at the Meeting of the Shareholders of the said corporation, to be held on ×× or any adjournment thereof, for the transaction of any business which may legally come before the meeting, and for me and in my name, to act as fully as I could do if personally present; and I herewith revoke any other proxy heretofore given.

WITNESS my hand and seal this ×× day of ××, 20××.

Signed:

二、传票

法院传票（summons）是指由原告（plaintiff）准备、由法庭下达的、用来通知答辩人（defendant）其被起诉信息的法定文件。通常情况下，法庭传票要求答辩人在指定期限内向法庭提交文件作出回应；或在小额钱债法庭中，该答辩人可以仅在法庭传票中指定的特定日期到庭参加法庭听证审理；答辩人也可选择对法庭传票不作任何回应，即任由法庭下达缺席判决，但需要承担输掉该诉讼的风险。

中华人民共和国××市第二中级人民法院

传票

案号	2009××二中民五（知）初字第202号2009
案由	商标侵权纠纷
被传唤人	A. B. C. 有限公司
工作单位或住址	[省略]
传唤事由	宣判 [或：开庭。是具体事由而定]
应到时间	2009-12-29 上午 10：30
应到处所	×××市中山路567号C201法庭

注意事项：
1. 被传唤人必须准时到达应到场所。
2. 本票由被传唤人携带来院报道。
3. 被传唤人收到传票后，应在送达回证上签名或盖章。

审　判　长：×××
审　判　员：×××
代理审判员：×××
书　记　员：×××
（印章）
2009年12月23日

本联送达被传唤人

×× No. 2 Intermediate People's Court, People's Republic of China

SUMMONS

CASE NO.	×× Erzhong Minwu (Zhi) Chuzi No. 202, 2009
CAUSES	Dispute on trademark infringement
SUMMONED	A. B. C. Co.
WORK UNIT OR ADDRESS	[Omitted]

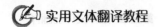

SUMMONED FOR	Rendering Judgment [or:]
TIME OF APPEARANCE	10:30 am, December 29, 2009
REPORT TO	Court C201, 567 Zhongshan Road, ×× City
NOTE: 1. The summoned must arrive at the designated location on time. 2. The summoned should report to the court with this summons. 3. The summoned must sign or stamp on the proof of service upon receipt of the summons. Chief Judge: ××× Judge: ××× Acting Judge: ××× Court Clerk: ××× (Seal of the Court) Dated: December 23, 2009	

This copy shall be served on the summoned.

此外值得一提的是与法律文书"送达"有关的词汇。在英联邦国家和美国的法律制度中,"送达"是由 service 来担当的。法庭的一切文书,如传票、命令、判决、各种诉状,都是以 service 或 serve 这两个同根的普通词来实现,例如:serve a court order 或 serve an injunction or restraining order。

三、民事起诉状

民事起诉状,是指公民、法人或其他组织,在认为自己的合法权益受到侵害或者与他人发生争议时或者需要确权时,向法院提交的请求依法裁判的法律文书。在我国,民事诉讼状的内容和结构大致如下:

(1)首部:包括标题("民事诉讼状"或"民事诉状")和当事人基本情况。

(2)请求事项,即案由:主要写明请求解决争议权益的事物。

(3)事实和理由:事实部分围绕诉讼目的,全面反映案件事实的客观真实情况;理由部分主要是列举证据,说明证据的来源、证人的姓名和地址。

(4)尾部及附项。

(一)我国民事起诉状及其翻译

民事起诉状

原告: 被告:
住所: 住所:
法定代理人: 法定代理人:
职位: 职位:
诉求:

(1)要求被告为已发出货物支付人民币××元,加利息××元,总计××元。

（2）诉讼费用由被告承担。

事实和理由：

被告是原告在国内××地区的产品分销商。自2007年9月至2008年10月，原告向被告发出了各种货物共计××元。（见证据一）

上述每笔交易均由被告正式签署和接受（见证据二）。尽管原告多次催讨货款，被告仍未能清偿到期债务。

原告认为，因原告与被告之间交易引起的债务应由中国法律管辖。被告在收到上述货物之后拒付约定货款，给原告带来巨大经济损失（见证据三）。因此，根据中华人民共和国有关法律规定，被告应承担因未付货款而造成的相应民事责任。

基于以上原因，根据《中华人民共和国民法通则》第106条和第112条、《中华人民共和国民事诉讼法》第108条及其他适用法律、法规的规定，原告特向贵院提起本案诉讼。

原告：

日期：

附：

（1）原告营业执照复印件一份

（2）法定代理人证书原件一份

（3）委托书原件一份

（4）证据一：每笔交易发票

（5）证据二：每笔交易收据

（6）证据三：损失清单

CIVIL COMPLAINT

To: _____ People's Court

Plaintiff:	Defendant:
Domicile:	Domicile:
Legal Representative:	Legal Representative:
Position:	Position:

CLAIMS:

(1) To order the Defendant to pay to the Plaintiff the due amount of RMB ××× for the dispatched products, plus the interests of RMB ××× thereon, in the aggregate of RMB ×××;

(2) To order the court fees to be borne by the Defendant.

FACTS AND REASONS:

The Defendant was one of the distributors of the Plaintiff for various kinds of products in the territory of ×××, China. From September, 2007 to October, 2008, the

Plaintiff dispatched various kinds of products in the aggregate values of RMB ×××. (see Exhibit I)

Each of the said transactions was duly signed and received by the Defendant (see Exhibit II). Though the Plaintiff has repeatedly demanded payment, the Defendant fails to liquidate the outstanding debts in due time.

It is the Plaintiff's position that the indebtedness arising out of the transactions between the Plaintiff and the Defendant shall be under the jurisdiction of the China's laws. The Defendant's refusal to satisfy the agreed amounts after receipt of the above-mentioned lubricants resulted in tremendous economic losses on the side of the Plaintiff (see Exhibit III). Therefore, pursuant to the relevant PRC laws and regulations, the Defendant shall assume the civil liabilities accordingly for such nonpayment.

By reason of the forgoing, in accordance with Articles 106 and 112 as set forth in the PRC General Civil Law, Article 108 as set forth in the PRC Civil Procedural Law and other applicable laws and regulations, the Plaintiff hereby files this case with the Court for your adjudication.

Plaintiff:

Date:

ATTACHMENTS:

(1) One copy of the Plaintiff's business license;

(2) One copy of the original Certificate of the Legal Representative;

(3) One copy of the original Power of Attorney;

(4) Exhibit I: Invoices for each transaction;

(5) Exhibit II: Receipts for each transaction;

(6) Exhibit III: List of Losses.

（二）英美国家民事起诉状基本格式及翻译

IN THE UNITED STATES DISTRICT COURT
FOR THE EASTERN DISTRICT OF PENNSYLVANIA

Plaintiff(s) VS. Defendant(s)

Cause of Action (e.g. Complaint for Breach of Contract)

Case No.

CIVIL COMPLAINT

    (1) JURISDICTION AND VENUE

    (2) ALLEGATION

    COURT I/FIRST CAUSE OF ACTION

    COURT II/SECOND CAUSE OF ACTION

(3) PRAYER FOR RELIEF

Dated ×××

RESPECTFULLY SUBMITTED,

(Signature)

Attorney for Plaintiff(s):

宾夕法尼亚东部地区美国联邦法院

原告 VS. 被告

案由（如：违约）

案件编号

民事起诉书

（1）管辖权与审判地

（2）原告诉称的事实和理由

第一案由

第二案由

……

（3）请求事项/请求得到的判决

日期：

此致！

（原告签名）

原告的诉讼代理律师：（姓名、执业证编号、所在律师事务所地址、电话等）

在实践中，由于案情的差异，具体民事起诉状的内容会有所不同。比如：如果起诉状很长，往往在标题之下附上一个"内容目录"（Table of Contents）以方便阅读；如果原告一方要求案件由陪审团裁决，则在 PRAYER FOR RELIEF 部分后增加标题为 DEMAND FOR JURY TRIAL（要求陪审团裁决）的一项内容，然后在该项内容下写明：Plaintiffs demand a trial by jury on all issues of fact and damages in this action.（原告要求本案中所涉的所有事实及损害赔偿的问题交由陪审团裁决。）[15]

四、民事答辩状

民事答辩状，是民事被告、被上诉人针对原告或上诉人的起诉或上诉，阐述自己认定的事实和理由，予以答复和辩驳的一种书状。我国民事答辩状包括首部、答辩理由和结尾三个部分：

（1）首部。标题写"民事答辩状"；答辩人的基本情况，包括答辩人姓名、性别、年龄、民族、籍贯、职业或职务、单位或住址；答辩事由，具体行文为"因某某一案，提出答辩

15　李克兴、张新红. 2006. 法律文本与法律翻译. 北京：中国对外翻译出版公司.

如下:",然后转入正文。或:"答辩人于某年某月某日收到某某人民法院交来原告因某某一案的起诉状,现答辩如下。"

(2)答辩理由。答辩状的内容没有统一的规定,要根据原告的诉状内容来确定。除被告愿意承认原告的诉讼请求外,答辩状的理由部分要针对原告在诉状中提出的事实和理由进行答辩,并可提出相反的事实、证据和理由。

(3)结尾。在答辩理由后,另行写"此致",再另一行写"某某人民法院"。由答辩人签名盖章,注明年月日。

(一)我国的民事答辩状及其翻译

答 辩 状

答辩人:××人民医院

住址:××市××路七号

因×××要求×××人民医院人身损害赔偿一案,现提出答辩意见如下:

1. 答辩人与×××之间不存在直接的合同关系,答辩人于1998年6月10日与××第二建筑安装工程公司订立了一份口头合同,由××第二建筑安装工程公司负责把答辩人的一个高压电表柜拆除,×××是受××第二建筑安装工程公司的委托来拆除高压电表柜的,与答辩人之间不存在直接合同关系。

2. ××的伤害赔偿应由××二建筑安装工程公司负责。其一,根据我国法律和有关司法解释规定,××第二建筑安装工程公司对其职工在履行合同的范围内所受到伤害应负责任,×××的伤害并不是由于合同客体以外的事物造成的。其二,受××第二建筑安装工程公司委托的×××在拆除高压电表柜的过程中,存在严重违反操作程序的行为,未尽一个电工应尽的注意义务。

3. 答辩人对×××伤害赔偿不应承担责任。根据我国《民法通则》的规定,从事高度危险作业的人致他人损伤的,应负赔偿责任。而本案中答辩人与××第二建筑安装工程公司订有合同,高度危险来源已通过合同合法地转移给××第二建筑安装工程公司,××第二建筑安装工程公司成为该危险作业物的主体。××在操作过程中受到伤害,这是××第二建筑安装工程公司在履行合同过程中,合同客体造成自己员工的伤害行为,与答辩人无关。

综上所述,×××人民医院为不适合被告,请贵院依法驳回原告起诉。

此致

××市中级人民法院

答辩人:×××人民医院

日期:

ANSWER TO COMPLAINT

Respondent: ××× People's Hospital

Address: No. 7, ××Road, ×× City

The following answer is hereby given to the claim of ××× for compensation by the ××× People's Hospital for personal injuries:

1. The respondent does not have a direct contractual relationship with ×××. The respondent entered into an oral contract with ×× No. 2 Construction and Installation Company on June 10, 1998, whereby ×× No. 2 Construction and Installation Company shall be responsible for removing the high-voltage meter cabinet. ××× was engaged in removing the high-voltage meter cabinet as entrusted by ×× No. 2 Construction and Installation Company and therefore has NO direct contractual relationship with the respondent.

2. The liabilities for compensating ×× for the damage shall be born by ×× No. 2 Construction and Installation Company for the following reasons. Firstly, pursuant to PRC laws and relevant judicial interpretations, ×× No. 2 Construction and Installation Company shall be liable for any injuries suffered by its employees to the extent of the contract performance. The injuries of ××× was not caused by anything other than the object of the contract. Thirdly, ×××, who was entrusted by ×× No. 2 Construction and Installation Company, seriously violated the operational procedure in removing the high-voltage meter cabinet and failed to pay due attention thereto.

3. The respondent shall not be liable for compensating the injuries of ×××. In accordance with the General Principles of the Civil Law, any person engaged in highly dangerous operation shall be liable for compensation in the event of any damages. In this case, however, the respondent entered into a contract with ×× No. 2 Construction and Installation Company, whereby the source of high danger shifted to ×× No. 2 Construction and Installation Company legitimately. ×× No. 2 Construction and Installation Company became the subject of the dangerous operation, and therefore any damages caused in the contract performance by ×× No. 2 Construction and Installation Company has NO connection with the respondent.

By reason of the foregoing, ××× People's Hospital is not legible for becoming the defendant. We hereby request the court to reject the plaintiff's action according to law.

To:

×× City Intermediate People's Court

Respondent: ××× People's Court

Date:

（二）英美国家的民事答辩状及其翻译

IN THE CIRCUIT COURT OF COOK COUNTY, ILLINOIS COUNTY DEPARTMENT

INDEPENDENT TRUST CORP. Plaintiff VS. LAURENCE W. CAPRIOTTI et al., Defendants

No. 00 CH08270

ANSWER TO COMPLAINT

NOW COME the Defendants, Laurence W. Capriotti et al., by and through his attorney, ××, and for his Answer to the Complaint of the Plaintiff, states as follows:

1. The Defendant invokes his Fifth Amendment privilege against self-incrimination as to each and every allegation contained in Paragraphs 1 through 75 inclusive.

2. As to Count I, the Defendant makes no answer, as the allegation in Court I are not directed towards Defendant.

3. As to Count II, the Defendant invokes his Fifth Amendment privilege against self-incrimination as to each and every allegation contained in Court II.

……

WHEREFORE, the Defendant prays that the Complaint of the Plaintiff be dismissed in its entirety and that no relief be afforded whatsoever thereunder.

Respectfully submitted,

By ××

Attorney for Defendant ××

库克县巡回法院伊利诺县分庭

独立信托公司（原告）V. 劳伦斯·W. 卡普里奥蒂等（被告）

案件编号：00 CH08270

答辩状

被告劳伦斯·W. 卡普里奥蒂等现到庭，通过其律师××就原告的诉称做出如下答辩：

1. 被告援引《美国联邦宪法第五修正案》规定的"不自证其罪权"对抗原告在其起诉状中第一至第七十五段所包含的每一种诉称。

2. 对于原告在起诉状中的第一项案由，被告不做任何答辩，因为原告起诉状中的第一项案由并未直接针对被告。

3. 被告援引《美国联邦宪法第五修正案》规定的"不自证其罪权"对抗原告在其起诉状中第二项案由所包含的每一种诉称。

……

由此，被告请求法院驳回原告的所有请求事项，不给予原告任何一种救济。

此致

（被告签名）

（被告律师签名）

需要说明的是，民事答辩状一般可翻译为 Answer to Civil Complaint，但实践中也经常采用其他的表达，比如：Answer to Complaint、Reply Brief for Defendant(s)、Answer on Merits 等。

与民事起诉状相似，英美国家的民事答辩状也会经常使用一些惯用语。如在开始陈述答辩内容之前，经常会以"Now comes/Comes now the Defendant, ××, by and through his attorney, ××, and for his answer to the Complaint of the Plaintiff, states as follows: ..."开头。大致可译为："被告××现到庭，通过其律师××，就原告的诉称作出如下答辩：……"[16]

总之，法律文体与普通文体的翻译不同，既要关注语言，还要关注法律文化，只有把二者结合起来才能翻译出质量合格的作品。

练习五

一、将下列句子译成英文。

1. 贪污贿赂犯罪，国家工作人员的渎职犯罪，国家机关工作人员利用职权实施的非法拘禁、刑讯逼供、报复陷害、非法搜查的侵犯公民人身权利的犯罪以及侵犯公民民主权利的犯罪，由人民检察院立案侦查。
2. 辩护律师自人民法院受理案件之日起，可以查阅、摘抄、复制本案所指控的犯罪事实的材料，可以同在押的被告人会见和通信。其他辩护人经人民法院许可，也可以查阅、摘抄、复制上述材料，同在押的被告人会见和通信。
3. 第三十五条 合伙的债务，由合伙人按照出资比例或者协议的约定，以各自的财产承担清偿责任。合伙人对合伙的债务承担连带责任，法律另有规定的除外。偿还合伙债务超过自己应当承担数额的合伙人，有权向其他合伙人追偿。
4. 省、自治区、直辖市人民政府对国家污染物排放标准中未作规定的项目，可以制定地方污染物排放标准；对国家污染物排放标准中已作规定的项目，可以制定严于国家污染物排放标准的地方污染物排放标准。地方污染物排放标准须报国务院环境保护行政主管部门备案。
5. 被告人是盲、聋、哑或者未成年人而没有委托辩护人的，人民法院应当指定承担法律援助义务的律师为其提供辩护。

---

16 李克兴、张新红. 2006. 法律文本与法律翻译. 北京：中国对外翻译出版公司.

二、将下列句子译成中文。

1. The valuation determined by the Independent Appraiser shall be the valuation adopted by the Parties for purposes of this provision save that where the valuation is a State-owned asset valuation required by Applicable Laws, the Parties may agree an adjustment to such valuation where and to the extent permitted under Applicable Laws.

2. The Assigning Party shall acknowledge and agree that to the extent that the Affiliate Assignee fails to perform any obligation hereunder, the Assigning Party is not released from, and remains jointly and severally liable with the Affiliate Assignee for, the full performance of the provisions of this Contract and any damages for the breach thereof.

3. In the event that the Company's operations are reduced substantially from the scale of operation originally anticipated by the Parties, or the Company experiences substantial and continuing losses resulting in negative retained earnings not anticipated by the Parties in the agreed Business Plan, or in any other circumstance permitted under Applicable Laws or agreed by the Parties, the Parties may agree to reduce the registered capital of the Company on a pro rata basis.

4. Given the requirement that all transfers of registered capital must be approved by the original examination and approval authority, and because such original examination and approval authority will require signed consents, waivers of pre-emptive rights and unanimous board resolutions, it is very difficult to achieve and put into effect a deemed consent to any transfer as provided in this Article 5.6 (b).

5. When any dispute occurs and is the subject of friendly consultations or arbitration, the Parties shall continue to exercise their remaining respective rights and fulfil their remaining respective obligations under this Contract, except in respect of those matters under dispute.

三、将下面的短文译成英文。

　　法律保护市民不被错误地剥夺自由的权利。如果警察或其他州或联邦官员无合理原因、违反规定对你实行逮捕，或者有人非法剥夺你的自由，你可以提起诉讼，要求赔偿损失（包括要求对方支付律师费和其他费用）。你的权利受美国宪法以及州普通法的保护。认为自己被错误逮捕的人通常会抗议这种错误关押。如果警察没有正当理由逮捕了你，你可以以错误关押为由提起诉讼。错误逮捕属于错误关押的一种。当有足够证据表明行为人正在犯罪或者已经实施了犯罪行为时，警察就有了合理逮捕行为人的理由。为了迅速将案犯逮捕以便对犯罪活动进行调查，这个结论必须证据充分而非仅仅是怀疑。如果认为自己被错误关押或错误逮捕时，你也许希望能和律师联系。时间在许多案例中会成为至关重要的因素，一些过往案例表明，如果在案情发生后较短时间内没有提出诉求，法庭将会拒绝审理。需了解更多信息可向律师咨询。

四、将下面的短文译成中文。

  Juveniles, or people under the age of eighteen, are usually tried in a juvenile court for misdemeanor offenses. Misdemeanor offenses are not serious crimes like murder, rape, or assault, but they are still serious enough to warrant punishment. Crimes are usually classified as felonies and misdemeanors. Generally speaking, felonies are the more serious crimes and are usually punishable by imprisonment in a penitentiary. Misdemeanors are offenses of a less serious nature and are punishable by a fine or imprisonment in a county or local jail. Committing a forgery is a felony, but driving an automobile in excess of the speed limit is a misdemeanor. The criminal statutes define the acts that are felonies and misdemeanors. Occasionally, the same offense may be either a misdemeanor or a felony, depending on its degree. For example, the first offense of a crime may be a misdemeanor. After a certain number of convictions for that same crime, the state may prosecute the next violation as a felony. Punishment for juvenile misdemeanor offenses can range from probation to reform school, depending on the seriousness of the crime and if there was any prior criminal behavior. If the juvenile has a long record of serious crimes, he or she may be tried in a regular court as an adult. For more information on juvenile law, consult an attorney.

第六章 新闻文体的翻译

新闻文体一般指报刊、电视、广播、网站等大众媒体所做的报道,是常见的实用文体,在语言上具有自己的特点。新闻常可分为"硬新闻"(hard news)和"软新闻"(soft news)两大类:硬新闻一般题材严肃,关系国计民生和人们的切身利益,时效性强;软新闻一般轻松幽默,娱乐性强。在报道形式上,新闻体裁主要分三大类:消息、特写和评论。[1] 本章将重点探讨新闻文体的文体特点及其翻译技巧。

第一节 新闻文体概论及其特点

什么是新闻,人们众说纷纭,看法不一。《现代汉语词典》(第5版)将"新闻"定义为报纸或广播电台等报道的国内外消息。《辞海》(第6版缩印本)对"新闻"的解释是:报社、通讯社、广播电台、电视台等新闻机构对当前政治事件或社会事件所作的报道,要求迅速、及时、真实、言简意明、以事实说话,形式有消息、通讯、特写、记者通信、调查报告、新闻图片、电视新闻等。Oxford Advanced Learner's English-Chinese Dictionary (7th Edition)(《牛津高阶英汉双解词典(第7版)》)给出的定义是 reports of recent events that appear in newspapers or on television or radio(报纸、电视、电台上有关新近发生事件的报道)。以上定义分别从不同的角度对新闻进行了阐释:《现代汉语词典》主要从新闻传播媒介、发生区域及分类角度进行了解释;《辞海》的定义涉及新闻的传播媒介、分类、客观性、时效性等,比较全面具体;Oxford Advanced Learner's English-Chinese Dictionary (7th Edition) 的定义则侧重于新闻的传播媒体和时效性。

虽然这些定义不尽相同,但都有助于我们了解新闻的一些基本属性:一是时效性,即是"新"闻而不是"旧"闻;二是客观性,即实在发生了的而不是虚构杜撰的;三是大众性,即借助媒体向新闻受众即大众进行传播。新闻的属性从根本上决定了新闻语言的表达形式及特点。

---

1 张健.1998.新闻英语文体与范文评析.上海:上海外语教育出版社.

一、新闻报道的结构形式

新闻报道的主体结构一般由标题、导语、正文三部分组成。标题（headline）浓缩概括全文的中心实质话题；导语（lead or introduction）通常为文章的第一段，提供最主要的事实；正文（body）在导语的基础上，引入更多的与主题相关的事实，使之更加翔实、具体，有时也展开评论，并进而得出结论。

新闻体裁的多样性决定了新闻文体组织形式的多样性。即使同类体裁的新闻，作者也会依据背景、内容、目的、受众等因素灵活组织篇章结构。以我们最为熟悉的新闻形式"消息报道"为例，常见的有"倒金字塔"结构、"金字塔"结构、"菱形"结构、"放射型"结构等。由于消息报道的时效性强，题材相对严肃，"倒金字塔"结构（the Inverted Pyramid）成了最常用的一种结构，即按事实的重要程度或受众关心程度依次递减的次序，先主后次地安排消息中各项事实内容，犹如倒置的金字塔或倒置的三角形，因而得名（如下图）。软新闻由于其题材多样，写法灵活，人情味较浓，易于引起读者情感上的呼应，故结构往往不拘一格。

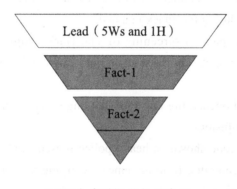

"倒金字塔"结构示意图

二、新闻英语文体特点

（一）语言风格

新闻的基本属性决定了新闻英语语言的风格。新闻是对事实的反映，这要求新闻语言必须客观、准确，慎用夸张、渲染、主观性强的词汇。同时，新闻面向的对象是大众，这就要求新闻语言具有朴实易懂、大众化的特点。为节约时间和成本，新闻语言要精练。此外，为吸引眼球，争取读者，也要考虑到趣味性，这就要求新闻语言尽可能生动、形象。这些特性，即客观性、大众性、经济性、趣味性，共同构成了新闻语言的总体风格，并渗透到新闻语言的各个层面上。请看一篇有关美国丹佛市电影院枪击案的报道。

例1

Masked Gunman Kills 14 at U.S. Cinema[2]

A masked gunman killed at least 14 people and injured 50 more when he opened fire on a midnight screening of the new Batman film near the U.S. city of Denver, local police said.

Dan Oates, police chief in the Denver suburb of Aurora, told reporters that 10 people were killed at the cinema and four others were reported to have died in hospital.

"Witnesses tell us he released some sort of canister," the Associated Press news agency quoted Mr. Oates as saying. "They heard a hissing sound and some gas emerged and the gunman opened fire."

The police chief said a suspect, thought to be in his early 20s, had been detained after being found in the car park of the mall where the shootings occurred in the early hours of Friday. The suspect was found with a rifle, handgun and the gas mask he reportedly wore during the attack.

Local radio station KOA quoted witnesses as saying that the assailant had set off a smoke or gas bomb during the attack in a mall.

A witness at the packed screening of The Dark Knight Rises told CNN the gunman was wearing a bulletproof vest and a riot helmet and was "completely covered in black with goggles".

The gunman had opened fire during a shooting scene in the film, witnesses said, apparently sowing confusions.

Footage of the scene showed a heavy police presence. One witness said he had seen a police officer emerging from the cinema carrying the body of young girl. One officer said witnesses were being taken to a nearby school.

One local hospital, the Swedish Medical Center, said it had put its disaster plan into effect.

这是一篇典型的突发事件新闻报道，可以让我们对英语新闻的语言特点了解一二。首先，新闻标题为一简单句，短短7个字就把新闻的主要内容、人物、事发地点交代清楚，言简意赅，短小精悍。对于惜时如金的人们，仅仅浏览标题就可大致了解新闻事件的主要内容。其次，全篇的实词以单、双音节词为主，如masked、killed、injured、opened、died、released、detained、suspect、attack、witness、wearing、sowing、seen、emerging、taken等，都是日常生活中使用频率很高的词汇，既易于理解，又节省了版面。再次，从句法角度看，全篇基本上以简单句为主，同位语、介词短语等的使用有效扩展了简单句，信息量完整；从语态上看，多为主动态，使得新闻事件贴近读者。最后，大量使用引言以

---

[2] 此例引自金融时报中文网 2012-07-20。

及很少使用富有感情色彩和主观判断的词汇使得新闻报道真实、可信，体现了新闻报道的客观性要求。

（二）词汇特点

1. 常用词汇旧"貌"换新"颜"

新闻报道常使用某些词汇来叙述事实和事件，这些词汇经过长期使用后逐渐被赋予特殊含义，具有了特定的新闻色彩，成为常见新闻词汇。例如：media=the press and TV network（媒体，主要指报刊和广播电视）、loom=appear（出现）、shock=astonish（震惊）或 blow（打击）、bar=prevent（阻止）、comb=search（搜查）、operation=activity（活动）、upper=drug used as a stimulant（兴奋剂）、umbrella=protective shield（核保护伞）、throwaway=wasteful（浪费成风的）、streetwalk=do something as a mere formality（毫不费力地走过场）等。

2. 小词常受青睐

新闻工作者为节约时间、节省版面，对单音节词青睐有加，这些词一般具有短小精悍、简单易懂、生动灵活的特点。例如：back=support（支持）、ban=forbid（禁止）、curb=control（控制）、boost=increase（增加）、clash=controversy（争论）、vow=promise（誓言）、rap=criticize（批评）、fake=counterfeit（伪造）、voice=express（表达）、talk=negotiation（谈判）或 conference（协商、会议）、cut=reduce 或 curtail（减少、缩减）等。

3. 临时造词

世界时刻变化，新事物层出不穷，现有词汇有时很难满足表达的需要，同时为了追求新奇，吸引读者，新闻工作者常会临时造词。[3] 例如：moonscape（月景）、moonquake（月震）、atobomb（原子弹）、heartmen（换心人）、cyberphobia（网络恐惧症）、cyberwidow（网络寡妇）、cross-dresser（伪娘）、empty-nester（空巢老人）、seckilling（秒杀）、Euromart（European market 欧洲市场）、Reaganomics（Reagan-economics 里根经济学）、Liconomics（李克强经济学）、Ameritocracy（American-aristocracy 美国寡头政治统治）、haves and have-not（富人和穷人）等。值得一提的是，美国 NBA 2011—2012 赛季，华裔球员林书豪爆发，表现神勇，各大媒体和球迷为此造出了不少生动有趣的"林氏英语"：Lisanity 被翻译成"林来疯"，此外还有 Lincredible（=Lin+incredible "林神奇"），Linner（=Lin+winner "林赢家"）等。

4. 广泛使用缩略语和复合词

新闻报道中大量使用缩略语和复合词。常用的缩略语如：NBA（National Basketball Association 全美篮球协会）、IOC（International Olympic Committee 国际奥委会）、

---

3 刘金龙. 2011. 汉语报刊超 IN 新词英译例话. 北京：国防工业出版社.

START（Strategic Arms Reduction Talks 裁减战略武器谈判）、WB（World Bank 世界银行）等。复合词如：yearlong（长达一年的）、thumb-suck（安抚）、on-site-service（现场服务）、most-favored-nation treatment（最惠国待遇）、free-range kid（自由放养儿童）、close-off management（封闭式管理）、last-gasp goal（绝杀）、low-carbon economy（低碳经济）、water-intensive industry（耗水产业）、dusk-to-dawn curfew（宵禁）、get-rich-quick scheme（快速致富的骗术）、the off-and-on-again civil war（断断续续的内战）等。

5. 大量使用新闻套语

新闻报道中存在各种套语，例如：according to (eyewitness, AP reports, sources concerned, etc.)（据目击者，美联社报道，有关方面等）、informative sources or well-informed source（消息灵通人士）、on the brink of a breakthrough（即将取得进展）、quoted/cited as saying（援引……的话说）、preferred not to be identified（不愿透露姓名的）、in response to allegation in *The New York Times*（就《纽约时报》的提法发表评论）等。

6. 巧妙措辞，收获奇效

为吸引读者，在不违背新闻报道客观性的前提下，作者常在措辞上煞费苦心，以使行文生动有趣、幽默诙谐。如美国《时代周刊》刊登的一篇亚洲金融危机使华尔街股票大跌的报道采用了这样的标题："Catching the Asian Flu"（华尔街患上"亚洲流感"）。该标题将亚洲金融危机比作流感，形象地反映了金融危机给美国带来的影响，仿佛感染了"亚洲流感"；可谓独具匠心，令读者忍俊不禁。

7. 大量使用各种专业词汇和外来词

英语新闻文体大量借用体育、军事、商业、科技、文学、娱乐业等方面的专业词汇或外来词。例如：schmuck（蠢货，源于意大利语）、macho（有伟男子气概的，源于墨西哥语）、the odds（可能性，体育用语）、showdown（摊牌，赌博用语）、package deal（一揽子买卖，法律和金融用语）、dark horse（指出人意料的获胜者，赛马用语）、throw somebody a curve ball（虚晃一招，江湖行骗用语）、get to first base（取得初步成功，棒球用语）、throw in the sponge（认输或投降，拳击用语）、play for high stakes（下大赌注，牌戏用语）、hit the jackpot（获得大笔赌注或取得巨大成功，赌博和彩票用语）等。

（三）句法特点

1. 多用现在时

英语新闻中大量使用现在时，让读者感觉事件正在发生，现实感强。有时宾语从句应该用过去时也会被现在时或将来时代替。例如：

例2 Magnitude 6.0 quake kills 57 in eastern Turkey.

例3 Thailand's central bank governor said on Monday that the country's economy is poised to make a strong recovery from debilitating floods.

2. 较多使用省略句和扩展的简单句

新闻英语写作倾向于使用结构简单的语言形式，体现在大量使用简单句和省略句，同时为了达到信息浓缩的效果，常使用分词短语、同位语、介词短语等语言成分扩展简单句。[4] 有时还较多地使用插入语代替从句，简化句子结构。尤其在新闻标题中，很多成分都会被省略，如冠词、介词、系动词、连词、代词等功能虚词。

例4 Holiday safety checks to protect travelers (=Holiday safety checks are to protect travelers)

例5 The holiday, which begins on Saturday, often brings increased commodity prices, creating additional pressure for low income urban families who are already struggling to get by.

3. 大量使用被动语态

著名语法学家 Svartvik 通过研究发现，被动语态在新闻英语语篇中的使用频率是很高的。[5] 这是因为被动语态能够起到保持中立态度、避免麻烦冲突、缓和语气等交际效果，并且被动语态"更远离说话者"，类似小说"叙述"过去发生的事件。但这并不意味着主动语态在新闻英语语篇中的地位弱化，实际上，主动语态在实时报道语篇中大量出现，这样表达直接生动，富有感染力，具有生动展现事件的临场戏剧效果。

例6 A second UN school has been attacked by Israeli shells with Gaza's emergency services saying "dozens" killed as fresh ceasefire attempts are made.

例7 Sudan declared a two-week ceasefire in the restive state of South Kordofan, where 200,000 people have fled from their homes in recent months.

4. 大量使用前置修饰语修饰名词

为简化句子结构，节省篇幅，同时帮助读者提高阅读速度，新闻报道往往大量使用带连字符的复合短语作定语，这种前置修饰语结构灵活。例如：

例8 Precisely on time and target, NASA's Curiosity rover touched down safely on Mars Monday to begin <u>an ambitious two-year</u> trek through a mountainous crater that promises to reveal whether the red planet was ever hospitable to life.

例9 The men have spent 68 days in the hot, humid bowels of a small gold and copper mine in <u>Chile's far northern Atacama</u> desert after <u>an August 5</u> collapse, and now face a harrowingly claustrophobic journey to the surface in <u>specially-made</u> capsules.

4　孙致礼. 2005. 新编英汉翻译教程. 上海：上海外语教育出版社.
5　曾丽芬. 1994. 试论被动语态的功能及其使用的语境. 外语教学，（2）：57–64.

第二节
新闻文体的翻译原则和方法

一、新闻文体翻译的一般原则

新闻翻译不能任意而为，要遵循一定的翻译原则。严复提倡的"信、达、雅"一直是中国翻译界广为推崇的翻译原则。"信"指意义不背离原文，即译文要准确，不能歪曲遗漏，不得随意增减；"达"指不拘泥于原文形式，译文通顺明白；"雅"指译文语言要优美典雅、富有品味，追求文章本身的简明古雅，强调其文学艺术价值。显而易见，"雅"并不太适用于新闻文体翻译，"信""达"却不失为新闻翻译的指导原则。总的说来，翻译新闻时，应该选择最接近原文、最自然的语言形式，使译文既能再现原语所传递的信息，又能符合目的语的表达习惯，让读者易懂。

二、新闻标题的翻译

（一）新闻标题的特点

标题常被视作新闻的"眼睛"，好的标题能快速吸引读者的注意力，激发他们强烈的阅读兴趣。标题一般短小精悍，言简意明，新颖独特，富有吸引力。此外，为了吸引读者，标题还会灵活运用多种修辞技巧。

由于受不同的文化习惯、思维模式、语言系统等因素的影响，中英文新闻标题也有各自的风格。第一，中英新闻标题详细程度不同。中文标题比较具体，习惯综述新闻的各个要点；而英文标题关注事件焦点，精悍短小。第二，措辞手法不同。中文新闻标题喜欢以动词开头，常用修饰语来加强语气，营造氛围；而英文新闻标题中名词却受到重用，起到动词、形容词等的作用，具有很好的延展性，虚词则常被省略。第三，时间概念表达不同。中文标题常借助时间词来表达不同的时间概念；而英文新闻标题常用现在时来突出已发生事件的现实感和新鲜感，在使用将来时态时，最常见的形式是省略 be 的不定式结构，即 to+V。针对中英文新闻标题的特点，翻译时常用的方法有直译法、意译法、增删法、重拟法等。

（二）新闻标题的翻译

1. 直译法

如果新闻标题的含义明白直接，一目了然，没有太多具有民族色彩的词汇，并且在翻译转换后不会造成读者理解困难，那么可以采用直译法。例如：

例1 Spanish convents use social media to recruit new nuns[6]
西班牙修道院利用社交媒体招募修女

例2 京高校开设艾滋病教育课程[7]
Beijing colleges give AIDS classes

2. 意译法

由于中英文化不同，英汉表达形式有异，翻译新闻标题时，有时很难做到形式上的对等。此时可以把重点放在标题意义的所指上，不拘泥于原标题的语言结构和形式，进行适当的变通。例如：

例3 The Chinese market, a bottomless pit[8]
中国市场潜力巨大

原标题中 a bottomless pit 意为"无底坑"，此说法接近汉语中的"无底洞"，带有贬义，若在译文中用此表达，感情色彩不符。因此，翻译后的标题舍弃了原文的修辞形式，进行了意译。

例4 塞国球迷"看不起"世界杯[9]
Soccer fans in Senegal can't afford World Cup tickets

原标题使用了双关的修辞手法，一指塞国球迷囊中羞涩，支付不起观赏世界杯的费用；二含有鄙视、不在乎"世界杯"的意思。双重意思给翻译带来了难度，不如把握重点，采用意译的方法，将作者的真正意图直接翻译出来。

例5 Slipping into darkness[10]
贝卢斯科尼在劫难逃

英文原标题的表面意思是"（正在）滑向黑暗"，表达了意大利前总理贝卢斯科尼受情色丑闻的影响支持率下滑，政治生命正走向穷途末路。但对中文读者而言，初读此标题可能会不知所云。因此，翻译时使用意译法，明确表达贝氏所处的窘境。

3. 增删法

中英标题概括程度不同，详尽差异有别。英文新闻标题一般比较精练简短，常以点代面，而中文标题则很详细，往往求大求全。因此，英文标题汉译时，译者可以结合中文标题的

6　此例英文标题引自 *Guardian*, 2015-03-16.
7　此例引自 http://www.doc88.com/p-2532076634935.html.
8　此例引自王晓、黄春兰. 2009. 从功能对等理论看英语新闻标题常用修辞的翻译. 湖北广播电视大学学报，（12）：92–93.
9　此例引自许明武. 2003. 新闻英语与翻译. 北京：中国对外翻译出版公司.
10　此例引自《经济学人》中英文对照版，2011-09-24.

特点，适当增加一些词语，使标题的形式更趋汉化，意义更趋完整，利于中国读者理解。[11] 反之，新闻标题中译英时，则须提炼要点，简化语义，删除意义空泛的词语，使之符合英文标题的表达习惯。例如：

例6 Older, wiser, calmer[12]

人愈老，智愈高，心愈平

例6的新闻聚焦于当今老龄化社会，尤其是老人们退休后在处理各种问题时表现出来的睿智和冷静。若按照原文逐字翻译成"更老，更明智，更冷静"，也可以接受。但如果根据中国读者阅读习惯，增加"人""智""心"三个字，意义则更明确，句式也更整齐。

例7 航空燃油附加与煤油价联动

收取标准、时间由各航空公司自定 [13]

China announces new pricing mechanism of fuel surcharge

原文标题信息量丰富，符合中文新闻标题的传统，而西方新闻读者一般从个人角度看待问题，常关心事件核心要点及其对自身利益的影响。因此，翻译时须进行提炼简化，突出重点。

例8 临沧县24名小学生因挤压致死 [14]

24 children killed

中文标题常带有背景知识，信息比较全面，而英文标题简洁凝练，常聚焦事件最有价值的部分，即新闻焦点。本例中，中文标题就像一个微型故事，不仅包括了事件发生的具体地点、多少名小学生失去生命，而且也道出了致死原因，可谓"麻雀虽小，五脏俱全"。在英译时，需进行删减，抓住事件焦点，即儿童的死亡。

4. 重拟法

中英新闻标题在概括程度、突出的重点、语法结构、组织形式上有着明显的差异。比如，中文标题结构有时很复杂，对于一些重要事件，可能会出现对偶对仗的结构形式，十分醒目；有时还会包含引题和主题，结构形式更加复杂。鉴于此，译者在英译时可以灵活调整，放弃原文标题形式，根据新闻内容重新拟定题目，以满足新闻受众的阅读心理需求。重拟法在新闻标题中译英时尤为常见，例如：

例9 现代汽车气囊问题难涉中国 维权力度弱致不重视 [15]

Hyundai motor recall excludes China

---

11 许明武. 2003. 新闻英语与翻译. 北京：中国对外翻译出版公司.
12 此例引自张健. 1998. 新闻英语文体与范文评析. 上海：上海外语教育出版社.
13 此例中文标题引自人民网，英文引自新华网英文版，2009-11-13.
14 此例中文标题引自大众日报，英文引自 China Daily, 1996-09-14.
15 此例中文标题引自新浪财经，英文引自人民网，2012-08-12.

此例中文标题符合求大求全、信息量大的传统，不仅说明现代汽车召回不包括中国市场，而且点出了质量缺陷以及召回难的症结所在。译者在翻译时对标题进行了重拟，突显了新闻事件的焦点，即"现代汽车召回不包括中国市场"。英文标题措辞简明扼要，重点突出，照顾到了西方读者对于标题潜在的阅读心理需求。

例10 肩负神圣使命 忠实履行职责 [16]

CPC delegates urged to faithfully perform duties

此例中文标题使用了对仗结构，醒目而隆重，但英文标题很少使用此种结构和措辞，故而翻译时，译者进行了结构调整，以简化繁，聚焦事件要点。

例11 大坝出现"大裂缝"？
资金是个"无底洞"？
三峡总公司辟谣：空穴来风 [17]

Big rift and fund shortage: A rumor

此例中文标题结构形式更加复杂，包含引题和主题，其中引题又包含两个设问，答案则在主题中得到了揭晓。这种引题加主题、自问自答的结构形式，是汉语重大时事新闻报道的常见形式之一。然而英文标题很少使用引题形式，因此翻译时有必要把引题和主题合二为一。译者抓住了事件的三个要点"大坝裂缝""资金短缺"和"谣言"，对原标题进行了调整，仅用三个名词性词组，就解决了所有的问题，凝练醒目，符合英文报道拟题习惯。

5. 修辞法

中英新闻标题经常采用各种修辞手段，以增加新闻的趣味性和生动性。常见的修辞手段有押韵、比喻、拟人、对比、双关、借代等。翻译时，应尽可能再现原标题的修辞特点。然而，由于语言文化上的差异，往往很难让译文读者得到与原文读者在义、音、形等方面几乎一样的感受。此时，译者的首要任务是保证源语信息得到准确、充分地表达，然后尽可能根据目的语的文化特点，寻求能够达到类似效果的表达方式。例如：

例12 After the booms everything is gloom [18]

繁荣不再，萧条即来（或：一别繁荣，一片愁容）

原标题中的 boom 和 gloom 构成尾韵（rhyme），而汉语译文通过"再"和"来"（或者"荣"和"容"）也达到了押韵的效果，读来朗朗上口，并且四字形式的运用突出了主题。

例13 "史上最牛的钉子坟"今日迁坟 [19]

Last tomb standing in construction site relocated

---

16 此例中文标题来自新华网，英文来自新华网英文版，2012-08-13.
17 此例引自许明武. 2003. 新闻英语与翻译. 北京：中国对外翻译出版公司.
18 此例引自刘金龙. 2011. 英语新闻标题中的修辞格及其翻译. 中国科技翻译，（2）：45–49.
19 此例引自中国日报网，2012-12-18.

此例标题译文中使用了拟人的修辞格，standing 一词和原文中的"钉子"一词相对应。

汉语表达形式灵活多样，有许多植根于民族文化、广为人们熟知的诗词歌赋、谚语等，言简意赅，生动形象，形式多样，朗朗上口，有着丰富的语义内涵，深受人们喜爱。翻译英文新闻标题时，灵活运用这些语言，会收到意想不到的效果。

例14 Doleful[20]

愁云惨淡万里凝

原标题只有一个单词，意为"悲哀的、阴沉的、忧郁的"。如直译，平淡无奇，味同嚼蜡。此处译者借用了唐朝诗人岑参的诗句，翻译后的标题不仅含蓄朦胧兼有诗意，诱使读者想要读下去，同时也很好地烘托了主题，即经济惨淡、失业率飙升如同一层挥之不去的阴霾，使年轻人深受其害。

三、新闻导语的翻译

（一）新闻导语的特点

新闻导语"立片言以居要"，是新闻的第一部分，是对新闻内容的提炼概括。主要涉及六个要素（who、what、when、why、where 和 how），主要特点是精练、准确、直接。好的导语可以让读者在最短时间内抓住新闻的主要内容，并判断是否深入阅读，因此，导语是新闻的灵魂和视窗。导语的写作灵活多变，引人入胜，并没有统一的模式。总体上看，"倒金字塔"结构模式始终占据主导地位，尤其是在时效性强的新闻报道中最为明显。但不管何种结构的导语，翻译时一定要做到言简意赅，通俗易懂，让读者能迅速掌握新闻的主要信息。

（二）新闻导语翻译的原则

1. 弄清导语语义结构

从导语语义结构来看，导语一般包括两方面的内容：未知信息和已知信息。未知信息是导语传达的主要内容，是导语要突显的主要部分，是必须部分；而已知信息则提供相关的背景知识，可以有，也可以根据需要省略。未知信息和已知信息之间有着主次轻重之分。弄清二者之间的关系，则可避免主次颠倒。现摘引一例如下[21]：

例15 A bomb explosion caused the crash of an Air India jumbo jet off Ireland last year in which all 329 people aboard were killed, investigation for the Boeing Company and the Indian government have testified.

---

20 此例引自《经济学人》中英文对照版，2011-08-20。
21 朱伊革. 2008. 英语新闻的语言特点和翻译. 上海：上海交通大学出版社.

a. 去年一枚炸弹爆炸使印度航空公司的一架大型客机在爱尔兰离岸坠毁；造成机上329人遇难。这是波音公司和印度政府调查人员证实的。

b. 据波音公司和印度政府的调查人员证实，印航的一架大型客机去年在爱尔兰离岸坠毁，造成机上329人死亡；原因是机上炸弹爆炸。

c. 据波音公司和印度政府的调查人员证实，去年印航大型客机在爱尔兰离岸坠毁的事件是由于炸弹爆炸造成的；该次空难使得机上329人全部丧生。

原导语包含的主要内容（即未知信息）是"印航空难的原因是炸弹爆炸"，次要内容（即已知的相关背景信息）是"印航大客机去年在爱尔兰离岸坠毁，机上329人遇难"。有鉴于此，译文 c 更恰当，因为译文 a、b 都把已知信息当成了新闻。

对语义结构的分析，实际上涉及导语内各信息的价值差异或重要性的问题。由于东西方思维模式的不同，中英新闻导语的信息排列顺序有明显差异。中文导语一般遵循先介绍相关背景信息后切入主题的写作模式；而英文导语则不同，重视层次性，以重要性或受关心程度依次递减的顺序，先主后次地安排各项事实内容。例如：

例16 公安部在全国36个大、中城市实施的道路交通"畅通工程"今天下午在北京拉开帷幕。[22]

A program to ease city traffic got under way in Beijing this afternoon. This program, run by China's Public Security Ministry, will involve thirty-six cities across the country.

此例中，中文导语句子长，信息量大，首先介绍了项目的范围以及性质，然后才切入到正题，这符合中文导语的写作模式，符合汉语思维表达的传统。翻译时，译者对各信息点进行了调整，把原文拆分成两句话。首先，把新闻的主要内容放在第一句话里直接点题，开门见山，即 A program to easy city traffic got under way in Beijing this afternoon；然后，把次要信息安置在第二句话中，作为补充背景信息，符合英文导语先主后次的写作传统。

2. 使用简明的句法结构

英语新闻导语常使用扩展的简单句和主动结构，语言客观凝练，语法严谨清晰。英译汉时要尽量使译文简明扼要，忌晦涩费解、冗长拖沓。可多使用主谓宾或主谓结构，少使用复合句、从句。相反，汉语翻译成英语时，则需整合新闻要素，合并句式。例如：

例17 Siemens, the German company which sliced 20% of the Chinese telecommunications market last year, expects to continue being bullish about the world's biggest market.[23]

去年在中国已经占有20%市场份额的西门子公司，目前仍然看好这个世界上最大的市场。

---

22 此例引自于航. 2004. 中英文新闻导语语篇结构差异分析. 北京第二外国语学院学报，（2）：5–8.
23 此例引自朱伊革. 2008. 英语新闻的语言特点和翻译. 上海：上海交通大学出版社.

例18 外交部发言人华春莹 12 日表示，关于中方将有关南京大屠杀和日军强征慰安妇的一些珍贵历史档案向联合国教科文组织申报世界记忆名录，联合国教科文组织已受理中方申报。[24]

China said on 12 June UNESCO has accepted its application to register records of the 1937 Nanjing Massacre and Japan's wartime sex slaves on the Memory of the World Register.

3. 分清逻辑层次

英语汉语分属不同的语言系统。英语属于"形合"语言，在表达中往往使用不同的衔接手段来表达各种各样的逻辑关系，比如连词、从句、非谓语结构等；句子比较长，呈树状结构，常把最重要的内容放在开始位置。汉语属于"意合"语言，句子简短，是线性结构，上下语义连贯，很少使用连接词，句子的重要内容一般放在最后。因此英译中时，首先要弄清句子的逻辑关系、语法形式，掌握基本意思，然后对复杂句型进行位置调整，灵活整合各要素，以满足读者的阅读习惯。总体上说，常见的处理方式有长句拆分、信息换位。反之，中译英时，则处理方式相反，常进行短句合并、信息换位。例如：

例19 Widespread violence marred the first phase of voting in the general election yesterday, with at least 22 people killed and dozens injured in clashes around the country.[25]

由于到处发生暴力冲突事件，昨天大选第一阶段投票工作受阻，全国的冲突至少造成 22 人丧生，数十人受伤。

从语法角度看，原文导语句式简明，为简单句后加一独立主格结构作状语表示结果。从语义角度看，原句各部分有清晰的因果关系，widespread violence 是"因"，marred the first phase of voting in the general election 和 at least 22 people killed and dozens injured 是"果"，与汉语表达习惯相符，翻译时应该明确此关系，保留原文形式。译者添加了逻辑词汇"由于"和"造成"，使逻辑关系清晰明确，把长句处理成四个小句，简练而不拖泥带水，较为成功。

例20 The President said at a press conference dominated by questions on yesterday's election results that he could not explain why the Republicans had suffered such a widespread defeat, which in the end would deprive the Republican Party of long-held superiority in the House.[26]

在一次记者招待会上，问题集中于昨天的选举结果，总统就此发了言。他说他不能解释为什么共和党遭到了这么大的失败。而这种情况最终会使共和党失去在众议院中长期享有的优势。

24　此例引自新华网，2014-06-12.

25　此例引自朱伊革．2008．英语新闻的语言特点和翻译．上海：上海交通大学出版社．

26　此例引自 http://www.douban.com/group/topic/39212178/?type=like.

本例原句很长，结构复杂，由一个带分词短语的主句、两个宾语从句和一个非限制性定语从句组成，此外还有几个不同功能的状语。如果翻译成汉语里的一句话，就会显得冗长晦涩。因此，译文对句型和各要素做了拆分整合。原句被分成了三句话来译，分词短语前置，两个宾语从句翻译成一句，非限制性定语从句译成一句。这样，原句中复杂的逻辑关系便变得清晰明确了。

四、新闻消息的翻译

（一）新闻消息概述

消息以简要的文字迅速报道新闻事实，是最广泛、最常用的新闻体裁。消息报道的对象常常是最新发生的重大政治、经济、自然灾害等事件，故题材较为严肃，重在迅速传递信息。因此，消息写作一般要求开门见山，一开始就把最具新闻价值的内容写入导语中。消息的写作要求主题明确，思路清晰，措辞精练，笔调客观，不含任何议论抒情，让事实说话，增强新闻的可信度。消息报道的常见形式主要包括单一事件报道、综合报道、连续报道和深度报道等。记者在采写消息时，常根据事件的重要性、素材的多少等因素灵活选取合适的报道形式。其中单一事件报道是最基本、最常见的形式。

（二）新闻消息翻译

1. 新闻消息的结构处理

中英文消息报道多采用"倒金字塔"式的结构，把重要新闻事实尽量安排在前面，其他新闻事实则以重要程度依次摆放。因此，在翻译时，可以尽量保留原文报道的结构。从段落形式上看，英文消息段落短，一个段落通常只讲一个要点，节奏明快，跳跃性强；中文消息报道则不同，一般段落较长，一个段落内可以有几个要点，通常把相关内容集中到一起来讲，节奏比较慢，逻辑严密、连贯，很少有跳跃式思维。因此，在进行消息翻译时，应以"事实"为准则，以"准确"为核心，确保内容准确无误；在行文方面，不必拘泥于原文语言形式，务必做到言简意赅，文字流畅，通俗易懂，使译语读者能顺利阅读、理解。另外，英文消息报道非常重视直接引语的使用，以示客观、真实。在翻译时，一方面要调整说话人的位置（英文消息中，说话人的位置比较灵活，可出现在引语的前、中、后位置上，而中文的说话人位置一般要放在引语前）；另一方面，翻译直接引语时要"忠于原文，保持说话人的原意和风格，在行文方面力求符合中文的表达习惯"[27]。下面是一篇有关加拿大欲退出《京都议定书》的消息报道。

---

27 朱伊革. 2008. 英语新闻的语言特点和翻译. 上海：上海交通大学出版社.

例 21

Canada to Pull out of Kyoto Protocol[28]	加拿大宣布将正式退出《京都议定书》
Canada will pull out of the Kyoto protocol on climate change, Environment Minister Peter Kent said on Monday, dealing a symbolic blow to the troubled global treaty. Canada will become the first country to formally withdraw from Kyoto, which it says is badly flawed because it does not cover all major emitters of greenhouse gasses. The news came as little surprise, especially since Kent said last month that "Kyoto is the past." The right-of-center Conservatives took power in 2006 and made it clear they would not stick to Canada's Kyoto commitments. "As we've said, Kyoto for Canada is in the past ... We are invoking our legal right to formally withdraw from Kyoto," Kent told reporters after returning from talks in Durban, South Africa, on extending the protocol. He gave no details on when exactly Ottawa would pull out, but said Canada would be subject to enormous financial penalties under the terms of the treaty unless it withdrew. The announcement will do little to help Canada's growing reputation as an international renegade on the climate. Green groups awarded the country their Fossil of the Year award for its performance in Durban. Ottawa says it backs a new global deal to cut emissions of greenhouse gases, but insists it has to cover all nations. Canada's former Liberal government signed onto Kyoto, which obliged the country to cut emissions to 6 percent below 1990 levels by 2012. By 2009 emissions were 17 percent above the 1990 levels. Kent says the Liberals should not have signed up to a treaty they had no intention of respecting. Environmentalists quickly blasted Kent for his comments. "Mr. Kent does not understand what he is sentencing our children to. Catastrophic climate change will cost them far more," said John Bennett, executive director of the Sierra Club Canada.	加拿大环境部长彼得·肯特本周一宣布，加拿大将退出有关气候变化的《京都议定书》，这对目前麻烦不断的这一全球条约来说无疑是沉重打击。 加拿大将成为首个正式退出《京都议定书》的国家，并称该条约有严重漏洞，并未覆盖全部的温室气体排放大国。 加拿大的退出在人们的预料之中，特别是自上月肯特说出"《京都议定书》对加拿大而言已经成为过去"之后。中间偏右的加拿大保守党自2006年上台后，明确表态不会遵守加拿大对于《京都议定书》所做的承诺。 肯特从南非德班的气候会议返回后告诉记者："《京都议定书》对加拿大而言已经成为过去，我们将行使我们的合法权利正式退出。"南非德班气候会议旨在延长《京都议定书》的承诺期。 肯特没有给出加拿大退出的准确时间，但表示如果不退出，按照目前的协议条款，加拿大将面临巨额罚款。 加拿大在气候保护方面的"国际叛徒"的名气越来越大，而肯特的表态更恶化了这一形象。由于在德班的表现，加拿大还获环保组织评选的"年度顽固不化奖"。 加拿大表示支持新的温室气体减排条约，但坚称这一条约必须覆盖全部国家。 此前，加拿大自由党政府签署加入《京都议定书》，承诺截至2012年，在1990年的基础上减排6%。但截至2009年，加拿大的温室气体排放仍然比1990年高出17%。 肯特表示，自由党本就不该签署一份自己都不重视的条约。 环保人士迅速对肯特的评论予以抨击。 加拿大塞拉俱乐部的常务董事约翰·本奈特说："肯特先生不明白他给我们的孩子宣判了什么。灾难性的气候变化会让他们付出更惨重的代价。"

这是一篇典型的英文消息报道。首先，语篇结构呈现"倒金字塔"式的结构。先是直

---

28 此例引自 *Reuters*，中文翻译引自中国日报网，2011-12-13。

接给出加拿大将退出《京都议定书》的消息，接着谈及退出的原因，然后指出加拿大的退出并不出人意料，最后提及加拿大在减排方面的负面形象以及相关人士的评价。这种"倒金字塔"结构在中文消息报道中也广为采用，因此，译文保留了原文的结构模式。

其次，原文中出现了许多直接引语和间接引语，这是新闻文体的重要特点之一，显示了新闻的客观性、真实性。翻译这部分内容时，要考虑三个方面：第一，发话者的位置调整。英语新闻的发话者置于句末，这正好与汉语的行文习惯相反，翻译时需要进行处理。第二，内容的处理。对于直接引语，不能断章取义，更不能歪解误译，要保持话语的完整性，一定要加上引号，保持新闻报道的客观性和完整性。第三，发话者的"说"的表达。在英语里，"说"有许多表达形式，常见的有50多个，为了保持报道的客观性，一般以中性的"say"居多，但有时也会出现一些带有强烈感情色彩的"说"，翻译时要注意理解。

最后，原报道句子较长，但结构较简单，多为扩展式的简单句。分词短语、定语从句、介词短语等成分的使用加大了信息量。翻译时，译者根据它们之间的语义关系和逻辑关系，进行了灵活的整合。对于关系密切的定语从句、同位语处理成了前置定语，对于不够密切的非限制性定语从句，则分成两句话处理。

2. 编译和摘译处理

中英新闻消息在内容处理和结构安排上不尽相同，翻译时，应以目的语受众的阅读习惯为准绳，对原文进行结构和信息上的整合，不必逐字逐句翻译。因此，译者常使用编译和摘译的方式。编译是编写和翻译的有机结合，在操作时，译者应首先压缩全文，择其精华，弃之繁琐。编译者可以使用原文的原句，也可以根据消息的内容提炼观点，可以重组段落，但不可以随意打破原文的篇章结构，更不可以发表个人的看法。[29] 编译对译者的要求很高，既需要新闻专业知识，又需要语言的整理能力。摘译则不同。摘译时，译者会摘取一些自己认为重要的新闻段落或内容作为翻译对象进行翻译，一旦抽取之后则必须完整地将其翻译出来。下面是新闻报道编译的例子：

例22

习近平会见北戴河暑期休假专家[30]	Chinese VP Greets Experts, Grassroots Talents
本报北戴河8月5日电（记者杜榕）<u>中共中央政治局常委、中央书记处书记、国家副主席习近平5日在北戴河会见了在</u>这里参加暑期休假活动的优秀专家和基层一线人才，<u>向全国各条战线各个领域的专家和广大基层一线人才表示诚挚问候和崇高敬意</u>，勉励大家为党和国家事业作出新的更大贡献，以优异成绩迎接党的十八大胜利召开。	BEIDAIHE, Hebei, Aug. 5 (Xinhua)—Chinese Vice President Xi Jinping on Sunday greeted a group of renowned experts and grassroots talents and encouraged them to contribute more to the country's development.

---

[29] 吴波、朱健平. 2011. 新闻翻译：理论与实践. 杭州：浙江大学出版社.
[30] 此例引自人民网，英文翻译引自新华网英文版，2012-08-06.

| 党中央、国务院对各领域高级专家和专门人才十分关心。暑期邀请专家到北戴河休假，是中央关心、联系和服务人才的一项重要制度性安排。2001年以来，已分10批次共邀请600多名专家携家属休假。为体现对广大一线基层人才的关心爱护，党中央、国务院专门邀请62位长期工作在教学、科研和生产一线，特别是长年扎根在艰苦边远地区、边疆民族地区和革命老区的优秀专家和人才代表参加。休假专家中，有勇攀科技高峰、做出突出贡献的两院院士，有为祖国铸利器、保和平的国防科技专家，有潜心研究、著述等身的社科专家，有辛勤耕耘、桃李满天下的教学名家，有德艺双馨、为群众喜爱的文艺名家，有刻苦钻研、技术精湛的知识型人才，有自学成才、革新多项工艺的农民发明家，有无私奉献、感动中国的最美乡村教师和最美边疆医生，有"上九天揽月"归来的"神舟"航天员，他们是全国各地各行业各领域广大基层一线人才的优秀代表。 中共中央政治局委员、国务委员刘延东，中共中央政治局委员、中央书记处书记、中央组织部部长李源潮，国务委员兼国务院秘书长马凯，以及中央组织部、人力资源和社会保障部负责同志参加会见。 会见活动结束后，中央组织部听取专家意见。专家们结合自身成长成才经历，围绕加强基层一线人才队伍建设、造就创新创业人才、优化人才发展环境、重视青年拔尖人才培养、加大对西部地区和边疆民族地区人才工作支持力度等方面提出了意见建议。专家们感谢党中央、国务院对基层一线人才的重视和关怀，表示将始终把祖国和人民放在心中，把个人理想与国家发展、事业追求与人民需要、人生价值与社会进步融为一体，扎根一线、不懈奋斗，为推动科学发展、促进社会和谐，作出自己应有的贡献。 | Those experts and talents were invited by the central authority to a routine high-profile holiday program in Beidaihe, a popular northern seaside resort close to the Chinese capital, as a form of recognition and reward for their works. Since 2001, over 600 experts and their family members had been invited under the program to gesture country's resolution in talent cultivation. Among the 62 invited this year, there are leading scientists in defense technology, renowned educators, artists, workers, village teachers, rural medical staff and astronauts. A seminar was also held Sunday for the experts to give suggestions to the country's human resources programs. |

以上是习近平会见北戴河暑期休假专家的报道。仔细对比中英报道可以看出，译者对原文进行了编译处理，译文中删去了大量与新闻核心事件关系不大的内容或套话等，短小精悍，不拖泥带水。整体上看，译文内容严格按照信息价值编排，属于"倒金字塔"式的结构，符合英语消息的篇章结构特点。鉴于中文报道很重视党和国家领导人的身份、职衔，而这些信息英文读者可能不太感兴趣，译文对此也进行了删减，只选择保留了最重要的职衔。译文平铺直叙，句式以简单句为主，简练地道，措辞明快，客观真实，符合英文消息的语言特色。虽然译文在形式上与原文有别，但反映的信息与原文基本一致，可读性很强，做到了中心突出、层次分明，整体上收到了意义相符、功能相似的效果。

3. 模糊语的处理

模糊性是语言的基本属性之一。模糊性是由客观事物的多样性、复杂性和不确定性以及人们认识的局限性决定的。模糊语在新闻文体里有着重要的作用。模糊语具有生动、含蓄、凝练、灵活等特点，运用得当，可以使新闻语言更加形象、简洁，概括力强，不但不会影响到新闻报道的准确性，反而会增强报道的可信度和可读性。一般来说，语言愈凝练，模糊性就愈强。反映在消息报道里，标题的模糊性最强，导语次之，正文最弱。[31] 中英语言中都有类似的模糊语，但也存在不对应的部分。因此，在对模糊语进行翻译时，我们应根据实际情况，作灵活处理。处理的方法基本上有两种：模糊对模糊，精确对模糊。例如：

例23 The new rules have drawn protests from some women's rights groups, arguing the government has stepped beyond its mark.[32]

新的规定已经引起了一些妇女权益组织的抗议，她们争辩道，当局已"出格"了。

此例中，beyond the mark 系英语成语，含义是"超出界限、过度、过分"。但在此译中可以套用"出格"二字。言简意赅，模糊中透出了精确。

4. 语态的处理

英汉新闻语言语态不同。总体上看，主动语态在新闻文体中占据主导地位，远多于被动语态。这是因为主动语态表意更加自然、直接、生动，富有感染力，符合人们的亲身体验，易为人们接受。但是，主动语态的主导地位是相对而言的。实际上，被动语态也广泛存在于新闻文体中。被动语态可以突出新闻事件的结果，容易抓住读者的兴趣，使行文更加凝练客观。被动语态常用于一些灾难、犯罪的新闻报道中，有主动语态无法比拟的优势。但汉语受语法系统的影响，主动语态的使用更见优势，甚至一些明显的被动句也要处理为不带"被"字但含被动意义的主动句。因此，在英译汉时要灵活处理主动被动的关系，除非要强调动作的受动者或结果，一般还是以主动形式为好。例如：

例24 Hundreds of people involved in the rioting that swept through London and other English cities were processed swiftly through the courts, though concerns were raised that some of the sentences were too harsh and would not have been handed down for similar offences committed outside the riots. Senior police officers continued to bristle at government criticism that they reacted poorly to the disorder.[33]

法庭对成百上千参与了伦敦及其他城市骚乱的人进行了迅速审判，尽管有人担心有些判决过重且对骚乱外的类似罪行的量刑不具参考价值。高级警局官员对政府关于其骚乱处理不力的批评表示愤怒。

---

31 陈明瑶、卢彩虹. 2006. 新闻文体语体与翻译研究. 北京：国防工业出版社.
32 此例引自毛荣贵、范武邱. 2005. 语言模糊性与翻译. 上海翻译，（1）：11–15.
33 此例引自《经济学人》中英文对照版, 2011-08-20.

原文有两句话，被动态共出现了 3 次，全部集中在第一句。如果将它们都译成汉语被动式，一方面难以进行信息整合，另一方面会让译文读者觉得行文佶屈聱牙、难以理解，所以不如处理为主动态，更符合人们熟悉的认知经验，通顺自然，易于理解。

五、新闻特写的翻译

（一）新闻特写概述

新闻特写是新闻体裁的三大支柱之一，包括的范围很广，凡不属于硬新闻（hard news）范畴的稿件都可称为特写。特写不注重时效性，采写对象往往是一些富有典型意义的事件或人物，通过撷取其中某个最能反映其特点或本质的片段、剖面或细节，运用文学笔法放大、渲染，从而更集中地表现主题。正因如此，特写往往具有强烈的感染力。特写的分类多种多样，粗略地讲，可分为人物特写和事件特写。

新闻特写与文学作品相类似，但二者本质不同。特写必须遵守新闻真实性原则，须如实描绘真人真事，细节也必须是真实的，像新闻摄影一样再现现场真实情景，捕捉典型瞬间的生动形象，使作品具有强烈的现场感。因此，在写作上要求集中、突出，忌面面俱到。

特写与消息的不同之处在于二者报道的目的、范围和写作手法不同。消息告诉读者发生了什么事情。为了把新闻事件交代清楚，消息往往需要给出新闻的各个要素，给读者展现一幅粗略的全景图。特写比消息读来更细腻，提供的信息更详尽，给读者展现的则是一幅极尽色彩和画意的近景图。消息注重事件报道的时效性和经济性，写作时往往平铺直叙，不加主观判断，语言简洁精练，谋篇常采用"倒金字塔"结构；而特写结构不拘一格，表现手法灵活多样，语言生动形象，富有感染力，在篇幅上可长可短。

（二）新闻特写翻译

1. 新闻特写开场白的翻译

尽管中英新闻特写在篇章结构上一般没有特定的格式可循，但成功的特写开篇，即导语或引语（prelude），往往是最有魅力、最吸引人的地方，要么进行提纲挈领式的概括，要么突出一个事实要点，要么描写一个生动情节，要么进行一段情感抒发，然后在此基础上引导读者追源问后。翻译时，要尽量做到意义相符，功能相似。例如：

例25 The two warring images will be linked forever, each denying—and completing—the other: Christopher Reeve, built and beautiful in his superman suit, roaring invincibly into the stratosphere. And Christopher Reeve, strained and drawn, hooked to a ventilator and living another motionless day in his wheel chair. The cartoon hero had suffered a horrible fall and emerged as a real-life hero.[34]

两个相互抵触的形象将永远地联系在一起：互相否定又互相补充。一个克里斯

34　此例引自 http://www.for68.com/new/2006/4/su691922643101460022794-0.html。

多夫·里夫,在超人电影里英俊、刚健,总是以胜利者的姿态冲入云霄;另一个克里斯多夫·里夫,身体僵硬、面部走形,带着呼吸器,日复一日地坐在轮椅上一动不动。太多的不幸降临在这位卡通般的英雄身上,但最终使他历练成一位真正的英雄。

原文是《华盛顿邮报》2004 年对"超人"里夫所作的人物特写的开场白。作者采用了概括对比的手法,通过对里夫电影内外"超人""残疾人"典型形象的描写,一个历经辉煌又饱受磨难的英雄形象跃然纸上,让人印象深刻,暗生佩服,急于往下细读。译文措辞精练,再现了两种典型的截然不同的里夫形象,具有很强的感染力。一次"摔落"并不能塑造出英雄,只有"艰难困苦,玉汝乃成",因此,译文中译者并没有直译 had suffered a horrible fall and emerged as a real-life hero,而是采取了意译的方式进行处理,效果很好,易于读者理解。

2. 新闻特写全译和编译

特写是新闻消息的继续,主要从新闻事件中一个富含典型意义的角度进行深挖,以便给读者提供详尽的背景信息,因此特写往往翔实和深入。译者必须在遵守"忠实""通顺"的原则上尽可能地传达信息,在翻译时一般采用全译的手法。不过有时候,由于语言表达习惯不同,有些信息过于累赘,因此,译者有一定的创作空间,可适当进行编译。同时,由于特写往往是叙述描写并重,语言细腻生动,形象优美,具有很强的感染力,特写翻译应尽量再现原文的语言风格。例如:

例 26

72 岁老农自学拿下法律本科[35]	**Farmer, 72, Gains Degrees Through Self-study**
72 岁,可以儿孙绕膝地享天伦之乐;可以没事在院子里晒晒太阳;可以读读报纸看看闲书……然而,却有这样一位已经 72 岁的老大爷,于今年获得了高自考的毕业证。这位大爷名叫齐洪珍,是天津武清区南蔡村镇田辛庄的农民。只上过 3 年小学的齐大爷从 1997 年参加高自考,拿下汉语言文学的专科学历后,经过 4 年苦读,今年又拿下了法律的本科学历。记者昨日走近了这位普通而又传奇的老人。 **动机:从未放弃大学梦** 说到自己的求学之路,齐大爷告诉记者,他只上过 3 年小学,也就是"初小"文化水平,但从来没有放弃过上大学的梦想。因为在农村生活,齐大爷年轻时要下地干活,挣钱养家,读书这个梦想也就一直没能实现。等到孩子们都独立成家了,齐大爷肩上的担子终于放了下来,他这才又重新拾起了课本开始读书。	Qi Hongzhen, a 72-year-old farmer from Tianjin is not spending his golden years enjoying the sunshine in his yard, reading newspapers or visiting with his friends, all in their 70s. Instead, the farmer, who only has three years of primary school education, has absorbed himself with law-related books and is preparing to take the national judicial examination on September 16 this year, the Tianjin-based *City Express* reported on August 24.

---

35 此例引自搜狐新闻,英文版引自 *China Daily*,2006-08-24.

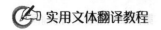

转向：为帮乡亲弃文从法 齐大爷最初选择的专业是汉语言文学，他2001年念完了所有的课程，并拿到了汉语言文学专业专科的毕业证书。拿到了梦寐以求的毕业证书，齐大爷却没有轻松起来，他发现，汉语言文学在现实生活中，特别是在农村中并没有特别实用的价值。 思考了几天，齐大爷决定重读一门新专业——法律。"我看到很多农村人因为不懂法律而犯法的事情，所以就想学法律，这也能帮助乡亲们多懂点法律。" 就这样，经过4年学习，齐大爷自学了22门课程，于今年7月24日拿到了法律专业本科的毕业证书。齐大爷骄傲地说，虽然他们这个村只有一百户左右的人家，但乡亲们遇到什么法律上的疑问总是来咨询他，他特别有成就感。 **秘诀："干活"听"笔记两不误** 记者问他有没有学习"秘诀"，对此齐大爷笑着说，他并没有感觉到学习有多辛苦，在学习的过程中，他也确实自创了一些适合自己的学习方法。齐大爷告诉记者，每天他趁着早晚凉快的时候去地里干一两个小时的农活，然后就在家看书学习。 "我不像孩子们还有教室和自习室，家里人要吃饭、看电视，乡亲们也要来聊天串门，这些打扰总是避免不了的，所以我就特别喜欢晚上看书。"由于年纪大，眼睛看书时间长了比较累，齐大爷就自创了"录音笔记"学习法，就是把笔记本上的内容录到录音机里，这样可以边下地干活边听录音，充分利用了闲散时间和劳动时间。 **目标：准备参加司法考试** 拿到法律本科毕业证书后，齐大爷又有了新目标。目前，他正在为今年9月16日的司法考试做准备。齐大爷说，由于年龄原因，他报名时还遇到了一些麻烦。原来，齐大爷让自己的孩子为他在网上报名，然而国家对于考生年龄虽然不设限制，但报名软件却把年龄上限设定在1935年出生，即1935年之前出生的人会因为软件原因无法正常报名。为此，齐大爷为了报名的问题就来回折腾了很多次。后来，在天津司法考试中心一个老师的帮助下，他终于报上了名。	Qi has obtained a diploma in Chinese Language and Culture after he took the examination in 1997 and gained a law degree in 2006 following four years of study. "I have never given up my determination to pursue a university," Qi says, adding that he loved studying when he was a child. According to the paper, he had to quit school to work and make a living for his family. After his children grew up, he was able to concentrate on books. But Qi found his diploma in Chinese Language and Culture was not applicable in the countryside. "I find lots of locals in the countryside commit crimes due to a lack of legal knowledge so I focused on law," the farmer told the paper. Qi has finished 22 lessons so far, the paper says. There are only some 100 households in the village and he feels a sense of pride when villagers turned to him for legal consultation. The elderly man told the paper that he doesn't feel tired when studying, and hits the books until one or two in the morning, after his farm work is finished. "I don't have a room to study in, so I've learned to study at night when there are no distractions from my family or visitors," says Qi. "I record the contents of my notebook in a recorder and listen to it when I work, in order to make full use of free and working time." But examinations have never been smooth for him. When he applied to take the national judicial examination, he faced some problems, according to the paper. "Although there is not an age limit on the application, the application software puts a limit on applicants who were born before 1935, like me. With the help of a staff member at the Tianjin Judicial Examination Center, I succeeded applying to take the exam," says Qi. "No pain, no gain."

续表

说到这次报名风波，齐大爷幽默地说："好事多磨，所以我更应该好好学习。虽然我年龄、精力不占优势，但也要努力。"齐大爷告诉记者，司法考试是一门非常严格、录取比例很低的资格考试，录取比例一般只是7%左右。"虽然今年不一定会通过这次司法考试，但我不会放弃，我会一直努力。"	"I may fail the exam this year, but I won't give up," Qi says. According to the paper, less than one in ten applicants are likely to pass the exam.

在这篇中文特写中，记者分别从四个角度即动机、转向、秘诀和目标成功地塑造了齐大爷晚年勤奋学习、为人豁达幽默、乐于助人的形象。翻译时，译者对原文本进行了编译。首先，从结构上看，原文分为四大块，即四个角度来写；翻译时，译者并未改变顺序，只是对较长的段落进行了拆分、缩减。比如，中文特写第一段导语部分，在译文中被拆分成三个小段处理，即生活状况、学习情况和学习成就。在四大块的内部结构处理上，除第三块（"秘诀"）之外，译者也进行了拆分、删减。其次，从内容上看，中文特写比较详细繁琐，在翻译时，译者进行了简化、省略甚至改写。比如主人公年轻时没读书的具体原因、拿到汉语言文学文凭时的情况等被简化，但主要信息则被保留。再次，引语得到了有效处理。中文特写中的一些间接引语转换成了直接引语，一些直接引语得到精简。这一点体现出在翻译特写时译者具有一定的创作空间，转换后的形式更加符合目的语的表达习惯，有助于主人公的形象塑造，满足了读者的阅读心理需要。最后，从整体上看，译文结构逻辑性强，语言精练形象，满足了特写翻译对于"忠实""通顺"的要求。

六、新闻评论的翻译

新闻评论是新闻机构对新近发生的新闻事件所发表的言论的总称，集新闻性与政论性于一身，以传播意见性信息为主要目的，属于论说文的范畴。新闻评论往往立意新颖独特，逻辑严密合理，论述精当透彻，文字庄重典雅，让人过目难忘。新闻评论分类很多，大致可分为社论（editorials）、述评（commentaries）和专栏（columns），其中社论属于最重要的评论文章，代表编辑部就某一重大问题发表的权威性评论，被认为是编辑部的"灵魂"所在。新闻评论一般由引论、论证和结论三部分组成。引论一般以"开门见山"居多，直接进入正题，尽快引起读者兴趣；论证指的是摆事实、讲道理，证明引论的观点，以说服读者；结论即结尾，往往起到画龙点睛、突出论点、呼应主题和引人深思的作用。以下是来自《金融时报》中文网的一篇社论：

例27

| **Faster, Fatter**[36] | 奥运新精神——更快，更胖？ |

The International Olympic Committee admits that it had qualms about naming high-calorie, fast-food brands such as McDonald's and Coca-Cola official sponsors to the games. They and others have rightly asked how Big Macs promote the values expressed by the official motto—citius, altius, fortius, or faster, higher, stronger. But banning these brands from sponsorship, as some critics want, is not the answer.

Obesity is a growing problem around the world. In Britain—host to the 2012 games—almost two-thirds of adults and one-third of children are overweight. The ubiquitous offer of fast food—with its addictive combination of fat, sugar and salt—is contributing to our growing girth.

But, like most things in life, there is nothing wrong with chips and fizzy drinks in moderation. The blame lies instead in popular ignorance of good eating habits, while high prices can put healthier foods beyond the reach of some families. These are challenges that are best addressed by comprehensive government programmes to educate children from an early age and support hard-pressed families.

Yet, while it is not the IOC's responsibility to solve the problem of global obesity, it could do more to contribute to the battle of the bulge. It should start by being far more demanding of its sponsors in all sectors. Competition is fierce among global brands to win the right to sport the Olympic rings on product advertising. The committee should set higher hurdles for sponsors to demonstrate concrete commitment to behaviour underpinning Olympic values. This could apply as much to Rio Tinto on the environment as Coca-Cola on healthier lifestyles. Real people and real projects should be the foundation of any sponsorship bid.

For the high-calorie brands, the committee could also consider requiring ads using the Olympic logo to carry a health warning—much as for cigarettes—about the dangers of a regular diet of fast food. Finally the criteria on which all sponsors are chosen should be published. Public scrutiny is the best guarantee that money alone will not be the deciding factor.

国际奥委会承认曾对给予麦当劳、可口可乐等高热量快餐品牌奥运会官方赞助商资格有过犹豫。和其他人一样，这个委员会提出了一个应该提出的问题：如何使快餐巨无霸们弘扬奥运会更快、更高、更强的精神呢？但国际奥委会并没有如一些批评者所希望的那样，禁止这些品牌成为奥运会赞助商。

在世界各地，肥胖问题日趋严重。在2012年奥运会的东道主——英国，近三分之二的成年人和三分之一的儿童体重过高。快餐食品随处可见，以其高脂、高糖、重盐的配方令人欲罢不能，为我们日益增长的腰围做了不少贡献。

但薯条和碳酸饮料，和生活中大多数东西一样，只要吃得适量，就不会是大问题。导致问题的真正原因，是人们缺乏好的饮食习惯，而健康食品高昂的价格可能让一些家庭承受不了。要解决这些难题，最好是由政府推出综合计划，一方面从小培养孩子们良好的饮食习惯，一方面资助困难家庭。

然而，尽管解决全球肥胖问题并非国际奥委会的责任，但它还是可以为抗击肥胖做更多事情。国际奥委会应该从一个方面着手：大大提高对所有领域赞助商的要求。全球各大品牌都希望能在自己的产品广告中炫耀奥林匹克的五环标志，竞争十分激烈。奥委会应该设定更高门槛，要求赞助商拿出实际行动，体现奥林匹克精神。按照这个思路，奥委会可以要求巴西力拓公司在环境方面做得更好，也可以要求可口可乐积极推广更健康的生活方式。企业参加奥运赞助商竞标时，竞标的基础应该以人为本，拿出真正的实际行动。

对这些快餐巨无霸们而言，国际奥委会还可以考虑一点，那是要求他们在广告中使用奥运五环标志时加上健康警告（类似香烟广告），以提醒消费者注意经常食用快餐的种种危害。最后，奥委会应公开它选择赞助商的标准。公众的监督是保证金钱不成为决定因素的最好方法。

---

36 此例引自选自金融时报中文网，2012-07-10.

It may be that such tough conditions leave the IOC with a smaller pool of potential funders. The cost of the games has grown exponentially, even though the number of athletes has not changed much in a decade. This raises the question of whether too much money is being spent in increasingly inefficient ways. Bigger is not always better. Sometimes it can even be damaging to your health.	这样严格的要求可能会让国际奥委会只剩下较少的潜在赞助商。尽管奥运会参赛运动员数量过去十年来基本没变，但奥运会的举办费用一直呈指数增长。这让人们不禁要问：是不是有越来越多的资金由于低效而被浪费了？更大并不总意味着更好。有时候，更大甚至有损健康。

原文围绕奥运如何在控制肥胖问题上发挥积极作用展开评论。该评论主要由引论、论证和结论三部分组成。文章一开始就提出了问题所在，即奥委会的担忧——如何让快餐巨头们在弘扬奥运精神上有所建树。在接下来的几段，作者步步论证，层层深入，首先剖析了问题的症结所在——快餐店的高脂、高糖、高盐配方固然是体重增加的原因，但缺乏良好的饮食习惯才是真正的罪魁祸首。然后作者笔锋一转，指出政府固然对此问题是义不容辞、责无旁贷，但奥委会可以而且也应该在此问题上有所作为。比如，奥委会可以提高对赞助商的要求，可以在赞助商使用五环标志时加上健康警告提醒消费者，可以采用标准公开、舆论监督等措施。最后得出结论，画龙点睛，即"更大并不总意味着更好。有时候，更大甚至有损健康"，回应了主题，言已尽而意未绝，引人深思。整体上看，该评论立意新颖，引人思考，论证有理有据，让人信服，并且措辞上精练准确，富有哲理，不失为一篇典型的西方评论文。

新闻评论是以发表议论、阐明事理为主的文章，运用逻辑思维去说服读者。与消息报道和特写相比，新闻评论有自身的语体风格。一般说来，评论的语言正式典雅，语气严肃，语法结构繁琐，长难句较多。因此，在翻译时，译者应使译文在风格上尽量靠近原文。评论文章在篇幅上可长可短，短篇评论可以全译，而对篇幅很长的评论一般采用编译或摘译的翻译方法。

新闻作为一种正式语篇，承载着源语社会主流的意识形态，其重要特点之一就是具有一定的政治倾向性。[37] 在新闻三大体裁中，政治色彩的浓厚程度是不相同的，从整体上看，特写最淡，其次是消息，最浓烈的属新闻评论。因此，在翻译带有政治倾向性的关键词语时，译者要有高度责任感，政治立场坚定，坚决拥护党和国家的方针政策。在翻译策略上，译者可进行增删译或者改译，使之服务于社会的主流意识形态。比如，中国的"对外开放政策"，现在通常的译法为 the policy of opening to the outside world、the open policy 或者 the open-up policy，但是有的西方新闻媒体却使用 the open door policy。单从语义角度看，这些表达似乎差别不大，但 the open door policy 带有强烈的意识形态

---

[37] 陈宏薇、李亚丹. 2010. 新编汉英翻译教程. 上海：上海外语教育出版社.

色彩。在西方，这种说法特指鸦片战争后美国为了同欧洲列强争夺在中国的殖民利益而提出的臭名昭著的"门户开放政策"，有着强烈的负面意义，因此，翻译时要格外小心，不能随便望文生义。

对于属于我国领土的一些地名翻译，必须使用我国统一的标准译法，同时也要了解国际译名，以免阅读时误解。这就需要译者平时关心时事，多阅读，多积累，碰到问题多咨询多查阅。比如黄岩岛，为我国固有领土，我们将其翻译为 Huangyan Islands。还有西沙群岛、南沙群岛，统一译法为 Xisha Islands、Nansha Islands。

对于一些专属我们民族文化的"特产"，在翻译时应该坚持自己的特色，否则，"过多地依赖于简单类比的方式，只是将对方语言中类似的名称加上一个定语，则往往造成文化含义的缺位或意义传达的失真，坚持把自己的文化'特产'去附会外国的产品，无异于自我贬低，甚至毁坏自己的艺术"[38]。随着时代的发展，新的事物、新的表达会不断涌现，有些"国家关键话语"的对外表达，就显得十分重要。比如胡锦涛同志提出的"不折腾"，当代中国外交战略的"韬光养晦"，中国科技发展中的"自主创新"等。如何翻译这些"关键话语"，能够既让世界明白易懂，又能体现出中国特色，这是摆在所有新闻翻译者面前的重大课题。

七、结语

新闻英语作为英语的一种变体，具有自身独有的文体特征。本章在分析新闻文体词汇、语法、语篇特点的基础上，从标题、导语以及新闻语篇等角度对新闻翻译进行了探讨，总结出了一些规律性的内容。但是，在具体的实践中，由于中英语言系统的差异，加之新闻体裁灵活多样，内容包罗万象，翻译过程中总是充满了挑战和困难，有时译者甚至会发出"一名之立，旬月踯躅"的感慨，但这也凸显新闻翻译工作的必要性和重要性。作为译者，应该勤于学习，善于思考，广为涉猎，多加积累，不断提高自身的语言功底和学识素养，扎实掌握新闻翻译的标准、方法和技巧，发挥自身在新闻传播过程中的桥梁作用。建议大家平时多多关注以下网站，从点滴积累，方能制胜。

1. 世界主要通讯社

AP: Associated Press	美联社（美国）
AFP: Agence France Presse	法新社（法国）
Reuters: Reuters News Agency	路透社（英国）
DPA: Deutsche Presse-Agentur	德新社（德国）

---

37 赵启正. 2011. 公共外交与跨文化交流. 北京：中国人民大学出版社.

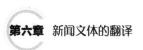

UPI: United Press International　　　合众国际社（美国）
KYODO: Kyodo News Agency　　　共同社（日本）
TASS: Telegraph Agency of the Soviet Union　　　塔斯社（俄罗斯）
CNS: China News Service　　　中国新闻社（中国）
PTI: Press Trust of India　　　印报社（印度）
Xinhua News Agency　　　新华通讯社（中国）
Yonhap News Agency　　　联合通讯社（韩国）

2. 英美国家部分主要报刊名称及网址

英文名称	中文名称	网址
New York Times	《纽约时报》	www.newyorktimes.com
USA Today	《今日美国》	www.usatoday.com
Washington Post	《华盛顿邮报》	www.washingtonpost.com
Time	《时代周刊》	www.time.com
The Times	《泰晤士报》	www.timesonline.co.uk
Guardian	《卫报》	www.guardian.co.uk
Daily Telegraph	《每日电讯报》	www.telegraph.co.uk
The Sun	《太阳报》	www.thesun.co.uk
The Wall Street Journal	《华尔街日报》	www.online.wsj.com
The Economist	《经济学人》	www.economist.com
International Herald Tribune	《国际先驱论坛报》	www.iht.com
The Christian Science Monitor	《基督教科学箴言报》	www.csmonitor.com

练习六

一、将下面的新闻消息译成中文。

Obama Spares Many Young Illegal Immigrants Deportation

About 800,000 young illegal immigrants who came to the United States as children could be spared deportation for at least two years under new rules announced on Friday by President Barack Obama that may appeal to Hispanic voters in an election year.

"This is not amnesty. This is not immunity. This is not a path to citizenship. It is not a permanent fix," Obama told reporters at the White House, adding that a permanent U.S. immigration policy solution would have to come from Congress.

The move comes as Obama, a Democrat, is courting the nation's fast-growing Hispanic population while trying to win re-election on November 6 against Republican Mitt Romney, who has taken a harsh stand against illegal immigration. Most U.S. illegal immigrants are Hispanics.

Under Obama's plan, those who qualify would be allowed to live and work in the United States for two years and could be eligible for extensions, the Obama administration said.

Obama has long supported measures to allow the children of illegal immigrants to study and work in the United States, but efforts to pass such measures in Congress have failed amid objections by Republicans.

The president's action sidestepped Congress and laid down a challenge to Republicans, many of whom view leniency on deportations as amounting to amnesty for illegal immigrants at a time when there are an estimated 12 million such people in the United States.

Republican lawmakers attacked the president's move, accusing Obama of encroaching into Congress' authority to set laws governing U.S. citizenship.

But Obama said, "This is a temporary stop-gap measure that lets us focus our resources wisely while giving a degree of relief and hope to talented, driven, patriotic young people."

Many of these illegal residents have lived most of their lives in the United States, attending American elementary and secondary schools. "They are Americans in their hearts and minds; in every single way but one—on paper," Obama said.

While campaigning in New Hampshire, Romney said, "The president's actions make reaching a long-term solution more difficult."

There are up to 2 million illegal immigrants who came to the United States as children and who remain in the country, according to immigration group estimates. U.S. officials said the new measures would affect roughly 800,000 people.

二、对下面两例新闻进行编译。

1. 汉译英

瓦杰帕伊结束访华回国　与中国多位领导人会晤

印度总理阿塔尔·比哈里·瓦杰帕伊（Atal Bihari Vajpayee）结束了对中国为期6天的正式访问，于27日下午乘专机离沪回国。

这是印度总理10年来首次访问中国。中国多位领导人与瓦杰帕伊在北京举行会晤、会谈，就双边关系和共同关心的地区及国际问题广泛交换意见。双方签署了《中华人民共和国和印度共和国关系原则和全面合作的宣言》等11个合作文件，加强了两国在各个领域的交流和合作。瓦杰帕伊于22日抵达北京。在京期间，他到北京大学和两国企业界人士举办的经济合作和发展研讨会上发表了演讲。

中印双方高度评价此次访问取得的成果。双方一致认为，访问增进了两国政府、两国领导人和两国人民之间的相互理解和信任，标志着中印双方为在新世纪加强全面合作迈出了新的步伐。

2. 英译汉

Singapore Says Disturbed by Double Standards of U.S. Human Rights Report

SINGAPORE, August 16 (Xinhua)—Singapore's Ministry of Foreign Affairs (MFA) on Thursday slammed the U.S. State Department's "Human Rights Practices 2011," saying that the report "again includes the same gross inaccuracies and misrepresentations of the Singapore government's policies."

"We are disturbed by the double standards applied to the U.S.' criticism of our Internal Security Act (ISA)," the ministry said in a statement.

The Internal Security Act, which has been in place in Singapore over the past decades, is meant to address threats to internal security, including threats to public order, communal and religious harmony, and subversive and terrorist activities, it said, hitting back on the criticism contained in the report.

The U.S. report alleged that Singapore used the controversial Internal Security Act, which allows preventive detention without trial under certain circumstances, against "alleged terrorists" in recent years. It also cited caning as a punishment for some crimes in Singapore as one of the "problems".

Singapore said it failed to understand how the United States reconciles its criticism of the act with the continued existence of U.S. detention facilities at Guantanamo.

"By contrast to the Guantanamo detention facilities, which exist outside the framework of U.S. law, the ISA provides a proper legal framework, and prescribes rules, for preventive detention," the statement said.

Singapore also reacted angrily to the annual U.S. human rights report last year, which it said contained the same misrepresentations and inaccuracies year after year.

"This seems to suggest that the U.S. Department of State is really not interested in the facts, and indeed does not want the facts to come in the way of the conclusions it wishes to reach, pursuant to its own ideology. This approach undermines the objectivity of the report," the Ministry of Foreign Affairs said.

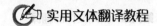

"Singapore does not claim that our system is perfect, or that our system would necessarily work in other countries. Our government is held accountable to the public through democratic elections and the rule of law," it said. "We will adapt our policies in the interests of our people and as the balance of rights and obligations evolve in our society."

第七章
广告文体的翻译

在全球一体化的进程中，不同经济和文化的交流日益密切，广告作为一种传递商品和劳务等信息、开拓国际市场、扩大市场份额的有效工具，显得尤其重要。[1] 无论是海外的商品和劳务想进入中国市场，还是中国的商品和劳务想登上国际舞台，都离不开广告。广告翻译在其中发挥着不可替代的作用。成功的广告翻译能使商品或劳务等在目的语国家得到更好地推广和销售。

广告的英汉互译不仅要考虑英汉两种语言和文化的特点及差异，还要注重广告功能的实现。本章将从广告的定义、功能、构成、语言特点和常见修辞等几方面讨论英汉广告文体的互译。

第一节 广告的功能和构成

广告的目的是推销某种产品、商品、服务或劳务，以促进销售、实现购买，或者推广某种观念或理念。广告具有信息功能、唤起需要功能、说服功能、促使行动功能和扶植信用功能。[2] 广告的对象是广大消费者，广告在为商家服务的同时也为消费者提供了方便，是消费者获得信息的重要来源，同时影响或改变消费行为。

广告种类繁多。从构成上看，完整的广告文本一般包含标题、正文、标语和附文四个部分。

广告的标题（Headline）是对广告宣传内容的高度概括，起着提纲挈领、吸引眼球的作用。广告标题字体醒目，内容简洁精练，重点突出。成功的广告标题能迅速锁定潜在客户，引起他们对广告主题的关注，激发他们阅读广告正文的兴趣。

广告的正文（Body Text）是广告文本的中心，是对广告标题的解释，是广告主题的具体展现。通常广告正文会较为详细地介绍广告标题中涉及的广告信息，例如：企业的历史、

---

1 包惠南. 2001. 文化语境与语言翻译. 北京：中国对外翻译出版公司.
2 王燕希. 2011. 广告英语. 2版. 北京：对外经贸大学出版社.

规模、技术、服务宗旨，或者商品的特性、功能、优点等诸多方面。广告正文具有解释性、说服性和鼓动性等特点，使广告受众进一步了解企业、商品、服务或劳务，建立信任，并产生消费的欲望，最终促使消费行为的产生。

广告的标语（Slogan）是为了加深受众对企业、商品、服务或劳务等的印象，在相当长一段时期内反复使用的固定宣传语句。广告标语通常精练简洁、通俗易懂、容易记诵、感召力强。一些好的广告标语甚至广为流传，能使读者对商品和企业形成固定的良好印象。[3]

广告的附文（Supplementary Items）是在广告正文之后的附加性文字，是对正文的补充，一般包含企业名称、地址、购买商品或接受服务的方法等。附文也称随文或尾文。

需要说明的是，由于受时间、场合、版面或广告要求等各种因素的影响，并非所有的广告都完整地含有标题、正文、标语和附文四个部分。

第二节
广告文体的语言特点及其翻译

广告是传播信息、促进消费的重要手段之一，这决定了广告文体语言的独特性。与其他文体相比，广告使用的词汇和句式兼有吸引、创造、说服和影响消费者的特点。因此，广告在词汇、句式的选用上通常遵循简洁精练、新颖生动和易于传诵的原则，以达到良好的宣传和推销效果。总的来说，英汉广告文本的词汇和句式具有某些共同的特点。

一、词汇特点和翻译

（一）简洁灵活的动词

英语广告多采用简洁的常用动词，尤其是单音节动词。这类动词简洁明快、通俗易懂，既能拉近广告商品与受众的关系，又能节省广告版面，经济实用。英语广告中常用的动词有：do/go/make/get/use/ give/have/want/set/hear/care/create/see/buy/come/go/know/keep/look/need/love/feel/take/begin/start/taste/serve/live/help/meet/save/choose/last/offer/think 等。[4]

汉语中动词独立性强，不但可以组词，也可单独出现。汉语广告中巧妙地使用动词，能使广告形象生动，精彩非凡。

因此，翻译英语广告中的动词时，可以适当挑选汉语中形象生动的动词；而翻译汉语

---

3 方梦之、毛忠明. 2005. 英汉—汉英应用翻译教程. 上海：上海外语教育出版社.

4 王海. 2011. 传媒翻译概论. 广州：暨南大学出版社.

广告中的动词时，则可以挑选英语中简洁通俗的单音节动词。例如：

例1 Capture life in detail. (Nokia N 8)

清晰地捕捉生活瞬间。

这是诺基亚公司 N8 型手机的广告标题。capture 一词形象地展现出该手机拍照功能强大，能迅速清晰地"捕捉"图像；同时也一词双关，预示该手机能牢牢"捕捉"消费者，俘获他们的心。

例2 不断创新，打造核心竞争力。（深圳发展银行）

Innovate, to build the core competitiveness.

这则深圳发展银行的广告用"创新"和"打造"两个动词形象地展示了该行努力创新、争做行业佼佼者的作风。英译时，选用了 innovate 和 build 直译，简洁明了。

例3 飞在春暖花开时……

国航踏青游丽人篇：女性出行必游地（中国国际航空公司）

Flights to celebrate spring...

Short trips designed just for women by Air China

这是中国国际航空公司 2012 年春季的一则广告。该广告用"飞"字形象地描绘了乘坐飞机出游、尽享自由的畅快感觉，让人无限憧憬。英译时放弃了原有的动词"飞"，取而代之的是名词 flights 和动词 celebrate，同样能使人联想到向着春天飞行的愉悦。

（二）褒义形容词

英语广告中常使用褒义形容词或其比较级和最高级，如：good/excellent/perfect/delicious/great/beautiful/exciting/fresh/clean 等。这些形容词能突出广告商品或服务的特点和优势，展现商家的自信，迎合消费者货比三家的心理，使其在与同类的竞争中脱颖而出。

汉语广告中也常用"更""至尊""超凡""超群""独特""优良""精湛""卓越"等词来展现广告商品或服务的优越性。

这些褒义形容词通常可直译，以保留源语广告的宣传效果。例如：

例4 Refined, elegant and timeless, the fragrance of eternal feminity. (Sisley)

精致、优雅、超越时光，夜幽情怀香水演绎出永恒的女性魅力。

这则法国希思黎的香水广告共使用了四个褒义形容词，形象地展现了该款香水的独特魅力，能引起无限美好的遐想，唤起购买欲望。汉语译文运用褒义形容词直译，在整体上保留了原广告的用词特点。

例5 只为优质生活。（蒙牛）

For a better life.

这则广告以"优质"一词不但展现了蒙牛乳制品公司的宗旨，而且能让消费者联想到拥有蒙牛就拥有了"优质"生活,简洁通俗。"优质"直译成 better,传达了与原文本等同的信息。

(三)意义积极和褒奖的名词

除形容词外,广告文本也会使用表达褒奖和积极意义的名词,以增强吸引力和说服力。这类名词能生动形象地展现广告商品或服务的优点和特质,树立良好的形象,吸引并劝说消费者消费。

对于这类名词,通常也可采用直译的方法,真实再现源语广告的内容。例如:

例6 The relentless pursuit of perfection. (Lexus)
不懈追求完美。

这则雷克萨斯汽车的英文广告用 perfection 一词,能让消费者联想到该品牌汽车近乎完美的特质,同时,也表明该公司在汽车制造方面对完美的一贯追求。译文将 perfection 直译成"完美",忠实地保留了原广告的效果。

例7 Intelligence everywhere. (Motorola)
智慧演绎,无处不在。

原广告以 intelligence 一词展现出摩托罗拉手机功能多样,智慧卓绝的特点;译文则采用四字短语,增添"演绎"一词,将"智慧"动态化,凸显该手机的灵动智慧。译文广告效果更胜一筹。

(四)复合词和新创词

广告中经常出现复合词和新创词,富有创意,能使广告文本倍加新颖、活泼。英语广告往往运用不同的词缀、时态或词组构成让人耳目一新的词汇。而汉语广告多用谐音来创造新词。这些复合词和新创词在灵活诠释广告内容的同时,能迅速吸引消费者,满足他们的猎奇心理。

英语或汉语广告中的这类词汇植根于各自不同的语言和文化,一旦翻译成其他语言,就会脱离原有的语言文化土壤,变得索然无味,甚至毫无意义。翻译时,此类复合词或创新词往往会被摒弃,在尽量保留原广告意义和功能的前提下,代之以译入语中的其他词汇或表达。例如:

例8 Offer your skin an intensive ultra-detox treatment. (Dior)
让肌肤悦享清肌赋活呵护。

原广告中复合词 ultra-detox 是"超级排毒"的意思,表明迪奥的这款面膜具有密集修护、排毒养颜的功效。汉译时,若按字面意义直接翻译成"超级排毒"会使广告失去部分美感,而选用"清肌赋活"来翻译,不但准确再现了商品的功效,而且极富美感。

（五）四字成语或短语

上述几点是英汉广告文本共有的特征。但四字成语或短语的使用，则只见于汉语广告文本。汉字的独立性强，组词灵活，字与字、词与词的组合不像英语那样受语法的严格约束。特别是四字结构，语言简练、艺术性强，深受汉语广告的青睐。因此，汉语广告中的四字成语或短语在译成英语时一般舍弃原有形式，多以准确表达原广告意义为重，例如：

例9 精彩国航，"里"尚"网"来。

2012年度国航里程额外奖励（中国国际航空公司）

Splendid Air China online mileage awards.

2012 Air China Extra Mileage Awards

原广告中"'里'尚'网'来"是由"礼尚往来"谐音而新创的词，符合汉语四字成句的特点，巧妙地介绍了国航网络购票送里程的优惠活动，鼓励消费者选择国航服务，获得额外里程的奖赏。由于文化的差异，英语国家消费者大多不能理解"'里'尚'网'来"的真正意义。因此，英译时需将原广告字里行间的意思直接表达出来，才能让广告受众一目了然。

例10 畅销全球 selling well all over the world

工艺精良 sophisticated technology

久负盛名 with a long standing reputation

美观大方 elegant and graceful

保质保量 quality and quantity assured

二、句式特点和翻译

英汉两种语言虽属不同语系，存在诸多差异，但在广告文本的句式方面却有一些共同特点。

（一）多用简单句，少用复合句

简单句结构简洁、语义明确，因而容易传诵。相反，复合句成分较为复杂、冗长，不太符合广告语言简练易记的特点。例如：

例11 Time always follows me. (Rossini)

时间因我存在。

例12 良好的口腔护理让你受益一生。（飞利浦 Sonicare）

Philips Sonicare: A lifetime of good oral care.

例13 卡夫食品中国 让今天更美味。（卡夫食品）

Kraft Foods China make today delicious.

例14 I 有一个梦想。（格力空调 I 系列）

I have a dream.

（二）多用祈使句

祈使句多用于表达请求、要求、劝告、叮嘱或建议，与广告文体的诉求、建议或劝说等特点一致。此外，祈使句一般无主语，符合广告"广而告之"的特点。另外，汉语祈使句常使用语气词，能增添广告语言的生动性和感染力。例如：

例 15 Let's build a smarter planet. (IBM)
让我们共建智慧的地球。

例 16 Let's make things better. (Philips)
让我们做得更好。

例 17 Obey your thirst. (Sprite)
服从你的渴望。

（三）多用疑问句

疑问句能引起读者兴趣，尤其是设问句，通过一问一答的方式吸引读者，然后以点睛之笔的回答让人恍然大悟，获得认可。例如：

例 18 Feeling stressed? Chew gum. (Wrigley)
有压力？嚼口香糖。

例 19 Looking to earn more money? Become an Avon independent sales representative. (AVON)
想挣更多钱吗？成为雅芳直销员吧。

（四）多用并列结构

在广告文本中，多个并列结构的词或短语单独成句，可使广告结构工整、重点突出，既节约了版面，又朗朗上口、利于记诵，宣传效果良好。例如：

例 20 Comprehensive, Thorough, Objective. (*China Today*)
综合、全面、客观

例 21 Golden heritage for golden moments. (Ferrero Rocher)
金色经典，金色时刻

例 22 百年中行，全球服务（中国银行）
A century of global service

例 23 同心同行 标新致远（标致）
Motion & Emotion

（五）多用省略句

广告文本中常使用省略句，省略主语、谓语、宾语或连词等。例如：

例 24 创造绿色低碳新生活。（三洋电视）
Creating a new living of low carbon

例25 中国南方航空
——你的、中国的、世界的（中国南方航空）
China Southern Airlines
—Yours, China's and the world's

总之，英汉广告互译时，如果原句是简单句、祈使句或疑问句，应尽量遵循与原广告句型一致的翻译原则；如果是并列结构或省略句，则需要多考虑语言文化差异以及不同广告受众的习惯等心理因素，灵活变通地进行翻译，使广告译文符合译入语读者的审美和表达习惯。

第三节
广告文体中的修辞与翻译

广告文体的特殊性决定了自身的独树一帜。除了新颖独特的词语和经典简洁的句式外，运用各类生动形象的修辞手法也是广告文体的一个显著特征。广告文本中常使用的修辞有：比喻、排比、拟人、双关、顶真、押韵和仿拟等。这些修辞手法使广告文本生动形象、妙趣横生、异彩纷呈。然而，修辞的运用离不开语言赖以生存的文化背景。因此，要做好广告文本的翻译，就要了解广告中使用的修辞所展现的不同文化心理、意识观念和风俗习惯等。在翻译时尽可能采用相同或相似的修辞手段，但要注意根据译入语消费者的文化和审美情趣做相应变化。[5] 在修辞意义表达较为直接，且两种文化相通的情况下，可采用直译；一旦原广告修辞所展现的内容仅适用于原语言文化的消费者，就需要采用其他翻译方法，使译文更易被译入语消费者理解和接受，实现广告最终的目的。

一、比喻

比喻就是打比方，用本质不同而又在某一方面或某些方面相似的事物或情境描绘另一种事物或情境。广告文本中常运用比喻的手法对广告商品的某种特征进行描绘和渲染，使该商品在消费者心中的形象从抽象变为具体、从陌生变为熟悉，进而促使消费行为的产生。当英汉对喻体含义解释一致时，可采用直译法对广告进行翻译；一旦源语喻体在译入语中有不同解释，或不能被译入语文化理解和接受时，则应通过转换喻体的方式进行翻译，在保留原广告的修辞特色的同时，准确而生动形象地表达广告内涵。例如：

例1 Life is a journey. Enjoy the ride. (Nissan)
生活就是一次旅行，祝您旅途愉快。（直译）

5　陈新.1999.英汉文体翻译教程.北京：北京大学出版社.

例2 Pick an Ace from Toshiba. (Toshiba)
选择品质,选择东芝。(意译)

二、排比

排比就是将三个或三个以上结构相同、意义相关的词组或句子并排,达到节奏和谐、层次明晰的效果。广告文本中通常使用排比,使描述清晰、条理分明,朗朗上口。此外,排比句工整而有气势,能强化表达效果,极具说服力。在翻译排比类型的广告文本时,多采用直译,选用并列结构,保持原广告的排比特色。例如:

例3 打造知识产权信息交流平台,
关注知识产权领域风云人物,
报道知识产权重大新闻事件,
传播知识产权先进文化理念。(中国日报网——知识产权频道)
Provide an arena for information exchange.
Put leading figures in the intellectual-property field in the spotlight.
Deliver the latest news on intellectual-property developments and highlight the big events.
Spread intellectual-property notions and culture. (直译)

三、拟人

拟人是将人的特征赋予人以外的他物,把事物人格化,使之具有人的思想、行为、个性或情感等。广告文本中经常使用拟人的手法,赋予广告商品人类才能拥有的特质,使商品形象生动、栩栩如生。对广告中的拟人手法的翻译一般采用直译,某些情况下也可使用套译等方法。例如:

例4 Apple thinks different.(Apple)
苹果电脑,不同凡"想"。(直译)

例5 汰渍到,污垢逃。(汰渍洗衣粉)
Tide's in, dirt's out. (套译)

四、双关

双关是指利用字词的多义或同音的特点,有意安排在表达中,使语句拥有双重含义。双关通常可分成意义双关和谐音双关。广告文体要求语言简练,双关的运用能使简短的语句拥有双重含义,寓意深刻、妙趣昂然,能引起消费者的联想,加深记忆。双关与其所在的语言文化有着深刻的联系。广告文本中的双关词多与广告品牌名有一定的联系,可采用直译和意译相结合的方法分别译出该词的多个含义。例如:

例6 From Sharp minds, come sharp products. (Sharp)
夏普产品，来自智慧的结晶。（意译）

例7 Live with focus. (Ford)
生活有"焦点"，才是真正的享受！（直译＋增补译）

例8 茅台王子酒——世界的王子（茅台）
Prince of Moutai—Prince of the world （直译）

五、顶真

顶真是指以上一句中结尾的字词作为下一句开头的字词，使相邻的两句首尾相连。广告文本中顶真的运用可以巧妙地使广告词环环相扣、别具一格。顶真多见于汉语广告中，是汉语广告的一大特点，对其进行结构等同的英译并非易事，因此，在结构和内容不能两全的情况下，还是应该以保留原广告主题为重。例如：

例9 你看世界，世界看你。（海伦·凯勒眼镜）
You view world. （直译＋删减译）

例10 嘉士利，利万家。（嘉士利）
Jiashili, benefiting every family!（意译）

例11 You like it, it likes you. (7 Up)
您爱它，它爱您。（直译）

六、押韵

押韵是指句首或句末的一个字或词使用相同或相近的发音，使朗诵时产生一种和谐的节奏感，常见的有头韵和尾韵。押韵能使广告文本音韵优美，宛如诗歌，易于传诵。由于英汉语言的差异，广告韵律的翻译难度较大，应在不改变原广告主题思想的前提下，尽量保留押韵的修辞，从译入语中选用适当的押韵方法灵活翻译，再现原广告的节奏美感。例如：

例12 It's blended, it's splendid. (Blue Ribbon Beer)
百味大成，百品不厌。（意译）

原文中 -ded 和 -did 押尾韵，汉译本选择了两个都以"百"开头的四字短语，可谓巧妙。

例13 Fresh-up with Seven-up. (7 Up)
痛饮七喜，清心爽气。（增补译）

例14 Every time a good time. (McDonald's)
每时每刻，欢乐时刻。

例15 No problem too large. No business too small. (IBM)
无关不克，无客不尊。（直译）

例16 牙好，身体就好。（高露洁牙膏）
Good teeth, good health. （直译）

七、仿拟

仿拟是指仿照人们熟知的成语、习语、谚语、名言等，创造新内容的一种修辞手法。广告文本仿拟这些家喻户晓的表述，创造新语句，能突出广告主题，加深消费者的印象，且便于记忆和流传，达到良好的宣传效果。运用了仿拟的广告文本与其所在的语言文化有着根深蒂固的联系，若生搬硬套地进行翻译，势必因背景文化的缺失而影响译入语消费者对广告主题内容的理解，使译入语广告丧失原有的功能。因此，仿拟的翻译首先要遵循原广告的主题思想，然后在译入语的文化背景下选用广为人知的谚语、诗歌或成语等进行套译，以再现原广告的主题和修辞特色。当然，如果在译入语中无法找到恰当的仿拟内容，那就只能舍弃形式，以准确表达原广告主题思想和内容为原则进行翻译。例如：

例17 Tasting is believing.

百闻不如一尝。（套译）

例18 Not all cars are created equal. (Mitsubishi Motors)

并非所有的汽车都有相同的品质。（直译）

例19 LUX every day keeps old hands away. (LUX)

力士洗手，青春不走。（意译）

例20 A Mars a day keeps you work, rest and play. (Mars)

一天一块Mars巧克力，令你精力充沛、生活愉快。（直译＋增补译）

例21 衣食住行，有龙则灵。（中国建设银行）

Your everyday life is very busy. Our Long card can make it easy.（意译）

第四节　广告文体的翻译方法

广告文体的翻译应该遵循应用翻译理论，采用灵活变通的翻译技巧，使译文广告具有感染力、艺术灵感和丰富的想象力，能在功能和效果上与原广告对等，达到传递信息、刺激需求、展现美感和创意、提升形象和敦促购买的目的。[6]

英汉两种语言既有共性也有差异。因此，在英汉广告文体互译时，首先要充分理解源语广告的内涵，了解广告商品或服务的特点，然后，按照译入语的表达习惯，选用恰当的词汇和句式等结构，灵活地翻译。一般来说，英汉广告文本的翻译可采用直译、意译、增补译、删减译、套译和创译这几种方法。

6　冯修文. 2010. 应用翻译中的审美与文化透视：基于商标品牌名和品牌广告口号的翻译研究. 上海：上海交通大学出版社．

一、直译

直译法多用来翻译语义明确、句法结构简单的广告，能最大限度地保留原广告的效果。例如：

例1 发现更多·体验更多（中国上海）
More Discovery More Experience

例2 The Philips AVENT range of pacifiers and teethers help to soothe and comfort your baby. They're designed to suit your baby's age and stage and are made to the highest safety standards, so you can feel at ease knowing that your baby is comforted and happy. (Philips)

飞利浦新安怡安抚奶嘴和牙胶系列有助于安抚您的宝宝。精心的设计能满足各个年龄阶段的宝宝。卓越的安全标准使您能够安心见证宝宝的舒适和喜悦。

以上两则广告原文表意清晰，句式简单，能够直译成相同句型结构的英语或汉语文本。因此，翻译时采用了直译法。

二、意译

由于英汉文化存在差异，语言表达的规则和习惯各有不同，源语广告文本无法直接翻译成译入语的现象也屡见不鲜。遇到这种情况，可以采用意译法，在保留源语广告精髓的前提下，将源语广告的内容和语言进行转化，使之符合译入语的语言文化特点，这样的译语广告较易为受众接受。例如：

例3 演绎生活智慧。（苏泊尔）
Smart thinking for smooth living.

例4 城市，让生活更美好。（上海世博会）
Better City, Better Life.

例5 Everybody on HP. (HP)
你我即世界。

这三则广告的译文虽然在语言结构和特点上与原文有很大差异，但是源语广告的深层意义却在译文中得到了展现。

三、增补译

增补译法在英汉广告文本互译中扮演着重要角色。增补译时，译语广告中增加的内容通常是对源语广告中隐含意义的深入挖掘和显现，或是为了符合译入语的语言文化习俗、迎合译语广告受众而进行的必要补充。这种译法多用于英语广告文本的汉译。例如：

例6 The Creative Life. (TCL)
创意感动生活。

例7　Absolue A Lancôme Legend.
　　　Absolue Quintessence of luxury.
　　　The Pleasure of Mixing
　　　Discover Absolue Regeneration. (Lancôme, Absolue)
　　　菁纯奢宠 演绎兰蔻传奇
　　　菁纯之美 奢华典范
　　　悦然新生 多重感官殿堂

　　这两则广告都采用了增补译法，使源语广告中的隐含信息在译语广告中得以生动再现。TCL 公司的汉语广告译文较原文添加了"感动"一词，增添了一抹人性的色彩，拉近了该品牌与广告受众的距离，使人们相信拥有 TCL 的产品，生活就拥有了无限创造性的享受。

　　例 7 原为法国著名化妆品品牌兰蔻的菁纯系列护肤品广告，文本在译成汉语时，新增了"奢宠""演绎""之美"和"悦然"等词语，符合汉语广告四字成句和多用褒奖的名词和形容词等特点，完美地传递了这款护肤品给肌肤带来的奢华感受以及堪称典范的高档品质。

四、删减译

　　删减译法一般用来处理原文本中过剩冗余的信息。使用删减译法时，需要充分考虑源语和译语的表达特点，以及源语广告和译语广告所针对的消费群体的特性和已有知识。有效的删减不仅使语言简洁精练，而且更能突出广告宣传的重点。例如：

例8　伦敦，盖特威克
　　　国航新开伦敦第二大机场盖特威克，从此轻松直达！
　　　开航首月惊喜预售价格往返 3880 元起。（中国国际航空）
　　　London, Gatwick
　　　Newly introduced air routes
　　　Surprising pre-sale round-trip prices in March 3880RMB up

　　这则广告是中国国际航空公司 2012 年推出的新航线的广告。汉语广告针对中国国民不熟悉英国机场的情况，特别提到盖特威克是伦敦的第二大机场。而在译成英语时，考虑到英语广告读者群体多熟知该机场，所以采用删减译法，删去了"伦敦第二大机场"等信息。

五、套译

　　套译是借助译入语已有的典故、谚语、习语、名言、诗句或歌词对原广告进行套用性翻译。这种翻译方法往往通过人们耳熟能详的语句使广告主题内容广为传唱，深入人心。例如：

例9 Where there is a way, there is a Toyota. (Toyota)

车到山前必有路，有路必有丰田车。

例10 East or west, Honda is the best. (Honda)

东奔西跑，本田最好。

例11 For the Road Ahead. (Honda)

康庄大道。

例12 有目共赏——上海电视

Seeing is believing.

六、创译

广告文体的翻译不同于其他实用文体的翻译。一般实用文体对源语文本的忠实要求严格，译者不能随意发挥；而广告文本本身就是创造力的显现，充满创意的广告才能在信息膨胀的现代社会中独树一帜，真正使广告商品、产品、服务或劳务得到广大消费者的青睐，因此，广告文体的翻译过程应该是一个再创造的过程。译者需要充分理解源语广告的内涵，深刻知晓译语风俗文化，并牢牢把握译语消费者的心理和消费观念，对源语广告进行创造性翻译，以达到译语广告效果的最大化。[7] 正如李克兴（2010）在《广告翻译理论与实践》一书中指出，广告翻译要遵循创造性的翻译原则，"任何广告的翻译都可以在原文的基础上，在原版广告字面及画面所提供的资讯框架内，必要时甚至可以离开这些框架，进行重新创作。"[8] 这种翻译方法，就是创译，它在广告文本的翻译中发挥着重要的作用。

例13 Make·Believe (Sony)

创新源于好奇，梦想成就未来。

例14 Connecting People (Nokia)

科技以人为本。

例15 Good to the last drop! (Maxwell House)

滴滴香浓，意犹未尽。

例16 心在更远处。（飞亚达）

Beyond the moment.

例17 《传媒》引领传媒（《传媒》期刊）

Media magazine——a channel to understand the China media industry

例18 精湛科技，轻松烹饪。（老板电器）

Enjoy cooking life.

以上几则广告文本的译文与源语少有相同之处，不论是用词还是句法结构，都很难在译文中看到源语广告的影子，如同原创。索尼公司原广告语仅有两个英语动词，译者脱离

7　李克兴. 2010. 广告翻译理论与实践. 北京：北京大学出版社.
8　同上。

源语广告的框架，以对偶句创造出新的汉语广告译文，传递的信息既不亚于源语广告，又符合汉语的语言表达习惯，生动形象，容易被中国的消费者接受。同样，老板厨房电器公司的这则汉语广告与其英语译文在结构和内容上也有所不同。汉语广告文本是传统的四字短语并列，英语译文则创造性地用 enjoy 一词，简洁明了地营造出一种轻松愉悦的烹饪氛围，让消费者自然联想到由老板厨房电器引领的美食人生。

创译可以说是广告文体特有的翻译方法。采用创译产生的广告译文通常更富有吸引力，创造出的意境也更加深远，有的甚至能超越源语广告，带来意想不到的收获。请看李克兴给出的两个例子：

例 19

I saw a city with its head in the future and its soul in the past;
I saw ancient operas performed on the modern streets;
I saw a dozen races co-exist as one;
I didn't see an unsafe street;
Was it a dream I saw?
—Singapore! So easy to enjoy, so hard to forget.[9]

译文 a：

我看到一个城市，她是过去与未来的结合。
我看到古老的歌剧在摩登的街头上演。
我看到不同种族融洽共存为一。
我看不到一条不安全的街道。
只疑身在梦中？
——新加坡！逍遥其中，流连忘返。

译文 b：

有一座城市，工业立足高科技，民间传统不忘记。
有一座城市，海边花园建高楼，摩登街头演古戏。
有一座城市，十余民族一方土，情同手足睦相处。
有一座城市，大街小巷无盗贼，夜不闭户心不惧。
是天方夜谭、痴人说梦？
啊，新加坡——如此享受，铭心刻骨。

原文是新加坡的旅游广告文本，不难看出译文 a 采取的是直译，既保留了源语广告的用词和句式特点，又沿用了原广告文本的排版格式，非常忠实于原文。译文 b 是李克兴采用创译的方法翻译的，不论是用词、句式，或是内容，都与源语文本有很大区别，是译者的再创作。两篇译文虽各有优点，但在译文 b 中，译者创造性地添加如"工业立足高科技"和"海边花园建高楼"等内容，不仅使汉语译文对仗工整，韵律优美，而且形象地展现了

9　此例引自李克兴. 2010. 广告翻译理论与实践. 北京：北京大学出版社.

新加坡的别具一格；另外，"情同手足""大街小巷""夜不闭户"和"天方夜谭"这些四字成语的应用，突出了汉语广告的用词特色，符合汉语读者的审美习惯，易于传唱。

例20

阳光唇膏[10]

  阳光唇膏有各种色泽，可根据不同年龄、肤色、口型、时间、场合选用。年轻的姑娘用色彩鲜丽显得活泼，中年人用色调较暗的橙红显得庄重，唇小可将唇线适当扩大，光线明亮宜用淡色，背景较暗宜用深色，该唇膏可使唇部获得健康美丽的光彩。

译文 a：

Sun Shine Lipstick

  There are many colors for choice according to the age, skin's color, mouth's pattern, time and occasion. Young girls use gay color which appears lively. Middle-aged ladies use somewhat dull orange red which appears solemn. Small lips may enlarge the contour of the lips by it. You may use light colors in bright condition and with deep colors under dark occasion. The lipstick makes the lips with healthy and beautiful gloss.

译文 b：

Sunshine Lipsticks

  Sunshine lipsticks. Various colors available. For different ages, complexions, lip-shapes, time and occasion. Bright colors make you a cute baby. Deep colors make you a dignified lady. If you have small lips, you can enlarge the lipline accordingly. In well-lit place, light colors are suitable. With gloomy background, deep colors are desirable. Sunshine Lipsticks make your face look vital with dazzling charm.

  两篇译文分别采用直译和创译的方法。译文 a 采用了直译，忠实再现了原广告的语言形式和内容。译文 b 主要采用创译，对原广告的句型和词汇等进行创造性地改造，译文句式简洁明了，易于记忆，忠实地传达了广告内容。特别是 Bright colors make you a cute baby 和 Deep colors make you a dignified lady 两句结构对仗，节奏感强，略去了原广告中对女性消费者年龄的划分，代之以 baby 和 lady，更符合女性心理，而且韵律优美，与 suitable 和 desirable 一样押尾韵。

  比较例 19 和例 20 两则广告的直译译文和创译译文可以看出，直译译文忠于原广告的主题思想和语言特色，广告译者只需对照原广告进行直接的语言转换就可完成翻译；而创译法则采用完全不同于原文的用词、句式甚至排版进行翻译，是对原广告已有内容的重新

---

10 此例引自李克兴. 2010. 广告翻译理论与实践. 北京：北京大学出版社.

整合和创造性加工，也是对译者创造性思维的考验。因此，能否成功地使用创译法在一定程度上取决于译者在源语和译入语方面的语言和文化功底。较为成功的创译文本能给广告增光添彩，甚至比原广告更能起到传递信息、吸引注意和刺激购买的作用。

练习七

一、将下列广告文本译成英文。

1. 中国吸油烟机领导者
   改善人类烹饪环境（老板电器）

2. 争创利润，力求发展
   重视科研，不断创新
   遵纪守法，保持声誉
   一视同仁，工作愉快（A.O. 史密斯公司）

3. 科技·创新家装（东易日盛家装）

4. 满堂红——以真诚为旨的家装企业。（满堂红家装）

5. 新一代的选择。（百事可乐）

6. 我们领先，他人仿效。（理光复印机）

7. 选择南航 粤享精彩
   尽享广州 72 小时国境免签。（中国南方航空）

8. SM 家电以其一如既往秉持的创新精神引领国际家电业，并以其在尖端技术的领先优势而蜚声全球。SM 家电代表着优良的品质、时尚的设计、可靠的性能，更重要的是我们只选用经层层筛选、严格测试的材料制造而成的产品，一切想消费者所想，一切为消费者所需。（西门子家电）

9. 都市人生活紧张，食无定时，又缺乏足够运动，难以通过日常饮食吸收每日所需的足够营养。要健康，便要日日食 F&H 营养补充品，日日补充身体所需营养。
   F&H 营养补充品，浓缩自天然食物营养精华，经高科技提炼而成；近百种不同产品，配合身体各种需要，为你日日补充足够营养，持久健康。（Fancl F&H）

10. 麦香风味，
    凝聚成纤巧身形。
    满心喜悦的巧克力味道，
    铸就了醇正百味之百醇。（百醇饼干）

二、将下列广告文本译成中文。

1. Arrow Ceramic Tiles—Good Taste, Best Choice. (Arrow Ceramic Tiles)
2. Transfiguration (hair spray)
3. Sophisticated design and revolutionary performance (laptop)
4. Let's build a smarter planet. (IBM)
5. Better Patterns, Better Jackets. (K-Boxing)
6. How to Reach Customers Near of Far?
   FedEx. Solutions Powered by People. (FedEx)
7. You're more powerful than you think. (Apple)
8. When chocolate flavor falls in love with red wine,
   The sweet flavor melts my heart,
   And makes me
   Forget the passing of time. (Pejoy)
9. Weighing only 158g (body only) and sporting an ultra slim (22.5mm) design, the NX mini can easily slip into almost any pocket or bag. It features a solid premium metal body with a luxurious leatherette finish, making the camera the natural choice for style-conscious shooters. (Samsung)
10. 1912–2012
    A Century of Tonneau-shaped Watches
    At Vacheron Constantin
    Four
    New Models
    In The Malte Collection

    In 1912, the first tonneau-shaped watch appeared at Vacheron Constantin, and has since become an iconic model in its collections.

    In 2012, the manufacture decided to redesign its Malte collection and to enrich it with four new models that are classic in spirit, yet contemporary in style. It is also an ideal opportunity to present a new form movement for the Malte Tourbillion, the 2795 caliber, developed and crafted by Vacheron Constantin and bearing the Hallmark of Geneva.

    With this new Malte Collection, Vacheron Constantin pays tribute to a century filled with a wealth of tonneau-shaped creations, and celebrates its fundamental values based on classicism, elegance and technical mastery. (Vacheron Constantin)

第八章
会议文书的翻译

会议文书是关于会议、会务工作的文书。具体地说，会议文书就是为会议的准备、召开及结束而撰写的公务文书。[1]

会议文书的翻译要求依据会议文书的类别而定。总的来讲，在遵循一般翻译对等原则的基础上，应使译文尽量做到语义清晰，语言简明，语体适当。

会议文书的种类非常多。会议性质、内容、形式、目的、规模和进程不同，对会议文书的要求也不同，会议文书范式也有所不同。应用比较广泛的会议文书主要有以下四类：

（1）会务文书：主要包括会议方案、会议通知、会议议程、会议须知及参会回条等。

（2）礼仪文书：主要包括邀请函、祝贺词、欢迎词、答谢词、欢送词、祝酒词等。

（3）事务文书：主要包括会议制度、会议提案、会议记录、会议纪要、会议简报、会议决议及会议公报等。

（4）话语文书：主要包括主持词、开幕词、闭幕词、颁奖词、会议报告等。

本章将在分析各种会议文书语言特点的基础上，根据会议文书的分类，通过丰富的译例，分别介绍各种会议文书的语言特点和翻译技巧，并指出不同类型会议文书的翻译应注意的问题。

第一节
会议文书的语言特点和翻译原则

一、会议文书的语言特点

会议文书作为一种实用文体，语言特色鲜明。首先，不同类型的会议文书具有不同的语言特色。比如，会务文书要求语言客观、严谨，表达简洁，力求做到通俗易懂；礼仪文书和话语文书则通常要求语言情感真挚，言辞恳切，生动形象，既要完成文书既定的会议功能，又要实现较好的会场效果；而事务文书，由于是用于记录会议期间具体问题、具体

---

[1] 李树春.2010.会议文书写作：方法·结构·最新例文.北京：中国纺织出版社.

事件，以及议程进展或决议决定，通常要求语言科学规范，内容详略得当，主次有序，以期能准确无误地传达会议精神。其次，会议文书的语言带有较强的程序性。不同类型和层次的会议文书通常都有约定俗成的固定表达范式，撰写各种会议文书通常都有一定的规范可循。

二、会议文书的翻译原则

在进行会议文书翻译时，应注意不同种类会议文书的语言特点，选择恰当的语言形式，既要忠实于原文本的内容，又不拘泥于其语言形式，力求内容准确，语言顺畅。要根据汉英两种语言各自的特点，有针对性地选择符合目的语规范的表达形式；还要根据会议的正式程度，选择不同的语体形式，确定译文的风格，灵活地进行翻译。会议文书中出现的专有名词，如人名、地名、组织机构名称等，可根据本书前面章节提到的原则进行翻译。另外，还要考虑中英文里同类文书的不同文体格式，应努力避免格式不同给信息传达造成的影响，务求准确反映原会议文书文本中的重要信息。

第二节 会议会务文书的翻译

会议会务文书是为了组织和服务会议而撰写的文书，主要包括会议方案、会议通知、会议议程、会议须知及参会回条等。本节将依次讨论上述会务文书的翻译以及中英互译中需注意的问题。

一、会议方案的翻译

会议方案是会议组织者在会议召开前，为使会议顺利进行并能取得预期效果而做出的预设方案。会议方案的内容因会议类型而异，但一般都包括三个部分：标题、正文和签署。标题分为单一标题和多要素标题；正文分为前言、主体和筹备事项；签署包括会议方案的制作单位和会议方案的成文日期。

（一）标题的翻译

会议方案的标题通常由会议的召开单位、会议内容或事由及文种（即"会议方案"）组成。例如：

例1 HARTHHORNE-BERGESON, INC.
　　　Meeting Plan of the Marketing Department Staff

哈松伯吉森公司营销部员工会议方案

例2 Plan of the 2nd World Congress on
Controversies in Diabetes, Obesity and Hypertension
第二届世界糖尿病、肥胖症及高血压学术大会会议方案

例3 Scheme of World Engineers Convention 2011 in Geneva
2011年度日内瓦世界工程师大会会议方案

例4 中国整形外科协会第七届国际学术大会会议方案
Scheme of the Seventh International Congress of Chinese Orthopaedic Association

  英文中关于"会议"的表达很多。按照会议正式程度、规模大小及讨论话题的不同，大致有 congress、conference、convention、forum、symposium、colloquium、seminar、workshop、panel 和 meeting 等。congress 和 conference 均可用于正式的学术会议或官方会议，convention 常用于每年一次或多年一次的例会，forum、symposium、colloquium 和 seminar 常用于某个专业领域或固定话题的研究会议，workshop 多为会议下设的分组讨论会议，meeting 是最普通意义上的会议。在翻译标题时，应根据会议的规模和正式程度来确定"会议"一词的英译词，然后在"会议"一词前面加上相关内容的翻译。"方案"一词在英文中也有多个，如 scheme、program、plan 等，其中 scheme 和 program 用法较正式。汉译英时应抓住主要信息，如不分主次，可能会造成题目过长。

（二）正文及签署的翻译

  会议方案的正文一般由前言、主体和筹备事项组成。前言通常说明会议的名称、目的、参会人员、召开的时间和地点等；主体包括会议基本内容、指导思想、主要任务、会议议程和日程等；筹备事项通常包括文件准备、会议安排、宣传报道、会场布置、后勤服务等，有时还包括食宿交通、参观娱乐等项目。学术会议的会议方案略有不同。通常会对会议的筹备指导委员会（steering committee）、大会涉及的学术议题以及与会人员向大会提交论文摘要或对全会的期限做出说明。正文的内容通常分模块逐条列出，翻译时应注意语言地道准确、简明易懂。下面请看一个一般会议方案的例子：

例5

青年志愿者队伍创建策划方案

一、指导思想

  一年级新生为财会系增添了新鲜血液。作为新一代青年，你们拥有青春的朝气，阳光的气息，让社会感受你们的热情，青年志愿者是你们最好的选择！财会系青年志愿者活动为系团总支社工部重点工作之一，同时也是院青年志愿者总队一支青春蓬勃的分队。为提高我系志愿者活动影响力，调动广大志愿者积极性，我系团总支特在各班团支部内成立青年志愿者服务支队，各支队将秉承"受系队领导、不受其干涉"的原则开展志愿工作。只要你拥有一颗炽热的心，

只要你肯付出不怕累,欢迎加入青年志愿者队伍!

二、目标任务

1. 召开志愿者支队成立仪式。
2. 要求大一各班新志愿者均要参加。
3. 社工部成员作为各支队驻班志愿者,指导各班级支队开展工作,制定一系列激励制度,对突出支队和个人给予表彰。
4. 11月5日前务必完成各班志愿者招募工作,统一填表交至社工部,各支部做好参加成立仪式志愿者的召集工作,做好考勤。
5. 各支部要在本班内成立领导机构,选出支队长、支队宣传委员、支队组织委员各一名。(支队长可由团支书兼任)

三、财会系各班志愿者支队成立仪式安排

1. 时间:2010年11月5日(星期三)下午4:00。
2. 地点:财会系(一号楼)楼前。
3. 大会主持人:吕友谊
4. 议程:
   1) 主持人介绍与会领导和嘉宾。
   2) 社工部负责人介绍志愿者支队的宗旨与概况。
   3) 财会系领导讲话。
   4) 财会系青年志愿者代表发言。
   5) 财会系辅导员宣读各班支队负责人名单。
   6) 全体志愿者宣誓。
   7) 财会系老师以及团总支干部为各班志愿者支队授旗。

财会系团总支社工部
2010年11月1日

Program to Found Youth Volunteer Society Detachments (YVSD)

Guideline

Freshmen, the new generation of youth with courage and warmth, have just entered our Accounting Department. Now we are welcoming them to join the Department Youth Volunteer Society (DYVS), a young and vigorous group, a key part of the Social Work Section under the Department General Youth League Branch (DGYLB) which is led by the College General YVS. To enhance and motivate our volunteering work, our DGYLB has planned to found its detachments within every class and make them work with much independence. Dear freshmen, come and join us!

Aims and Tasks

1. To hold Volunteer Detachment Founding Ceremony.
2. All new volunteers from first-year classes should attend.

3. Social Work Section members should join detachments as volunteers to guide their work and make motivation regulations by awarding the excellent.
4. The recruiting work of new members should be finished before Nov. 5, and volunteers' ceremony attendance should be recorded.
5. Each detachment should select its leaders including a head, a publicity commissary and an organizing commissary. (The Youth League Branch secretary of the class can act as detachment chair).

Agenda of the Founding Ceremony
Time: 4 o'clock p.m. on Wednesday, Nov. 5th, 2010
Venue: In front of Accounting Department (Building No.1)
Host: Lv Youyi
Agenda:
    1) Host introduces leaders and guests present.
    2) Social Work Leader introduces missions and gives general information of YVSD.
    3) Department leader speaks.
    4) Department Volunteer representative speaks.
    5) Department counselor declares roll of heads for each detachment.
    6) All volunteers take an oath.
    7) Accounting Department Teachers, GYLB leaders present flags to all detachments.

Social Work Section of General Youth League Branch,
Accounting Department
Nov. 1, 2010

二、会议通知及会议议程的翻译

会议通知是会议组织者向与会者发出的告知性文书，告知会议召开的有关事项和会议要求等。通知一般由四部分组成：标题、受文单位、正文和签署，受文单位和签署有时会省略。会议通知的语言具体明确、通俗易懂。会议议程是会议对即将审议、讨论、通过的各项文件、议案或议题的顺序安排。一般由标题、题注和正文组成。对会议议程进行翻译时应注意有无题注。下面请看几个翻译实例：

例6

Meeting Notice

To: All salespersons
From: Marina Pennel, Secretary to Sales Director

Date: December 1, 2012

Subject: A Meeting of Sales Planning for 2013

In view of the more and more fierce competition and the approaching of the New Year, the Sales Division will hold a meeting to make the sales planning for 2013 on Friday, December 7, 2012 at 4 p.m. at the conference room of this company. Enclosed is the agenda for the meeting.

You are expected to be here on time. If you are unable to attend, please let me know before December 5.

会 议 通 知

接收人：全体销售人员

发送人：玛丽娜·彭内尔（销售部经理秘书）

日期：2012 年 12 月 1 日

主题：2013 年销售计划会议

鉴于市场竞争日益加剧，新年又即将到来，销售部定于 2012 年 12 月 7 日星期五下午 4:00 在公司会议室召开会议，编制 2013 年销售计划。随函附本次会议议程。

请按时到会。如若不能参加，请在 12 月 5 日前通知我。

例 7

HARTHORNE-BERGESON, INC.

Meeting of the Marketing Department Staff

Tuesday, March 6, 2013

9:00 to 12:00 a.m.

The Third Conference Room

AGENDA

1. Call to order by Chairperson, Henry Walker

2. Reading and approval of the minutes of the February meeting

3. Old Business

   1) Discussion of the results of the market research for Product No. 321

   2) Discussion of the direct-mail campaign

4. New Business

   1) Selection of employee incentives

   2) Discussion of strategies to win new accounts

   3) Other business

5. Adjournment

Contact: Nancy Brown, Extension 3287

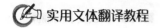

哈松伯吉森公司会议议程

营销部员工会议

时间：2013年3月6日星期二上午9:00—12:00

地点：第三会议室

1. 会议主席亨利·沃克宣布会议开始
2. 宣读并通过2月份会议的记录
3. 讨论过去的工作
   1）讨论321号产品市场调查结果
   2）讨论直接邮件促销活动
4. 讨论新的工作
   1）选择激励员工的方式
   2）讨论赢得新客户的策略
   3）其他业务
5. 休会

联系人：南茜·布朗（分机3287）

例6是公司内部职员会议的通知，内容、格式都较简单，标题没有题注。直接对应原文的格式翻译即可。例7是典型的会议议程模式，内容简洁，层次分明，翻译时应严格按照议程顺序逐条翻译。

三、会议须知及参会回条的翻译

会议须知是会议组织者告知与会人员应当了解和遵守有关会议活动事项的规定文书，通常由会务人员在会前发给与会人员。会议须知一般由标题和正文两部分组成。标题分单一性标题和多要素标题。单一性标题只有文种，如"会议须知"；多要素标题由会议主办单位、会议内容及文种组成。正文结构较简单，通常是按顺序分别写清会议的注意事项，包括会议组织机构及负责人的联系方式、会议日程、纪律及安保事项、后勤服务等。翻译时一般按顺序逐项翻译即可。参会回条通常同会议通知一起发送或邮寄给参加会议的人员，由参加者填写后发回至会议组织者，内容包括与会人员的个人简介、参加会议的意向、对会议的特殊要求、个人联系方式等。翻译时无须改变格式，按会议回条的具体样式进行翻译即可。例如：

例8

中华医学会第九次全国老年医学学术会议
暨第三届全国老年动脉硬化与周围血管疾病专题研讨会（2009）
会 议 须 知

会议时间：2009年4月24日至27日
会议地点：湖南长沙中共湖南省委九所宾馆

学分授予：中华医学会Ⅰ类学分
主办单位：中华医学会老年医学分会、《中华老年医学》杂志编辑委员会
协办单位：中南大学湘雅二医院、湖南省医学会老年医学专业委员会
咨询电话：010-58294398（注册）；58115073（投稿）；
84205137、85158123（学术）
会议网站：www.cma-epvd.com 详情请登录网站或电话咨询。
具体安排：24日全天报到，25—26日学术会议，27日上午12:00前离开
各种费用：会务费代表800元，学生500元（凭学生证），会务组统一安排食宿，费用自理。
会场地址：长沙市韶山北路16号（410011），0731-2263888
乘车路线：从黄花机场乘坐旅客大巴（票价15元，全程35分钟左右，从6:20至20:30，每30分钟一班车）到火车站的民航大酒店，转乘的士到长沙九所宾馆（车费大约6元）。从火车站可搭乘1路、136路、142路、168路公交车到袁家岭站下车。
传　　真：010-58294398
E-mail：58294398@163.com

The 9th National Geriatrics Conference & The 3rd National Old Age Arteriosclerosis and Its Ambient Vascular Disease Symposium by Chinese Medical Association (2009) Conference Brochure

Date: April 24th–27th, 2009
Venue: CPC Hunan Provincial Committee Jiusuo Hotel, Changsha, Hunan
Credit: CMA Class I Credit
Organizers: CMA Geriatrics Branch, Editorial Board of *Chinese Journal of Geriatrics*
Co-organizers: Central South University Xiangya Second Hospital, Hunan Provincial Medical Association Geriatrics Specialized Committee
Telephone: 010-58294398 (registration); 010-58115073 (contribution); 010-84205137, 010-85158123 (academic)
Website: www.cma-epvd.com. For further information about the conference, please visit the website or consult us by telephone.
Schedule: Check in, 24th; Meeting, 25–26th; Check out, before 12:00, 27th
Expenses: Symposium Fee, representative 800 RMB/ students 500 RMB (student ID needed). Catering and accommodations will be arranged by organizers and paid by participants.
Address: No. 16 Shaoshan North Rd., Changsha City, Hunan (410011), 0731-2263888

Travel: Participants can take airport shuttles from Huanghua Airport to Minhang Hotel at the Railway Station (Airport shuttles leave every 30 minutes from 6:20 a.m. to 8:30 p.m. Ticket price: 15 RMB. The journey will take about 35 minutes.), then transfer to a taxi to Jiusuo Hotel (The taxi expense is about 6 RMB). Participants can also take No. 1/136/142/168 buses at the Railway Station and get off at Yuanjialing Stop.

Fax: 010-58294398

E-mail: 58294398@163.com

例9

2011年两岸特殊教育学术研讨会回条

单位名称：

姓名	性别	职称或职务	联系电话	E-mail	是否需协助联系住宿	备注

注：请于2011年9月20日前将参会回条e-mail至：cqnutj@163.com 或传真：+86-23-65363469

2011 Taiwan and Mainland Academic Seminar on Special Education Return Receipt

Organization:

Name	Gender	Title or Position	Phone	E-mail	Accommodation Aids (Yes/No)	Remarks

Ps: Please send the receipt to e-mail address cqnutj@163.com before Sept. 20, 2011 or fax it to +86-23-65363469.

"会议须知"的表达在英文中并不固定，常用的有：conference brochure、general information、notice、hints、instruction 等。其中，brochure 和 information 正式些，多用于规模较大的国际学术会议，notice 等正式程度要低些。"参会回条"又称参会回执，英文中类似的表达有 return slip (receipt)、acknowledgement slip (receipt)、acknowledgement 等，翻译时可灵活选择。

会议会务文书注重会议相关信息的传递，强调实效性，因此语言主要以说明为主，没有太多感性因素，条理性和逻辑性也很强。翻译时首先要准确再现原文本信息，比如时间、地点、日程、议程、行程等。其次，需要考虑恰当的对等表达，从词汇到句式均应以朴素、简明为好。

第三节
会议礼仪文书的翻译

会议礼仪文书是为了做好会议前、中、后的礼节性工作而撰写的文书，主要包括邀请函、祝贺词、答谢词、欢迎词、欢送词、祝酒词等。不同类别的礼仪文书有不同的语言特点，翻译时应注意把握用语措辞得体、准确。

一、邀请函、祝贺词、祝酒词的翻译

邀请函是为邀请相关人员参加学术性会议、商务会议或政府主办的贸易洽谈会等专业性会议而撰写的礼仪文书，语言一般要谦恭、客气。此外，还要向被邀请者介绍会议概况，说明会议特色，语言应准确、严密。例如：

例1 I am writing to ask whether you would deliver a speech in English at the plenary session. Invited talks will be twenty minutes long, followed by a five minutes question and answer session.
给您写信是想邀请您在全体人员大会上做一次英语演讲，时间大概20分钟，之后有一个5分钟的问答环节。

例2 Your local expenses, including hotel accommodations, meals, and the conference fee will be covered by the organizers.
您在会议期间的所有费用，包括住宿、用餐以及会务费，将由主办方支付。

例3 We hope that you can spare time from your tight schedule to attend this forum.
我们真诚希望您能拨冗参加本次论坛。

邀请函也是信函的一种。众所周知，英文信函有信内地址，地址的写法有固定的格式，通常为由小到大，小的在前，大的在后。汉语地址的书写习惯与英文相反。翻译邀请函时应注意两种语言地址写法的转换。例如：

例4

A Letter of Invitation[2]

School of Electronics & Information Engineering
Tongji University
1239 Siping Road
Shanghai 200092
P. R. China

Prof. Roger Lee

---

[2] 董琇. 2011. 国际会议交流英语. 上海：同济大学出版社.

College of Science & Technology
Central Michigan University
ET Building 200
Mount Pleasant, MI 48859
U.S.A.

Dear Prof. Lee,

On behalf of the School of Electronics and Information Engineering at Tongji University, I am very happy to invite you to be a keynote speaker at the 3rd IEEE International Workshop on E-Activity to be held on May 10–15, 2011, at our university. This workshop will focus on theory, systems, and applications for all electronic activities such as e-learning and e-commerce. You are an internationally acclaimed scholar and your participation will be among the highlights of this workshop.

We enclose more detailed information on this workshop which you might need. If you have any questions about this workshop, please do not hesitate to contact our convener, Mr. Wu, at 86-21-65980000. We sincerely hope you can honor the invitation.

We are looking forward to hearing from you soon.

Yours sincerely,
Haoran Liu
Dean of the School
Chair of the Organizing Committee

邀 请 函

美国密歇根州芒特普莱森特市东部大厦200号
中央密歇根大学科技学院李·罗杰教授
邮编：48859

亲爱的李教授：

我代表同济大学电子信息工程学院，诚挚邀请您作为大会主旨发言人参加2011年5月10日至15日在我校举行的"第三届电气和电子工程师协会网络活动国际研讨会"。本次研讨会的主要议题为网上学习与电子商务等网络活动的相关理论体系及其应用。作为国际上享有盛誉的专家学者，您的参与一定会成为本次研讨会的焦点。

随函附寄本次研讨会的详细情况。如果您对本次研讨会有任何疑问，请随时通过电话86-21-65980000联络本次会议的召集人吴先生。真诚地希望您能接受我们的邀请。

期待尽快收到您的佳音。

刘浩然　敬启
院长兼组委会主席
同济大学电子信息工程学院
中国上海四平路 1239 号
邮编：200092

祝贺词也称贺词，是机构或个人在参加重大会议时发表的对会议的祝贺语。以函件形式送达的贺词叫贺信，借助电报发出的贺词称作贺电。贺词长短灵活，语言富有感情，措辞与祝贺方的身份密切相关。翻译时应弄清祝贺方与会议的身份关系，注意用语准确，措辞恰当。祝酒词是会议举办方或个人作为东道主在欢迎客人到访的酒会或宴会上宣读或即席发表的祝贺文稿。祝酒词语言生动、感情真挚，翻译时应注意选词的感情色彩。

例5 值此二〇〇一年亚太经合组织妇女领导人会议召开之际，我谨代表中华人民共和国政府和中国人民，并以我个人名义，向远道而来的与会代表表示热烈的欢迎，并对大会的胜利召开致以衷心的祝贺！

On the occasion of 2001 APEC Women Leaders Convention, on behalf of the Government of the People's Republic of China and the Chinese people, and in my own name, I hereby give my warmest welcome to the delegates coming afar, and my heartfelt congratulations to the successful convening of the Meeting.

例6 医院管理学会成立五年来，努力加强自身建设，积极开展理论研讨、专题研究和学术交流，团结广大医院管理人员，严格自律并维护医院合法权益，为我国医院管理事业的发展做出了重要的贡献。

During the five years after its founding, the Hospital Management Society has made great contributions to the development of our career of hospital management by taking efforts to strengthen self-construction, actively carrying out theoretical, monographic studies and academic exchanges, as well as uniting hospital managers, strictly self-disciplining and maintaining legislative interests of the hospitals.

例7

祝 酒 词

各位领导、各位嘉宾，女士们、先生们：

湘江欢歌庆盛会，麓山红装迎嘉宾。在风景怡人的湘江之滨，在钟灵毓秀的岳麓山下，我们相聚雷锋家乡希望之城，隆重举办湘台经贸交流与合作高峰论坛，同叙友谊，共谋发展，其情真真，其意切切。借此机会，我谨代表中共长沙市委、市人民政府和620万长沙人民，对远道而来的各位嘉宾贵客表示最热烈的欢迎和最诚挚的问候！

友谊架通合作桥，开放拓宽发展路。近年来，湘台两地之间的交流与合作不断深化，并取得了丰硕成果，此次论坛的成功举办就是最好的证明。我们将以此为契机，积极开辟合作新途径，不断拓宽发展新空间，加快对外开放步伐，降低市场准入门槛，提升政务服务水平，使长沙成为经济社会快速发展、核心竞争力不断增强的区域性中心城市，成为台湾资本输出、产业转移的重要基地。我相信，在湘台两地的共同努力下，友谊的桥梁一定会化作腾飞的翅膀，真诚的合作一定会敲开成功的大门！

相聚星城喜事多，酒逢知己千杯少。我提议：让我们共同举杯，为美好的明天，干杯！

Words for a Toast

Ladies and gentlemen,

Xiang River sings and celebrates the great event while the Yuelu Mountain dresses up for our guests. At the pleasant riverside of Xiang River and the foot of the witty Yuelu Mountain, we are gathering at the hometown of Lei Feng, city of hope, to have this grand Forum on Hunan-Taiwan's Economic and Trade Exchanges and Cooperation. Our friendship is sincere, and our desires to develop are equally strong. Please allow me to take this opportunity to express my warmest welcome and cordial greetings to our dear guests on behalf of the Changsha Municipal Committee, the Changsha Government and the 6.2 million Changsha people.

Friendship paves the cooperation bridge while opening-up broadens the way of development. The successful convening of this Forum best proves the deepening of exchanges and cooperation between Hunan and Taiwan which has led to fruitful achievements. We shall take this opportunity to improve our cooperation and development in new areas through new mechanisms and at greater speed. We shall lower the market entrance thresholds and improve our services to make Changsha a regional center with fast economic development and strengthened core competitiveness. Hunan will become an important base for Taiwan to invest and transfer industries. I believe that our friendship and cooperation will bring success to both areas with our joined efforts.

At last I'd like to ask all present to make a toast to our bright future. Cheers!

祝酒词最后通常是邀请宾客一起举杯干杯，下面请看常见的有关"干杯"的表达：

- Let us drink to the 20th anniversary of the founding of our Society.
  让我们为庆祝本协会成立20周年干杯。
- Hold your glass please. Now let's drink to president Jackson for his successful organization of the conference.
  请举起酒杯，现在让我们为杰克逊会长成功组织本次大会而干杯。

- Now ladies and gentlemen, may I ask you all to join me in raising the glass to the health of Dr. Johnson.
  下面,请大家共同举杯,为约翰逊教授的健康干杯。
- Let me propose a toast to our members' health and success in research activities.
  让我们为诸位会员的健康和研究成功干杯。

二、欢迎词、答谢词、欢送词的翻译

欢迎词是会议举办方或个人以东道主身份出面,在公共场合对宾客的到来表示欢迎的讲话文稿。欢迎词针对性强,与其使用的场合密切相关,语言风格随场合而定,或轻松活泼,或严肃庄重。翻译时应首先弄清欢迎词的使用场合,确定恰当的基调。答谢词是在会议或酒宴上,主人致辞后,宾客为答谢主人的热情欢迎或款待所做的发言。答谢词通常感情真挚,措辞得体精练。

例8

Welcome Speech[3]

Ladies and gentlemen,

It is a great honor for us to have Dr. Harrison with us. First of all, please allow me on behalf of all present here to extend our warm welcome and cordial greetings to our distinguished guest, who has been our good friend for decades.

Dr. Harrison is well known to the world for his achievements in the field of electronics. It was with his full assistance that our laboratory came into being. It is with his sincere support that we have trained so many experts in electronics who are now undertaking important tasks of this field all over the country.

Now, let us invite Dr. Harrison to speak to us.

欢 迎 词

女士们、先生们:

今天能与哈里逊博士在一起,是我们莫大的荣幸。首先,请允许我代表在座的各位向我们的贵宾、几十年来的老朋友表示热烈的欢迎和真诚的问候。

哈里逊博士以他在电子方面的卓越成就而闻名全球。是他的鼎力帮助促成了我们实验室的建成。正是有了他的真诚帮助我们才培养了众多的电子专家,他们现在已经是全国各地电子界的栋梁。

下面,有请哈里逊博士讲话。

---

3 何乔. 2006. 秘书英语. 合肥:中国科学技术大学出版社.

例9

Speech of Thanks[4]

Ladies and gentlemen,

I feel very pleased to attend your meeting and have the opportunity to talk with our Canadian friends here, and thank you for your warm welcome.

Following the continuous development of the friendly relations between our two countries, many government officers, scientists, artists and businessmen exchange their visits. I have been looking forward to this trip, and now I have been more than rewarded.

I feel much honored to be given this opportunity to meet so many well-known personages like you. I am sure my stay here will be a fruitful and enjoyable one. I do hope to learn much from you while I am here.

Thank you.

答 谢 词

女士们、先生们：

能参加此次会议，有机会与在场的加拿大朋友交谈，我感到十分高兴。非常感谢你们的热烈欢迎！

随着两国友好关系的不断发展，许多政府官员、科学家、艺术家和商人互访。我一直盼望着这次旅行，现在总算如愿以偿了。

特别荣幸有机会认识如此多的知名人士。我坚信这次访问将是卓有成效和令人愉快的。我真心希望在此期间能多向各位请教。

谢谢。

下面是一些欢迎词和答谢词中常用到的句子：

- It is my pleasure to extend to all of you a cordial welcome on behalf of all the staff members of the company.
  我代表公司全体员工向大家致以热烈的欢迎。
- It is with a profound feeling of pleasure and privilege that I'd like to express a hearty welcome to all of you, especially to many distinguished guests from abroad.
  我非常愉快而荣幸地向大家表示衷心欢迎，尤其是许多来自国外的贵宾。
- Please allow me to offer my hearty thanks to the Chairman Mr. Washington for his kind welcome.
  请允许我对本次会议的主席华盛顿先生表示真诚的感谢，感谢他的热烈欢迎。
- I wish to express my sincere gratitude to the Organizing Committee for the general way in which it has extended its hospitality to all of us.

---

4 何乔. 2006. 秘书英语. 合肥：中国科学技术大学出版社.

我要对组委会给予我们的热情款待表示衷心的感谢。

欢送词是会议即将或已经结束之际，会议组织者欢送参加会议的团体或重要宾客的讲稿。如果是在欢送宴会上使用的欢送词，也可以称作祝酒词。欢送词和祝酒词一样，语言生动，感情真挚，简洁明快。翻译时用语不要过于文气，通俗为好。

例10

A Send-off /Farewell Speech[5]

Ladies and gentlemen,

How time flies! It was here that we gave Prof. Smith a hearty welcome two weeks ago. We are now here again to bid him farewell.

As you know, Prof. Smith is well-known for the computer software development. During his stay here, he visited many universities and colleges and gave many great lectures on the subject. He will leave for home tomorrow morning. I sincerely hope that Prof. Smith will benefit us with his valuable suggestions.

Finally, I want to take this opportunity to ask Prof. Smith to convey our profound friendship and best regards to his people. We wish him a pleasant journey home and good health.

Now let's welcome Prof. Smith to address us.

欢 送 词

女士们、先生们：

时间过得真快。两个星期前我们在这里热烈欢迎史密斯教授，现在我们又要在这里向他道别。

众所周知，史密斯教授因为计算机软件的研发而闻名于世。来访期间，他访问了很多大学和学院，做了很多软件研发方面的讲座，非常精彩。明天早上他就要回国了。我真诚希望史密斯教授的建议能让我们每个人受益。

最后，借此机会我想请史密斯教授向美国人民转达我们深厚的友情和美好的祝愿。祝他一路顺风，身体健康。

下面，让我们欢迎史密斯教授讲话。

会议礼仪文书首先强调礼仪功能，即在既定的场合表达既定的情感。因此，有别于会务文书和事务文书等说明文体多强调信息性和逻辑性的特点，礼仪文书更多要求抒情。所以，礼仪文书中会较多地使用抒情性的形容词和副词，以表达邀请、欢迎、感谢、祝贺及离别等不同场合下宾主双方的真挚情谊，对彼此美好的祝福和将来继续合作的愿望。翻译时应把握具体礼仪文书所蕴含的情感，恰当地选用对等的形容词和副词，尽可能周详地将

---

5 何乔. 2006. 秘书英语. 合肥：中国科学技术大学出版社.

原文中的情感还原，有时还应注意再现原文的语言风格，比如有的礼仪文书幽默活泼，有的则情真意切，有的甚至会引经据典。翻译时，在达意的基础上，应着力保证在风格上与原文对等。

第四节
会议事务文书的翻译

会议事务文书是指为处理会议的事务性工作而撰写的文书，主要包括会议制度、会议提案、会议记录、会议纪要、会议决议及会议公报等。会议事务文书一般要求语言客观规范、条理清楚。翻译时要注意语言的明确、规范，避免含混不清和语体失当。

一、会议制度和会议提案的翻译

会议制度是会议组织机构为保证会议质量和效果，对会议工作的任务、内容、程序、规则、分工等方面所作的规范性文书。会议提案是指在各类代表大会上，参加会议的代表按照规定程序提交大会的书面意见和建议。会议制度和会议提案都有明确的规定性，语体正式，内容翔实，用语明确，没有过多的修饰词藻。翻译时应参照中英文中同类会议文书的规范用语进行翻译。

例1

公司会议管理制度

第一条　为加强公司会议纪律，规范公司会议管理，提高会议质量，降低会议成本，特制定本制度。

第二条　公司会议包括公司年终会、周例会、部门会议等。

第三条　公司年终会每年召开一次，具体时间由综合管理中心根据董事长指示安排执行。年终会议由董事长主持，全体员工参加，若有事不能参加的，应提前向综合管理中心请假并经执行总经理批准。

第四条　年终会议由各部门各自总结本部门年度工作情况。如工作的具体内容、工作任务的完成情况及所取得的业绩与成效，按照公司总体工作要求和指标提出下一年度的工作计划等。年终会议由综合管理中心进行会议记录。

第五条　周例会由综合管理中心根据执行总经理的指示召集，时间暂定为每周一上午9:00。特殊原因需要延期召开的，由综合管理中心另行通知。

第六条　周例会由部门主管及以上员工出席，特殊情况由全体员工出席。若有事不能出席的，应当提前向综合管理中心请假并经执行总经理批准。

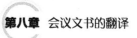

......

第十三条 本制度未尽事宜，由综合管理中心负责解释、补充。

第十四条 本制度由公司执行总经理批准后生效，自颁布之日起执行。

Administration Regulations for Corporate Meetings

Article 1　Regulations are hereby made to strengthen the meeting discipline and management, to improve the meeting quality as well as to lower the meeting costs.

Article 2　Corporate meetings mentioned here include year-end meetings, weekly meetings and departmental meetings, etc.

Article 3　Year-end meeting should be held once a year with time arranged by the Administrative Center under the direction of board chairman. The year-end meeting will be hosted by board chairman himself and attended by all the staff. Anyone who cannot attend should ask for leave ahead of time and get permission from the chief executive manager.

Article 4　Year-end meetings are mainly about departmental work sum-ups for the year such as work contents, task progress, the results and effects as well as work plan for the next year according to the company's overall requirements and plan. The Administrative Center is responsible for the minutes of the year-end meeting.

Article 5　Weekly meetings should be convened by the Administrative Center under the chief executive manager's directions. Time for weekly meetings is temporarily set at 9:00 a.m. on Monday every week. Extension notices should be given by the Administrative Center in advance.

Article 6　Weekly meetings are attended by departmental head and above level and by all staff under special circumstances. Anyone who cannot attend meetings should ask for leave at the Administrative Center and get permission from the chief executive manager.

…

Article 13　The Administrative Center is responsible for the explanation and supplementation of the regulations.

Article 14　The regulations above shall take effects after approval of the chief executive manager and be executed immediately after enactment.

例2

关于建议设立十二中心理咨询室的提案

案由： 由于青少年所处的特殊阶段以及他们所处的学习环境，其心理健康的发展变化正处在不稳定阶段,因此在中学设立心理咨询室对增强学生的心理健康有特殊意义。

提案建议:
1. 学校建立心理健康教育课制度。
2. 设立"心理咨询室"并配备专职的心理健康教育教师。
3. 心理健康教育教师必须由经过专业培训、取得心理咨询资格证书的专职人员担任。

Proposal on Establishing Psychological Counseling Room at No. 12 High School

Summary of the Case: High school students' psychological conditions and their learning environment, have led to their unstable stage in psychological health development. Therefore, it is of special significance to establish Psychological Counseling Room at the school to improve students' psychological health.

Proposals of the Case:

Article 1　The School should establish a system for psychological health education.

Article 2　The School should establish Psychological Counseling Room with full-time psychological counselors.

Article 3　Psychological counselors are required to have years of professional trainings and certificates in psychological counseling.

二、会议记录和会议纪要的翻译

会议记录是由会议的组织者指定专人,如实、准确地记录会议的组织、进程、研究讨论的议题、报告发言的主要内容和议定有关事项的一种重要书面材料。会议记录要求内容真实和完整,常作为相关决议的依据,也是查阅与会者发言等内容的依据。会议纪要是正式的法规性公务文件,是在会议记录、会议相关文件及其他相关材料基础上,对会议研究的问题和事项综合整理而成的,内容包括会议的基本情况、主要精神和中心内容等。会议纪要比会议记录文体上更加正式,在翻译中应注意这种区别,尤其在体例和措辞上。

例3

德育领导小组会议记录

主要议题:学期德育工作总结

日　　期:2010年1月20日

地　　点:办公室

出席人员:赵慧文、王素婷、赵琨、邵建英、赵晓云、耿婷婷、姬巧文

主 持 人:杨晓琳

本年度，围绕我校整体工作目标，在深入开展社会主义荣辱观教育，切实加强对学生品德教育、纪律教育、法治教育、心理健康教育、习惯养成教育等方面做了大量的工作，为顺利创建苏州市教育现代化学校做出了贡献。主要工作有以下几方面：

1. 进一步强化德育队伍。

2. 加强安全、法纪教育，培养学生安全意识、遵纪守法意识和自我保护意识。

3. 开展主题教育月活动。努力培养学生的文明素养、社会公德，争做合格的小公民。

4. 继续学习、实践"八荣八耻"的荣辱观教育，充分利用国旗下致辞、板报、宣传栏、德育实践基地等作用，引导学生在社区开展健康有益的文化文娱活动。

5. 进一步加强校园文化建设，营造良好育人环境。

6. 开展德育课题的研究活动。

德育工作任重而道远，我们将不断学习先进学校的成功经验，团结一致，创新工作，努力使我校德育工作再上新台阶。

会议主持人：××
记录人：××
2010 年 1 月 20 日

Moral Education Leading Group Meeting Minutes

Subject: Summary of moral education work

Date: January 20, 2010

Venue: Moral Education Office

Attendance: Zhao Huiwen, Wang Suting, Zhao Kun, Shao Jianying, Zhao Xiaoyun, Geng Tingting, Ji Qiaowen

Moderator: Yang Xiaolin

This year, centering on the overall objectives of the school work, our school has made great progress in the building of Education Modernization School of Suzhou City by spreading socialist concepts of honor and disgrace and strengthening education in areas like students' morality, discipline, law, mental health and good habits. The work done mainly includes:

1. Further strengthening moral education team;

2. Strengthening education in law and security to foster awareness of security, laws and regulations, and self-protection;

3. Conducting monthly education activities to foster students' civility, social morality and sense of honor in being a qualified citizen;

4. Continuing the campaign of learning and practicing "Eight Honors and Eight

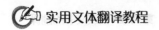

Shames" and encouraging students to participate in healthful cultural and recreational activities such as under-the-national-flag speech-making, bulletin board designing, publicity column preparation, moral education base construction, etc;

5. Pushing forward campus culture construction to create a good educational environment;

6. Conducting research activities on moral education.

All in all, moral education is very important that requires us to keep learning from successful schools, be united and work creatively so as to update our work to a higher stage.

Moderator: ××
Recorder: ××
January 20, 2010

例4

Mid-Winter Meeting in Moscow
IFLA Acquisition and Collection Development Section
MINUTES

Standing Committee meeting held at the Russian State Library in Moscow on Thursday, March 4, 2010 (10:00–12:45)

1. Attendance and General Introductions

Standing Committee members attending were:

Sharon Johnson, Glenda Lammers, Natalia Litvinova, Susanne Maier, Judy Mansfield, Johannes Rudberg, Nadia Zilper.

Standing Committee members not attending were:

Joanna Ball, Corrado Di Tillio, Kazuko Fukubayashi, Julia Gelfand, Joseph Hafner, Judy Jeng, Klaus Kempf, Helen Ladron de Guevara Cox, Dudu Nkosi

The Chair expressed her sincere thanks to Natalia Litvinova and Irina Gayshun for all their efforts in preparing the meeting and the previous day's workshop.

2. Adoption of the Agenda

The proposed agenda was approved with the addition of three questions: a brief evaluation of yesterday's workshop, the issue of committee meeting times in Gothenburg and the issue of the questionnaire about the general conferences.

3. Approval of Minutes of the Annual Meeting of the Standing Committee, held in Milan, 22 and 26, August 2009.

The Minutes of the Milan meetings were approved with one correction: Susanne Maier and Regine Schmolling are implementing a German translation of the Gift Guidelines.

4. Announcements

The Chair announced that the Committee's first meeting during the General Conference in Gothenburg is scheduled for August 10 at 8:30–11:20. A second meeting might be held sometime during the conference.

5. Gothenburg Programme—2010

On behalf of Joseph Hafner, Judy Mansfield reported that the working group for the Gothenburg Programme had voted on the thirteen delivered proposals, and six of these had been chosen.

…

12. Adjournment

The meeting was adjourned at 12:40.

国际图联采集和馆藏发展组
仲冬莫斯科会议
会议纪要

2010年3月4日，星期四，上午10:00—12:45，在莫斯科俄罗斯国家图书馆举行常务委员会会议。

1. 出席会议人员

出席会议的常务委员会成员：

莎朗·约翰逊、格伦达·拉默斯、纳塔利娅·利特维诺娃、苏珊·迈尔、朱迪·曼斯菲尔德、约翰内斯·鲁德贝里、纳迪亚·希伯

未出席会议的常务委员会成员：

乔安娜·波尔、科拉多迪·提里奥、福林合子、朱莉娅·盖尔芬德、约瑟夫·哈夫纳、朱迪·政、克劳斯·肯普夫、海伦拉德恩·格瓦拉考克斯、杜杜·恩科西

大会主席向在会议筹备期间和前一天召开的研讨会中付出巨大努力的纳塔利娅·利特维诺娃和伊琳娜·盖伊沙恩表示衷心的感谢。

2. 通过议程

大会通过了拟定的会议议程及另外三个议题，即对前一天研讨会做的简要评价、关于哥德堡委员会会议日程的议题以及有关大会的问卷调查的议题。

3. 通过2009年8月22日和26日在米兰举行的常务委员会年会的会议纪要

大会批准通过了米兰会议的会议纪要并做出一处更正：应为苏珊·迈尔和雷吉娜·施莫琳负责"购物指南"的德语翻译。

4. 公告

大会主席宣布，国际图联委员会哥德堡大会第一次会议时间定于8月10日8:30—11:20举行，第二次会议将于大会期间的某个时间进行。

5. 关于2010年哥德堡计划的进展

朱迪·曼斯菲尔德代表约瑟夫·哈夫纳向大会报告，哥德堡大会会议方案工作组已对十三项已提交提案进行了投票，其中六项提案已经被采纳。

……

12. 休会

会议于12:40休会。

三、会议决议和会议公报的翻译

会议决议是会议组织方经过讨论通过的针对重要事项所做的决策和安排的公文，常见于政府机关、企事业单位。会议决议的内容具有决策性、权威性和程序性，语言严谨、准确。会议公报是国家机关就重要会议或重大决定公开发布的告知性文书。会议公报的发布机关级别很高，因此内容上比会议决议更具权威性和重要性；另外会议公报的内容还具有很强的公开性和新闻性。会议公报的语言通常准确、全面、活泼，富有感染力。翻译时应注意以上两种文本区别于其他事务文书的语言特点。

例5

CORPORATE RESOLUTION

I _____ Secretary of _____, a corporation organized under the laws of the Country of _____ (the "Corporation"), do hereby certify that at a meeting of the Board of Directors of the said Corporation, held in accordance with its charter and by-laws on the date at which a quorum was at all times present and acting, the attached resolutions were duly adopted, that said resolutions have not been amended, rescinded or revoked, and are in no way in conflict with any of the provisions of the charter or by-laws of the said Corporation.

RESOLUTION

Name_____ Title_____

Each of them or such other person as this Corporation may designate from time to time either in writing or by their apparent authority be and hereby are authorized to trade in OTCFX account for risk of this Corporation through and with FXCM ASIA, as the said Corporation is now constituted or may be hereafter constituted, the authority hereby granted including the power to do any of the following:

(a) To open an account with FXCM ASIA for the purpose of FXCM ASIA's carrying, clearing, and settling all securities transactions undertaken by the Corporation;

(b) To buy and sell foreign currency positions for present delivery, on margin or otherwise, the power to sell including the power to sell "short";

(c) To deposit with and withdraw from said firm money, currencies, contracts, for the purchase or sale of currencies, securities and other property;

(d) To receive requests and demands for additional margin, notices of intention to sell or purchase and other notices and demands of whatever character;

(e) To receive and confirm the correctness of notices, confirmations, requests, demands and confirmations of every kind;

(f) To place oral orders with any authorized representative of FXCM ASIA for the execution of securities transactions on behalf of the Corporation on any marketplace FXCM ASIA is permitted to effect transaction on;

(g) To pay FXCM ASIA all fees, commissions and mark ups or downs incurred in connection with any such transactions and all amounts as may be requested by FXCM ASIA formative to time as margin or equity for the Corporation's account;

(h) Further Resolved, that the foregoing resolutions and the certificate actually furnished to FXCM ASIA by the Secretary/Assistant Secretary of the Corporation pursuant thereto, be and they hereby are made irrevocable until written notice of the revocation thereof shall have been received by FXCM ASIA.

I further certify that the foregoing resolutions have not been modified or rescinded and are now in full force and effect and that the Corporation has the power under its charter and by-laws and applicable laws to take the action set forth in and contemplated by the foregoing resolutions. I do further certify that each of the following has been duly elected and is now legally holding the office set opposite his/her signature.

Signature of President
Signature of Vice-President
Signature of Secretary

公司决议

本人 _____，为 _____ 公司秘书，本公司为根据 _____ 国法律成立的合法公司。本人特此证明本公司董事会已于本决议所载之日，根据公司章程及公司规则召开董事会会议。出席会议的董事自始至终符合法定人数；会议通过以下所附各项决议；各项决议自通过后未被修改、终止或撤销，并且与公司章程及公司规则并无任何冲突之处。

决议内容

姓名 _____ 职务 _____

任何一位上述人士或本公司以书面或表见代理的形式授权的其他人士可以通过福汇亚洲为本公司进行杠杆式外汇买卖。本公司为此目的授权上述人士从事下述任何行为：

1. 于福汇亚洲开立账户，以便福汇亚洲执行本公司所有证券交易并进行有

关的清算及交割;

2. 进行外汇现汇、保证金或其他交易,售出外汇的权力包括卖空;

3. 向本公司账户存入或从本公司账户提取货币、现钞、合约以用于买卖现钞、证券或其他财产;

4. 收取请求或要求支付额外保证金通知、买卖意图通知或任何其他性质的通知或要求;

5. 收取并确认各类通知、确认书、请求要求及各种确认书的更正;

6. 向福汇亚洲的任何授权代表人发出口头指令,以便于后者在福汇亚洲有权进行交易的任何市场代表本公司进行证券交易;

7. 向福汇亚洲支付与此类交易有关的所有费用、佣金、溢价和折价,及福汇亚洲不时要求的与本公司账户有关的保证金或其他款项;

8. 本公司进一步决议,除非福汇亚洲收到书面撤销通知,前述决议及根据前述决议由本公司秘书/助理秘书向福汇亚洲实际送达的确认,不得撤销(不论上述主管是否已不再担任本公司的主管或雇员);

本人进一步证明前述决议未被修改或撤销,全部有效;本公司依据公司章程、公司规则及适用法,有权采取前述协议中所列行动。并且本人证明以下各位人士经正式选举,并合法担任与其签名对应的职务。

总　　裁　签名:

副　总　裁　签名:

公司秘书　签名:

下面请看中国共产党十七届五中全会会议公报部分内容的原文及译文:

例6

- 中国共产党第十七届中央委员会第五次全体会议,于2010年10月15日至18日在北京举行。
  The Fifth Plenum of the 17th CPC Central Committee was held in Beijing from October 15 to 18, 2010.

- 出席这次全会的有,中央委员202人,候补中央委员163人。中央纪律检查委员会常务委员会委员和有关方面负责同志列席了会议。党的十七大代表中部分基层同志和专家学者也列席了会议。
  Present at the plenum were 202 members and 163 alternate members of the CPC Central Committee. Members of the Standing Committee of the CPC Central Commission for Discipline Inspection and leading officials of relevant departments attended the meeting as non-voting delegates. Some delegates to the 17th CPC National Congress, including a few from the grass roots and a few experts and scholars, also attended the meeting as non-voting delegates.

- 全会由中央政治局主持。中央委员会总书记胡锦涛作了重要讲话。
  The plenum was presided over by the Political Bureau of the CPC Central Committee. Hu Jintao, General Secretary of the CPC Central Committee, delivered an important speech at the plenum.

- 全会听取和讨论了胡锦涛受中央政治局委托作的工作报告，审议通过了《中共中央关于制定国民经济和社会发展第十二个五年规划的建议》。温家宝就《建议（讨论稿）》向全会作了说明。
  The plenum listened to and discussed the working report delivered by Hu Jintao, who was entrusted by the Political Bureau of the CPC Central Committee, and adopted the "CPC Central Committee's Proposal for Formulating the 12th Five-Year Program for China's Economic and Social Development (2011–2015)". Wen Jiabao made an explanatory speech on the draft proposal to the plenum.

- 全会提出，文化是一个民族的精神和灵魂，是国家发展和民族振兴的强大力量。要推动文化大发展大繁荣、提升国家文化软实力，坚持社会主义先进文化前进方向，提高全民族文明素质，推进文化创新，深化文化体制改革，繁荣发展文化事业和文化产业，满足人民群众不断增长的精神文化需求，基本建成公共文化服务体系，推动文化产业成为国民经济支柱性产业，充分发挥文化引导社会、教育人民、推动发展的功能，建设中华民族共有精神家园，增强民族凝聚力和创造力。
  The plenum pointed out that culture is the spirit and soul of a nation, and is the power to propel development of a country and the revitalization of a nation. Efforts should be made to help the culture sector prosper, to boost the country's soft power in cultural fields, to consistently advance the development of the socialist culture, and to improve the Chinese people's civil education. The plenum also called for efforts to promote cultural innovation, to deepen the reform of the cultural system, and to boost cultural undertakings and the cultural industry. Efforts should also be made to satisfy the people's ever-growing demand for cultural products, to basically build up a public service system of culture, to make the culture industry one of the pillar industries for the national economy, to give full play to the role of culture in guiding, educating people and promoting development, to build a spiritual home for the Chinese nation, and to boost cohesion and creativity of the nation.

会议公报的内容涉及国家大政方针，语言表达既要合乎英语国家同类文本的规范要求，又要生动活泼，体现汉语的表达特色。对于一些表达早已模式化的固定用语，要多查资料，避免生造新的不符合通用习惯的表达。

会议事务文书与会议的主旨内容、决议决策以及会议产生的效应及影响紧密相关，具有严肃性和规范性的特点。因此，在文体上与礼仪文书和话语文书有较大的差别；与会务文书相比，也更加正式。会议事务文书措辞总体要求客观规范，严谨全面。在翻译的过程中，应严格按照惯例及固定格式范本进行翻译。在词汇和句式的选择上，应多参照已经发表的正式文本或官方认可的相关表述，力求做到准确规范，严谨全面。

第五节　会议话语文书的翻译

　　会议话语文书是指为完成会议议程而提前撰写的用于会议期间口头表达的文书，主要包括主持词、开幕词、闭幕词、颁奖词、会议报告等。话语文书因为用于口头表达，具有明显的口语特征，句式语法比较简单，措辞相对通俗易懂。翻译时应特别注意话语文书的语体特征。本章第三节中谈到的欢迎词、欢送词、感谢词、祝酒词等也具有话语文书的特点，可与本节结合起来学习。下面列出主持词、开幕词、闭幕词、获奖词中常用到的表达。

一、主持词

例1　I am delighted that so many of you have joined us for this conference.[6]
很高兴大家共聚一堂参加此次会议。

例2　令我感到荣幸的是，在此次会议上我们将听到20个研究报告。
I am indeed proud to recognize the fact that 20 research presentations at this conference will be made.

例3　诸位，下面我们休息十分钟。
Now, ladies and gentlemen, we would like to take a 10-minute intermission.

例4　By taking this opportunity of intermission, let me announce that Prof. Coles, who is supposed to give us a lecture, has already arrived.
利用休息的时间通知大家，将要做演讲的科尔斯教授已经到达会场了。

例5　下面的报告来自东京大学的田中先生和佐藤先生，题目是"关于色彩的心理影响研究"。
The next presentation will be "A Study of Psychological Effects of Colors on Humans" by Mr. Tanaka and Mr. Sato of Tokyo University, Japan.

例6　Mr. Keaten is an eminent scholar and professor of Information System at MIT.
基顿先生是麻省理工学院信息系统专业的著名学者和教授。

例7　接下来，我们来听下一场报告。报告人是来自美国西北大学的阿什比教授。
Next, we are going to move on to the next presentation. The speaker is Prof. Ashby from North Western University.

6　以下所举译例均出自石井隆之著，陈丝伦译．2011．国际会议英语表达实例．北京：外文出版社．

二、开幕词

例8 It's so nice to have so many participants from all our branches in 32 countries of the world. I declare our assembly of 2005 open.

来自世界上32个国家分支机构的与会者齐集一堂,真是令人欢欣鼓舞。现在我宣布2005年年度大会开幕。

例9 Welcome all to the Third Annual Conference of the International Abnormal Psychology Association.

各位,感谢光临"国际变态心理学第三届年度大会"。

例10 Ladies and gentlemen, I would like to announce the opening of the 20th Annual Convention for the Japan Association of Language and Culture.

诸位,下面我宣布"日本言语文化学会第20届年度大会"现在开始。

三、闭幕词

例11 各位,请大会委员长致闭幕词。

Ladies and gentlemen, let us have a closing address given by the chairperson of this convention.

例12 诸位,请允许我在此做闭幕词。

Ladies and gentlemen, please allow me to give you a closing address here.

例13 诸位,今天的会议到此结束,希望大家都度过了愉快的一天。

Ladies and gentlemen, today's session is now over. I hope you have had a pleasant day.

例14 非常高兴我们有一个很好的结果。最后我要特别感谢科尔曼先生、杰克逊先生、卡莱尔小姐和詹金斯博士。谢谢诸位的参加。

I am happy to have a good finale. Finally I'd like to express my special thanks to Mr. Coleman, Mr. Jackson, Miss Carlyle and Dr. Jenkins. And thank you all for joining us.

四、颁奖词

例15 We would like to award the Best Research Prize to Prof. Adams.

我们将授予亚当教授"最佳研究奖"。

例16 We would like to present Dr. Kipling with a small remembrance as a token of thanks for what he has done for our association.

为感谢吉普林博士对本学会做出的贡献,我们为其献上一份纪念品。

例17 为纪念我会成立十周年,特向全体与会者赠送小礼品。

We just want to bestow this small gift on every participant to commemorate the 10th anniversary of the establishment of our society.

下面请看学术会议报告中常见的表达:

例18 今天我们报告的目的是精确地调查河流自净是怎样完成的,其原因是什么。

The purpose of our presentation today is to probe how and why the self-purification of a river progresses.

例19 就被害妄想症这一问题作为焦点，我将对此提出可能的解决方法。
I would like to focus on the problem of a persecution complex and present a possible solution to it.

例20 本研究使用的方法基于定量分析。
The method employed in this research is based on quantitative analysis.

例21 本研究依据的假说如下：
The assumptions on which this research is based are as follows:

例22 It is generally assumed that the extinction of dinosaurs was caused by the collision of an asteroid against the earth.
一般假想认为，恐龙灭绝的原因是小行星撞击地球。

例23 Extensive research has recently been done on the healing effects of classical music.
最近，对经典音乐的治疗效果有了广泛的研究。

例24 首先，我将稍微介绍一些在此之前关于地震预测的研究及讨论的信息。
First of all, allow me to introduce some of the information concerning what has been studied and discussed so far about earthquake prediction.

例25 在进入此报告正题之前，我将就关于股票公开收购的先行研究做一个概括性陈述。
Before going into the main part of my presentation, let me give an overview of the previous studies on TOB. (TOB =takeover bid)

例26 By contrast, we can say the white hole is a hypothetical celestial body that emits radiation of all wavelengths.
与此相对，我们可以说白洞是可以发出所有波长射线的假想天体。

例27 Here we will illustrate the difference in views of the world after death between Buddhism and Shintoism.
在此我们将说明佛教和神道对死后世界的看法差异。

例28 在阐述新开发的人工透析器这一重点之前，首先对人工透析做一些相关的预备性说明。
Before going further into the crucial point of our newly developed hemodialyzer, let us first give some preliminary explanation about hemodialysis.

例29 我认为此项观察可作为充分证据证明我们关于新药对前列腺癌有效的主张。
It seems to me that this observation has enough evidence for our claim that the new drug is efficacious against prostate cancer.

例30 这张表格清晰地说明，如果现在日照再持续5天以上，就会引起水供应不足。
As is clear from the table, we have to say that if the present drought continues for longer than five more days, water will be in short supply.

例31 这里的重点是，在日本神话中，男性原理会被女性原理所抵消。

What is important/ noteworthy here is that the male principle can be offset by the female principle in Japanese mythology.

例32 这些例子并不能有效地证明光在重力场中会弯曲。

These examples do not necessarily show that light is deflected in a field of gravity.

例33 So far we have discussed the fact that deep-sea animals endure the pressure several hundred times greater than that at the surface of the water.

之前我们所讨论的事实是，深海动物可以忍耐数百倍于海面的压力。

例34 The results of this study showed that the generation of an ant cow alternate between sexual reproduction and asexual reproduction.

此项研究的结果表明蚜虫的繁殖在有性生殖和无性生殖之间交替变化。

对于学术会议上的会议报告，研究者通常会从研究目的、研究方法、研究基础、过程分析、数据分析、研究结论等几个方面来阐述自己的研究成果。因此掌握以上常用表达很重要。

会议话语文书在文体上与礼仪文书有相似之处，有一定的礼仪功能，但也有一定的程式性，比如开幕词、闭幕词和颁奖词等所使用的语言是有既定的范式可循的。学术会议报告有自己独特的文体特点，即语言是研究性的、学术性的。翻译的过程中，必须弄清楚报告内容所涉及的学科知识、理论方法等的正确表述，才能保证译文地道、准确。

练习八

一、将下列句子译成英文。

1. 全会综合考虑未来发展趋势和条件，提出了今后五年经济社会发展的主要目标：经济平稳较快发展，经济结构战略性调整取得重大进展，城乡居民收入普遍较快增加，社会建设明显加强，改革开放不断深化，使我国转变经济发展方式取得实质性进展，综合国力、国际竞争力、抵御风险能力显著提高，人民物质文化生活明显改善，全面建成小康社会的基础更加牢固。

2. 第十二条　公司会议室由综合管理中心统一管理。各会议召集人需占用会议室时，须向综合管理中心主任或副主任口头申请。若出现多个会议同时召开的情况，则根据会议的大小、轻重缓急由综合管理中心统筹安排。

二、将下面的会议记录译成中文。

Forest Residues Session

Facilitator: Jingxin Wang
Recorder: Amy Welch
Participants: Jingxin Wang, Amy Welch, Jude Liu, Tony Nekut

The Forest Residues working group discussed the current best feed-stocks in this category currently available in the northeastern U.S. These feed-stocks can be divided into three categories: Primary (logging residues, fuel treatments, tree trimming), Secondary (mill residues and pulping liquors) and Tertiary (urban wood residues). The group consensus was that the best sources of information for determining quantities of these feed-stocks are state agencies that focus on energy or forestry and universities (especially forestry or natural resources related departments). There are also state-level inventories. For example, West Virginia—statewide inventory on logging and mill residue is available at county level. In addition, spatial analysis tools are available and detailed.

三、将下面的祝酒词译成中文。

Words for a Toast

Ladies and gentlemen:

Good evening.

To celebrate the opening of the 2nd Training Course on Urban Sustainable Development and Disaster Management sponsored by the Shanghai Municipal Government and UNCRD, we happily gather here and host this welcoming banquet. First, on behalf of the Shanghai Municipal Government, please allow me to extend my warm welcome to all the foreign and Chinese government officials, experts, scholars and friends coming from afar. Allow me to express my sincere thanks to every friend from UNCRD and their colleagues, for their efforts to hold this training course on time.

There is a Chinese saying: "Is it not a delight to have friends come from afar?" Dear distinguished guests, although we all come from different countries and are not acquainted with each other, today we come here together for the sustainable development and for the common cause of disaster prevention and reduction. I feel especially honored to be here today and I believe this conference will surely promote friendship, cooperation and exchange between China and other Asian countries.

In closing, I would like to ask you to join me a toast to the success of the Training Course on Urban Sustainable Development and Disaster Management and to everyone's good health and family happiness.

Cheers!

四、将下面的会议通知译成英文。

会 议 通 知

主题：信息安全委员会会议通知

亲爱的委员会会员们：

　　现诚挚邀请您参加美国律师协会科技部信息安全委员会的会议。会议将于2006年10月18日至19日（星期五、星期六）在波士顿举行。委员会将推动其发展的商业密钥托管指引，以及在一些既定州和其他司法管辖区考虑数字签名的立法措施，并继续审议数字签名的证据和法律责任。根据政策条款，信息安全委员会参加者必须同时是美国律师协会及其下属科技部信息安全委员会的成员。关于会员资格的详细信息请咨询美国律师协会芝加哥办事处科技部部门经理安·科瓦尔斯基（电话：+1-312-988-5599，传真：+1-312-988-5628，电子邮箱：sciencetech@attmail.com）。在会议当天可以成为美国律师协会及其下属信息安全委员会的会员。信息安全委员会成员丹·格林伍德同意主持在马萨诸塞州联邦信息技术部举办的会议。您可以通过电话6179730071或电子邮箱DGreenwood@state.ma.us向他咨询相关后勤服务信息。

　　会议安排如下，期待与您聚首波士顿。

迈克尔·S.鲍姆
美国律师协会科技部
信息安全委员会主席

第九章

礼仪文书的翻译

礼仪是礼节和仪式的总称。千百年来，礼仪在规范人际交往方面发挥着重要的作用。所谓人际交往，或曰交际。南宋朱熹在《四书集注》中说："际，接也。交际谓人以礼仪币帛相交接也"，即人与人交往过程中，互待以礼仪或互赠礼物，以促进人与人之间的双向交流。礼仪一般需借助口头或书面的载体来实现，这书面的载体，便是礼仪文书。

简单说来，礼仪文书就是人们在交际过程中为了符合礼仪的要求而使用的各种文本，常包括祝词、贺卡、欢迎词、欢送词、请柬、名片、祝贺信、慰问信、感谢信、喜报、祝酒词、祝寿词、礼笺、讣告、悼词、唁电、碑文等。

礼仪文书的主要功能并不是传递信息，而是表达感情。因此，感情真挚是对礼仪文书的首要要求。几千年来，围绕着各种人际交往活动，已经形成了一整套的礼仪习惯。相应地，为满足不同类型人际交往活动而产生的各种礼仪文书也发展出了相对固定的格式和表达方式。因此，能否满足这种格式或表达方式上的要求，是判断礼仪文书合格与否的重要标准之一。

从先秦到明清的几千年间，大体有四类社交礼仪文书对中国礼仪文化的发展和繁荣产生了重要影响：一是以传递信息、沟通情感为主的书札信函类文书；二是以挽悼逝者、寄托哀思为内容的丧祭哀悼类文书；三是以庆贺、道谢、应酬为内容表达人际友情的祝告答赠类文书；四是以立身、处事、治学为内容，训诫后辈儿孙的家训格言类文书。四类文书中，本章将只选取几种与我们日常生活密切相关的礼仪文书进行讨论，包括：邀请函、请柬、名片、丧吊类文体。

第一节
礼仪文书的文体特点及翻译技巧

礼仪文书是现代社交礼仪的基本方式之一。在现代社会中，个人、机关、企事业单位及社会团体之间时常发生各种交往，有时需用书面形式沟通、联络。例如：邀请客人出席招待会、开业典礼、座谈会、宴会、交易会、沙龙、学术讨论会的柬帖；迎来送往、喜庆场合的欢迎词、答谢词、欢送词、祝酒词；还有书信、名片、题词及婚丧寿诞方面的文书等。

礼仪文书的特殊社交功能决定了其独特的文体特点。

（1）交际性。礼仪文书主要体现交际双方（有时甚至是多方）的愿望、喜好、情感，反映的是一种"双边"关系，以书面的形式互通信息、交流情感，为增进友谊、加强合作、促进人际关系的和谐起催化作用。

（2）礼节性。礼仪文书注重"以礼相待"，强调因人、因事、因地、因时地待人接物。在对人生的各种美好祝愿上，多以全社会通行的人生重大礼仪方式进行；在日常交际应酬中的小礼，大多是用书面文字材料加上礼仪活动来展示丰富的礼仪内容。

（3）规范性。礼仪文书一般都具有比较固定的格式和用语，是规范化的文体。比如书信，不仅称谓语、开头结尾的应酬和问候祝颂语有很多讲究，而且行文格式也要注意，即以抬头表示尊敬，以侧写表示谦逊等。如果用错了对象、场合或不合于情境名分，就会伤感情，影响交际效果。当然，礼仪文书并非像正式公文一样有相关的规定，而全凭民间约定俗成。

礼仪文书是实用文体的一种，有着明确的写作目的，也有比较固定的语篇特征。礼仪文书的翻译应以翻译目的论为指导，译文必须满足目的语文化背景下承担相同或相似功能文本在语篇上的要求，遵循惯常的格式，使用一些相对固定的表达方式，以完成一种内部结构特征明显、高度约定俗成的交际实践，实现特定的交际目的或功能。

翻译礼仪文书时，在词语层面我们需注意以下几点：

（1）注意正确使用情态动词，以便表达委婉的语气。西方思维习惯往往是客体思维模式，即要求写信人持有 your attitude，而非 our attitude，同时力求语言客观、公正、严密。采取客体思维的英语在表示意见的时候，倾向于间接婉约，用劝说建议的方式（persuasive）表示肯定或否定。在英语语法中，情态动词与动词原形及其被动形式一起使用，增添某些情态色彩，表示说话人对有关行为或事物的态度和看法。个别情态动词有过去式和现在式两种形式，过去式用来表达更加客气、委婉的语气，时态性不强。这一点符合客体思维方式。因此在礼仪文书中，应多使用情态动词为句子润色。

例1 十分遗憾的是，我们因有约在先无法接受您的邀请。

Most unfortunately, we shall be unable to avail ourselves of your kind invitation on account of a previous engagement.

本例句中，译文使用情态动词 shall，使整句的语气更加委婉，客气而得体地拒绝了对方的热情邀请。

（2）正确使用情绪动词，使感情真实真切。商务礼仪文书是为了表达发函方对某个事件的主观情绪，所以在该类文书中，最常见到各类情绪动词。在现代英语中，情绪

动词的现在分词 -ing 和过去分词 -ed 多数都已经形容词化，构成分词形容词。这些词已失去了动词的性质，大多可被副词 very 或 too 所修饰，有的还有比较级形式。在商务礼仪文书如祝贺信、致谢信、邀请信等信件中，正面情绪的形容词使用较多，如 amaze、delight、charm、encourage、excite、interest、impress 等。这类动词的形容词形式表达积极正面的情绪，使用得体会使礼仪文书措辞热情、诚恳，使收信人感到写信人真心实意的祝贺、致谢或邀请。

例2 我很高兴您多年来一直致力于全球旅游和营销的服务得到了认可和赞赏。
I am so happy that the many years of service you have dedicated to global travel and marketing has been recognized and appreciated.

译文使用了 appreciate 和 recognize 两个正面的情绪动词，感情真实，赞扬恳切，恰如其分。

翻译礼仪文书时，在句子层面也有特殊考量。

（1）礼仪文书中圆周句、松散句、平衡句使用较多。圆周句（periodic sentence）把关键信息放在整句末尾，将次要信息放在句首，如从句在前，主语在后，多用于正式语体。松散句（loose sentence）把主要信息首先提出来，随后附加修饰语或补充细节。礼仪文书要求表达简洁高效，要使用信息量极大的简单句、并列句、复合句等。因此，在商务应用文中，散句使用较多。

例3 鉴于数年来你一直是营销团队的优秀成员，我很高兴地通知你从 11 月开始你将被提升为市场总监。
Because you have been an outstanding member of the marketing team, I'm glad to inform you that you will be promoted to the position of Director of Marketing from November.

例 3 中，圆周句的使用使句子更严谨，语气更有力，信息内容更明确。在商务礼仪文书中善用圆周句与松散句，可以使句式结构错落有致，增加行文美感。

（2）使用被动句，使文书客观有力。无论是用 it 作形式主语，还是用人或物作主语，人称的变换避免了主观性，所以商务礼仪文书中的被动句使用较多。

例4 遗憾的是，由于三月份的日程安排我无法参加这个重大的庆祝活动。
Unfortunately, I'm not allowed by my schedule in March to attend this significant celebration.

除上述所介绍的几点，我们还需考虑到礼仪文书独特的文体特点，对译文进行润色修饰。译者应该遵循译文读者的语言习惯，将原文格式转化成译入语的语言格式，即采用译入语的格式套译原文，这样才能做到源语和目的语的功能对等。

第二节
邀请函的翻译

邀请函是写信人对收信人的一种盛情邀约，一般有正式和非正式两种。邀请函通常分以下三个部分：首段陈述写作意图，说明与收信人的相关性；主体段交代情景，包括受邀之人、邀请朋友参加的活动、地点及具体的时间等，一般会解释邀请的原因；结尾段表达对朋友回复的期待。

一般而言，正式的邀请函往往具有公务的性质，通常为公司或机构所发，所涉及的事情比较复杂，非短短数语可以说清楚，所以文字比较多，语言比较规范。翻译时一定要注意语言的规范，须使用正式的书面语，语气客观。相比之下，非正式的邀请函语言相对随意，语气也更随和亲昵，翻译时要使用比较口语化的语言，语气应透着亲切。

在翻译邀请函时需注意几个方面：（1）在翻译文本的同时，需要体现应用文体翻译过程中的文本结构和文本功能的等值；（2）行文措辞礼貌得体，态度诚恳热情；（3）注意英语多用名词和介词、汉语多用动词的特点。此外，翻译时还需注意动态到静态的表达逻辑的转换。在汉译英时可以将汉语有动态倾向的句子翻译成英语有静态倾向的句子，反之亦然。

例1 我荣幸地代表武汉科技大学，并以我个人名义诚挚地邀请您于2014年11月对我校进行友好访问。
On behalf of WUST and in my own name, I have great honor in extending our warm invitation to you for a friendly visit in November, 2014.

译文中用了on behalf of、for a friendly visit等静态化介词短语代替了汉语里"荣幸地代表""进行友好访问"等动态化短语。

在翻译时还需注意情感意义的转化，兼顾措辞和情感意义的表达。

例2 我殷切企望与您会面。
I much look forward to meeting you.

下面举例说明几种邀请函的翻译。

一、论坛邀请函

例3

中国经济发展高层论坛
——全面开放时代：中国经济发展策略
邀 请 函

亲爱的先生/女士：

  为了使中外企业能够及时、准确、全面地了解和掌握世界经济环境与中国的有关经济和产业政策，更好地把握和推动经济发展，由世界经济发展宣言组委会主办、中国国际跨国公司研究会承办的"中国经济发展高层论坛"将于2007年8月18～19日召开，主题为"全面开放时代：中国经济发展策略"。

  "中国经济发展高层论坛"以前瞻性、权威性、互动性为特点。本次论坛拟邀请联合国官员、中国政府官员及国内外权威专家共同对全球经济、上半年中国经济动态、货币政策、外资外贸政策、产业发展趋势和国家政策进行解读和展望。

  本次论坛还将特别举办"金融变革与企业融资圆桌会议"，组委会将邀请中国人民银行、银监会、证监会、发改委等相关领导出席，同时邀请部分中外工商知名人士参加这一圆桌会议。

  世界经济发展宣言组委会曾于2003年11月组织发表了迄今为止世界上第一份全球性经济发展宣言——《世界经济发展宣言》。

  我们珍视您的关注，期望您能积极参与这一盛会！

世界经济发展宣言组委会
中国国际跨国公司研究会
2007年6月17日

High-Level Forum on China's Economic Development
—China's Economic Development Strategy in the Full Opening-up Era
Invitation

Dear Sir/Madame,

  The High-Level Forum on China's Economic Development organized by the Organizing Committee of World Economic Development Declaration (WEDD) will be held from August 18th to 19th, 2007 in order to make Chinese and foreign enterprises well-informed of the world economic situation and China's economic and industrial policies timely, accurately and comprehensively as well as to drive the development of economy. On behalf of the WEDD Organizing Committee, China International Institute of Multinational Corporations hereby invites you to take part in the High-Level Forum on China's Economic Development. The theme will be China's Economic Development Strategy in the Full Opening-up Era.

  Prospectiveness, authoritativeness and interactiveness are characteristics of this Forum. UN officials, Chinese dignitaries and renowned Chinese and foreign economists will be invited and they will offer their practical knowledge and penetrating insights on the issues concerning global economy, China's economic trends in the first half of 2007, monetary policy, policies on foreign investment and foreign trade, industrial development tendency and other related national policies.

A Roundtable on Financial Reform and Corporate Financing Strategy will be specially held. Leaders from the People's Bank of China, China Banking Regulatory Commission, China Securities Regulatory Commission and National Development and Reform Commission together with some elites from commercial circles will be invited to attend the meeting.

The Organizing Committee of World Economic Development Declaration organized and issued the World Economic Development Declaration in November, 2003 which is the first global economic development declaration in the world up to now.

We value your attention and look forward to your participation in this Forum.

WEDD Organizing Committee
China International Institute of Multinational Corporations
June 17, 2007

例4

The Hubei Communication and Media Forum 2011

We are pleased to invite you to participate in the Hubei Communication and Media Forum 2011 to be held on September 17th, 2011 in Wuhan, China.

Hubei Communication and Media Forum has been held twice. The theme of this Forum is "A Harmonious Society and Mass Media". The 2011 Forum will commit to providing an excellent opportunity for scholars and professionals to discuss and share their knowledge and experience.

Your participation will contribute to the ultimate success of the Forum. RSVP as soon as possible.

2011年湖北传媒论坛

我们非常高兴地邀请您参加将于2011年9月17日在中国武汉举办的2011年湖北传媒论坛。

湖北传媒论坛业已举办过两届。本次论坛的主题是"和谐社会和大众传媒"。本次论坛将努力为各位专家学者交流知识经验提供良机。

您的参与将助力本次论坛的成功举办。请赐复。

以上两例都是比较正式的邀请函。翻译时要注意措辞，同时语气要庄重。主要注意以下几个方面：Correctness（准确）——译文要表达准确，不能言过其实；Conciseness（简洁）——应避免使用冗长的表达，用语尽量简洁；Clearness（清楚）——应选用简明易懂的词语，避免模糊和歧义，且内容须条理清楚，逻辑性强；Completeness（完整）——应提供给对方所需的完整信息，不能遗漏；Concreteness（具体）——为给受邀方留下明确具体的印象，翻译时应避免使用抽象或笼统概念的词语。

正式的邀请函在措辞和语气上讲究礼貌、委婉、严谨，所以，英译汉时，常用"承蒙""恭请""敬请""烦请""期待"等礼貌用语。

二、宴会邀请函

例5

亲爱的琼：

我打算于2012年2月4日（星期六）在我家举行一个晚宴，庆祝我母亲六十大寿。这对我们全家来说是一件大事。你是我们的好朋友，我们真诚地希望你能来参加，分享我们的快乐。

晚宴将于7点开始。首先会有一个小型的演奏会，届时我们将欣赏到乐队演奏的流行和古典歌曲。8点左右我们开始用餐，朋友们可以随便聊天欢笑。最后所有的朋友们一起照相作为纪念。

我知道你最近很忙，但我真的希望你能来，我们全家都期待你的光临。

你的老朋友
刘珊

Dear Joan,

    I am going to have a dinner party at my house on Feb. 4, 2012 (Saturday) to celebrate my mother's 60-year-old birthday. It is an important occasion for our family, and as you are a close friend of us, my parents and I do hope you can come and share our joy.

    The party will start at seven o'clock in the evening. There will be a small musical soiree, at which a band will perform some popular and classical songs at first. At around eight o'clock, we will start our dinner, during which we can talk and laugh together. And then all the friends will take some photos together.

    I know you have been busy these days, but I do hope you can make it. My family and I look forward to the pleasure of your company.

Yours affectionately,
Liu Shan

例6

Dear Mrs. Jones,

    My husband and I should be very much pleased if you and your daughter would dine with us next Saturday at 6:30. I would hope we may have some Karaoke after dinner. If Marie would merely consent to bring some DVDs, I am sure we will have a wonderful evening.

    We do hope you can come and are expecting to see you then.

Yours cordially,
Rose

亲爱的琼斯夫人：

我们夫妇诚邀您和令千金下周六6:30到寒舍赴家宴。我希望宴后我们一起唱卡拉OK娱乐。如果玛丽能同意带上DVD，我相信我们将会度过一个难忘的夜晚。

我们希望您能来，期待见到您。

罗斯谨上

邀请某人参加宴会虽然是施人恩惠，但在翻译时要避免流露出傲慢的语气，应尽量采用商量和试探的口吻。落款没用全名，是为了表示亲昵，翻译时要注意对应。

另外，信函在内容的表达上要考虑对方的感受，在选词上注意分寸，经常会使用如 I、We、You 等第一、第二人称的代词，please、would、kindly、respectfully 等委婉表达方式也常用于信函中以示礼貌客气。翻译时要注意尽量表达礼貌和委婉的语气。

例7

亲爱的史密斯先生：

如您能够出席为中国代表团举行的招待会，我们将感到十分荣幸。

招待会定于10月4日星期二在市政厅举行。6点钟准时举行鸡尾酒会，随后在8点钟举行正式晚宴。

我们期待您的光临。请提前告知您能否出席。

琳达谨上

Dear Mr. Smith,

It would give us great pleasure to have your presence at a reception in honor of the Chinese delegation.

The reception will be held in the City Hall, on Tuesday, October the fourth. Cocktails will be served promptly at six to be followed by dinner at eight.

We sincerely hope you can attend. Let us know.

Sincerely yours,
Linda

三、开工典礼

例8

Dear Mr. Harrison,

Our new factory will be commencing production on April 10 and we should like to invite you and your wife to be present at a celebration to mark the occasion.

As you will appreciate, this is an important milestone for this organization, and is the result of continued demand for our products, both at home and overseas. We are inviting all those individuals who have contributed all their power to the success of our company and trust that you will pay us the compliments of accepting.

Please confirm that you will be able to attend by advising us of your time—we can arrange for you to be met. All arrangements for your stay overnight on April 10 will, of course, be made by us at our expense.

Yours faithfully,
Martin

亲爱的哈里森先生：

  本公司新厂将于4月10日开始投产，希望能邀请贤伉俪前来参加新厂开工典礼。

  如您所知，新厂的设立是本公司的一个里程碑，而这正是海内外对本公司产品需求不断的结果。我们邀请了所有对本公司的成功贡献力量的个人，我们相信，您一定会赏光。

  如您确能参加，请来函告知您抵达的时间——以便我们为您安排会晤。当然，您在4月10日夜宿的所有费用，皆由公司支付。

马丁谨上

  邀请函的翻译大多可以采用套译。套译可从词语、句子和篇章格式三个层面着手：一方面可用内容、形式、语用色彩大致相符的礼貌用语、文体标记词语和相关专用词语进行套译；另一方面应在译入语中寻找相应的句型；此外，还应在格式上与目的语中承担相同或相似功能的语篇保持一致。事实上，有些英语表达形式已经在汉语中沉淀成固有的表达，因此翻译时可以作为参照。

  通过上述例子不难看出，翻译邀请函时除了要遵循忠实原文、语言通顺的翻译标准之外，还需要注意套语的表达。应用文既是信息性文本，也是交际性文本。大量使用礼貌词语和标记词语是应用文交际性内涵的表现形式。因此，翻译时要仔细斟酌，尽量使译文符合语用和体式要求。在很多情况下单靠字斟句酌无法解决问题，行之有效的方法是套用译入语中惯常使用的礼貌用语和固定表达。

第三节
请柬的翻译

  请柬又称请帖，是一种用来邀请有关人员出席社交活动而发出的礼仪性通知。请柬表示对被邀者的尊重，亦表示邀请者对此事的郑重态度。凡召开各种会议，举行各种典礼、仪式和活动，均可以使用请柬。

  请柬与邀请函都是用于邀请有关单位或个人参加某种活动而使用的礼仪文书，因此人们往往将这两者等同起来使用，并认为二者写法上也没什么区别。事实上，这种观点是错误的。

请柬作为对客人发出邀请的一种专用函件，规格颇高，但也有一个缺陷，即内页篇幅有限，所以正文部分除写明邀请的意向、活动的内容、时间、地点以及提醒被邀请者注意的有关事项外，不会对活动的内容作进一步的介绍。被邀请者阅读请柬，只知道被邀参加某一活动，但很难从中了解这一活动的来由和具体情况。如果是一些宴请活动或常规活动，被邀请者又是主办者的老朋友，这似乎并无大碍。但如果是一些内容较新颖的专题性会议，被邀请的对象中又有不少对主办单位不很了解者，一份请柬就显得不够了。由于对活动内容及主办者缺乏了解，许多人可能会弃邀请于不顾，不如期赴会。在这种情况下，就需要用到邀请函。

邀请函最大的优点是有足够的篇幅（一页或多页），可对一次会议（或活动）的背景情况、具体内容以及规模和形式等做较为详尽的介绍和说明，从而引起被邀请者的关注，激发被邀请者的兴趣。此外，请柬和邀请函在以下几方面还有重要的差异：

（1）内涵性质差异

邀请函一般是为实质性工作、任务或事项发出的，如学术研讨会等；而请柬一般是为礼仪性、例行性、娱乐性活动发出的，如庆典、晚会等。

（2）邀请对象差异

邀请函一般由社会组织出面，邀请对象的范围往往不能确指，一般是某个行业或较大的范围，被邀请的人员较多，使用称谓大多为泛指。请柬可以由社会组织出面发出，也可由个人发出，邀请对象一般是上级领导、专家、社会名流、兄弟单位代表、友好亲朋等，请柬的称谓一定要确指。邀请函和请柬在邀请对象上的差异在于：邀请函的邀请对象与主人是宾主关系，而非上下级关系或管理与被管理的关系；而请柬的邀请对象与主人有时存在着上下级关系或管理和被管理的关系。

（3）身份礼仪差异

邀请函和请柬的相同之处在于两者均属礼仪文书，文首文尾处须使用敬语，但由于二者在邀请对象身份上的差异，因此在礼仪表达方面存在着很大的不同。为了表示对被邀请者的尊重，邀请函可以使用重要的敬语，也可以使用一般的敬语。请柬既表示对被邀请者的尊重，又表示邀请者对此事的郑重态度，因此请柬一定要使用重要的敬语。

（4）结构要素差异

邀请函往往对事宜的内容、项目、程序、要求、作用、意义等进行介绍和说明，结构复杂、篇幅较长。函尾常附邀请者的联络方式，有些以回执的形式要求被邀请者回复是否接受邀请。请柬内容单一，结构简单，篇幅短小，可用两三句话写清活动的内容要素。

（5）语言差异

邀请函的文字容量大于请柬。从整体而言，对事宜的内容、项目、程序、要求、作用、意义做出详细的介绍和说明,务必使被邀请者明确其中的意思,达到正常交流交际的效果,语言要求准确、明白、平实。

请柬的文字容量有限,十分讲究对文字的推敲。语言务必简洁、庄重、文雅,切忌堆砌辞藻;语气尽量热情和口语化,但切忌俚俗的口语;请语以文言词语为佳,但切忌晦涩难懂。要求话语简练、达雅兼备、谦敬得体。

英文请柬标题可有可无,如有标题,Invitation 放在正文顶端。称谓一般用全称,不用缩写词。邀请人与被邀请人姓名之前一律加上头衔。如无爵位、官衔、职称时,Mr. 写在 Mrs. 前。如果以公司单位名义发出邀请,可写公司、单位全名,不加称呼。这些都是翻译请柬时应该注意的。

中英文请柬本身也存在一定的差异,我们在翻译中一定要注意以下几点:(1)两者的结构要素的表述位置不尽相同。汉语请柬中的来宾称呼与结尾套语在英语文本中一般都不单独出现,而是嵌套在请柬正文中。(2)两种文本中各个内容要素的呈现顺序不尽相同。汉语文本的顺序为"被邀请人—邀请事由—时间地点—活动内容—结尾套语—邀请人";英语请柬常见的呈现顺序为"邀请事由—邀请人—被邀请人—活动内容—时间地点"。富有格式特征的应用文不能简单地以词和句子为单位进行翻译,而应从整个篇章的角度去把握,遵循译入语请柬格式特点。

由于英汉请柬都是邀请亲朋好友或知名人士、专家等参加某项活动时所发的邀约性书信,因此,英语请柬汉译应遵循功能对等原则,即不求文字表面的死板对应,而应在两种语言间达成功能上的对等。

规范的格式既是请柬的文体标志,也是实现其功能的必要手段。因此,为达预期目的,译者在翻译请柬时,应遵循目的语的语言习惯,采用目的语请柬的格式套译原文。英文请柬是分行式的,邀请者、被邀请者、邀请之意、活动内容、时间、地点等各占一行,一目了然;而汉语则是段落式的,邀请事项、时间、地点包含在同一个段落里,被邀请者和邀请人分别置于开头和结尾。翻译时要注意行文格式的转换。

下面以一则汉语请柬翻译成英文的过程为例说明。

例1   兹订于三月八日(星期三)下午四时在柳林街
二十五号为小儿施洗礼,敬请光临。
爱德华·斯通夫妇谨订

第一步:基于英汉请柬在词汇层面的差异,对原文用词做省略处理:

三月八日(星期三)下午四时在柳林街二十五号
为小儿施洗礼,敬请光临。
爱德华·斯通夫妇

第二步：基于英汉语言、思维、文化（心理）的差异，对原文进行换位、合句处理，使其符合英语表达习惯。

爱德华·斯通夫妇
爱德华·斯通夫妇敬请您光临小儿的洗礼，
星期三，三月八日下午四时柳林街二十五号。

第三步：英文的生成，包括冠词与部分介词的增补、称谓的替代与格式的调整，因为汉语里没有冠词，介词的使用频率也不及英语高。另外，英文请柬用固定的分行式，中文请柬则用"兹定于"开头，"敬请光临""谨订"结尾，体现请柬的正式性。

Mr. and Mrs. Edward Stone
Request the pleasure of your company
At the christening of their son
On Wednesday, March eighth
At four Clock
At 25 Willow Street

请柬的种类也很多。这里列举一些与我们日常社会生活密切相关的一些请柬的翻译。

一、结婚请柬的翻译

结婚请柬往往多以父母的名义发出，新婚夫妇的姓名是请柬当中的焦点，应置于醒目位置，婚礼的举办地点和日期是关键信息。

例2

Mr. and Mrs. Jack Sparrow
request the honor of your presence
at the marriage of their daughter
Miss Elizabeth Smith
to
Mr. John Frederick Hamilton
son of
Mr. and Mrs. Martin Thomas
on Saturday, the fifth of May
2012
at seven in the evening
Church of the Heavenly Rest
New York, New York State
R.S.V.P

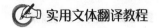

兹定于二〇一二年五月五日星期六下午七时在纽约天安教堂为小女伊丽莎白·史密斯与约翰·弗雷德里克·汉密尔顿先生举行婚礼，届时恭请光临。敬请赐复。

杰克·斯帕罗夫妇谨订

二、毕业典礼请柬的翻译

在西方很多国家，人们极为重视子女的毕业典礼，主要的家庭成员一般都会全部出席，也会邀请亲朋好友参加。

例3

Mr. and Mrs. Bernard Herrmann
are proud to announce
the graduation of
our son
Stephen Jones
Class of 2011
We should be honored
to have your share in the
Commencement Exercise
Saturday, May 28, 2011
at 7:30 p.m. in the
Stanford High School
Auditorium

伯纳德·赫尔曼夫妇诚邀您于2011年5月28日下午7点30分于斯坦福中学礼堂参加犬子史蒂芬·琼斯的2011届毕业典礼。

基于功能对等原则，英语请柬汉译宜采用归化策略，即：用汉语读者习惯的表达方式，传达邀请之意。对照上文的英汉请柬，不难发现译者主要采用了增补、省略、替代、拆句、换位等技巧。

三、派对请柬的翻译

无论在中国，还是在英美国家，邀请重要人物参加派对一般都要送上请柬。

例4

请　柬

兹定于2014年5月10日星期六下午六时在武汉科技大学第一教学楼103室举行英语晚会，恭请帕里斯先生及夫人大驾光临。

请赐复！

英语系学生会

Invitation Card

The Students' Union
of the English Department
requests the honour of the company of
Mr. & Mrs. Paris
at the English Evening
on Saturday, 10 May, 2014
at 6 p.m.
Room 103, Classroom Building One
Wuhan University of Science and Technology
R.S.V.P.

从上面三个例子可以看出,中英文请柬都有固定的格式和措辞,在请柬的开头、结尾、署名等方面都有一套约定俗成的规则。因此,翻译时,不能简单地以单句为单位,而应从整个篇章的角度去把握,使译文符合目的语的表达习惯。

第四节
名片的翻译

名片,是陌生人互相认识、自我介绍的快捷有效的方法。交换名片常是商业交往的第一个标准动作。名片上常印有个人的姓名、地址、职务、电话号码、邮箱等。例如:

例1

> **The University of Sydney**
>
> **John Adams** *PhD*
> Director, TEFL Research network
> Professor in TEFL
>
> **Faculty of Education and Social Work**
> Sydney NSW 2006 Australia
> Telephone: +61 2 9999 8888
> Facsimile: +61 2 9999 7777
> E-mail: j.adams@edfac.usyd.edu.au

例 2

```
天地人和新技术有限公司

          张慕景    总经理

电话：+86 27 4567 8910
电邮：tiandirenhe@sina.com
地址：湖北省武汉市和平大道 1023 号
```

在现代社会，名片的使用相当普遍，通过方寸空间准确交代相关信息，以达到顺利沟通的目的。中英名片有同有异。共同点在于中英名片都印有个人的基本信息，包括姓名、单位名、职务、电话、电子邮箱、联系地址等，以便联系；不同点在于受中国几千年官本位的影响，中国人在印制名片时喜欢罗列一大串官职、头衔或称号，以抬升自己形象，扩大个人影响。虽然中文名片有罗列官职、头衔或称号的习惯，但在中文名片英译时，却不能将所有的官职、头衔或称号都译成英文印制在英文名片上。这是因为：其一，英文名片只是为了便于联系的小卡片，其主要特征就是简明扼要；其二，英美文化崇尚人人平等，罗列太多官职、头衔或称号只能给人自我膨胀、庸俗无聊的印象，还不如只选择一两个比较重要的官职、头衔或称号翻译出来即可。

此外，名片翻译还要注意以下这些方面：

1. 人名的翻译

按照惯例，汉语姓名英译时通常采用音译，仍然按照汉语名字姓在前、名在后的次序，复姓的要拼在一起，不需要连字符。例如：

李建军：Li Jianjun
王刚：Wang Gang
诸葛亮：Zhuge Liang
欧阳长风：Ouyang Changfeng

英美国家的姓名拼写习惯是名在前、姓在后，汉译时也通常采用音译的方法，次序不变，名和姓之间通常加"·"。例如：

Barack Obama：巴拉克·奥巴马
William Shakespeare：威廉·莎士比亚
George W. Bush：乔治·W. 布什
John Forbes Kerry：约翰·福布斯·克里

汉语姓名音译时，有时也可以将"姓"全部大写，以与"名"区分。例如，李建军可以译为 LI Jianjun。

2. 职务的翻译

我国许多职业称呼和行政职务在英语里都有功能等值词。对于这些词，可以采用定译的方法，如：教授 professor、省长 governor、总经理 general manager 等。还有一些职务的翻译则见仁见智。比如"局长"，有人译成 Bureau Director，有人译成 Bureau Chief，还有人译成 Bureau Manager。对于那些没有对应英语职称职务的词汇，首先要仔细查证单位和行政职务的级别，再酌情选择合适的英语词汇来翻译。比如"局长"一词，国家质量监督检验检疫总局局长和广州市教育局局长虽然同为局长称呼，但从级别上来讲，前者是部级单位，后者是处级单位，所以质检总局的局长要翻译成 Minister，广州市教育局的局长适合翻译成 Director。[1]

3. 机构名称的翻译

中文单位、机构名译成英语时，首先要查阅有关资料，弄清其具体职能，确定是否已有为大众所接受的定译；如有定译，不需重译或改译，照用即可。如我国中央党政机关各部门的"部"，英语中的对等词有 department 和 ministry。但因分工不同，中央所属各部译为 department，如组织部 Organization Department、宣传部 Publicity Department、中共中央统战部 United Front Work Department，而国务院所属各部则译为 ministry，如外交部 Ministry of Foreign Affairs、国防部 Ministry of National Defense、教育部 Ministry of Education、公安部 Ministry of Public Security、司法部 Ministry of Justice 等。如果是委员会，通常用 commission，如国家发展和改革委员会 National Commission of Development and Reform、国家民族事务委员会 State Ethnic Affairs Commission、国家卫生和计划生育委员会 National Health and Family Planning Commission。[2] 如果是总局，通常用 administration，如国家税务总局 State Administration of Taxation、国家林业局 State Forestry Administration、国家旅游局 National Tourism Administration 等。

4. 地址和地名的翻译

中国地名的英译一般采用汉语普通话拼音表示，例如：

武汉：Wuhan

上海：Shanghai

西安：Xi'an

太原：Taiyuan

但有些地名的翻译要遵循约定俗成的原则，应沿用传统译名，避免因采用汉语拼音而造成混乱，如：

---

1 郝俊杰.2011.名片翻译的策略和技巧——兼论几类专有名词的翻译.南昌高专学报，（2）：48–50.
2 颜秉乡.1999.名片翻译漫谈.平原大学学报，（3）：89–90.

西藏：Tibet
香港：Hong Kong
澳门：Macao
呼和浩特：Hohhot

翻译地址时，要注意英语和汉语的表达顺序完全相反。例如："浙江省台州市黄岩区天长路18号201室"翻译成英文是 Room 201, 18 Tianchang Road, Huangyan District, Taizhou, Zhejiang Province。

5. 缩略语的翻译

由于名片只有方寸，所以英文名片会使用一些缩略语，在翻译的时候一定要熟悉这些缩略语及其汉语意思。常见的有：

Prof.: Professor（教授）
Dr.: Doctor（博士、医生）
Tel: Telephone（电话）
Co.: Company（公司）
Res.: Residence（住所）
Sect.: Section（科、段、室）
Aly.: Alley（胡同、巷）
Ngbd.: Neighborhood（小区）
Bldg: Building（楼、栋）
Ave.: Avenue（大道）
Dr: Drive（道、大道）
St.: Street（街）
I.Z.: Industrial Zone（工业区）
D.Z.: Development Zone（开发区）
S.: South（南）
N.: North（北）

CEO: Chief Executive Officer（首席执行官）
Add.: Address（地址）
Cbl.: Cable（电报）
Inc.: Incorporation（公司）
Rm.: Room（房、室）
Ln.: Lane（胡同、巷）
Vil.: Village（村）
Apt: Apartment（房、室、公寓）
Fl./F: Floor（层）
Blvd: Boulevard（大道、林荫大道）
Rd.: Road（路）
Sq.: Square（广场）
I.P.: Industrial Park（工业园区）
E.: East（东）
W.: West（西）
No.: Number（号、第 × 号）

下面请看几个名片翻译实例：

例3

青岛大学
李伟 教授
地址：中国青岛市宁夏路308号
邮编：266071
电话：（0532）89993680（办公）
　　　（0532）89993231（住宅）
传真：（0532）89993688
电子邮箱：lwei@qdu.edu.cn

Qingdao University
Professor Li Wei
308 Ningxia RD., QINGDAO
266071 P. R.CHINA
TEL: (0532) 89993680 (Office)
(0532) 89993231 (Home)
FAX: (0532) 89993688
E-mail: lwei@qdu.edu.cn

例4

Joanne C. Sokolski
Chief of Protocol
Orange Country Office of Protocol
Joanne.Sokolski@ocgov.com
Phone (714) 834-5654
Voice Mail 4-5134
Fax (714) 834-4465
10 Civic Center Plaza, Suite 106
Santa Ana, California 92701

美国加州橙郡礼宾司司长
琼安·苏克斯基
电子邮箱：Joanne.Sokolski@ocgov.com
地址：加州圣塔安那市市政中央广场10号106室
邮编：92701
电话：（714）834-5654
语音邮箱：4-5134
传真：（714）834-4465

第五节
丧吊类文体的翻译

  丧吊类文体是礼仪文书中比较特殊的一类，通常包括讣告、碑文、悼词、哀祭文和生平。虽然相对而言不是很常见，但也是礼仪文书中一个重要的类别。
  古人云："死生亦大矣"。死亡是每个人都要面对的现实，亲朋好友的离去，是人生中不可避免的最为悲痛的事，而所引发的感触也是相当强烈而复杂的。中国古代非常重视有关丧事的礼仪、礼制。《周礼·春官·大宗伯》说："以丧礼哀死亡"。哀祭文不但源远流长，也是最为重要的文体类别之一。虽然哀祭类文体的实用性很强，但由于其特殊的用途与内容，该文体与其他应用文体相比，具有抒情色彩和强烈的文学性。

一、吊唁信的翻译

吊唁信是指给逝者家属的慰问信，表达对逝者的哀悼和怀念。吊唁信的文字朴素，感情真挚，简明扼要。例如：

例1

陈女士：

　　得悉您母亲因长期患病，不治去世，不胜哀悼。我无法用语言来表达我深切的悲伤。我谨向您和您全家表示深切的慰问，万望节哀。

露西

Miss Chen,

　　I heard with profoundest sorrow that your mother, after protracted illness, passed away. There were no words that can express my deep sorrow. I hasten to offer you my most profound sympathy for the great grief that has fallen on you and your household.

Lucy

例2

亲爱的玛格丽特：

　　今天听说您的父亲去世了，我知道这件意外的事情对您一定是沉重的打击，我无法用言语表达自己难过的心情。

　　我真希望我能做些什么或说些什么来减轻您的痛苦。

　　向你们全家致以最深切的慰问。

你亲爱的，
鲍勃

Dear Margaret,

　　Today I heard you had lost your father. I know the suddenness of it must have been a dreadful shock; and I just can't tell you how sorry I am.

　　I wish there were something I could do or say to soften your grief.

　　With the deepest sympathy to you and all your family.

Affectionately,
Bob

从以上两例可以看出，吊唁信涉及的场合非常庄重，读信人的心情也比较特殊，所以翻译吊唁信时，措辞要严肃庄重，文字朴素，行文应简洁。请再看两例：

例3

Dear Mr. Forrest,

　　Word of the recent death of your brother has just come to me, and I hasten to offer condolences.

　　I had the privilege of knowing your brother in years past, and I realize your great loss. He was a fine and brilliant man, and he will not be forgotten by the many who admired and respected him.

　　Please convey my sympathy and my warm personal regards to all your family.

Cordially yours,
Jack

亲爱的弗雷斯特先生：

　　惊悉您哥哥最近逝世的消息，特此吊唁。

　　多年前我有幸结识您哥哥，我知道他的逝世对您是巨大损失。他是一位高尚的、出类拔萃的人。那些钦佩他、尊敬他的人是不会忘记他的。

　　请向您全家转达我的慰问以及亲切的问候。

您热诚的，
杰克

例4

Dear Jackson family,

　　It is with great sadness that we learned of the untimely death of Michael Jackson. Michael became close to us after he started visiting and performing in South Africa regularly. We grew fond of him, and he became close—a close member of our family. We had great admiration for his talent and that he was able to triumph over tragedy on so many occasions in his life. Michael was a giant and a legend in the music industry. And we mourn with the millions of fans worldwide. We also mourn with his family and his friends over the loss of our dear friend. He will be missed and memories about him cherished for a very long time. My wife and I, our family, our friends, send you our condolences during this time of mourning. Be strong.

Nelson Mandela

致亲爱的杰克逊家族：

　　得知迈克尔的死讯，我非常悲伤。他在南非进行定期访问和演出之后，就与我们全家建立了非常密切的关系，我们非常爱他。我们对他的才华赞叹不已，并且对他在面对人生的诸多坎坷时所展现出的勇气表示敬意。在音乐界，迈克尔是个传奇人物，我们和全世界亿万歌迷、他的家人和朋友们都为失去这样的挚友而共同表达哀思，我们会长久地思念他，铭记他。我和我的妻子、朋友，还有我们全家人在今天致以我们最深切的慰问，希望大家能够坚强！

纳尔逊·曼德拉

二、悼词的翻译

悼词是对逝者表示哀悼的话或文章，有广义和狭义之分。广义的悼词指向逝者表示哀悼、缅怀与敬意的一切形式的悼念性文章，狭义的悼词专指在追悼大会上对逝者表示敬意与哀思的宣读式的专用悼文。

悼文一般包括以下三方面的内容：

（1）点明悼念对象，简要介绍其生前身份、简历、因何逝世、逝世时间、终年岁数等；

（2）扼要介绍逝者生前的事迹，突出其对社会的贡献，恰如其分地评价其一生；

（3）对逝者表示哀悼，并勉励生者化悲痛为力量。悼词一般由较有威望或地位的人宣读。

例5

We're here to memorialize 29 Americans: Carl Acord, Jason Atkins, Christopher Bell, Gregory Steven Brock, Kenneth Allan Chapman, Robert Clark, Charles Timothy Davis, Cory Davis, Michael Lee Elswick, William I. Griffith, Steven Harrah, Edward Dean Jones, Richard K. Lane, William Roosevelt Lynch, Nicholas Darrell McCroskey, Joe Marcum, Ronald Lee Maynor, James E. Mooney, Adam Keith Morgan, Rex L. Mullins, Joshua S. Napper, Howard D. Payne, Dillard Earl Persinger, Joel R. Price, Deward Scott, Gary Quarles, Grover Dale Skeens, Benny Willingham, and Ricky Workman.

Nothing I, or the Vice President, or the Governor, none of the speakers here today, nothing we say can fill the hole they leave in your hearts, or the absence that they leave in your lives. If any comfort can be found, it can, perhaps, be found by seeking the face of God—who quiets our troubled minds, a God who mends our broken hearts, a God who eases our mourning souls.

Even as we mourn 29 lives lost, we also remember 29 lives lived. Up at 4:30 a.m., 5:00 in the morning at the latest, they began their day, as they worked, in darkness. In coveralls and hard-toe boots, a hardhat over their heads, they would sit quietly for their hour-long journey, five miles into a mountain, the only light the lamp on their caps, or the glow from the mantrip they rode in.

Day after day, they would burrow into the coal, the fruits of their labor, what so often we take for granted: the electricity that lights up a convention center; that lights up our church or our home, our school, our office; the energy that powers our country; the energy that powers the world.

And most days they'd emerge from the dark mine, squinting at the light. Most days, they'd emerge, sweaty and dirty and dusted from coal. Most days, they'd come home. But not that day.

These men—these husbands, fathers, grandfathers, brothers, sons, uncles, nephews—they did not take on their job unaware of the perils. Some of them had already been injured; some of them had seen a friend get hurt. So they understood there were risks. And their families did, too. They knew their kids would say a prayer at night before they left. They knew their wives would wait for a call when their shift ended saying everything was okay. They knew their parents felt a pang of fear every time a breaking news alert came on, or the radio cut in.

But they left for the mines anyway—some, having waited all their lives to be miners; having longed to follow in the footsteps of their fathers and their grandfathers. And yet, none of them did it for themselves alone.

All that hard work, all that hardship, all the time spent underground, it was all for the families. It was all for you. For a car in the driveway, a roof overhead. For a chance to give their kids opportunities that they would never know, and enjoy retirement with their spouses. It was all in the hopes of something better. And so these miners lived—as they died—in pursuit of the American Dream.

There, in the mines, for their families, they became a family themselves—sharing birthdays, relaxing together, watching Mountaineers football or basketball together, spending days off together, hunting or fishing. They may not have always loved what they did, but they loved doing it together. They loved doing it as a family. They loved doing it as a community.

That's a spirit that's reflected in a song that almost every American knows. But it's a song most people, I think, would be surprised was actually written by a coal miner's son about this town, Beckley, about the people of West Virginia. It's the song, *Lean on Me*—an anthem of friendship, but also an anthem of community, of coming together.

That community was revealed for all to see in the minutes, and hours, and days after the tragedy. Rescuers, risking their own safety, scouring narrow tunnels saturated with methane and carbon monoxide, hoping against hope they might find a survivor. Friends keeping porch lights on in a nightly vigil; hanging up homemade signs that read, "Pray for our miners, and their families." Neighbors consoling each other, and supporting each other and leaning on one another.

I've seen it, the strength of that community. In the days that followed the disaster, emails and letters poured into the White House. Postmarked from different places across the country, they often began the same way: "I am proud to be from a family of miners." "I am the son of a coal miner." "I am proud to be a coal miner's daughter." They were always proud, and they asked me to keep our miners in my thoughts, in my prayers. Never forget, they say, miners keep America's lights on. And then in these letters, they make a simple plea: Don't let this happen again. Don't let this happen again.

How can we fail them? How can a nation that relies on its miners not do everything in its power to protect them? How can we let anyone in this country put their lives at risk by simply showing up to work; by simply pursuing the American Dream?

We cannot bring back the 29 men we lost. They are with the Lord now. Our task, here on Earth, is to save lives from being lost in another such tragedy; to do what must do, individually and collectively, to assure safe conditions underground—to treat our miners like they treat each other—like a family. Because we are all family and we are all Americans. And we have to lean on one another, and look out for one another, and love one another, and pray for one another.

There's a psalm that comes to mind today—a psalm that comes to mind, a psalm we often turn to in times of heartache.

"Even though I walk through the valley of the shadow of death, I will fear no evil, for You are with me; your rod and your staff, they comfort me."

God bless our miners! God bless their families! God bless West Virginia! And God bless the United States of America!

我们在这里，悼念29位美国人，他们分别是：卡尔·阿克德、杰森·阿金斯、克里斯多夫·贝尔、格利高里·史蒂夫·布洛克、肯尼斯·艾伦·查普曼、罗伯特·克拉克、查尔斯·蒂莫西·戴维斯、克里·戴维斯、迈克尔·李·埃尔斯维克、威廉·I.格里菲斯、史蒂芬·哈拉、爱德华·迪恩·琼斯、理查德·K.雷恩、威廉·罗斯福·林奇、尼古拉斯·达利尔·麦考斯基、乔·马克姆、罗纳德·李·梅尔、詹姆斯·E.姆尼、亚当·基斯·摩根、雷克斯·L.姆林斯、乔什·S.纳皮尔、霍华德·D.佩恩、迪拉德·厄尔·波辛格、乔尔·R.普莱斯、迪华德·斯科特、加里·考拉斯、格罗佛·戴尔·斯金斯、本尼·威灵汉姆以及里奇·沃克曼。

无论我、副总统、州长，或是今天致悼词的任何一个人，无论我们说什么，都无法填补你们心中因痛失亲人而留下的创伤。如果有任何可以找得到的安慰，也许只能从上帝那里寻找：上帝安慰我们痛苦的心灵，修复我们破碎的心，让我们哀伤的心得到些许平复。

我们在这哀悼这29条逝去的生命，我们要记得这29条生命曾生活在我们这个世界。他们凌晨4点半最迟5点起床，开始一天的生活，他们在黑暗中工作。穿着工作服和硬头靴，头戴安全帽，静坐着开始一小时的征程，去到五英里远的矿井，唯一的灯光是从他们头戴的安全帽上发出的，或是进入时矿山沿途的光线。

夜以继日，他们挖掘煤炭，这也是他们劳动的果实，我们以之为当然：照亮会议中心的灯光；点亮教堂或家庭、学校、办公室的灯光；这是让我们国家运转的能源；也是让世界运转的能源。

大多时候，他们从黑暗的矿里探出头，眯眼盯着光亮。大多时候，他们从矿里探出身，满是汗水和尘垢。大多时候，他们能够回家。但不是那天。

这些人，这些丈夫、父亲、祖父、弟兄、儿子、叔父、侄子，他们从事这份工作时，并没有忽视其中的风险。他们中的一些已经负伤，一些人眼见朋友受伤。所以，他们知道有风险。他们的家人也知道。他们知道，在自己去矿上之前，孩子会在夜晚祈祷。他们知道妻子在焦急等待自己的电话，通报今天的任务完成，一切安好。他们知道，每有紧急新闻播出，或是广播被突然切断，他们的父母会感到莫大的恐惧。

但他们还是离开家园，来到矿里。一些人毕生期盼成为矿工，他们期待追随父辈走过的道路。然而，这并不是他们为自己而做的选择。

这艰险的工作，其中巨大的艰辛，在地下度过的时光，都是为了家人；都是为了你们；也为了在路上奔驰的汽车，为了头顶上天花板的灯光；为了能给孩子的未来一个机会，日后享受与伴侣的退休生活。这都是期冀能有更好的生活。所以，这些矿工的生活就是追寻美国梦，他们也因此失去了生命。

在矿里，为了他们的家人，他们像家人一样工作生活在一起：庆祝彼此的生日，一同休憩，一同观看橄榄球或篮球赛，一同消磨时间，打猎或是钓鱼。他们可能不总是喜欢这些事情，但他们喜欢一起去完成。他们喜欢像一个家庭那样去做这些事。他们喜欢像一个社区一样去做这些事。

这正是美国人熟知的一首歌里所表达的精神。也许，让大多数人惊讶的是这首歌实际是一名矿工的儿子所写，关于贝克利这个小镇，关于西弗吉尼亚人民。这首歌曲，《靠着我》，是友谊的赞歌，也是关于社区、关于相聚的赞歌。

灾难发生的几分钟、几小时、几日之后，这个团体终被外界关注。搜救者冒着风险在充满沼气和一氧化碳的狭窄地道里搜寻，抱着一线希望去发现幸存者。朋友们打开门廊的灯守夜；悬挂着自制的标语，上书"为我们的矿工和他们的家人祈祷"。邻居们彼此安慰，相扶相依。

我看到了，这就是团体的力量。在灾难后的几天，电子邮件和信件涌入白宫。邮戳来自全国各地，人们通常都是同一开头："我很骄傲来自一个矿工的家庭。""我是一名矿工的儿子。""我很自豪能成为一名矿工的女人。"……他们都感到自豪，他们让我关护我们的矿工，为他们祈祷。他们说，不要忘了，矿工维持着美国的光亮。在这些信件里，他们提出一个很小的要求：不要让这样的事再发生。不要让这事情再发生。

我们怎忍让他们失望？一个依赖矿工的国家怎能不尽全力履行保护他们的职责？我们的国家怎能容忍人们仅因工作就付出生命；难道仅仅是因为他们追求美国梦吗？

我们无法让29条逝去的生命回来。他们此刻与主同在。如今我们的任务，就是防止有生命再在这样的悲剧中逝去。去做我们必须做的，无论个人或是集体，去确保矿下的安全，像矿工对待彼此那样对待他们，如同一家人。因为我们是一家人，我们都是美国人。我们必须要彼此依靠，守望彼此，爱护彼此，为彼此祈福祈祷。

今天，我想起一首圣歌，在我们心痛时会想起这首歌。"我虽行过死荫的幽谷，但心无所惧，因你与我同在。你的杖，你的竿，都在安慰我。"

上帝保佑我们的矿工！上帝保佑他们的家人！上帝保佑西弗吉尼亚！上帝保佑美国！

这首悼词是2010年4月25日奥巴马总统为悼念当月西弗吉尼亚州遇难的29名矿工而在纪念仪式上发表的演讲。悼词语言简单、朴实，情感真挚、充沛。翻译时，一定要注意对译文语言的把握，再现这种真诚、充沛的情感。

悼词的翻译，有时也要考虑当地的文化因素。例如：

例6 Apple has lost a visionary and creative genius, and the world has lost an amazing human being. Those of us who have been fortunate enough to know and work with Steve have lost a dear friend and an inspiring mentor. Steve leaves behind a company that only he could have built, and his spirit will forever be the foundation of Apple.

译文a：一位富有远见、充满创意的天才离开了Apple。一位杰出的、了不起的人物告别了世界。曾有幸与他结识并共事的我们，从此失去了一位挚友、一位精神导师。Steve留下了一家唯有他才能创建的企业，他的精神将成为Apple永续前进的基石。

译文b：Apple失去了一位创意天才、创见先驱，世界失去了一位杰出奇才。有幸认识及曾与Steve共事的我们，失去了一位挚友、一位启蒙导师。Steve留下了一间由他一手创立的企业。他虽然离开了，但他的精神将永远长存，永远是我们的基石。

译文c：Apple深悼一位眼光远大且创意独具的天才离开了我们，一位了不起的人物离开了世间。何其有幸认识并与Steve共事的伙伴，则失去了一位挚友与精神导师。Steve身后留下一间唯有他才可能创立的公司，他的精神将永远长存并成为Apple永恒的基石。

译文a是苹果公司大陆官网发布的。译文重组了原文语序和行文结构，改变了前两句的主语突出主体；将amazing增译为"杰出的、了不起的"，使排比句更显对称整齐。译文的措辞多样化，分别使用"离开""告别"和"失去"，展示了汉语词汇的丰富多彩。

译文b是苹果公司香港官网发布的。该译文得体地运用了重复的修辞手法，重复"失去了"三次，重复"一位"四次，烘托了无尽的惋惜之情。最后一句运用转折句型"虽然……但"并重复"永远"，表达了很高的评价。

译文 c 是苹果公司台湾官网发布的。译文增加了"深悼""何其"等情感浓厚的词语，符合台湾民众的语言表述习惯。

在翻译吊唁信和悼词的时候，我们需要了解到在此类文体中经常会出现讳饰。讳饰是一种修辞方法。讳，即避忌、隐瞒，对有的事情不敢说或不愿意明说，改用一种含混的说法去掩盖；饰，是掩饰、美饰，为避开犯忌的话，改用别的话来装饰美化。所谓讳饰，就是在说话或写文章时遇到犯忌触讳的事物，不直说出这种事物，而用另外一个说法来回避掩盖或装饰美化。讳饰在应用文体特别是礼仪文书写作中也很常见。英语中对死亡的委婉表达有：grounded for good、to do one's bit、to lay down one's life、to make the ultimate/last sacrifice、to have one's name inscribed in the Book of Life、to be gone、to depart from life、to return to dust/the earth 等。汉语里也有许多委婉的表达，如："辞世""长眠""与世长辞""辞去人世""百年之后""寿终正寝"（男）"寿终内寝"（女）"成为故物""呜呼哀哉""已故""作古""大去""仙逝""安眠""安息""溘然长逝""风去楼空""天妒英才""南极星沉""驾返瑶池""音容宛在"等。

练习九

一、将下列句子译成中文。

1. May many fortunes find their way to you!
2. I want to wish you longevity and health!
3. Take good care of yourself in the years ahead.
4. Wish you many future successes.
5. On this special day I send you New Year's greetings and hope that some day soon we shall be together.
6. I would like to wish you a joyous new year and express my hope for your happiness and good future.
7. May the New Year bring many good things and rich blessings to you and all those you love!

二、将下面的邀请函译成中文。

Dear Sir/Madam,

　　Thank you for your letter of Jan. 9, 2011. I'm glad that you are also going to Wuhan next month. It would be a great pleasure to meet you at the exhibit trade fair.

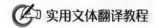

  Our company is having a reception party at Holiday Inn on the evening of Jan. 13, 2011 and I would be very pleased if you could attend.

  I look forward to hearing from you soon.

Yours sincerely,
Mike
CEO

三、将下面的邀请函译成英文。

亲爱的苏珊：

  我知道您对国画很有兴趣，所以我相信您对谢鹏夫妇也会感兴趣。他们将于9月12日（下星期日）来做客，我们很希望您和马克也能同来。

  谢鹏夫妇人很好。我们是去年夏天在伦敦认识的。他们收集了各个不同时期精美的国画作品。谢鹏先生在国画研究方面颇有权威。我深信您和马克会很高兴认识他们。

  我们准备6点开饭，这样有更长的聊天时间，如果事前没有得到您的回信，我就默认你们当天会来。

四、将下面的请柬译成英文。

请　柬

  兹定于11月8日（星期日）10时在文化广场举行舞会，敬请光临，恭候回音。

侯磊博士及夫人 谨订

第十章 启事文书的翻译

启事是一种常见的应用文体。我们每天都会在报纸、杂志、网络上读到寻人、寻物、招领、征婚、开业、征稿、招聘等各种各样的启事。启事已经成为我们生活中不可缺少的一部分，许多生产经营活动都需要借助启事来进行。当今，随着经济全球化步伐的进一步加快，跨国、跨地区的生产与经济活动迅速增多，启事的翻译就显得尤为重要。

从概念上讲，启事就是公开的简便告示。"启"是陈述、告知的意思，"事"即事情，"启事"就是把事情陈述出来，告诉大家。启事具有广泛性、公开性、自愿性的特点，但是它不具备法令性、政策性、强制性和约束性。启事的对象可参与启事中所要求的事，也可以不参与。

英语中，启事即 notice 或 announcement。但 notice 一词含义较多，《牛津英汉双解词典》对该词的释义为：① (sheet of paper) written or printed news or information, usually displayed publicly 布告、公告、告示、启事；② warning of what will happen 通知、警告；③ formal letter, etc., stating that sb. is to leave a job at a specified time 辞职书、辞呈。由此可知，英语中的 Notice 一词既有"启事"又有"公告"的含义，因此可用 Written Announcement 来对应汉语中的"启事"，但也可用 Notice。

汉语的启事和英语的 Written Announcement 或 Notice 都具有不同于文学、法律等其他文体的特征，在翻译启事文书之前，应首先了解汉语与英语启事文书的文体特征。

第一节 启事文书的文体特征

一、汉语启事的文体特征

（一）汉语启事的结构

尽管启事内容丰富、种类繁多，但其结构大体相同，通常包括标题、正文、落款三部分。

1. 标题

首行的正中写标题，要用大字醒目写出，如"招领启事""招聘启事""征稿启事"等。可以在"启事"之前加上一些修饰性的形容词，例如"重要""紧急"等以强调启事的性质；还可以将"启事"两字略去，只写"招领""招聘""征稿"。标题的写法比较灵活，常见的有以下几种写法：

1）笼统式：启事

2）事由式：招聘、寻人、征婚

3）事由＋文种：开业启事、招聘启事

4）单位名称＋文种：××公司启事

5）单位名称＋事由＋文种：×××公司招聘启事

6）加敬词表诚意：诚聘、敬聘、清华同方人工环境有限公司诚聘

启事的标题应简短、新颖、醒目，主旨鲜明突出，高度概括，能吸引人们的注意力并抓住其阅读心理。尤其是广告性、宣传性的启事，标题更要注意艺术性。

2. 正文

标题下一行空两格开始写正文。正文的内容一般包括目的、原因、具体事项、要求、特征、条件、时间期限等。正文必须将有关事项一一交代清楚，要写得具体、明白、详细，细节要交代清楚，不能含糊。如果内容较多，可分条列项，逐一交代。正文部分是体现各种启事不同性质和特点的关键部分，应依据不同启事的内容和要求，灵活处理，注意突出启事的有关事项，不必强求一致。

启事的正文内容要严密、完整，不能遗漏重要细节，表述要清楚，不能引起歧义。主题要单一，做到一事一启。

3. 落款

在启事末尾的右下方分两行写明启事单位名称或个人姓名和启事日期。注意落款处必须写个人姓名或单位名称的全称，不可写简称。如果标题或上文中已写明单位名称，此处可以省略。凡以机关、单位的名义发布的启事，必须加盖公章，以示对启事内容负全责。

（二）汉语启事的语言特点

汉语启事的措辞有着严格的要求。

第一，应使用正式文体。汉语启事应使用书面标准用语，少用口语、俗语，不用俚语。启事的语言注重实用性，以传递信息为主要目的，应避免明显的好恶、夸张的溢美与隐恶之词。

第二，用语应力求简洁。启事的语言少文饰，少修辞，少评论，用尽可能少的篇幅来告知公众尽可能详细的信息（为保密起见，招领等一些启事不能传达详细信息）。因此，

要精简细节，略去无关或关系不大的细节；提高语言的概括能力，可以适当使用一些缩略语。例如下面这则招领启事的用语就十分简洁：

例1

招 领 启 事

　　本人于5月8日上午在校园拾得皮包一个，内有若干证件、若干人民币、一些文件资料，望失主前来认领。联系电话：13212345678。

李同学

2014年5月9日

　　第三，用语应明确无误。启事文书要做到语意清晰，不能含糊其辞、模棱两可，应避免使用"相关部门""类似条件""时机成熟""事出有因，查无实据""大致时间"等表达含糊的词。在启事文书中，应写明启事缘由，逐一列出启事事项。例如，在招聘启事中，必须写明招聘者、招聘对象、招聘条件与要求、报名截止日期、面试地点与时间、联系方式和地址等事项。又比如，在招领启事中，需要写明何人、何时、何地、捡到什么东西、联系方式等事宜。

　　第四，用语应礼貌得体。启事文书的语言要热情、恳切、文明。另外，启事没有强制性和约束力，需特别注意使用礼貌用语，适当运用一些表示欢迎、希冀、感谢之类的词语。

二、英语启事的文体特征

（一）英语启事的结构

英语启事通常包括标题、日期、正文、落款四个部分。中文启事的日期包含在落款内，而英语启事的日期在标题的左下方，需单独列出。

1. 标题

英语启事的标题应该简短、醒目，能概括事由并吸引公众的注意。启事的标题可以只写一个字，如：Found、Lost、Notice 等；也可以加上事由，如：International Forum Call for Papers、Subscribing Announcement 等。

2. 日期

标题下一行的最左边写日期。一般情况下，日期应该包括年、月、日，以方便公众查看。英语的日期有两种方式表达，可以用"日+月+年"，如：2nd March, 1996；也可用"月+日+年"，如：March 2, 1996。前者为英式表达法，后者为美式表达法。在美式写法中，不使用 1st、2nd、3rd 的 st、nd、rd。全部用数字表达日期时，英式英语和美式英语也有差别。如"1998年5月6日"按照英式写法应写成 6/5/1998，而按照美式写法应写成 5/6/1998。在写英文启事时，应特别注意日期的写法。

3. 正文

正文的写法和中文启事一样,需具体说明启事的内容,必须将有关事项写清楚。这部分要写得具体、详细,尤其是细节要交代清楚,避免歧义。

4. 落款

在启事末尾的右下方写明启事单位名称或个人姓名。如果标题或上文中已写明单位名称,此处可以省略。

(二)英语启事的语言特点

英语启事用词简洁,较多使用短句,很少使用长句,定语从句、状语从句、非谓语动词等复杂结构则更为少用。此外,英语启事常使用省略结构,言简意赅。例如:

例2

Found

Oct. 28, 2011

　　A brown leather bag, in the reading room on the morning of Oct. 2. Owner can claim at the Lost and Found Office, Rm. 406 of the Office Building.

Lost and Found Office

从这则启事可以看出,英语启事用词简洁,启事的第一句省略了谓语动词 was found,仅保留主语,这在英语启事中是很常见的。

第二节　启事文书的翻译原则与注意事项

一、启事文书的翻译原则

启事文书的翻译首先应遵守忠实、通顺的一般翻译原则。此外,因启事的主要目的在于传递信息并吸引相关人参与其中,所以启事文书的翻译与文学等其他类型的翻译存在较大区别。季羡林教授在谈到翻译时曾指出:"凭我自己的经验,不同门类的翻译有不同的要求。有的需要严格对应,有的无须或很难对应,能较准确达意即可。"[1] 不同文体需要遵循体现其目的与要求的翻译原则。德国功能学派翻译理论家卡特琳娜·莱斯(Katharina Reiss, 1923—)根据功能的不同,将文本分为描述性文本(descriptive text)、表达性文本(expressive text)和祈使性文本(vocative text),并指出不同的文本在翻译时的侧重点

---

[1] 张光明. 2009. 英语实用文体翻译. 合肥:中国科学技术大学出版社.

和要求不同。描述性文本主要包括新闻报道、商业信函、官方文件、法律文书等非虚构的文本，这类文本注重内容信息，强调译文必须准确传达原文的内容，符合目的语的表达习惯。表达性文本即小说、戏剧、诗歌等文学文本，这类文本注重用各种语言形式来表达作者的情感与立场，译文要求符合原文的美学特征。祈使性文本即宗教和政治上的宣传，强调文本的渲染与影响效果，译文要求符合原文的宣传效果和鼓动性力量。[2]

按照莱斯的分类方法，启事属于描述性文本，注重"说什么"，强调原文与译文内容信息的完全对等，重视译文的规范性与程式性。具体来讲，启事的翻译应遵循以下几个原则：

第一，语言简练，表达准确。启事的内容有很强的针对性，强调实用，不重视遣词造句的审美效果。因此，在翻译时，必须做到语言简洁，就事论事，明白易懂，不做过多修饰，不追求不必要的美学效果。启事的翻译需条理清楚，层次分明，表达准确，避免使用晦涩难懂和模棱两可的词语，确保译文不会产生歧义。下面这则英文启事的翻译就符合此项要求。

例1

Lost

Mar. 23, 2013

I was careless and lost my mobile phone when studying in the reading room of our library yesterday. The finder can contact me to fetch it back, please. Many Thanks.

Address: Room 308, Dorm Building 6
Tel: 86350491

Mary

寻物启事

由于失主不慎，昨天在图书馆阅览室丢失一部手机，请拾到者联系失主去取，不胜感激。失主地址：第6宿舍308室，电话：86350491。

玛丽

2013年3月23日

第二，译文与原文的语体风格一致。汉语与英语均有不同的语体风格，语体风格从极正式到极不正式渐进过渡，语言学家们将之称为不同的等级。通常而言，中间一级是标准语体，其上有正式语体和极正式体，其下有不正式语体和极不正式体（口语体、粗俗体等）。请看以下几个例子[3]：

- I beg, sir, that you will offer him my sincerest apologies.
  敬请阁下向他传达在下最诚挚的歉意。

2　陈琴. 2007. 英汉汉英翻译基础. 郑州：河南出版集团.
3　同上。

- Please send my sincerest apologies to him.
  请向他传达我最诚挚的歉意。
- Tell him I'm awfully sorry.
  告诉他我很抱歉。

汉语和英语的启事都是标准语体，遣词造句比较规范。英汉互译时，不应使用口语体和粗俗体，也不宜使用极正式语体，应使用标准语体。

第三，译文符合目的语的格式要求。启事有固定的结构与格式。汉语与英语的启事格式上大同小异，在翻译时可以照搬，但在遇到差异时，可以根据译文的格式规范进行适当的调整，使译文符合目的语的格式要求。比如本节例 1，英文启事的日期位于左上角，但是在中文译文中，根据中文启事的格式习惯，将该日期放在了右下角的签名下面。

二、启事文书翻译的注意事项

中英文启事文书在格式和内容表达方面存在差异，这是翻译时需要特别注意的地方。

首先，英文启事中，经常会使用省略结构，用名词短语来代替完整句子；但中文启事中，很少使用省略结构。例如：

例2

Found

Oct. 28, 2011

  A black notebook PC in the reading-room of library on the evening of Oct. 27th. Owner please claim at the Library Office, Room 101 of the Library Building.

                     Library Office

招 领 启 事

  10 月 27 日晚上在图书馆阅览室发现一台黑色笔记本电脑。请失主前往图书馆楼 101 室认领。

                    图书馆办公室

                    2011 年 10 月 28 日

从上面这则招领启事中可以看出，英文启事用语非常简练，第一句省略了谓语动词，这是英文启事中常用的句法；但中文启事则很少用省略结构。在翻译时，需要做适当调整。

其次，翻译时要对格式做适当调整，以符合目的语的规范。在时间写法上，中文通常先写年、月、日，再写星期几，而在英文中，通常是星期几在前，日、月或者月、日在后。比如，"2011 年 5 月 28 日星期三"，应被译为 Wednesday, May 28, 2011。除此之外，英文启事的标题很少用全称，Notice 或 Announcement 很少出现在标题中，而中文启事既可以用全称，如"招领启事""征稿启事"等，也可以略去"启事"二字，直接把"招领""征稿""寻物"等作为标题。如例 2 所示,英文标题简洁,译为中文时,标题为"招领启事",也可直接译为"招领"。

第三节
常用启事文书的翻译

一、征稿启事与征订启事

(一)征稿启事

征稿启事中,应写明征稿单位、征稿的主题与内容、征稿要求、投稿邮箱或地址、截止收稿日期等具体内容。下面通过几个例子来具体说明征稿启事的翻译。

例1

International Forum Call for Papers

Topic: Language Issues in English-medium Universities: A Global Concern

Date: June 18–20, 2008

Venue: The Chinese University of Hong Kong

Content:
　　☆ The dynamics of English and other local, foreign and minority languages in higher education;
　　☆ Integrating language and content in higher education contexts;
　　☆ The use of English across disciplines;
　　☆ Language identity and its impact on learning.

Notes: Abstract no more than 300 English words. Please attach a separate page indicate the name, title, address, telephone and other personal information.

Deadline: January 31, 2008

Contacts: Miss Scarlet Poon

E-mail: scarletws@hku.hk

国际论坛征稿启事

议题:大学英语教学中的语言问题:一个全球性话题

日期:2008 年 6 月 18 日—20 日

地点:香港中文大学

内容:
　　☆高等教育中的英语及其他本地语、外语和少数民族语言的动态研究;

☆高等教育语境中语言与内容的整合；
☆跨学科的英语运用；
☆语言认同及其对学习的影响。

要求：摘要不多于 300 词。请另附页注明姓名、职务、地址、电话和其他个人信息。

截止日期：2008 年 1 月 31 日

联系人：斯嘉丽·潘小姐（Miss Scarlet Poon）

电子邮箱：scarletws@hku.hk

以上这则英文征稿启事摘自香港中文大学的网站，内容略有删减，汉语译文由编者翻译。从此例可以看出，征稿启事的翻译务求准确，应尽量采用严格的逐词对应的翻译。例如，the dynamics of English and other local, foreign and minority languages in higher education 一句，根据汉语的表达习惯把状语 in higher education 放在句首，原句中的 other local, foreign and minority languages 采用逐词对应的翻译方法，译文为："高等教育中的英语及其他本地语、外语和少数民族语言的动态研究"。这样做，既保证了译文符合汉语的表达习惯，又确保了信息的完整准确。

（二）征订启事

征订启事需要介绍杂志或报纸的主要信息，包括：主办方、内容、栏目、发行周期、订阅价格、地址、邮政编码、联系电话等具体事项，方便读者了解和订阅。下面通过例子来具体说明征订启事的翻译事项。

例 2

The Sunday Times[4]

Editor: John Witherow

The Sunday Times is known for the rigor of its political coverage, the vigor of its editorials, and its commitment to providing a platform for a diverse and pluralistic range of options. At the same time the newspaper offers great value to readers with Culture, which covers all of the arts and entertainment and style which sets the pace in fashion, gossip and social comment.

The Sunday Times is Britain's leading quality Sunday newspaper and plays an important role in the lives of over 2.8 million people every week.

 Subscriptions: help@timesplus.co.uk

 Post: 3 Thomas More Square

  London.

  E98 1XY

4　此例引自 https://niadsdirect.com/advertising/paperBlurb.do?id=1.

《星期日泰晤士报》

主编：约翰·威瑟罗

《星期日泰晤士报》以严肃的政治报道、犀利的社论以及致力为多元化的意见提供发表平台而著名。此外，报纸的《文化》专栏涵盖艺术、娱乐、时尚等多个领域，引领时尚，集最新社会传闻和大众舆论为一体，为读者提供富有价值的阅读空间。

《星期日泰晤士报》是英国品质领先的星期日报纸，每周在280万余人的生活中发挥着重要作用。

订阅邮箱：help@timesplus.co.uk

通信地址：伦敦托马斯·莫尔广场三号 E98 1XY

此则英语征订启事摘自英文《泰晤士报》的网站，内容略有删减，中文译文由编者翻译。原启事较为简单，略去了价格等信息。翻译时需要注意几点：第一，报纸杂志名等专名的翻译，须以约定俗成的译法为准，比如这里的 The Sunday Times 一般译为"《星期日泰晤士报》"，而不是"《泰晤士星期日报》"或"《泰晤士报星期日版》"；第二，撰写征订启事的目的是吸引读者订阅，因此翻译时，在忠实于原文的基础上，可以有意识地使用一些带褒义的词语和表达方式，如此处译文中的"犀利的""引领时尚""集最新……为一体""富有价值的"等；第三，汉语地址与英语地址的表达有较大差别。例如此则启事中 3 Thomas More Square 包含了一个专有名词 Thomas More，是以英国思想家"托马斯·莫尔"命名的一个广场，而前面的"3"，指的是这个广场的"三号"。如果不知道这个文化信息，翻译就会出现问题。

例3

征订启事

《台湾研究》是中国社会科学院台湾研究所主办的综合性学术刊物，是中国人文社会科学核心期刊、中文社会科学引文索引（CSSCI）来源期刊。《台湾研究》现为双月刊，主要刊登有关台湾政治、经济、法律、历史、宗教、社会、教育、文学、艺术及有关两岸关系、祖国统一等问题的学术论文，兼载台湾人物介绍、书刊评价以及其他重要研究资料。

本刊欢迎各界订阅。2012年每期订费11.5元（含邮寄费），全年六期共69元。订阅者，请直接汇款至北京海淀区中关村东路21号台湾研究所发行部，邮政编码：100083；如经银行汇款至中国工商银行北京海淀区西区支行，账号89160118，开户名：中国社会科学院台湾研究所。请务必注明汇款用途及订户所在地邮政编码。凡欲订阅者，请与本刊发行部联系，电话：（010）82864903。

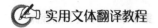

Subscription Announcement

Taiwan Research is a comprehensive academic journal sponsored by Taiwan Institute of Chinese Academy of Social Sciences. It is a source journal for both the Humanities & Social Science Core Journals in China and Chinese Social Sciences Citation Index (CSSCI). *Taiwan Research* is now bimonthly published, carrying research papers on Taiwan's politics, economy, law, history, religion, society, education, literature, arts, cross-strait relation and reunification of China, etc. It also publishes profiles of Taiwan celebrities, book reviews and other important research materials.

All subscribers are welcome. Subscription fee for each issue is 11.5 yuan (including postage) in 2012, and annual cost is 69 yuan. Subscribers may remit subscription fee via post office to Taiwan Institute Circulation Office, 21 Eastern Zhongguancun Road, Haidian District, Beijing 100083, China, or through bank to the Account No. 89160118 of Western Haidian District Branch, Industrial and Commercial Bank of China, with the account name of Taiwan Institute of Chinese Academy of Social Sciences. Please make sure to indicate the remittance is for subscription only and inform us of your detailed post code.

Subscribers may contact our Circulation Office at (Tel.) 010–82864903 for any information they are interested in.

这则中文征订启事摘自《台湾研究》杂志的封底，内容略有删减，译文由编著者翻译。如前所述，汉语征订启事英译时，应特别注意专有名词的翻译，例如："中国人文社会科学核心期刊"应译为 The Humanities & Social Science Core Journals in China；"中文社会科学引文索引"应译为 Chinese Social Sciences Citation Index。这些专有名词都有固定的、约定俗成的译法，翻译时务必使用固定的译法，否则容易引发歧义。

二、开业启事与招聘启事

（一）开业启事

开业启事一般由三部分组成：标题、正文和落款。开业启事的标题通常有两种构成形式：由文种名直接构成，如"开业启事"；由开业单位和文种名共同构成，如"××酒店开业启事""×××公司开业启事"。开业启事的正文包括：开业的具体时间、地点和联系方式；具体经营范围、服务项目、设备状况、环境气氛、发展前途等有关内容；盛情邀请顾客惠顾的礼貌用语，如"欢迎广大顾客前来选购""欢迎惠顾"等。落款要注明发文单位的称呼并署上发文的具体日期。下面通过例子来具体说明开业启事的翻译。

第十章 启事文书的翻译

例4

Opening Notice

Mar. 4, 2011

We have opened a new branch in this district, for the convenience of our customers who live here, and for residents who wish to obtain clothing of the newest style and most reliable quality at reasonable prices. Our store is located on No. 8, London Road. We start our business on the 12th of this month. Welcome all customers!

Chanel Company

开业启事

为方便居住在本地的顾客，我公司特在本地区开设分店，供应品质可靠、款式新颖、价格公道的服装。新店位于伦敦路8号，本月12日开始营业，敬请光临。

香奈儿公司

2011年3月4日

这则开业启事摘自香奈儿公司的网站，译文由编者翻译。翻译时，应注意具体信息的准确性和文体风格的一致性。

例5

国美商城夜间服务部开业启事

为满足广大市民夜间购物的需要，本商场决定从2011年7月1日起开设夜间服务部。服务部主要经销烟、酒、糖果、糕点和日常生活用品。敬请惠顾。营业时间：19:00—23:00。服务部地址：国美商城4楼。

国美商城

2011年6月10日

Gome Mall Running Night Service

June 10, 2011

To meet the needs of our customers for night shopping, we decide to operate night shopping service from July 1, 2011. We offer cigarettes, wines, candies, pastries and daily articles for our customers' choice. Welcome all customers!

Business Hours: 7 p.m.–11 p.m.

Address: 4/F, Gome Mall.

Gome Mall

这则汉语开业启事摘自西祠胡同网站，译文由编者翻译。开业启事的翻译较为简单。翻译时需特别注意信息的准确性，要根据英语和汉语的表达习惯，对地址和日期进行适当调整。

（二）招聘启事

招聘启事是用人单位面向社会公开招聘有关人员时使用的一种应用文书。招聘启事通常包括标题、正文和落款三部分。标题由事由和文种名称构成，如"招聘启事""招工启事""招聘科技人员启事"等。还可以在标题中写明招聘的单位名称，如"××服装厂招聘启事"。正文包括四个方面的具体内容：招聘方的情况，包括招聘方的业务、工作范围及地理位置等；对招聘对象的具体要求，包括招聘人员的工作性质、业务类型，以及年龄、性别、文化程度、工作经历、学历等要求；待遇与福利事项；应聘的具体时间、联系地点、联系人、联系方式等。落款要求在正文右下角署上发表启事的单位名称和启事的发文时间。下面通过例子来具体说明招聘启事的翻译。

例 6

SENIOR CONSULTANT RECRUITMENT[5]

Job Description: Senior Consultant, IBM Corporation, Somers, NY and at various client sites throughout the U.S.: Provide industry experience and technical skills around the SAP Extended Warehouse Management (EWM) application. Implement the SPA EMW module. Understand the client requirements related to warehouse management processes. Prepare process design, functional design and functional specifications according to SAP EWM module functionality. Analyze requirement gaps and provide customized solutions. Configure the EWM system for inbound, outbound, internal, yard management and transportation processes. Perform unit testing and integration testing. Utilize SAP R/3 and ECC, SAP EMW, SAP WM and SAP ABAP.

Required: Bachelor's of Science degree or equivalent (employer will accept three years of post-secondary study plus one year of IT experience in lieu of a Bachelor's degree) and two years of experience as a Consultant, Senior Business Consultant, Software Consultant, Senior Consultant or related. Before Oct. 1, 2012, send resumes to IBM, box #X164, 71 Fifth Avenue, NY, NY 10003

招聘高级顾问

职位描述：IBM公司高级顾问，工作地点为萨默斯、纽约和全美各地的客户站。为SAP EWM应用程序提供行业经验和技术技能；执行SPA EMW模块；理解客户涉及仓库管理过程的需求，根据SAP EWM模块功能，准备过程设计、功能设计和功能说明；分析客户需求并提供定制的解决方案；配置EWM系统用于入库、出库、内部、堆场管理和运输过程；执行单元测试和集成测试；使用SAP R/3和ECC、SAP EMW、SAP WM及SAP ABAP。

要求：理学学士学位或同等学历（没有学士学位但接受了三年高中教育且

5　此例引自 http://jobview.nytimes.monster.com/SENIOR-CONSULTANT-Job-Somers-US-110192321.aspx.

有一年在 IT 行业工作经验的亦可）及两年从事顾问、高级业务咨询、软件顾问、高级顾问或相关工作的经历。有意者请于 2012 年 10 月 1 日前将简历发送到纽约第五大道 71 号 IBM 公司 X164 信箱，邮编 10003。

这则 IBM 公司的招聘启事摘自美国《纽约时报》的招聘专栏，内容略有删减，汉语译文由编者翻译。启事中对职位和要求的描述非常具体。翻译时，应采用逐词翻译的方法，根据汉语的语法与表达习惯，准确传递原启事的信息。例如：two years of experience as a Consultant, Senior Business Consultant, Software Consultant, Senior Consultant or related，在翻译时，根据汉语表达习惯将定语 as a Consultant, Senior Business Consultant, Software Consultant, Senior Consultant or related 置于 experience 之前，译为："两年从事顾问、高级业务咨询、软件顾问、高级顾问或相关工作的经历。"

例7

扬州报业广告公司人员招聘启事

为适应扬州报业广告公司发展的需要，现面向社会公开招聘广告经营人员 10 名，男女不限。

一、应聘条件

1972 年 1 月 1 日以后出生，身体健康，大学专科以上学历，具有良好的职业道德和社会责任感，有户外广告从业经历者优先。

二、待遇

1. 考试合格者先行试用，试用期内底薪加提成。

2. 试用期满经考核合格后，按规定办理聘用手续，与扬州报业广告公司现有从业人员同岗同酬。

三、报名方法

应聘者请于 2012 年 5 月 21 日至 31 日，将个人资料（复印件）邮寄或送至扬州市文昌西路 525 号扬州报业传媒集团人力资源部，邮编 225009。初审合格者，将另行通知考试时间。一个月内未收到通知，视作初审未通过，应聘材料恕不退还。

扬州报业传媒集团人力资源部

2012 年 5 月 21 日

Yangzhou Newspaper Advertising Company Recruitment Ads

May 21, 2012

Yangzhou Newspaper Advertising Company is now recruiting 10 advertising personnel, male or female, to meet the needs of the company development.

I. Requirements

Born after Jan. 1, 1972. Healthy. Holding a junior college degree or above & displaying sound professional ethics and good sense of social responsibility. Applicants with outdoor advertising work experience are preferred.

II. Salary

1. Applicants who pass the company evaluation will be subject to a term of probation, during which they will receive basic salary plus commission.

2. After the probation term, qualified applicants will be formally employed and enjoy the same salary package as other employees doing the same work in the company.

III. Application

Those interested should post or send their application materials (photocopies) to Human Resources Office of Yangzhou Newspaper Media Group Company, 525 West Wenchang Road, Yangzhou 225009, China. Applicants who have passed the first-round screening will be informed of test time, and those who haven't received any reply within a month may deem that they have failed the first-round screening. Application materials won't be returned.

Yangzhou Newspaper Media Group Company

以上这则汉语招聘启事摘自扬州报业集团网站，内容略有删减，英文译文由编者翻译。翻译时需注意词和句子要简洁易懂，不必把启事中的省略句全部译为完整句子。例如，"1972年1月1日以后出生，身体健康，大学专科以上学历，具有良好的职业道德和社会责任感"，在翻译时，就处理为并列的几个短语：Born after Jan. 1, 1972. Healthy. Holding a junior college degree or above & displaying sound professional ethics and good sense of social responsibility. 另外需要注意项目编号的翻译。由于英语中没有"一、二、三"这样的数字表达方法，在翻译时，需要转换为罗马数字 I、II、III 或 A、B、C。由于中英文中都有阿拉伯数字，所以阿拉伯数字表示的项目编号不必转换。

三、寻人启事、寻物启事与招领启事

（一）寻人启事

寻人启事需要写明丢失人的姓名、年龄、性别、口音、走失时穿的衣服款式和颜色、走失的地点和时间，有无精神病史，联系人的姓名、电话、酬谢方式等信息。除此之外，还需附上丢失人的照片。下面通过例子来具体说明寻人启事的翻译。

例8

寻人启事

杨江，男，67岁，身高1.75米，较壮不胖。白发，头戴黑色帽子，脸部有短的白色胡须；上身穿蓝色拉链无帽运动服，内穿乳白色秋衣；下身穿黑色牛仔裤，黑皮鞋。老人于2012年4月29日从莘县县城走失，语言表达能力较弱。请见到该人者与家属联系，定重谢！

联系人：杨先生，联系电话：13662316749。

MISSING

Yang Jiang, male, 67 years old, 1.75 meters high, strong but not fat. He had white hair and wore a black hat, with short white beards on his face. He wore a blue zipper sportswear without cap and ivory-white autumn clothes beneath, black jean pants and a pair of black leather shoes. He was last seen in Shenxian County on April 29, 2012. He cannot express himself well. If you have seen him, please contact his family members. A great reward will be offered.

Contact: Mr. Yang at (Tel.) 13662316749.

在翻译寻人启事时，应特别注意信息准确和语气恳切。

（二）寻物启事

寻物启事须写明丢失物品的名称、形状、大小、颜色等特征，丢失的大致地点和时间，联系人的姓名、地址、电话，以及发现后交还的办法和酬谢方式等。

例9

Suitcase Lost

Due to carelessness, Mr. Perkin lost his suitcase in his bus ride to the Jin Ancestral Temple from Yingze Street at 9:30 a.m. last Saturday. The suitcase is square, orange in color and made of leather. It has a metal handle to which a label is attached, and on the label is Perkin's name. Inside the suitcase are a camera made in Japan, several rolls of film and two woolen jackets. In the packet on the front cover are a Chinese-English dictionary and two letters from U.S.. In the back packet are a wallet containing 1,000 dollars and a train ticket from Taiyuan to Beijing. Would the finder contact Mr. Perkin, please? His telephone number is 7075441. Many thanks!

寻手提箱

上周六上午九点半，Perkin先生从迎泽街乘公共汽车去晋祠时，不慎将手提箱丢失。手提箱为方形、橘色、皮制。提箱上有一个系着标签的金属提手，标签上写着Perkin的名字。箱内有一日本相机，几卷胶卷和两件毛料夹克。箱前的口袋里放着一本汉英词典和两封美国来信。箱后有一装有1000美元的钱包和一张从太原到北京的火车票。请拾到者与Perkin先生联系，他的电话号码是7075441。Perkin先生将不胜感激！

翻译寻物启事时，应特别注意丢失物品的细节描述，力求准确无误。

（三）招领启事

招领启事由标题、正文和落款三部分组成。标题可以写为"招领启事"，或写明招领物品名称，如"招领自行车启事"。正文要求写明启事的具体内容：一是拾到的东西及有关情况,包括时间、地点、名称等;二是联系的时间、地点、方式。落款处署上招领启事人和日期。

例10

招领启事

本人于6月18日在大连市一辆红色出租车上捡到一个钱包,内有现金若干、银行卡、身份证、驾照等物品。望失主速与本人电话联系。电话:13265894213。

李先生
2014年6月19日

Found

June 19, 2014

I found a purse from a red taxi in Dalian on June 18. In it were some cash, bank card, ID card, driving license, etc. Whoever lost this wallet can call me as soon as possible. Tel: 13265894213.

Mr. Li

从以上翻译实例中可以看出,寻人启事、寻物启事与招领启事的翻译务求准确、简洁,译文经常使用短句和并列结构。

四、招生启事

与其他启事一样,招生启事也包括三部分:标题、正文和落款。标题可以直接用"招生启事",也可加上学校或培训机构的名称,如:"新东方暑期英语夏令营招生启事""中央音乐学院招生启事"等。正文应包括招生范围、条件、考试或面试的内容、课程设置、报名时间和地点、录取人数、联系电话等具体信息,方便报名者报考。落款包括招生单位名称和日期,需要加盖公章。

例11

北京四中国际部招生

北京四中国际部定于2003年10月正式招生,拟招初一、初二、初三、高一、高二、高三共6个班,每班15人。自入学开始,外籍学生在四中的学习时间达到2—3年,考试合格者颁发北京四中毕业证书,并根据外籍学生意愿,负责推荐报考北大、清华等国内知名大学。

四中国际部还拟招高等教育预备班(15人),汉语起点班(15人),高中毕业拟上中国大学者均可报名。

初、高中、大学预备班均以报名顺序择优录取。

报名时间:2003年10月—2004年1月办理缴费注册手续,2004年2月正式开课。

四中国际部招生简章、报名手续、收费标准请见四中网站 http://www.bj4hs.edu.cn/

Recruitment Notice
International Department of Beijing No. 4 High School

The International Department decides to recruit new students in October 2003. There will be 6 classes: Grade 1, Grate 2 and Grade 3 of Junior High School and Grade 1, Grade 2 and Grade 3 of Senior High School with 15 students in each class. The international students will study at No. 4 High School for two or three years and then take relevant exams. The International Department will issue those qualifiers with certificate of graduation from Beijing No. 4 High School, and based on the wish of the foreign students, recommend them to take entrance examinations of such prestigious universities as Peking University and Tsinghua University.

The International Department is also going to have a preparatory class and a Chinese beginning class with 15 students in each class. High school graduates who wish to study at colleges in China are welcome. The preparatory class at junior high school level, senior high school level and college level will enroll students based on their academic competitiveness.

Time: Register and pay tuition from October 2003 to January 2004. Class starts in February 2004.

For more information, please login to the website of No. 4 High School at http://www.bj4hs.edu.cn/.

例 12

法学专业招生启事

如果你以追求公平和正义为人生价值，如果你正在培养逻辑推理分析事物的能力，如果你愿意为你身边的人排除纠纷与困扰，东北财经大学法学专业向你敞开怀抱。

一、专业说明

1. 专业介绍

法学专业是东北财经大学法学院设立的本科专业。学生主要学习法学的基本理论和基本知识，进行法学思维和法律实务的基本训练，运用法学理论和方法分析解决问题。

2. 主要课程：法理学、中国法制史、宪法、行政法与行政诉讼法、民法、刑法、民事诉讼法、刑事诉讼法、商法、知识产权法、经济法、国际法、国际私法、国际经济法。

3. 修读年限：四年

4. 授予学位：法学学士

二、报名事宜

1. 报名条件：详见《东北财经大学招生简章》。

2. 报名方式：网上报名（网址 http://www.dufe-law.com）

咨询电话：0411-84715324

邮箱地址：faxueyuan@dufe.com

东北财经大学法学院（公章）
2012 年 3 月 10 日

Enrollment for the Undergraduate Program of Law
AVAILABLE Now

March 10, 2012

If you believe in fairness and justice, if you want to develop your logical, reasoning and analytical abilities, if you desire to resolve interpersonal disputes for the people around you, you are welcome to enroll for the undergraduate program of law in the Law School of Dongbei University of Finance and Economics.

I. Program Details

1. Program Introduction

The undergraduate program of law in the Law School of Dongbei University of Finance and Economics was launched to help students study basic law theories and knowledge, get trained in legal reasoning and legal practice, analyze and solve problems by using law theories and methods.

2. Main Courses

Jurisprudence, History of Chinese Legal Systems, Constitution, Administrative Law and Administrative Procedure Law, Civil Law, Criminal Law, Civil Procedure Law, Criminal Procedure Law, Commercial Law, Intellectual Property Rights Law, Economic Law, International Law, International Private Law, and International Economic Law.

3. Duration: Four Years

4. Degree Awarded: Bachelor of Law

II. Application

1. Requirements: For detailed information, please refer to the Enrollment Brochure of Dongbei University of Finance and Economics.

2. Application Procedure: Please apply on our website http://www.dufe-law.com

Inquiries: Please call 0411-84715324

Email address: faxueyuan@dufe.com

Dongbei University of Finance and Economics (Official Seal)

这则招生启事摘自东北财经大学的网站，内容有删减，英文译文由编者翻译。翻译时，对一些专业、学校或单位名称、组织、机构等专有名词，需要遵循已有的、约定俗成的译法，不能随意翻译。例如："东北财经大学"不能根据意义翻译为 Northeast Finance and Economics University，而应该登录东北财经大学的网站，查看其固定的译法 Dongbei University of Finance and Economics。

五、出售启事与出租启事

（一）出售启事

出售启事比较灵活，内容上一般包括要出售的物品、物品描述、价格、联系方式等具体信息。出售信息可以落款，也可以不落款。

例 13

For Sale

May 5, 2011

　　A second-hand computer for sale. I plan to buy a new computer, so I want to sell my old one bought in 2009. It is still in good condition, but works a little slowly. I want to sell it at about 800 yuan. Whoever interested can call me at 45671230 for more information.

John

出　售

　　出售二手电脑。本人欲添置新电脑，所以打算卖掉 2009 年购买的旧电脑。旧电脑性能完好，但速度有些慢。价格在 800 元左右。感兴趣者请打电话询问详情。电话：45671230。

约翰
2011 年 5 月 5 日

（二）出租启事

出租启事也叫招租启事，格式非常灵活，包括标题、正文两个部分。标题可以是"出租启事"或"招租启事"，也可写明出租的物品，如"房屋招租""房屋出租""商场招租"等。正文应该包括：价格、出租物品描述、联系方式、联系人等具体信息。与其他启事所不同的是，出租启事无须落款。

例 14

To Let [6]

Mar. 21, 2011

　　☆ Lovely three-bedroom apartment

---

[6] 此例引自 http://www.rightmove.co.uk.

☆ Lift service
☆ Fully integrated modern kitchen
☆ Modern bathroom with separate WC
☆ Furnished

Set within a prestigious residential development in a highly desirable area of Ealing, this well proportioned three-bedroom first floor flat (with lift) features spacious reception room with balcony overlooking well maintained communal gardens. It is within easy reach of the shops, bars and restaurants along Ealing Broadway. Ealing Broadway Station (National Rail, District and Central lines) is nearby. To view this property or request more details, contact Chasemore Lettings, Ealing (Tel:) 0843 315 1449.

招　　租

☆有三个卧室的舒适公寓
☆带电梯
☆装备齐全的现代厨房
☆带独立卫生间的现代化浴室
☆带家具

房子位于伊令黄金地段的一个高档居民小区内。房子位于小区二楼，三居室，空间设计合理，带电梯，客厅带阳台非常宽敞，从阳台上可以看到小区花园。可以很方便地到达伊令大道沿线的商店、酒吧和饭店。伊令大道车站（可乘坐国铁、地区铁路和地铁中央线）近在咫尺。欲看房或了解更多信息，请联系伊令 Chasemore 租赁公司，电话：0843 315 1449。

2011 年 3 月 21 日

翻译出售启事和出租启事时，需要准确描述出售或出租物品或房屋的细节，避免模糊不清。此外，还需注意街道和小区名称的翻译。需要先查阅有关资料以确定有无固定的习惯表达。如果没有固定译法，可以根据发音进行翻译，中文的地名大多采用汉语拼音。如果有固定译法，则需沿用既有翻译方法，如 Ealing 是英国的一个地名，国内已有固定译法"伊令"，在翻译时，就应采用这种译法。

六、更正启事与鸣谢启事

（一）更正启事

更正启事是报纸、杂志、网络等媒体正式登载的，更正文章、论文、业务等信息的一种应用文体。更正启事和其他启事一样，也包括标题、正文和落款三个部分。标题可以直接是"更正启事"，也可以写明单位或事由，如"网络中心更正启事"或"姓名更正启事"。正文部分需要明确指出错误之处及应如何改正。落款部分需要注明更正单位和发布更正启事的日期。

例 15

Correction: Whales and Wind Farms [7]

June 1, 2012

  Prof Ian Boyd, of the University of St Andrews, said the construction of offshore renewable energy sites is likely to cause some species to move to other areas and to disturb their feeding and reproductive cycles. At present it is not possible to predict precisely how this will affect their populations.

  However, he wished to correct a report on this website this week that said there was a proven link between offshore wind farms and strandings.

  The professor said a quotation attributed to him in a press release issued by the university, which suggested renewable energy sources contributed to the disturbance of whales, had been taken out of context.

  We are happy to make this clear.

The Telegraph

更正启事：鲸鱼搁浅和风力发电厂

  圣安德鲁斯大学教授伊恩·博伊德认为，建立近海可再生能源工厂可能会干扰一些物种的捕食和繁殖周期，迫使它们迁移至其他地区。目前还不能准确预测这将如何影响这些物种的数目。

  然而，他希望更正本周在本网站发表的一个报告，该报告称已有确凿证据证明鲸鱼的搁浅和近海风力发电厂之间存在联系。

  伊恩教授指出，圣安德鲁斯大学发布的新闻稿声称引用了他的观点，该新闻稿指出可再生能源工厂导致了鲸鱼生活习性的紊乱，这个引用实为断章取义的。

  我们很高兴澄清这一点。

《英国电讯报》
2012 年 6 月 1 日

  这则英文更正启事摘自《英国电讯报》网站，中文译文由编者翻译。该更正启事的标题注明了更正事宜，即鲸鱼和风力发电厂两者之间的关系。在翻译长句 The professor said a quotation attributed to him in a press release issued by the university, which suggested renewable energy sources contributed to the disturbance of whales, had been taken out of context 时，将其处理为若干短句，以符合中文启事言简意赅的表达习惯。

例 16

更 正 启 事

  8 月 4 日出版的《青年参考》B01 和 B02 版误将德国前外长费舍尔的图片当

---

[7] 此例引自 http://www.telegraph.co.uk/earth/energy/windpower/8388273/Correction-whales-and-wind-farms.html.

成金融大鳄索罗斯的图片刊登。经编辑部查实，发现所引用的中文图片说明有误，本报编辑未能及时发现错误。特此更正，并向读者致以歉意。

《青年参考》
2011年8月10日

Correction

August 10, 2011

The picture of the former German Foreign Minister Fischer was mistakenly used as that of Soros, the financial magnate, on Pages B01 and B02 of *Youth Reference* published on August 4. The Editorial Department re-checked and confirmed the mistake. We are sorry that our editors have failed to identify the mistake promptly. We are here to correct this and offer our sincere apologies to our readers.

Youth Reference

在翻译这则更正启事时，应注重礼貌用语的翻译，将"特此更正，并向读者致以歉意"翻译为：We are here to correct this and offer our sincere apologies to our readers.

（二）鸣谢启事

鸣谢启事是单位或个人在报纸、杂志、网络等媒体正式登载的，表示感谢的一种应用文体。鸣谢启事和其他启事一样，也包括标题、正文和落款三个部分。标题可以是"鸣谢启事"，也可以是"鸣谢"。正文部分应写明需要感谢的人或单位，并说明感谢事由。落款部分需要注明发布鸣谢的单位或个人以及发布更正启事的日期。

例 17

Acknowledgements [8]

June 24, 2010

The Chinese Cultural Association of Saint John (CCASJ) has been awarded a grant of $3,000 under the Saint John Community Arts Funding Program administered by the Saint John Community Arts Board (SJCAB). This is the third time the CCASJ received the funding support from the SJCAB. The grant is given in support of the Association's cultural and arts programming for 2010–2011. Projects aimed at introducing the general public to the rich Chinese culture and Asian heritage through language, displays, public lectures, arts, cultural workshops, and performances.

The entire CCASJ community greatly acknowledges the Grant Support from the SJCAB Funding Program.

The Chinese Cultural Association of Saint John (CCASJ)

8　此例引自 http://www.ccasj.org/553/acknowledgement-2/.

鸣　　谢

　　圣约翰中华文化协会（CCASJ）荣获圣约翰社区艺术基金资助的 3000 美元赠款。本基金由圣约翰社区艺术局（SJCAB）管理。这是圣约翰中华文化协会第三次得到 SJCAB 的资金支持。这笔赠款将用于支持本协会 2010 年至 2011 年的文化艺术项目，通过语言学习班、文化展览、公开讲座、艺术、文化研讨会和文艺表演等形式向公众介绍丰富悠久的中华文化和亚洲传统。

　　圣约翰文化协会全体成员对 SJCAB 给予的资金支持表示诚挚的谢意！

圣约翰中华文化协会（CCASJ）
2010 年 6 月 24 日

翻译鸣谢启事时，应注意信息准确和语气恳切。

例18

致　　谢

　　我要对导师李云教授表达我诚挚的感谢，没有她的帮助，我无法开始和完成该论文。我论文选题的灵感来自一部改编自童话的美国电视连续剧《童话镇》。从李教授那里，我得以了解巴塞尔姆的《白雪公主》，并很快迷上了这部小说。在写论文的过程中，李教授深厚的学术功底和丰富的文学经验帮了我很多。她的指导、鼓励和耐心帮助使我能够更深入地研究这部小说。我还想感谢我的父母，他们为我提供了一个良好的环境，并一直支持我的论文写作。我还要感谢所有给我上过课的教授们，他们不仅使我领略了英国文学与文化中最璀璨的部分，也使我的大学时光更加珍贵。

王璐
2012 年 6 月 12 日

Acknowledgements

June 12, 2012

　　I'd like to express my sincere thanks to my supervisor, Professor Li Yun, without whom I would not have started and finished this thesis. I was inspired to choose this topic for my graduation thesis by an American TV series called *Once Upon a Time*, which is adapted from fairy tales. And from Professor Li I got to know Barthelme's *Snow White*, and soon became addicted to this novel. During my writing of this thesis, Professor Li helped me a lot with her profound academic knowledge and rich experience in literary studies. Her guidance, encouragement and patience contributed to my deeper understanding of the novel. I also want to thank my parents, who gave me unfailing support throughout the process and provided me with a good environment. Besides, I'd also like to thank all the professors who have shared with me their knowledge in all the lectures. Their efforts have not only led me to the most beautiful part of the world of English literature and culture, but also made my years in this university a most precious time in my life.

Wang Lu

这则论文鸣谢选自编者所指导的学生的学位论文，人名等具体信息做了一些改动，英文译文由编者翻译。该鸣谢启事用词简洁，态度诚恳，对论文导师、父母和其他老师们都表达了诚恳的谢意。在翻译时，应注意用词朴实中肯，避免华丽的词句。

练习十

一、将下列启事译成中文。

1.

Call for Papers

The 16th Asian Games Science Congress, which is to be jointly hosted by the General Administration of Sport of China, the 16th Asian Games Organizing Committee and China Sport Science Society and to be organized by Guangzhou Sport University, will take place in Guangzhou from 11 to 12 October, 2010. The theme of this Congress is "Asian Sport: Science and Development". Sport science specialists and experts home and abroad will be invited to give keynote speeches. We are glad to invite submission of papers from all countries and regions in Asia.

Contents: Sports Management; Sports Media and Media Communications; Economics and the Sports Industry; Sports History; Sports Law & Legislation; Olympic Focus; Sports Tourism; The Past, Present and Future of the Asian Games.

Important Dates: Submission period for Abstracts begins on 20 March, 2010, and ends on 30 June, 2010

Contact Information:

Mailing Address: 1268 Guangzhou Dadao Zhong, Guangzhou, 510500, China

Official Website: http://www.agsc.gz2010.cn

The 16th Asian Games Science Congress Secretariat

Tel: +86 20 38025032 / 38025033

Fax: +86 20 38024567

E-mail: gztykyc@163.com

General Administration of Sport of China
Guangzhou Asian Games Organizing Committee (GAGOC)
China Sport Science Society
Guangzhou Sports University

2.

Be the First to Review the *Reviews*

Subscribe to *The New York Times Book Review* and receive it before Sunday.

For as low as $1.75 per week, subscribe to *The Book Review* and get a head start on everything new and noteworthy in the literary world.

The latest book reviews and *The New York Times* Best Sellers lists: Stay on top of titles and authors that are all the buzz

Children's Books: Find great reading for kids of all ages

Summer Reading: Spot the titles you'll enjoy at the beach, on the plane or on your day off

Holiday Books: Get in the spirit with an overview of the season's best titles

All this for as little as $1.75 per week.

To contact us by phone, please call our Service Center at 1-800-698-4637. Customer Care Agents are available 5 a.m.–12 p.m. from Monday to Friday or 5 a.m.–5 p.m. on Saturday and Sunday.

3.

Administrative Support Specialist Recruitments

Responsibilities: Working primarily with Excel worksheets performing data entry keying tasks that are associated with billing processes; Generating invoicing data and attachments; Sending out quote requests for out-sourced products; Verifying project quantities, pricing assistance to Sales; Generating monthly reports; Verifying selling prices and invoicing instructions; Assist Project Managers as needed; Other administrative duties as assigned.

Required Skills: 2–3 years experience clerical/administrative support, emphasis in billing/finance is preferred; Computer literacy including skill in Excel; Good organizational and communication skills required.

Company: RR Donnelley

Location: Hyde Park, MA

Status: Full Time Employee

Job Category: Administrative/Clerical

4.

Found

At about 8 a.m. on April 6, 2010, a staff of our airport found a purse at the security check. More specifically, it is a black purse made of ox leather, whose brand is

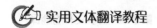

LV. Inside the purse, there is an air ticket of Flight EU2218 from Shenzhen to Chengdu, a credit card, an ID card and some Hong Kong dollars. We hope to find out the owner, so if you are the very one we are looking for, please call us at 0755-23235666 or come to the consultation service at our airport directly.

Shenzhen International Airport

二、将下列启事译成英文。

1.

征稿征订启事

  自本刊创办以来，深受广大作者厚爱，我们表示衷心的感谢。为了方便及时和您联系，请在投稿的同时，详细注明联系地址、邮箱及联系电话。

  由于我们的人力及电邮容量有限，请尽量采用打印邮寄方式投稿，避免未及时打开电邮而影响您的稿件录用。切勿反复邮寄同一篇文章，否则会给我们的工作带来诸多不便。请您自留底稿，本编辑部概不退稿。

  欢迎您订阅2012年《安徽体育科技》，全年6期，每期10元，年订价60元，公开发行，国内统一刊号CN34-1153/N，国际刊号ISSN1008-7761。

  本刊地址：合肥市包河区人民大街1号，安徽体育运动职业技术学院《安徽体育科技》编辑部，邮编：230051，联系电话：0551-3686559。

《安徽体育科技》编辑部

2.

校医招聘启事

  苏州工业园区仁爱学校是一所主要面向智障儿童、青少年的特殊教育学校。因学校发展需要，面向社会招聘校医1名。

  一、报名时间：2012年5月15日—6月15日

  二、岗位要求：

  1. 遵纪守法，工作认真，身心健康，服务态度好，关爱特殊儿童，具有良好的职业道德；

  2. 医学及相关专业，中专以上学历；优秀者可适当放宽条件，有校医工作经历者优先录用。

  三、应聘方法：

  有意者请将个人简历、各项证明材料复印件（含学历证书、职称证书、资格证书等）以及近期二寸照片1张寄至学校或直接到学校面谈。

  四、联系方式：

  1. 地址：苏州工业园区扬东路211号 邮编：215021

  2. 电话：0512-86660212 联系人：顾老师

3. 学校邮箱：sipras@163.com
4. 学校网站：www.sipras.net

3.
寻人启事

李×，男孩，11 岁，中等个子，短黑头发，小圆脸，眼睛不大，戴眼镜。身穿白色 T 恤，蓝色牛仔裤，脚穿黑色运动鞋。李× 于 1 月 8 日在前门大街走失。请见到孩子者与李先生联系，定重谢。电话：010-65885962。

李先生
2012 年 1 月 10 日

第十一章 公示语的翻译

公示语是一种常见的应用文体，涉及社会生活的方方面面。公示语种类繁多，但都具有简洁、准确、目的性强的特点，所以，公示语翻译也应当表达简练、信息明确、合乎规范。鉴于公示语翻译主要是以汉译英为主，因此，本章主要讨论公示语的汉译英问题。

第一节 公示语的定义和类型

一、公示语的定义与应用范围

公示语是指张贴于公众场合，旨在引起人们注意以达到某种交际目的的特殊文体。与公示语意义相近的语汇包括"标志语""标示语""标识语""标语"等。标志语与标志相结合，广泛应用于交通运输、旅游等公共领域；标示语在IT行业已经被广泛接纳，几乎成为这个行业的语言分支；标识语属于市场营销、广告促销中的推广语，经常和企业标识一起使用；标语则是人们比较熟悉的公益性、政治性、宣传性的文字语言。

公示语与标志语、标示语、标识语及标语有某些共同的使用特点，但公示语的应用更为广泛，在日常生活中随处可见，诸如：公共设施方面如地铁、机场、加油站、公交站、高速公路等；旅游景点如公园、博物馆、名胜、古迹等。公示语还应用在服务机构，如商店、超市、银行、餐厅、电影院、剧院、网吧等；科教机构的中小学、高校、研究所等；卫生设施的医院、急救中心等；治安监督的紧急警务、消费者投诉等。

二、公示语的语言功能和文本类型

文本类型与文本的语言功能密切相关，文本的语言功能决定文本的类型所属，因此，公示语的语言功能也决定了公示语的文本类型。公示语作为一种以社会公众为直接交际对象的文本形式，满足的是社会、行为和心理需求，其语言功能在实际应用中有以下几种具体表现，并且通过不同的语言形式体现出来：

（一）信息指示性公示语

信息指示性公示语主要是为公众提供指示性信息，用于指明道路、方向、处所、内容等，常见于街道、车站、机场、医院、学校、电影院、旅游景点等公众场所，主要表现形式为指示语。例如：

Underground/Subway	地铁
LANE FIRE	消防车道
Smoking Seat	吸烟席
General Hospital	综合医院
Baggage Depository	存包处
International Departure	国际出发
Forest-friendly building timbers	环保木材

（二）说明提示性公众语

说明提示性公示语意在对公众的行为加以指导和规范，告知公众采取何种行动，主要表现形式为各种提示语。例如：

Press for Assistance	需要帮助，请按钮
Sensor Tap	伸手出水
Reserved	预留席位
Handle with Care	小心轻放
Please Pay Here	请在此交款
Please Wear Life Vest	请您穿好救生衣
Recycled	回收利用

（三）要求限制性公示语

要求限制性公示语通过向公众发布信息或提出要求，以提醒公众按照文本意图采取相应的行动，主要表现形式是各种告示语。例如：

Admission by Ticket	凭票入场
Women and Children First	妇女儿童优先
Keep Clear	保持通畅
Keep Your Space	保持车距
Keep Clear of the Edges	勿靠两侧（电动扶梯）

（四）禁止强制性公示语

禁止强制性公示语主要是对相关公众的行为加以约束和限制，或"禁止"公众某种行动，语气比较强硬，毫无商量的余地，常用于道路交通和其他涉及安全的公共场所，主要表现形式为警示语。例如：

Ladies Only	男士止步
No Spitting	严禁随地吐痰
No U Turn	严禁调头
No Photography	禁止拍照
NO TRUCKS	卡车禁止通行
Police Line Do Not Pass	警戒线勿超越

（五）劝导推荐性公示语

劝导推荐性公示语主要是为公众提供服务和消费信息，使公众加深对商业经营机构的理解和好感，使他们按照文本意图行动，从而促进商业经营场所的销售，主要以各种广告形式出现在街道、商店、超市、酒店等场所。例如：

Duty Free	免税店
Cosmetics and Perfume	化妆品和香水
Frozen Food	速冻食品
Daily Special	今日特价
Daily Service	当日可取

（六）召唤宣传性公示语

召唤宣传性公示语主要用于营造声势、渲染气氛，号召公众采取相应行动以服务社会，主要表现形式为各种标语口号。例如：

One World, One Dream	同一个世界，同一个梦想
Better City, Better Life	城市，让生活更美好
Donate Blood to Save Lives	一滴血，一片心，一份爱
East or west, Guilin landscape is best!	桂林山水甲天下
Working together, we can make a world of difference.	共同努力，世界更精彩

第二节
公示语的语言特点

从语言学的角度来看，公示语是话语交际的一种特殊形式，旨在表达对公众的某个要求或引起公众的某种注意。话语交际既是一个信息交流的过程，也是一种社会交往活动。公示语的话语交际过程是指说话人（发布公示语的人或机构）根据社会规范和情景语境，用相应的言语或非言语的表达方式，向听话人传达话语信息，实现交际目的。作为一种具有指示、提示、限制、禁止、劝导和号召宣传等呼唤功能的特殊文体，公示语通常为寥寥几字，或简明易解的图示，或文字与图示兼用，短小精悍，一目了然。

一、语言表达简洁、精确

（一）名词或名词短语的使用

表示指示、说明、服务性质的公示语多用名词以及结构简单、组合多变的名词短语，能够直接、准确地传达特定信息。例如：

Cashier	收银处
Taxi Stand	出租车招手停靠站
Specialists	专家门诊
Leisure Center	休闲中心
Information	咨询服务

（二）动词、动名词及动词词组的使用

表示要求、限制性、禁止性的公示语多用动词或动词词组及动名词，将公众的注意力集中在公示语文本所要求采取的行动上。例如：

Slow	减速行驶
Keep Walkway Clear	旅客通道　请勿滞留
Queue up	请自觉排队
No Littering	请不要乱扔杂物
No Parking	禁止停车
Hold the Hand Rail	紧握扶手

（三）常用词汇的使用

考虑到公众和旅游者的认知与文化水平，公示语的表达以自然直接为准则，强调信息服务效果。公示语的词汇选择注重公众化，大量使用常用词汇，避免使用生僻词语、古语、俚语及术语等。例如：

Lost & Found	失物招领
GE Food	转基因食品
Warning: Anti climb paint	注意：（栅栏）涂有防攀油漆
Display Only	此商品仅供展示
Automatic Door	全自动门
Arriving passengers, please get off at the front door.	到站的旅客请在前门下车

（四）虚词及非核心词汇的省略

英语公示语词汇简洁，措辞精确，在不影响公示语准确体现特定的功能、意义的情况下，可以仅使用实词、关键词、核心词汇，省略冠词、代词、助动词等。例如：

Passengers Only	送客止步
Mind the Gap	小心脚下间隙
Out of Service	暂停使用
Please Stand on the Right	请右侧站立（自动扶梯）
No Hunting	景区内禁止狩猎
Water Polluted	水已污染

（五）缩略语的应用

公众和旅游者最常接触和使用的公共设施和服务的公示语，会较多使用缩略语，令人一目了然。例如：

P	停车场
I	旅游咨询
B & B	旅馆服务
YHA	青年旅馆
ATM	自动取款机
EXP	失效

（六）规范性和标准性语汇

由于公示语在公众生活中具有重要意义，若存在任何歧义和滥用，都会导致不良后果。与日常生活相关的英语公示语都是约定俗成的规范和标准表达的语汇。例如：

No Graffiti	禁止乱涂乱画
Ophthalmology Hospital	眼科医院
Yellow Pages	电话号码簿
DANGER HIGH VOLTAGE	高压危险
TAXI RANK PLEASE QUEUE THIS SIDE	出租汽车站 请在此排队等候

二、英、美公示语表达不同

少数英语公示语在英、美国家具有明显的本土意义，此类词汇的使用因而具有鲜明的地域局限。例如：

	英	美
垃圾箱	Litter	Trash
电梯	Lift	Elevator
药房	Chemist's Shop	Pharmacy
管理学院	Faculty of Management	School of Management
邮资已付	Post-Free	Postpaid

三、句式上高频度使用祈使句

公示语处于特定环境，针对的目标公众十分明确，所以公示语避免了程式化的客套，大量使用祈使句。例如：

Let Birds Be Your Friends	让我们做鸟类的朋友
Leave Your Bags in the Locker	进入超市请先存包
Come in and Win	进门赢大奖
Please do not take away	请勿带走
Please Take Your Belongings When Leaving	离开时请您带上您的包

四、时态上仅限于使用现在时

公示语提供给所处特定区域范围的公众，对现实行为加以指示、提示、限制、强制、推荐及宣传，因此，公示语的时态仅限于现在时。例如：

Life jackets to be worn	必须穿救生衣
Fasten Your Seat Belt	系好安全带
No Pets Allowed	禁止携带宠物
We are open	营业中
Recycle your rubbish, it's a resource	废物利用　能源再生

五、书写上作多种处理

公示语词汇书写有特殊要求，以突出重要、关键的信息，服务于特定的功能。

（一）首字母大写

通常，公示语每个词开头的第一个字母要大写，或句首字母大写。例如：

Staff Only	闲人免进
Alcohol Free Zone	禁酒区
Complain Box	意见箱
Do not speak to the driver	请勿与司机攀谈
Please conserve natural resources	请保护自然资源
Turn off the light before you leave	人走灯灭

（二）个别单词大写

某个单词大写，包括警示性、指示性、宣传性信息。例如：

NO food	严禁携带食物
Please Wait HERE	请在此等候

（三）所有字母大写

表示指示性、警告性及提示性的英语公示语则会以所有字母皆大写的形式，使特定公示语更加正式、严肃、重要，从而起到指示、提示、限制或警示的作用。例如：

CAUTION DO NOT CLIMB	小心！禁止攀爬
PRESS SWITCH TO OPEN	按键开启
BAGGAGE CLAIM	行李提取区
USE SIDE WALK	使用边道
CAUTION HOT	小心高温
NO SOMKING EXCEPT IN DESIGNATED AREAS	非指定地点严禁吸烟

（四）大小写结合

部分公示语也会采取大小写结合的方式，关键词、核心词大写有助于突出信息重点和要点，更容易引起公众对信息主体的关注与兴趣。例如：

NO RESTROOMS (Restrooms are located in the parking lot area)	无洗手间（洗手间位于停车场）
RED ROUTE No stopping at any time	红线区内 严禁停车

（五）全部小写

指示性及指令性信息公示语大多为宣传、呼唤性信息，一般全部小写，富有亲和力也便于识别。例如：

line forms here	请在这里排队
seat by number	对号入座
to avoid congestion please do not stand near the stairs	楼梯附近 请勿停留 以防堵塞

（六）标点符号省略

以上诸多实例反映出公示语的另一书写特点，即结尾一般不用标点符号，这丝毫不会影响公示语的意义完整，也会让公众感觉轻松、自然。例如：

Please mind your step	请小心台阶
Please use in an emergency	请在紧急情况下使用
Sorry We Don't Have Restrooms	抱歉 此处没有卫生间
Sorry We cannot accept personal checks	谢绝个人支票

第三节
公示语翻译中存在的问题

公示语是在公共场所书写或设置的各种警语和标牌，应用广泛，在对外宣传中发挥着不容忽视的作用。随着全球经济一体化进程的不断推进，国际交流日益频繁，国内很多城

第十一章 公示语的翻译

市尤其是大城市都需要良好的国际化语言环境，特别是北京、上海等大城市的公示语都在逐步双语化。这样做不仅能为来中国进行文化交流、经贸洽谈或观光旅游的外籍朋友提供信息，也能显示中国对外开放的诚意和力度。但是，令人遗憾的是，公示语的汉英翻译中出现的错乱现象，不仅没有给外国友人们带来方便，反而增加了很多不必要的麻烦，有的甚至成为国际笑话，已经严重影响到了信息的传递和交流。本节拟就当前公示语翻译中存在的诸多问题进行归类分析和探讨。

一、语言方面

（一）拼写错误，书写不规范

公示语中英语单词拼写错误比比皆是，主要表现为字母漏写或直接用汉语拼音代替。例如，某火车站的双语标识牌"饮水处 Drinking Wate"（如下图）：

显然，正确的拼写应该为 Drinking Water。这类错误是由于译者或制作人员的大意，不仔细校对所导致。

还有某些火车站和汽车站的双语标识牌直接使用汉语拼音。例如，"请勿随地吐痰"，就用 QINGWUSUIDITUTAN 标识。看到这种双语标识牌，让人哭笑不得。既然用双语，就是为了让外国人看懂；如果全用拼音，还不如不用。

（二）词汇使用不当

公示语用词不当，表达方式不准确，会导致所要传达的信息不能取得预期效果。某些词语有固定说法，不能按字面硬译，如"干手机"是一种专门设备，有专门用词，不可拆开进行翻译，不能译成 Dry Hand Machine，而应该译为 Hand Dryer。

还有一些英语公示语的词义搭配令人产生误解。例如，"残疾人专用电梯"被译为 Disabled Lift，字面意义好像是电梯出了问题。可以直接英译为 Wheelchair Accessible，表示无障碍设施。

（三）语法错误

公示语汉英翻译中的语法错误通常表现为单复数错误、词性错误、时态错误及句法搭配错误等。例如，某地铁上的标语"请勿靠车门"的译文为 DO NOT LEAN ON DOOR，就有明显的英语语法错误：动词 lean 在此语境下其后不可接介词 on，而名词 door 作为可数名词单数不能单独使用。建议改为 DO NOT LEAN AGAINST THE DOOR。

（四）语用失误

英语文体有正式与非正式之分，英语词汇中也存在大量同义词，在不同的场合应区分对待。如果视为等效而混用，则会令人啼笑皆非。如"小心"译为 Look out，译文过于口语化，应改为 Caution/Warning/Danger。但是，这三个英语词汇虽然属于同义词，也不一定适用于同一场合。一般情况下，如在施工地有人高空作业，需要提示他人"注意安全"，可以用 Caution；一些人喜欢在自然水域游泳，但并非所有的水域都是安全的，所以"注意安全"应选用 Warning；还有一些人喜欢冬季在冰面上滑冰，但是入冬和冬末的冰面都很薄，不适合滑冰，这时"注意安全"则要使用 Danger。

再如，有一公司名为"上海万象服饰公司"，该公司的英文名被翻译为 Shanghai Elephant Garment Co., Ltd。大象在中国人的眼里是忠诚、憨厚、可爱之物，而在西方人眼里是愚昧、凶猛、鲁莽之物，将之译成 elephant garment，谁会穿上"凶猛、愚昧"的衣服呢？虽然译文保持了源语中的信息，但是未能顾及文化差异，导致了意义上的误解，译语读者无法正确领会信息。其实只要译为 Shanghai Wanxiang Garment Co., Ltd 即可。

（五）同一标识译文不统一

同一标识语在不同场合下的译文尤其要注意前后的一致性，否则易使人产生误解。例如，广州中山大学就有两种译本 Sun Yat-set University 和 Zhongshan University；广州白云山上的"摩星岭"也有两个不同的版本 Starscraping Summit 和 Moxing Summit。显然，这种一名多译的现象违背了地名的唯一性原则，容易造成混乱。

二、中式英语翻译

中式翻译指的是那些望文生义、不符合英语表达习惯的翻译。由于不懂英语的相应说法，便按照汉语的字面意思逐字对应硬译，看似语言形式对等，却常常错误百出。如"售票厅"译成 Sell The Ticket Hall，字字照应，十分生硬，而且还有语法错误；正确的译法应为 Ticket Office/Lobby 或 Booking Hall。

又如，"遇到火灾，勿用电梯" 在有些场所被译为"When there is a fire, don't use the elevator!" 从表面上看，此译文似乎没有问题，但是仔细分析就可发现，该翻译明显受中文语序和表达习惯的影响，不仅繁琐，而且还让人有不安全感，好像火灾随时可能发生。正确的翻译应该是 Don't use the elevator in case of fire，使用 in case of 表示"一旦"或者"万一"出现该情形，如此就能采取迅速有效的行动。

由于不同民族、不同国家间的文化差异，英语和汉语的表达方式、语气及选词等方面都有所不同，如果字字对译而不考虑意义是否对等，就可能引起外国朋友的不满。例如，"非本园车辆禁止入内"的译文 Unauthorized Vehicles Are Prohibited in This Park 中的 Prohibited（或者译为 Forbidden），有强烈的命令口吻，比较粗暴，不礼貌。汉语倾向从反面说"禁止",但英语却会从正面说"允许"。该公示语比较得体的译文应该为 Authorized Vehicles Only。再如,旅游景区常出现的双语标识牌"游人止步"的英译中如果直接使用 STOP 过于直接,建议改译为 Please Stop,语气较委婉,语言简洁。

公示语翻译之所以出现上述错误,主要与以下因素有关:译者的专业素质不够高,没有经过公示语撰写或翻译的专项训练;在译写过程中容易受到母语的负迁移干扰,且缺乏对目的语文化背景的了解。另外,管理者和翻译者的态度和责任心欠佳也是公示语翻译频频出错的重要原因。

第四节 公示语的翻译原则及方法

公示语担负着服务大众的交际任务。公示语翻译带有明显的实用性特征,其服务对象是目的语使用者,因而译文的表达应符合目的语读者的语用习惯。我们不仅要从拼写、语言表达形式及意义上考虑,也要重视中英文化差异,遵循忠实原文、合乎规范等原则,运用合理有效的翻译方法,使公示语翻译真正实现对外宣传和交流的效果。

一、公示语的翻译原则

(一)语言简洁原则

公示语的语言总体特点是短小精悍、简洁明了。公示语汉英翻译的简洁原则是指译文精准,不含晦涩词语和复杂长句。公示语的社会功能主要是指示、提示、限制、强制等。特定的社会功能决定了公示语英译必须简洁。例如,"为了您的安全,请走人行横道,勿在站场前随意穿梭",原译为 For your safety, please walk on the sidewalk. Do not cross the bus line at will. 此译文过于复杂,无法在最短的时间内传递信息,英语倾向于简明,建议译成 Keep to the Sidewalk。

(二)语境本地化原则

英语和汉语一样,同样的意思可以有多种表达方式,不同表达方式的差别往往取决于具体的语境。所以,公示语的翻译一定要充分考虑不同文化之间的异同,考虑具体的场合与对象,考虑读者的阅读心理与情感。如,汉语"严禁吸烟"能为中国人普遍接受,但是若被直译为 Forbid Smoking 或 Smoking is Forbidden,在英语语境中是非常不文明的表达。所以,该公示语的汉英翻译要遵循外国人的思维习惯,译为 No Smoking。No 经常被用在中性语境中,语气较委婉,更容易为外国朋友所接受。

（三）约定俗成原则

翻译公示语时，译者要尽可能遵循或参照译入语在同样情形下的习惯说法。例如，某超市的"收银台"被译成 payment area，应为 cashier；某广场上的垃圾分类回收箱上的"不可回收"译成了 Unable Recovery，应该译为 Non-recyclable Only；某著名景点的双语标识语"小心碰头"竟然被译为了 Watch out, Knock head（小心，笨蛋），事实上这里可直接采用英语国家常用的说法 Mind your head 或者 Watch your head。

二、公示语的翻译方法

公示语翻译过程中普遍使用直译和意译这两种方法。例如，"中西餐厅"被译为 Chinese and Western Restaurant；"请靠右侧站立"可译为 Please Stand on the Right Side；"看管好您的个人财物"的译文为 Take care of your personal belongings，都是直译。不过，由于中西文化的差异，为了遵循外国读者的文化表达和思维习惯，增强译文的可读性，译者在很多情况下不做逐字逐句的翻译，而采取意译的翻译方法。比如，"全心全力全为您"的译文 For Your Every Heart Everything 令人费解，可译为 Your Needs, Our Priority；"足下留情，小草常青"直接简单地逐字译为 Your Careful Step Keeps Tiny Grass Invariably Green，汉语表达颇具人情味，但是这样的英译却显得繁琐，反而无法达到预期效果，还不如意译成 Keep off the Grass，表达更直接、效果更好。

公示语作为一种独特、常用的应用文体，结构比较特殊，表达形式多样，其功能性也较强。为了使其更好地服务于社会和公众，提升中国国际形象，在公示语汉英翻译过程中，译者可针对不同的场合语境，采取灵活多样的翻译方法。

（一）音译

饮食类公示语翻译多体现为菜单上的菜名翻译。众多菜名往往浓缩了中华优秀文化并表现出极浓的民族特色，为了保留这些词语的"原汁原味"，译者可以采用快捷又准确的"汉语拼音"拼写。例如：

Jiaozi	饺子
Tofu	豆腐
Er Guo Tou	二锅头

（二）音译与直译结合

汉语拼音音译词语在公示语英译中的使用范围很广。一些具有独特的文化、习俗、观念与人文特征的地名、路名或物名，通常较难翻译或者不可译，而且一旦直译或意译，则难以保存当地的人文、习俗和传说，此时译者可以采取音译与直译相结合的翻译方法。例如：

| *Bailu* Hotel | 白鹭迎宾馆 |
| *Cangshan* Mountain | 苍山 |

JINGLAN Highway	京兰路
Hu Silk	湖丝

（三）释义

有些带有中国特色的景点介绍或号召宣传性公示语的内容较丰富，但如若英文译文过于简单，对于不熟悉中国国情的外国人来说就无法理解这些公示语的真正含义。比如，"三个臭皮匠，抵个诸葛亮"这一俗语，英译文有三个版本：Three cobblers combine would equal Zhuge Liang. / The masses have great creative power. / Three cobblers with their wits combined would equal Zhuge Liang, the master mind. 第一种版本是纯粹的直译；第二个版本省略了源语中承载文化的形象比喻，缺少了中国文化的讲述和推介；而第三个版本既有中国文化的含义，又添加了简单释义，使翻译生动清晰，效果最佳。

为了让外国游客更好地了解中国不同地域的饮食文化，一些难处理的地方风味特色菜名，译者也可以采用"音译/直译+释义"的方法进行翻译。比如，"叫花鸡"被译为 beggar's chicken (toasted chicken wrapped in lotus leaf and earth mud)—A name after a legend telling a beggar smeared a chicken all over with clay, and threw it into a fire. After a long while, he removed it and cracked it open, founding it had been baked into a delicious dish.[1]

（四）借用

在公示语汉英翻译中，译者可在了解汉英使用差异的基础上套用现成的英语表达法，以避免生译乱译，或片面追求与原文字面上的对等而使译文生涩难懂，闹出笑话，甚至引起误解。比如把"休息室"错译为 Restroom。在美国英语中，restroom 指的是公共建筑物内的公共厕所或盥洗室。"休息室"在英语里有现成说法即 staff room 或 common room（尤指在大学里），在一般公共场所里则为 lounge 或 lobby，翻译时应借用。再如，许多购物场所推出的优惠活动，"八五折优惠"不可译为 85% discount，而应译为 15% off；公交车上的"老弱病残专座"，英语中可借鉴的现成表达有 Courtesy Seats；而"数量有限，售完为止"也可直接套用 Subject to availability。

（五）零翻译

对于某些完全针对本地、本国公民需求和行为特点而设置的公示语，又或者在英语国家根本无法找到或看到的公示语，译者可以考虑干脆不译。比如，类似"严禁赌博""收费厕所""禁止在公园内随地大小便""禁止乱刻乱画"等就没有必要英译；若译成英文，反而影响了中国的形象。

---

1 任静生. 2001. 也谈中菜与主食的英译问题. 中国翻译，（1）：56–57.

第五节
常用公示语规范翻译实例

在 2005 年 9 月北京第二外国语学院举办的"首届全国公示语翻译研讨会"上,学者们针对公示语的理论和实践这一课题展开了热烈的讨论,呼吁重视和完善城市公示语翻译,建议成立由专业人员组成专门机构负责监控公示语的翻译质量。制定参照标准是确保翻译质量的有效措施。《标志用公共信息图形符号》国家标准(GB/T10001)系列及专家、学者编写的相关专著、工具书是各行业的参照标准。公示语英文译写应该组织各行业专家及译员结合本地特色制定行业标准和译写规范,并对其不断修改和完善。

这里提供一些依据道路交通、旅游景区、文化及商业等细则为标准的常见的公共场所双语标识英文译写,供读者参考。

一、道路交通

(一)警告提示信息

爬坡车道	Steep Grade
长下坡慢行	Steep Slope—Slow Down
陡坡减速	Steep Incline—Slow Down
追尾危险	Don't Follow Too Closely
小心路滑	Slippery When Wet
保持车距	Maintain Safe Distance
事故多发点	Accident Area
多雾路段	Foggy Area
软基路段	Soft Roadbed
堤坝路	Embankment Road
道路封闭	Road Closed
车辆慢行	Slow Down
道路施工	Road Work Ahead
车辆绕行	Detour
前方弯道	Bend Ahead
双向交通	Two-Way Traffic
单行交通	One-Way Traffic
禁止超越线	No Passing
此路不通	Dead End
道路或车道变窄	Road / Lane Narrows

禁鸣喇叭	No Horn
停车领卡	Stop for Ticket
请勿疲劳驾驶	Don't drive when tired
请系好安全带	Buckle Up
雨雪天气请慢行	Drive slowly in rain or snow

（二）道路与车辆信息

道（大道）	Avenue (Ave)
干道	Main Rd
国道	National Rd
一般道路	Ordinary Rd
城市道路	Urban Rd
路	Road (Rd)
公路	Highway
高速公路	Expressway (Expwy)
街（大街）	Street (St)
小街（条、巷、夹道）	Alley
斜街	Byway
胡同	Hutong
桥	Bridge
环岛	Roundabout
小型车道	Car Lane
大型车道	Large Vehicle Lane
行车道	Through Lane
避车道	Lay-by / Passing Bay
应急车道	Emergency Vehicle Lane
大型车	Large Vehicle
小型车	Car
非机动车	Non-Motor Vehicle
机动车	Motor Vehicle
起点	Start
终点	End
隧道	Tunnel
应急停车带	Emergency Stop Area

（三）基础设施信息

长途汽车站	Inter-City Bus Station

经济技术开发区	Economic-Technological Development Area
火车站	Railway Station
收费站	Toll Gate
加油站	Gas Station
急救站	First Aid Station
汽修	Automobile Service
洗车	Car Wash
客轮码头	Ferry Terminal
轮渡	Ferry
休息处	Rest Area
服务区	Service Area
检票处	Ticket Check
物品寄存	Left Luggage / Luggage Deposit
残疾人牵引车（升降平台）	Wheelchair Lift
硬币兑换处	Coin Change
自动售票机	Automatic Ticket Machine / Ticket Vending Machine
补票处	Fare Adjustment
IC 卡查询机	IC Card Analyzer
终点站	Terminus
始发站	Departure Station
站台	Platform
换票处	Ticket-Changing
自动查询机	Inquiry Machine
自动充值机	Refilling Machine / Recharging Machine
非常紧急手柄	Emergency Door Handle
×××公交站	×× Bus Station/×× Bus Stop
停车场收费处	Parking Fee Booth
换乘大厅	Transfer Hall/Transit Hall
车库	Garage
第 × 通道	Passage ×
出租汽车上下/停靠站	Taxi
候车厅	Waiting Hall / Waiting Lounge
全日（昼夜）停车场	24-Hour Parking
地下停车场	Basement Parking
路侧停车	Roadside Parking
计时停车	Meter Parking
临时停车	Temporary Parking

二、旅游景点

（一）警告提示信息

严禁倚靠	Stand Clear / No Leaning
严禁攀折	No Picking
严禁滑冰	No Skating
严禁携带宠物	No Pets Allowed
严禁中途下车	No Drop Off Between Stops
禁止钓鱼	No Fishing
禁止燃放烟花爆竹	No Fireworks Allowed / Fireworks Prohibited
禁止由此滑行	No Skiing Here
雷雨天禁止拨打手机	Cellphones Prohibited during Thunderstorms
殿内请勿燃香	Don't Burn Incense in the Hall
防洪通道，请勿占用	Flood Control Channel. Keep Clear!
非游览区，请勿进入	No Admittance / No Visitors
1米以下儿童须家长陪同乘坐	Children under 1 meter must be accompanied by an adult.
请您不要坐在护栏上边	Don't Sit on Guardrail
请自觉维护场内卫生环境	Please Keep the Area Clean / Please Don't Litter
请遵守场内秩序	Please Keep Order
请在台阶下等候	Please Stand Clear of the Steps
请您穿好救生衣	Please Wear Life Vest
请勿投食	Don't Feed the Animals
请勿惊吓动物	Don't Frighten the Animals
请按顺序出入	Please Line Up
请爱护景区设施	Please Protect Facilities
请爱护文物 / 保护文物	Please Protect Cultural Relics
请尊重少数民族习俗	Please Respect Ethnic Customs
门票价格 / 票价	Ticket Price
危险路段	Dangerous Area
游客须知 / 游园须知	Notice to Visitors
景区简介	Introduction
单行线	One Way
敬告	Attention
当日使用，逾期作废	Use on Day of Issue Only
凭票入场	Ticket Holders Only
临时出口	Temporary Exit

火警出口	Fire Exit
允许拍照留念	Photos Allowed
票已售完	Sold Out
票已售出，概不退换	No Refund. No Exchange
游客投诉电话	Complaints Hotline
游客咨询电话	Inquiry Hotline
1.2 米以下儿童免票	Free for Children under 1.2 Meters
原路返回	Please Return by the Way You Came

（二）功能设施信息

售票处	Ticket Office / Tickets
游客中心	Tourist Center
客房部	Guest Room Department
游船码头	Cruise Terminal
办公区	Administrative Area
公园管理处	Park Administrative Office
广播室	Broadcasting Room
休息处	Lounge
导游处	Guide Service
表演区	Performance Area
特色餐饮	Food Specialties
遗址	Historic Site
滑雪场	Ski Field
滑雪道	Ski Slope
无障碍售票口	Wheelchair Accessible
休闲区	Leisure Area
贵宾厅	VIP Hall
贵宾通道	VIP Only
员工通道	Staff Only
货币兑换	Currency Exchange
行李手推车	Trolley
电动游览车	Sightseeing Trolley
自行车租赁处	Bicycle Rental
租船处	Boat Rental
旅游纪念品商店	Souvenir Shop
无烟景区	Smoke-Free Scenic Area
收费停车场	Pay Parking

茶室	Tea House
残疾人客房	Accessible Guestroom
非吸烟区	Non-Smoking Area
浅水区	Shallow Water
深水区	Deep Water
游览观光车	Sightseeing Trolley / Sightseeing Bus
世界文化遗产	World Cultural Heritage

（三）服务类信息

导游服务 / 讲解服务	Tour Guide Service
照相服务	Photo Service
邮政服务	Postal Service
声讯服务	Audio Guide
票务服务	Ticket Service/Tickets
残疾人服务	Service for Disabled
免费	Free Admission
赠票	Complimentary Ticket
宣传资料	Tourist Brochure / Travel Brochure
半价	50% Off/Half Price / 50% Discount
谢谢合作	Thanks for Your Cooperation
信用卡支付	Credit Cards Accepted
提供拐杖 / 轮椅	Crutches / Wheelchairs Available
游程信息	Itinerary Information / Travel Info

（四）其他信息

碑记	Tablet Inscription
雕塑作品	Sculpture
石刻	Stone Carving
草原	Grassland
温室采摘	Greenhouse Fruit Picking
数字特技	Digital Stunt
野营露营	Camping
消闲散步	Strolling
郊游野游	Outing
垂钓	Fishing
登山攀岩	Mountaineering / Rock-Climbing
揽胜探险	Expedition

科普教育	Popular Science Education
游戏娱乐	Entertainment
水上运动	Aquatic Sports
滑水	Surfing
潜水	Scuba Diving
冰雪活动	Ice Skating & Skiing
滑草活动	Grass Skiing
滑沙	Sand Skiing
水上漂流	Rafting

三、服务业

（一）警示提示信息

暂停服务	Temporarily out of Service
顾客止步	Staff Only
禁止通过	No Admittance
营业时间	Open Hours/Business Hours
进入超市请先存包	Please Deposit Your Bags
请勿将饮料带入场内	No Drinks from Outside
禁止未成年人进入	Adults Only
请关闭通讯设备	Please Turn Off Cellphones
找零请当面点清	Please check your change before leaving
不外售	Not for Sale
请在此处开票	Get Your Invoice Here
先试后买	Try Before You Buy

（二）企业名称及业态类信息

××大厦	×× Tower / Plaza / Mansion / Building
贸易中心	Trade Center
百货商场	Department Store
购物中心	Shopping Center
大型购物中心	Shopping Mall
食品店	Food Store
电器城	Home Appliances Store / Home Appliances Center
音像制品店	Audio-Video Shop
眼镜店	Optical Shop
药店	Pharmacy
形象设计中心	Image Design Center

发型工作室	Hair Studio
餐馆	Restaurant
美食城	Food Palace
美食广场	Food Plaza
中式快餐	Chinese Fast Food

(三)经营类信息

产地	Place of Production / Place of Origin
品名	Product Name
单价	Unit Price
等级	Class / Grade
规格	Specifications
服务项目	Service Items
价目表	Price List
服务指南	Service Directory
特卖场	Special Sales
手语服务	Sign Language Service
义务导购服务	Shopping Guide
餐饮服务	Food & Beverages
退换商品	Returns
售后服务热线	After-Sale Service Hotline
信息查询	Information Services
礼品包装	Gift Wrapping / Gift Packing
首饰加工	Jewelry Processing
钟表维修	Watch and Clock Repair
皮鞋修鞋、皮鞋美容	Shoe Repair & Polish
改衣部	Clothing Alterations Service
旅游纪念品	Souvenirs
打折 / 优惠	Discount
特价	Sale / On Sale
促销	Promotion
代售电话卡、地图	Phone Cards & Maps
代售火车票	Train Tickets
代售民航机票	Airline Tickets
代售演出文体票	Tickets for Shows & Sporting Events

（四）商品名称类信息

服装饰品	Fashion and Accessories
女士服装	Women's Wear
男士服装	Men's Wear
儿童服装	Children's Wear
休闲服装	Casual Wear
运动服装	Sportswear
羊绒羊毛	Cashmere and Woolens
皮革皮草	Leatherwear and Furs
针棉内衣	Knitted and Cotton Underwear
鞋帽	Shoes and Hats
男鞋	Men's Shoes
女鞋	Women's Shoes
儿童鞋	Children's Shoes
旅游运动鞋	Sports Shoes
进口高档化妆品	Imported Cosmetics
精品腕表	Luxury Watches
钟表	Clocks and Watches
化妆品	Cosmetics
运动器械	Sports Equipment
休闲包	Casual Bags
旅行箱包	Luggage and Suitcases
时尚内衣	Lingerie
珠宝眼镜	Jewelry and Glasses
精品皮具	Luxury Leatherware

（五）服务人员名称类信息

营业员	Sales Clerk / Sales Assistant
收银员	Cashier
信息员	Messenger
导购员	Shopping Guide
理发师	Hairdresser
美容师	Beautician
美发师	Hair Stylist
验光师	Optometrist
摄影师	Photographer
保洁员	Cleaner

四、场馆

（一）警示提示类

小心轻放	Handle with Care
禁坐栏杆	Don't Sit on the Handrail / No Sitting on the Handrail
请勿外带食品	No Food from Outside
易碎	Fragile
报警指示牌	Police Alarm
消防指示牌	Fire Alarm
单号入口	Odd Numbers Entrance
双号入口	Even Numbers Entrance
场馆示意图	Map / Sketch Map

（二）功能设施类

桑拿浴房	Sauna
更衣室	Locker Room
女淋浴室	Women's Shower Room
男淋浴室	Men's Shower Room
按摩室	Massage Room
医务室	Clinic
贵宾休息室 / 贵宾厅	VIP Lounge
力量训练房	Strength Training Gymnasium
运动员休息室	Athletes' Lounge
运动员席	Athletes' Seats/Box
新闻发布厅	Press Conference Hall / Media Conference Hall
文字记者席	Press Seats / Press Box
电视评论席	TV Commentators
播音室	Broadcasting Room
广播席	Radio Commentators
摄影记者区	Photo Zone / Pool Positions (Pool Positions 仅用于奥运场馆内)
兴奋剂检查室	Doping Control Room
场地器材室	Venue Equipment Room
技术代表室	Technical Delegates' Office
裁判员室	Referees' Office
仲裁办公室	Jury's Office
运动员专用通道	Athletes Only

散场通道	EXIT / Exit
观众通道	For Spectators
检录处	Call Room / Call Area
观众席	Spectator Seats
贵宾席	VIP Box
主席台	Rostrum
等候区	Waiting Area
警卫室	Guard Room

五、医疗卫生

（一）警示提示信息

门诊区	Outpatient Area
住院区	Inpatient Area
实验区	Experimental Area
宿舍区	Staff Dormitories
清洁区	Clean Zone
半污染区	Semi-Contaminated Zone
候诊区	Waiting Area
男士止步	Female Only
患者止步	Staff Only
放射物品	Radioactive Materials
当心射线	Caution! Radiation
易燃物品	Inflammable Materials
血液告急	Blood Donors Needed
有害气体！注意安全	Caution! Noxious Gas
生物危险，请勿入内	Biohazard! No Admittance
闭路电视监视区域	Closed Circuit TV in Operation
请保持安静 / 禁止喧哗	Quiet Please
严禁明火	No Open Flame
亲友等候区	Visitor Waiting Area
危险物品	Hazardous Materials
剧毒物品	Poisonous Materials
禁止吸烟、饮食、逗留	No Smoking, Eating, Drinking or Loitering
进入实验区，请穿好工作服	Experiment Area! Wear Work Clothes
请在诊室外候诊	Please Wait Outside the Consulting Room

（二）功能设施信息

门诊楼	Outpatient Building
病房楼	Inpatient Building
收费处	Cashier
挂号处	Registration
（急诊）分诊台	Triage
（普通）分诊台 / 门诊接待室	Reception
登记处	Registration
划价处	Prescription Pricing
取药处 / 药房	Pharmacy / Dispensary
探视入口	Visitor Entrance
消防应急面罩	Emergency Fire Masks
放标本处	Specimen
取检查 / 检验结果处	Test Reports
医疗急救电话 120	First Aid Call 120
医疗急救通道	Emergency Access
门诊化验室	Laboratory / Lab
门诊手术室	Outpatient Operating Room
门诊注射输液室	Injection & Transfusion Room
门诊治疗室	Outpatient Treatment Room
取血室	Blood Drawing Room
隔离门诊	Isolation Clinic
特需门诊	VIP Clinic
内科	Internal Medicine Dept. / Internal Medicine
外科	Surgery Dept. / Surgery
外科抢救室 / 外科急诊室	Emergency Surgery Room
妇科	Gynecology Dept. / Gynecology
儿科	Pediatrics Dept. / Pediatrics
产科	Obstetrics Dept. / Obstetrics
老年病科	Geriatrics Dept. / Geriatrics
急诊科	Emergency Dept. / Emergency
中医科	Traditional Chinese Medicine (TCM) Dept. / TCM
中西医结合科	Integrated TCM & Western Medicine Dept.
心理科	Psychology Dept. / Psychology
放射科	Radiology Dept. / Radiology
药物咨询	Medication Enquiry

男诊室	Male Consulting Room
女诊室	Female Consulting Room
疫苗室	Vaccination Room
换药室	Dressing Room
候诊观察室	Waiting & Observation Room
常规化验室	Routine Test Lab
量血压处	Blood Pressure Measurement
B 超室	β-Ultrasound Room
心电图室	ECG Room
脑电图室	EEG Room

在中国，公示语的应用关系到汉语的地位、国际通用语的标准、国家语言政策、城市开放程度以及城市国际化的进程与市容管理等，公示语的译文直接影响到一个城市甚至国家的形象。因此，公示语翻译应引起社会相关人士及部门的高度重视。在翻译过程中，必须遵循一定的翻译原则和方法，并且做到翻译方法和译名使用的规范统一，以更好地发挥公示语传达信息、满足公众需求的功能。此外，相关单位和机构应及时发现公共场所英文标识存在的问题，解决问题并确定参照性文本，改善各地公共场所英文标识使用不规范的状况，最大程度地改善和净化城市语言环境，提高我国对外传播和交流的水平。

练习十一

一、将下列公示语译成英文。

1. 肉类
2. （机场的）扶梯
3. 持证停车
4. 宠物禁止入内
5. 欢迎购买异地各站车票
6. 仅限船员，闲人免进
7. 携带好容易滑落的物品
8. 提高生活质量，迈向美好未来
9. 为了您的安全，请勿在此坐靠，谢谢合作
10. 高高兴兴上班去，平平安安回家来

二、将下列公示语译成中文。

1. Plastics
2. Diet Pepsi
3. Reserved Parking
4. Food & Beverages Not Allowed
5. Casual Sportswear
6. Sale of the year
7. Save Everyday
8. Group Services
9. More or Less This Year (e.g. in the supermarket)
10. Build a modernized garden city of ecotype

专有名词的翻译

一、专有名词的概念

"专有名词,指人名、地名、机构团体名和其他具有特殊含义的名词或名词词组。"专名用来区分一个人或物与其他人或物,体现了描述性、指示性和随意性等特征。专名是特指,普通名词是泛指。专名的所指总是明显的,而普通名词或隐喻的所指则需要根据上下文才能确定。一般情况下,专名有意义,但没有隐含意义。它没有指示性限定词,没有限制性形容词。不过,专名和普通名词的界限不是固定不变的,专名可以当普通名词来用,如"鲁迅是中国的高尔基",这里的"高尔基"就是作为普通名词使用的。

专名通常都是简单、具体的小词,往往被认为是语言之外的东西,与使用这种语言的人的生活经验有天生的直接的联系,有些不收录在字典中,而是放在百科全书中。专名包罗万象,如人名、地名、国名、组织名、机构名、会议名、报刊名、作品名、商标品牌名、公司名、官职名等。专名是一个国家社会、文化、宗教生活的组成部分,与法律、商业、文学、历史、地理、风俗民情、自然科学等密切相关,"其语源广、典故多、文化负载重、词义容量大。"如果没有经过专门训练或受训不严格,往往可能翻译时犯了错误还不自知。无论是在研究生入学考试还是在英语四级、六级、八级考试中,专有名词翻译出错的情况都屡见不鲜。

二、专有名词的分类

专名的分类各种各样,本书把专有名词分为如下五种:(1)人名;(2)地名;(3)机构组织名;(4)书名及报纸杂志名;(5)其他专名如官职头衔、商标名、节日名等。

三、专有名词的翻译方法

2005年,国家质量监督检验检疫总局和中国国家标准化管理委员会联合发布"翻译服务译文质量要求"国家标准(GB/T 19682–2005),其中针对专用名词翻译制订的规范如下:

5.2 专用名词
5.2.1 人名、地名、团体名、机构名、商标名使用惯用译名（有特殊要求的按双方约定）。无惯用译名的，可自行翻译，必要时附注原文。

中国人名、地名、团体、机构名译为拼音语言的，按汉语拼音法或采用历史沿袭译法译出。译为非拼音语言的，按目标语言既定译法和惯用译法译出，译出后可附注汉语拼音名称。

商标名应优先采用目标语言地区的注册名称。

5.2.2 职务、头衔、尊称

按惯用译法译出。

5.2.3 法规、文件、著作、文献名称

国家、政府和国际组织重要的法律、法令、文件等名称应采用官方或既定译法，无既定译法的译出后应附注原文（原文为中文的，附注汉语拼音名称）。

其他法规、文件、著作、文献名称采用既定译法，无既定译法的译出后应附注原文（原文为中文的，附注汉语拼音名称）。

原文中的参考文献名称可不译出（特殊约定除外），引述出处等具有检索意义的文字可以译出，并应附注原文。

5.2.4 通信地址

通信地址可直接引用原文，必须译出时应附注原文。

中国通信地址附注原文时一般按汉语拼音法译出。

5.2.5 专有名词原文附注方法

译文中专有名词原文的附注可采取两种方法：

——在第一次译出处，附注原文；

——在译文的适当地方统一附注。

翻译界普遍认可的专名翻译原则有如下几个：（1）约定俗成原则：这一原则要求，如果某个专有名词已经有了约定俗成的译法，则采用该译法，无须另起炉灶重新翻译；（2）名从主人原则：即译音要尽量接近原文发音；（3）专名专译原则，即同名同译；（4）音译为主原则，音译也有一定的规矩可循，英译汉有各种译名手册和译音表，汉译英过去以威妥玛式拼法为准，现在以国家规定的汉语拼音为准。

专名翻译的方法主要有以下五点：（1）音译：突出主要音节以求简练，避免不必要的意义联想和褒贬意味（文学作品中追求特殊艺术效果者除外），以求准确，多用一定数目的常用字音以求规范易记；（2）意译：按外文名称的含义用汉语译出。报刊、部分科学术语和地名国名多用意译。意译的优点是"名副其实"，易懂易记；（3）音意译：部分音译部分意译，特点是译法简练，并有一定意味；（4）形象译：有些外文字母表示的事物并不指形象，而是有其内在含义，则必须保留原文的说法；（5）指类译：有些名称不便音译，意译又不清楚，可在音译或意译后加上类别词使之简单明了。

以下具体介绍各类专名的译法。

（一）人名的翻译

1. 英译中

多年前我国的人名翻译非常混乱。后来为了统一和规范，新华社和商务印书馆出版了许多工具书，如"英汉译音表""法汉译音表""德汉译音表"《英语姓名译名手册》《德语姓名译名手册》《世界人名翻译大辞典》等。翻译者只要一册在手，看一个外文名字，像字典般去翻阅，就可以找到中译名了，省力省事。

英汉人名翻译多数采用音译，一般遵循几个原则：（1）用字统一原则：除了约定俗成的人名外，必须用字统一，参考标准就是前述的译音表；（2）约定俗成原则；（3）名从主人原则。应该注意性别差异、辈分差异、文学作品中使用归化法或音意兼重译法等特殊情况。

具体翻译做法就是：（1）先名后姓，名与中间名和姓之间用间隔号"·"隔开；（2）注意选字，避免"汉化"，采用译音表所规定的汉字，不要用那些容易引起联想的字；（3）选用约定俗成的标准译名。

1）英语国家人名

在翻译英语国家人名时，首先要查清该人名有无约定俗成的标准译法。有些外国人，本身就取有中文名字，比如一些国外的汉学家，他们往往取优美、典雅的中文名，兼顾名称的"音"与"意"，显示他们对中国传统文化的深刻理解。如 Stephen Owen 的中文名宇文所安，据说"宇文"是胡人姓，而"所安"出自《论语》的"观其所由，察其所安"。请看下面例子：

Chris Patten 彭定康（香港总督）
John Chamberlain 约翰·张伯伦（英国前首相）
Ezra Vogel 傅高义（汉学家）
Jay Taylor 陶涵（汉学家）
Bryan Van Norden 万白安（汉学家）
William Theodore de Bary 狄百瑞（汉学家）
Irene Bloom 卜爱莲（汉学家）
Philip J. Ivanhoe 艾文贺（汉学家）
David L. Hall 郝大维（汉学家）
Henry Jr. Rosemont 罗思文（汉学家）
Thomas A. Metzger 墨子刻（汉学家）

2）非英语国家人名

有些非英语国家的人名，本身就是从其他语言翻译成英文的，所以英译汉等于是再次翻译。若是中国人或日本、韩国、越南、新加坡等亚洲国家人士使用的拼音译名，这种重复翻译往往就是回译。不过，由于语音体系的差异，加上汉语中同音字很多，以及历史原因形成的威妥玛式拼音和现代汉语拼音的混合使用，这类人名的翻译往往成为译者的陷阱，稍不注意就会出错。

（1）亚洲国家人名

亚洲国家人名的英译汉通常比较麻烦，一般都不能简单地译音，而需要查找相关的工具书，找到约定俗成的译法。比如：

Fung Yu-lan 冯友兰（著名哲学家的英文名）
Gao Panlong 高攀龙（明代文学家、东林党领袖之一）
Luo, Qinshun 罗钦顺（明朝理学家、教育家）
Zhang, Junmai / Chang, Carsun 张君劢（民国时期著名人物）
Chang Ping-lin 章炳麟
Chu His 朱熹（宋朝大理学家）
Kublai Khan 忽必烈汗
Tu Weiming 杜维明（曾是哈佛燕京学社社长，现任北大高等人文研究院院长）
Lee Hsien Loong 李显龙

把日本人名翻译成汉语，同样需要找到其对应的汉字而不能译音，如 Hidetoshi Nakata 应该被翻译成"中田英寿"，其中 Hidetoshi（ひでとし）是名，Nakata（なかた）是姓。除了查阅日语工具书外，还可以参考陆谷孙主编的《英汉大辞典》附录八"常见日本人姓名拉丁字母拼写法"。请看下面的例子：

Watanabe Soichi 渡边聪一
Shintaro Ishihara 石原慎太郎
Shinzo Abe 安倍晋三

回译很难。中国人名若被译成外文之后也很难再回译成汉语，通常只好音译并加以注明。《中国翻译》上曾讲到 WanHoo 的故事。这位生活在大约 15 世纪的中国官员是试验火箭上天的第一人。这个故事据说来自于一本流传到国外的我国古代手抄本。英译本上并没有注上 WanHoo 的中文名。英汉翻译时，有人认为 WanHoo 代表官职，就译成"万户"，并称他为明朝士大夫。后来又有人提出，15 世纪的明朝时代，还没有"万户"这一官职，所以不应叫"万户"，并认为 WanHoo 是工匠。于是现在 WanHoo 有"万户""万虎""万火""万福""王虎"等多种音译法。

（2）除亚洲外的非英语国家人名

非英语国家的人名还包括非英语本族语者，如法国人、德国人、西班牙人、印度人、巴西人的人名等。这些人名有可能具有不同于英语本族语者人名的一些特征，如法国人的姓名由教名和父名或家族名组成，名姓之间有个 de，姓前有冠词 le 或 la，有男子专用名或女子专用名。翻译这些非英语本族语者的英语人名时，需遵从"名从主人"原则，不能按照这些人名在英语中的发音进行音译，而需按照它们在母语中的发音来译。通常，我们阅读时遇见的人名有很多是名人，有约定俗成的译法。请看下面例子：

Karl Liebknecht 卡尔·李卜克内西

Metternich 梅特涅

Montesquieu 孟德斯鸠

Erich Honecker 埃里希·昂纳克

Nikita Khrushchev 赫鲁晓夫

Robespierre 罗伯斯比尔

Le Corbusier 柯布西耶

Machiavelli 马基亚维利

Saint Simon 圣西门

Spinoza 斯宾诺莎

Tocqueville 托克维尔

Leon Trotsky 托洛茨基

Alexander Solzhenitsyn 亚历山大·索尔仁尼琴

也有译者在翻译人名时犯过一些错误，如在《挑战孔子》中曾把法国汉学家 Jean-François Billeter 翻译成"让·弗朗索瓦·比勒特"，而这位汉学家的中文名实为"毕莱德"。后来因为特别注意汉学家的中文名，所以曾经把法国汉学家 Victor Segalen 译成"维克多·谢阁兰"，把 Marcel Granet 译成"马塞尔·葛兰言"，把德国汉学家 Richard Wilhelm 译成"理查德·卫礼贤"，把比利时汉学家 Pierre Ryckmans 译成"皮埃尔·李克曼"。但实际上，汉译名中黑点前面的内容全都应该删掉，因为既然是中文名，就不应该再包含"维克多"之类的内容。

2. 中译英

将中文人名译成英语同样涉及前文谈到的很多问题。为了叙述方便，本节将人名分为中国人名和外国人名，在外国人名中着重人名回译。

1）中国人名

1958 年，全国人大通过了"关于当前文字改革工作和汉语拼音方案的报告"，改用国际通用的拉丁字母来拼写和标注汉字读音。在此之前，中国和国际上流行的中文拼音方案是威妥玛式拼音法（Wade-Giles romanization），所以曾经有一段时间，国内的出版物中存在两种译名同时出现的情况，给读者造成困惑。

中国人名英译的基本做法是：先姓后名，按汉语拼音音译；双姓和双名之间不留空格，也不用英语连字符"-"；姓和名的第一个字母大写，其余字母一律小写，如"司马迁"Sima Qian。

英译时容易出问题的是约定俗成的译名。如著名翻译家杨宪益和戴乃迭夫妇的英文名字分别是 Yang Hsien-yi、Gladys Yang。杨夫人是出生于北京的英国姑娘，小时候回到英国，1940年牛津大学毕业，婚前名字叫 Gladys Taylor，她是在牛津读书时认识杨先生的。有些港澳台地区和海外华人通常都有自己的英文名，也有一些采用旧式的威妥玛拼音，如：

李泽楷 Richard Li
宋楚瑜 James Song
黄仁宇 Huang, Ray
柳存仁 Liu, Ts'un-yan
欧阳桢 Eugene Chen Eoyang

2）外国人名

在汉译英时，常遇到需要把外国人名翻译成英语的情况，如历史人物和新闻人物等。多数情况下这是一个回译的过程，即查找这些人的英文名，直接使用即可。比如：

利玛窦（意大利汉学家）Matteo Ricci
安徒生（丹麦童话作家）Hans Christian Anderson
李约瑟（著名汉学家）Joseph Needham

值得注意的是由几个或多个汉字组成的日本人名，它们和中国人名一样是姓前名后，在翻译成英语时，不能采用汉语拼音，而应使用与这些汉字在日语读音的假名中对应的罗马字母。如前首相小泉纯一郎，翻成英文时写成 Junichiro Koizumi。吉田研作是 Yoshida Kensaku，其中姓在前，名在后，但为了符合英语姓名的习惯，把姓放在后面变成 Kensaku Yoshida。但翻译成英语时，到底是姓在前还是在后，并没有固定的标准。

（二）地名的翻译

与人名翻译相比，地名翻译相对简单些，但是也有一些问题需要注意，尤其是在翻译敏感的、正式的、重要的文件时。英语中地名的单复数形式，是否使用冠词都可能有隐含意义在里面，译者必须对当事国家或地区人民的民族情感和爱国情绪非常敏感。还要注意地缘政治变化给语言带来的问题，存在领土争议时，译者往往应采取中立的立场。下面，我们将分别讨论地名英译中和中译英时需要注意的问题。

1. 英译中

1）英语国家地名

《外国地名译名手册》给出了外国地名的汉译原则：惯用的地名译名予以保留；马列著作或自然科学中影响较大的地名译名适当予以照顾；同一外国地名存在不同汉字译名时，取其符合《外国地名汉字译写通则》和"汉字译音表"的译名。

事实上，许多英语地名都有固定的译法，遇到地名的翻译，首先是要参考《外国地名译名手册》等工具书；如果找不到，可以到这个国家的官方网站上去看看，或者搜索该地区发行量最大的报纸和网站，然后再决定怎么译。

常见的地名翻译方法有：

（1）音译：这是最常见的地名翻译方法。音译时，可对汉字做适当处理，如汉字名超过六个字时，外文轻音可以不译。连接词可用"-"代替，如 Wade and Stinson 译为"韦德-斯廷森"。以人名命名的地名，人名各部分之间需加点。地名如果只有一个词时，音译时可适当增加汉字，如 Leh "列城"，Bonn "波恩"。朝鲜、日本、越南等国的地名，过去和现在用汉字书写的，应沿用，不按音译；原来不是用汉字书写的，按拼音译写。如：韩国首都 Seoul，过去称"汉城"，现在改称"首尔"；朝鲜首都 Pyongyang 译为"平壤"；日本首都 Tokyo 译为"东京"；越南首都 Hanoi 译为"河内"。

（2）释义：把反映地理特征或地域风貌的明确含义解释出来，如 The Pacific Ocean 太平洋、the Black Sea 黑海、the Mediterranean Sea 地中海、Cape of Good Hope 好望角。

（3）音译与释义相结合：如 St. Paul 译为"圣保罗"等。

下面是地名翻译中需要特别注意的一些地方。

（1）英文拼写类似的地名，必须弄清地名所指的确切位置。例如：

Alexander I. 亚历山大岛（南极洲）

Alexander Arch. 亚历山大群岛（美国）

Alexander Bay 亚历山大贝（南非）

Alexandra 亚历山德拉（南非）

Alexandra 亚历山德拉（新西兰）

Alexandra Fiord 亚历山德拉菲奥德（加拿大）

Alexandretta 亚历山大勒塔（土耳其）

Alexandria 亚历山大（埃及）

Bashi Channel 巴士海峡（台湾以南菲律宾以北，南海和太平洋之间的重要通道）

Bass Strait 巴斯海峡（澳大利亚维多利亚州与塔斯马尼亚岛之间的水道）

（2）有些词可以作为人名也可以作为地名；同一个英文地名，可能指不同的国家或地方。翻译成汉语时译名可能相同，也可能不同。

Cicero 西塞罗，美国地名，不是古罗马政治家哲学家

Darwin 达尔文，澳大利亚地名

London 伦敦，英国首都，但也可以指加拿大安大略省的一个城市

Greece 希腊，也可能是美国一地名格里斯

（3）地名中的专名部分一般音译。例如，Mariana Islands 译为"马里亚纳群岛"。但也有例外，比如以有衔称的人名来命名的地名，衔称意译，如 Prince Edward Island 爱德华

王子岛；对地名中专名部分起修饰作用的形容词，一般意译，例如：

Great Nicobar Island 大尼科巴岛
Lower Egypt 下埃及
East Chicago 东芝加哥
East End 伦敦东区
Eastern District 东部区（英属开曼群岛，所罗门群岛）
Eastern Province 东部省（斐济、肯尼亚、塞拉利昂、乌干达等国）
Eastern London 东伦敦（南非，不是伦敦东部）
East New Britain Province 东新不列颠省（巴布亚新几内亚）
East York 东约克（加拿大）

（4）跨国度的河流和山脉，分别按其所在国名称译写。

Mae Nam Khong / Mekong River / Menam Khong 湄公河（澜沧江 Lancang River）
Mount Qomolangma 珠穆朗玛峰

2）非英语国家地名

非英语国家的地名，除了法语、德语等印欧语系的地名保留不变外，大部分是从其他语言翻译成英文的，所以常常需要再次翻译。同人名一样，若是中国和日本、韩国、越南、新加坡等国家使用汉字的，这种重复翻译往往就是回译。

（1）亚洲国家和地区的地名

中国地名回译一般都不会构成问题，但小地方的名称常需要核实，因为单看拼音并不知道究竟是哪个汉字。如若遇到不是汉语拼音的地名就比较麻烦，如 Shek Kip Mei 是香港九龙北部的一个叫"石硖尾"的地方，Victoria Peak 是"太平山顶"，Causeway Bay 是"铜锣湾"，Wanchai 是"湾仔区"，Mongkok 是"旺角"。请看更多例子：

Stanley 赤柱
Admiralty 金钟地铁站
International Commerce Center 环球贸易广场
Governor's House 总督府
the Prince Charles building 威尔士亲王大厦
Changi Airport 樟宜机场
Aichi 爱知县
Agano 上野
Nagoya 名古屋
Fukuoka 福冈
Waseda 早稻田

Okinawa 冲绳（从前叫琉球群岛，英文是 Ryukyu Islands）
Narita Airport 东京成田机场
Matsue 松江（不是上海的松江区）

（2）除亚洲外非英语国家和地区的地名

欧洲、拉美和中东等地名在翻译成英语时有不少是保留了原语拼写形式的，除了村庄或偏僻小街的地名外，很多都有标准译法。有些译名因为兼顾了音和意而受到特别的推崇，比如巴黎南郊名胜 Fontainebleau，中译名十分雅致，叫"枫丹白露"，假如译成"封丹不罗"，相信前往该地游览的中国旅客会减少一半。请看其他一些例子：

Potsdamer Platz 波茨坦广场
Vincennes 凡尔赛宫
the Arc de Triomphe 凯旋门
Hardenberg Strasse 哈登堡大街
Lachine 拉辛河
Roquefort-sur-Soulzon 洛克福尔镇
Les Halles 雷阿勒区
Le Louvre 卢浮宫
Lake Baikal 贝加尔湖
the Wailing Wall 哭墙
Pompidou 蓬皮杜中心
l'hôtel de ville 市政厅

2. 中译英

中译英地名主要采用音译的方法，但中文中也有非汉语拼音的地名，如卢沟桥的英文是 Marco Polo Bridge。少数民族地区的地名往往不是汉语拼音，如"日喀则"Shigatse (Xigaze)、"乌鲁木齐"Urumqi、"塔什库尔干"Tashkurghan。另外，还有因为历史原因而出现的新旧地名混用的情形。这里将从普通地名和少数民族地区地名两个方面展开讨论。

1) 普通地名

中国普通地名使用汉语拼音拼写，通常可以利用工具书找到标准译法，读者需要注意的是一些特殊情况。

（1）单音节地名翻译时应该加上范畴词，比如"恒山"译为 Hengshan Mountain，"淮河"译为 the Huaihe River，"渤海"译为 the Bohai Sea。

（2）同一个汉字构成的地名的英译可能不同，比如"峨眉山"Mount Emei，"象鼻山"the Elephant Hill，"大屿山"Lantau Island。

（3）地名中的同一个汉字有不同的读音和拼写，必须按中国地名词典的读音和拼写进行翻译，如"洞庭湖"the Dongting Lake，"洪洞县"Hongtong County。

2）少数民族地区地名

中华人民共和国国家测绘局和中国文字改革委员会在1976年发布的文件《少数民族语地名汉语拼音字母音译转写法》中，提出了用汉语拼音字母拼写少数民族地名的标准，其中有这样的条款："汉字译名如果原先来自少数民族语，后来变成汉语形式并且已经通用，可以按照汉字读音拼写，必要时括注音译写的原名。其他特殊情况具体斟酌处理。"例如：

湘西土家族苗族自治州 Tujia-Miao Autonomous Prefecture of Xiangxi
西藏自治区 Tibet Autonomous Region
拉萨 Lhasa
拉孜 Lhaze
格尔木 Golumd
昌都 Chamdo
察隅 Zayu County
拉达克 Ladakh
喀什 Kashgar
布达拉宫 The Potala Palace
罗布林卡 Norbulingka Summer Palace
大昭寺 the Jokhang Temple
扎什伦布寺 Tashilumpo, the New Palace of Bancan Lama
塔克拉玛干沙漠 Taklimakan Desert
喀喇昆仑公路 Karakoram Highway

（三）机构组织名的翻译

机构组织是非常宽泛的概念，包括国家机关、社会团体、企业和事业单位等任何为实现共同目标、任务或利益而有秩序、有成效地组合起来而开展活动的社会单位。这些机构组织的名称往往有固定的官方译法，译者的主要任务是遵循约定的译法，而不是另起炉灶自行翻译。

1. 英译中

1）外国机构组织名

机构组织名大多由专名和通名组成，通常情况下，专名采用音译，通名采用意译。但是，许多英语机构的名称都有固定的汉语译文，译者可结合机构的专业特征查阅相关领域的工具书。如今很多机构都有官方网站，提供双语甚至多语对照材料，译者只要留心搜索，也能检索到准确译法。翻译方法包括以下几种：

（1）意译。例如：

Amnesty International 大赦国际
Fellowship of Reconciliation 和平联谊会
the Black Liberation Army 黑人解放军
Young Americans for Freedom (YAF) 年轻美国人争取自由组织
the House Un-American Activities Committee (HUAC) 众议院非美活动委员会
the President's Council on Bioethics 总统生命伦理学委员会
Ecole Normale Superieure 高等师范学校
Bibliotheque Nationale 法国国家图书馆

（2）音译。例如：

Martinus Nijhoff 马蒂努斯·尼约夫出版社

（3）音译＋意译。例如：

Random House 蓝登书屋
the Los Alamos National Lab 洛斯阿拉莫斯国家实验室
the Manhattan Institute 曼哈顿研究所
Goethe Institute 歌德学院

此外，多数机构都有首字母缩略语，例如：

American Telephone & Telegraph (AT&T) 美国电报电话公司
Public Broadcasting Service (PBS) 美国公共广播公司

遇到机构名称相同的情况时，要特别注意对机构所在国家和专业领域等具体特征进行甄别，具体问题具体分析。比如著名石油公司 Royal Dutch Shell，在香港的译名是"蚬壳"，而在大陆的译名却为"壳牌"，因为"壳牌"听起来像粤语的"抄牌"，不吉利，会破坏公司的形象。又如，the National Council for US-China Trade 是"美中贸易全国委员会"（不是"美中贸易全国理事会"）；负责药品管理责任的政府机构，在英国是 Medicines and Healthcare Products Regulatory Agency "药品和保健品管理局"，在美国是 Food and Drug Administration "食品药品监督管理局"。

2）中国机构组织名

中国的机构组织名英译汉，更是一种回译，多数情况下都可以很容易找到正确译名。需要特别注意两点：一是历史上的机构组织名的翻译，译者必须熟悉中国的历史和文化；二是港澳台的机构组织，需要译者查证。如 the China International Trust and Investment Corporation（CITIC）是"中国国际信托投资公司"，不能译成"中国中信公司""中信集团""中信银行"或其他。请看部分机构组织名的中译：

the Grand National Theater 国家大剧院
the Social Development Department of the State Development Reform Commission 国

家发展改革委员会社会发展司

State Council Rural Tax Reform Work Leading Group 国务院农村税费改革工作领导小组

Information Office of the State Council 国务院新闻办公室

Standing Committee of Political Bureau of the CPC 中央政治局常务委员会

the Central Discipline Inspection Commission 中央纪律检查委员会

the Imperial Academy 国子监

2. 中译英

机构组织名的中译英大致可分成两种情况：一是把用汉字表达的外国机构组织名回译成英文；二是直接翻译我国的组织机构名。值得注意的是，有些机构，如法国的机构名，无须翻译成英语，可直接使用法语名称。

1）外国机构组织名

大都会艺术博物馆 the Metropolitan Museum of Art

法国国际农业展 Salon de l'agriculture

法国社会科学高等研究院 the École des Hautes Études en Sciences Sociales

纽约洋基队 New York Yankees

圣公会 Anglican church

2）中国机构组织名

我国的机构组织还无法实现专名专译，只有少数机构有约定俗成的英译，如国务院和中央各部委、大学及其他学术科研院所、大型企业等。遇到这类机构名称的翻译，必须查找官方的固定译法，或者多数人普遍使用的译法。即便找不到专业参考书，还可以在网络上找到相关信息，有依据地借用，不要另起炉灶自行翻译。不过也要注意甄选网上的信息是否准确。例如：

北京市人民政府 the People's Government of Beijing Municipality

北京市公安交通管理局 the Beijing Traffic Management Bureau

香港房屋委员会 the Housing Authority

香港工业总会 the Federation of Hong Kong Industries

香港马会 the Hong Kong Jockey Club

（四）书名和杂志名的翻译

书名和杂志名是专有名词的重要组成部分，翻译起来有特殊的要求，也有困难。多数书名或文章标题名是包含典故和隐含意义的，往往涉及不同历史时期、不同语言、不同领域的作品，而一旦出现翻译错误，不仅会给读者造成很多麻烦，而且会给译者的声誉带来损害。

书刊名常见的翻译方法有：音译、直译、释义、加注或直译与释义并用等四种。名篇名著和杂志多数都有固定的译名，译者的任务是通过各种手段查找正确译名。遇到没有固定译法的专名，则需要译者熟悉相关背景，采用适当方法把书名和期刊名翻译得传神、贴切。

1. 英译中

1）书名和文章名

文学作品名称的翻译往往有再创作的色彩。译者可以根据情节需要或者个人兴趣对书名进行大胆处理，以引起读者的兴趣。

商务印书馆于 1981 年从林纾翻译的著作中选择十本进行重印，如英国作家狄更斯（Charles Dickens）的名著 *David Copperfield*《块肉余生述》，现在的通用译名是《大卫·科波菲尔》；查尔斯·兰姆（Charles Lamb）和姐姐玛丽·兰姆（Mary Lamb）编的 *Tales from Shakespeare*《吟边燕语》，现译名《莎士比亚戏剧故事集》；斯托夫人（Harriet Beecher Stowe）的 *Uncle Tom's Cabin*《黑奴吁天录》，现译名《汤姆叔叔的小屋》；司各特（Walter Scott）的 *Ivanhoe*《撒克逊劫后英雄略》，现译名《艾凡赫》；华盛顿·欧文（Washington Irving）的 *The Sketch Book of Geoffrey Crayon*《拊掌录》，现译名《杰弗里·克雷昂先生的见闻札记》。

香港翻译学者金圣华列举了美国作家菲茨杰拉德的代表作 *The Great Gatsby* 的不同中文书名，如王润华的《大哉盖世比》、朱淑慎的《永恒之恋》、乔志高的《大亨小传》、范岳的《大人物盖茨比》等，并进行了分析："王译本的书名表面上是最'忠'于原著的，却使人想起什么'盖世霸王'之类的角色，与原著主人翁 Gatsby 的形象大有出入；朱译本的书名译得太浪漫、太含糊，题意表现得不够明确；范岳的译法略显呆板；乔志高所译的《大亨小传》一名，既表达了原著的本意，又符合中国传统文字中对仗精简的特色，可说是神来之笔，也是书名翻译中少见的佳作。"

翻译名家的经验固然值得我们学习，但有些译者因为知识水平和工作态度等原因犯下的种种错误同样值得我们警惕。曾有译者把马基雅维利的 *The Prince* 翻译成《王子》而不是通行的《君王论》，把尼采的 *Beyond Good and Evil* 译成《善恶之外》而不是《善恶的彼岸》，把瓦格纳的 *Der Ring des Nibelungen by Richard Wagner* 译成《歌剧院现场欣赏》而不是《尼伯龙根的指环》，把斯宾格勒的 *Der Untergang des Abendlandes* 译成《西方沉沦论》而不是《西方的没落》，把萨特的 *Les chemins de la liberte* 译成《自由之路》而不是《通向自由之路》，把 *La Nausee* 译成《厌恶》而不是《恶心》，把 *Words* 译成《词汇》而不是《词语》，把福柯的 *Surveiller et punir* 译成《监视与惩罚》而不是《规训与惩罚》，把卢梭的 *Narcisse* 译成《水仙》而不是《自恋者》，给读者造成一定的困扰。

请看书名和文章名翻译的其他例子：

Catch-22《第二十二条军规》
Bobos in Paradise《天堂里的波波族》
The Road to Serfdom《通向奴役之路》
A Theory of Consumption Function《消费函数理论》
The Bell Curve《钟形曲线》
Brave New World《美丽新世界》
Sickness unto Death《致死的疾病》
The Rape of Nanking: The Forgotten Holocaust of World War II《南京暴行：被遗忘的大屠杀》
"On Bullshit"《屁话考》
"Stopping By Woods on a Snowy Evening"《林边驻马风雪夜》
"Cupid is Cast Aside as Prenuptial Agreements Become Common"《婚前合同成为家常便饭，爱神被扔进垃圾堆》
"Taste the Wind"《风中感悟》
"War-Zone Journalism, a 'One Way Ticket to Hell'"《战区新闻报道工作——通向地狱的单程车票》

中国人写的英文著作或者本来是中文著作被翻译成英文的，英译中时则要特别注意回译的问题。如林语堂所著《生活的艺术》的英文名是 *The Importance of Living*，曾经有人把该书翻译成《论生活的重要性》而贻笑大方。

2）报刊名

知名的报刊一般都有固定的译法。如果遇到生僻的或者译者没有把握的情况，则必须查工具书确认；如果无法查到，可以在译名第一次出现时将原报刊名放在括号里附在译名后。编者从经常浏览的网站 Arts & Letters Daily 上摘取一些典型的报刊译名，希望读者能从中了解报刊名的语言特征和常见的翻译技巧。

The Australian《澳大利亚人报》（不是《澳大利亚日报》或《澳大利亚报》）
Beirut Daily Star《贝鲁特每日星报》（黎巴嫩）（不是《贝鲁特日报》）
Boston Globe《波士顿环球报》（美国）
Globe & Mail《环球邮报》（加拿大）（globe 通常都翻译成"环球"，《人民日报》的子报《环球时报》的英文名是 *Global Times*）
National Post《全国邮报》（加拿大）
Washington Post《华盛顿邮报》（Post 通常翻译成"邮报"）
Financial Times《金融时报》（英国）
New York Times《纽约时报》（Times 通常翻译成"时报"）
Guardian / Observer《卫报》（英国）
CS Monitor《基督教科学箴言报》（美国）

The Independent《独立报》（英国）
New Zealand Herald《新西兰先驱报》
Chicago Tribune《芝加哥论坛报》（美国）（其中的专名通常音译）
American Journalism Review《美国新闻评论》
American Review《美国评论》
Boston Review《波士顿评论》
Commentary《评论》
Common Review《公共评论》
Fortnightly Review《双周评论》
The Economist《经济学家》（另有《经济学人》的译法）
New Scientist《新科学家》
New Statesman《新政治家》
Forbes《福布斯》
Harper's《哈波斯》（音译）
History Today《今日历史》
First Things《第一要务》
Hoover Digest《胡佛文摘》
New Atlantis《新亚特兰蒂斯》
New Criterion《新批评》
New Republic《新共和》
New York Magazine《纽约杂志》
NY Times Magazine《纽约时报杂志》
New Yorker《纽约人》
Scientific American《科学美国人》（中国科学技术协会有个刊物叫《科学中国人》Scientific Chinese）
Der Spiegel《镜报》
Philosophy Now《哲学此刻》
Newsweek《新闻周刊》
Weekly Standard《旗帜周刊》（weekly 通常翻译成"周刊"）
Open Letter Monthly《人文月刊》(montly 通常翻译成"月刊"）
Wilson Quarterly《威尔逊季刊》（quarterly 通常翻译成"季刊"）

2. 中译英

书刊名英译时，需要特别注意英语读者的需要，必要时需做一些补偿性解释以免造成误解。

1) 书名和文章名

有些名著有不同的译法，如《红楼梦》就有 The Dream of the Red Chamber、The Story

of the Stone、The Dream of the Red Mansion 等译法。《西厢记》被译为 The Western Chamber 或者 The Romance of Western Bower，《牡丹亭》被译为 Peony Pavilion 或者 Soul's Return，《西游记》被译为 Pilgrimage to the West 或者 Journey to the West。这是不同译者所为，译法各有千秋，很难笼统地说哪个好哪个坏。若遇到此种情况，选择自己喜欢的即可。下面是杨宪益夫妇译和霍克斯译的《红楼梦》两个章节名的对比，读者可以有个直观的印象。

第 4 回　薄命女偏逢薄命郎，葫芦僧判断葫芦案
An Ill-Fated Girl Meets an Ill-Fated Man / A Confounded Monk Ends a Confounded Case (Translated by Yang Xianyi)
The Bottle-goured girl meets an unfortunate young man, / And the Bottle-goured monk settles a protracted lawsuit (Translated by David Hawks)
第 116 回　得通灵幻境悟仙缘，送慈柩故乡全孝道
Pao-yu, His Divine Jade Recovered, Attain Understanding in the Illusory Realm / Chia Cheng Escorts His Mother's Coffin Home to Fulfil His Filial Duty (Translated by Yang Xianyi)
Human destinies are revealed in a fairy realm, and the Stone is restored to its rightful owner, / Mortal remains are transported to their terrestrial home, and duty is discharged by a filial son. (Translated by David Hawks)

有些作品如吴运铎的《钢铁是怎样炼成的》，讲述的是中国版革命者的成长，英文译名是 The Making of a Hero，比较贴切。如果直接翻译成 How Steel Is Smelted，人们可能认为这是一本技术著作。

有时为了避免出现误解，译者可能在译文之外保留汉语拼音，例如：

《敦煌大藏经》Dun Huang Dazangjing / Buddhist Manuscripts from Dunhuang
《国语》Guo yu / Conversations of the States
《女诫》Nu jie / Admonitions for Women

2）报纸杂志名

中文报刊通常都有固定的英文译名。需要注意的是同名或类似名刊物的翻译，彼此略有不同。比如：《社会科学报》（Social Sciences Weekly）是上海社会科学院办的周报，《中国社会科学报》（Social Sciences in China Press）是中国社会科学院办的报纸，《中国社会科学》（Social Sciences in China）是中国社会科学杂志社主办的综合性杂志，中国社会科学院还办了一份英文版季刊 Social Sciences in China，复旦大学社会科学高等研究院有一份刊物《中国社会科学季刊》Chinese Social Sciences Quarterly。其他常见的报刊及其刊名翻译如：

《文汇报》Wenhuibao

《南风窗》Nan Feng Chuang（音译）
《人民日报（海外版）》People's Daily (Overseas Edition)
《参考消息》Reference News
《译林》Translations
《译丛》Renditions
《南方周末》Southern Weekly
《科学时报》Science Times
《中华读书报》Chinese Reading Weekly
《光明日报》Guangming Daily
《新华每日电讯》Xinhua Daily Telegraph
《文汇读书周报》Wenhui Reader's Weekly
《新民晚报》Xinmin Evening News
《广译：语言、文学、与文化翻译》Guangyi: Lingual, Literary and Cultural Translation（音译+意译）

（五）其他专名的翻译

1. 英译中

1）官职头衔

遇到英文官职头衔时，首先要弄清楚该官职头衔是哪个国家的，因为不同国家有不同的官职体系。比如英国的 Minister of Defence 就不能译成"国防部长"而须译成"国防大臣"；英国的 Chancellor of Exchequer 译成"财政大臣"；Chief Secretary to the Treasury 则译成"财政部秘书长"。美国的 Minister of Finance 译成"财政部长"，但日本的则要译成"财政经济大臣"，而且在日本政府 2001 年改革前要译成"大藏相"。日本的 Foreign Minister 至今仍然译成"外相"而非"外交部长"，美国的 State Secretary 不是"国务秘书"而是"国务卿"，Chief Cabinet Secretary 通常翻译为"内阁秘书长"，但在日本则译成"内阁官方长官"。

其次要知道官职头衔属于哪个行业，不同行业的说法是不一样的。比如，President of the European Council 是"欧洲理事会主席"而不是"欧盟总统"；President of the Board of Trade 是"贸易委员会主席"；President of World Bank 是"世界银行行长"或"世界银行总裁"；President of the Supreme Court of the United Kingdom 是"英国最高法院院长"。

总的来说，译者要掌握相关背景知识，善于寻找所需的信息，具备严肃认真的工作态度，千万不要想当然的翻译。

2）商品商标

翻译商标品牌名应优先采用该产品在目标语言国或地区的注册名，这需要译者仔细查找、搜寻，而不是自行翻译。如果确需译者翻译，则要注意目标市场的特殊情况和文化心理需要，以免造成文化误读，破坏企业的形象，影响产品的销售。翻译商标品牌名时需要迎合人们讨吉利的心理，选择优美、简洁，读起来朗朗上口，不仅吸引人的注意而且能给人留下深刻印象的词汇。例如：

Winston 温斯顿香烟
Gillette 吉列剃须刀
Pepsi 百事可乐
Seven Up 七喜
Mazda 马自达
Sprite 雪碧
Pentium 奔腾
Arrow 雅乐
Avon 雅芳
Poison 百爱神

3）节日名

节假日名是最能反映文化色彩的专名。虽然今天很多节日的宗教色彩已经非常淡化了，但英文中的某些节日起源往往与基督教有关，它们也都有固定译法。例如：

Christmas (December 25th) 圣诞节
Thanksgiving (the fourth Thursday in November) 感恩节
April Fool's Day (April 1st) 愚人节
Mother's Day (the second Sunday in May) 母亲节
Father's Day (the third Sunday in June) 父亲节
Easter (One Sunday between March 22nd and April 25th) 复活节
Valentine's Day (February 14th) 情人节
Veteran's Day (the Fourth Monday of Oct) 退伍军人节
Shabbat (the seventh day of the Jewish week) 安息日

2. 中译英

1）官职头衔名

汉语中官职头衔的翻译往往令人头疼，因为很多汉语官职头衔在英语中没有对应的表达方式，需要根据官职头衔的职责和权利统筹考虑来进行翻译。下面是一些常见官职头衔的译法：

总参谋长 Chief of General Staff
总会计师 Chief Account
首席财务官 Chief Financial Officer (CFO)
首席谈判代表 Chief Negotiator
总书记 General Secretary

秘书长 Secretary-general
总领事 Consul-general
总教练 Head Coach
护士长 Head Nurse
中央军委主席 Chairman of the Central Military Commission
办公厅主任 Director of the General Officer
公安局局长 Police Commissioner
行政/执行秘书 Executive Secretary
高级讲师 Senior Lecturer
省长 Provincial Governor
顾问 Advisor
副总理 Vice Premier
副市长 Deputy/Vice Mayor
副处/科长 Deputy Division/Section Chief
名誉主席 Honorary Chairman
名誉校长 Emeritus President

中国古代历史官衔的翻译难度更大，往往需要译者查阅专门的工具书方能确定译名。常见的历史官衔的译法如：

宰相 Prime Minister
吏部尚书 Minister of Personnel
兵部尚书 Minister of Military Affairs
刑部尚书 Minister of Justice
户部尚书 Minister of Revenue
工部尚书 Minister of Works
太师 grand preceptor
太傅 grand tutor
太保 grand protector
经筵官 the expositor
参知政事 Assistant Administrator
郡守 Prefect
县令/县长 Magistrate
刺史/州牧 Inspector / Governor
太守 Prefect
巡察使 Inspector
都督 Governor
肃政廉访使 Judicial Commissioner

巡抚 Provincial Governor
布政使 Civil Governor
节度使 Military Commissioner
司寇 Minister of Justice
司空 Minister of Public Works in ancient China
司徒 Minister of the Interior

还有很多中国文化词语的翻译都是先音译，后意译：

秀才：*Xiucai*, who passed the imperial examination at the county level in Ming and Qing dynasties
举人：*Juren*, prefect / provincial graduate
进士：*Jinshi*, graduates
榜眼：Runner-up (in imperial examinations)
探花：Second Runner-up (in imperial examinations)
贵妃 *Guifei* (Precious Consort)
太宗 *Taizong* (Grand Ancestor)

2）商标品牌

常见的商标品牌的翻译方法有两类：

（1）"简单借用"：利用汉语拼音、英文词汇、原有商标等稍加变通进行翻译。例如：

胡庆余堂 Hu Qing Yu Tang
杏花村 Xinghuacun
老凤祥 Lao Fengxiang
中华烟 Chunghwa（威妥玛式拼音）
张裕葡萄酒 Changyu
夏新 Amoi
李锦记 LEE KUM KEE
白天鹅 White Swan
回力 Warrior

（2）"大胆创新"：根据商品的特点、性能和功效，结合语言、文化、市场、心理等因素创造新词进行翻译。例如：

科龙 Kelon
雅戈尔 Youngor
新飞 Frestec
美的 Midea
海信 Hisense
神奇 Maqik（根据英文 magic 变异拼写）

3）节日名

常见的译法仍然是音译和意译两种，例如：

清明节 Qingming Festival

古尔邦节 Corban

那吾鲁孜节 Noroz Festival

吐鲁番葡萄节 Turban Grape Festival（音译）

端午节 Dragon Boat Festival

火把节 Torch Festival

宰牲节 Animal Slaughtering Festival

藏历新年 Tibetan New Year

刀杆节 Knife-Pole Festival

泼水节 Water-sprinkling Festival（意译）

总之，专名虽然意义单一，但翻译起来并不容易，需要长时间的知识积累和能力的不断提高。即使译者十分小心，有时也会犯下令人尴尬的错误。虽然如此，了解并掌握专名翻译的原则和方法，不断提高自身的知识修养和文化水平，加上一丝不苟的工作态度，就一定可以将错误降至最少，为读者提供规范的专名译名。

出国留学文书翻译

一、留学申请资料的翻译

进入 21 世纪以来，中国与外界的交往越来越频繁，大学生的视野也越来越宽，他们渴望走出去，体验多元文化，出国留学就是毕业生常选择的方式之一。但出国留学的程序十分繁琐，尤其是需要准备诸如申请书、毕业证明、学位证明、成绩单、推荐信和个人简历等一大堆的申请资料。这些资料往往都需要翻译成英文，因此准确无误而又地道地翻译这些资料，将有助于准留学生们踏入他们心仪的学府。否则，可能会延缓甚至耽搁他们的求学计划。以下介绍几类常用的留学申请文书及其翻译。

（一）毕业证书、学位证书的翻译

例1

××省普通高中毕业证书

照片 ××市教育局/委员会（钢印）盖普通高中毕业证书应用章（钢印）有效 学籍编号：×× 证书编号：×× ××省教育厅印制	**毕业证书** 学生××，性别×，××年××月××日生，于××年××月至××年××月在本校高中修业期满，经考核符合毕业标准，准予毕业。 校长（签章）：××× 学校（公章）：××× ××年××月××日

×× General Senior High School Graduation Certificate

Photograph ×× Municipal Education Bureau / Commission (Steel Seal) Effective only with the stamp of the special-purpose seal (Embossed Steel Seal) of the Graduation Certificate of the General Senior High School Student No.: ×× Certificate No.: ××	**Graduation Certificate** This is to certify that ××, male / female, born on ×× (month) ×× (date), ×× (year), studied at this school from ×× (month) ×× (year) to ×× (month) ×× (year), having completed all the required courses with qualified standing, is hereby granted graduation and duly awarded this Graduation Certificate of Senior High School. Principal: ×× (Signature) School: ×× Senior High School (Official Seal) Date: ××

例2

普通高等学校 毕业证书 照片 中华人民共和国教育部监制 编号：××	学生××，性别×，××年××月××日生，于××年××月至××年××月在本校××专业四年制本科学习，修完教学计划规定的全部课程，成绩合格，准予毕业。 校（院）长：××（签章） 校　名：××（公章） ××年××月××日 学校编号：××

General Institutions of Higher Education Certificate of Graduation Photograph Authorized under the supervision of the Ministry of Education of the People's Republic of China No.: ××	This is to certify that ××, Male / Female, born on ×× (month) ×× (date), ×× (year), pursued his graduate studies with this University for four years between ×× and ××, majoring in ××, and having completed all the courses required of graduate students and passed the thesis defence, graduated. (Signed) President of ×× University Date: ×× School Code No.: ××

例3

国徽 学士学位证书 （普通高等教育本科毕业生） （或者） （成人高等教育本科毕业生） 中华人民共和国教育部	照片 学生××，男/女，××年××月××日生。自××年九月至××年七月在××大学××学院××专业完成四年制本科学习计划，经审核符合《中华人民共和国学位条例》的规定，授予××学士学位。 　　　　　××（大学）：（公章） 学位评定委员会主席：××（签章） 　　　　　　　　××年××月 证书编号：××
(The National Emblem of the People's Republic of China) Diploma of Bachelor Degree / Bachelor Degree Certificate (For Graduates of Regular Higher Education) / (For Graduates of Adult Higher Education) Issued by the Ministry of Education of the People's Republic of China	Photograph This is to certify that ××, male / female, born on ×× (month) ×× (date), ×× (year), studied with the School of ×× of this University between September ×× (year) and July ×× (year), majoring in ××, and having completed the four-year degree program, is awarded the Bachelor's Degree of ×× in accordance with the Academic Degree Regulations of the People's Republic of China. ×× University (Seal) Chairman of Degree Appraisal Committee: ×× (Signature and Stamp) ×× (month) ×× (year) Diploma No. / Certificate No.: ××

（二）成绩单的翻译

例4

××大学学生成绩单

院系：××学院　　　专业：英语

学号：×××　　姓名：××　　性别：×　　班级：×××

课　程	性质	成绩	学分	学时	绩点	课　程	性质	成绩	学分	学时	绩点
思想道德修养与法律基础	必修	70	3	54	2	毛泽东思想与中国特色社会主义理论体系概论	必修	83	6	108	3.3
计算机基础	必修	71	3.5	64	2.1	英语听力（四）	必修	64	3	54	1.4
英语语音	必修	94	1	18	4.4	综合英语（四）	必修	60	6	108	1
英语口语（一）	必修	95	3	54	4.5	英语写作（一）	必修	71	2	36	2.1
英语听力（一）	必修	79	3	54	2.9	体育（四）	必修	95	1.5	32	4.5
英语阅读（一）	必修	72	3	54	2.2	当代世界经济与政治	任选	79	2	36	2.9
综合英语（一）	必修	72	6	108	2.2	旅游英语	任选	77	2	36	2.7
体育（一）	必修	90	1.5	32	4	教育学	任选	83	2	36	3.3
军训	必修	优秀	2	0	4.5	涉外文秘	任选	93	2	36	4.3
中国近现代史纲要	必修	74	2	36	2.4	英语辩论	任选	95	2	36	4.5
计算机程序设计基础	必修	79	3.5	64	2.9	普通心理学	任选	63	1	20	1.3
英语口语（二）	必修	95	3	54	4.5	翻译理论与实践	必修	82	3	54	3.2
英语听力（二）	必修	86	3	54	3.6	第二外语（德语）（一）	必修	75	3.5	62	2.5
英语阅读（二）	必修	69	3	54	1.9	高级英语（一）	必修	71	3.5	62	2.1
综合英语（二）	必修	74	6	108	2.4	英语写作（二）	必修	73	2	36	2.3
体育（二）	必修	84	1.5	32	3.4	英美文学	必修	80	4	72	3
心理卫生与健康	任选	80	1	18	3	公益劳动	必修	优秀	2	0	4.5
公共关系学	任选	68	1	18	1.8	国际贸易实务	限选	60	2	36	1
马克思主义基本原理	必修	72	3	54	2.2	外贸英语函电	限选	72	2	36	2.2
计算机应用基础	必修	66	3.5	64	1.6	大学美育概论	任选	88	1	20	3.8
英语听力（三）	必修	78	3	54	2.8	冶金概论	任选	99	1	20	4.9
综合英语（三）	必修	68	6	108	1.8	英语语言学	必修	81	2	36	3.1
英美文化	必修	93	3	54	4.3	第二外语（德语）（二）	必修	78	3.5	62	2.8
体育（三）	必修	93	1.5	32	4.3	高级英语（二）	必修	61	3.5	62	1.1
英语语法	任选	77	2	36	2.7	国际商法	限选	83	3	54	3.3
英语演讲	任选	94	2	36	4.4	国际商务谈判	限选	90	2	36	4
网上英语自主学习	任选	84	2	36	3.4	毕业论文	必修	良好	12	0	3.5
合同法	任选	90	1	20	4	毕业实习	必修	良好	6	0	3.5
总学分：162.5　　必修学分：131.5　　限选学分：9　　任选学分：22　　平均学分绩点：3.0											

××大学教务处
×年×月×日

Official Academic Transcript Form of xx University											
College: Foreign Language College				Major: English							
Student No.: ××		Name: ××		Gender: ×		Class: ××			
Name of Course	Type	Score	Credit	Class Hours	GPA	Name of Course	Type	Score	Credit	Class Hours	GPA
Moral Cultivation & Basics of Law	Compulsory	70	3	54	2	Mao Zedong Thoughts and Theoretical System of Socialism with Chinese Characteristics	Compulsory	83	6	108	3.3
Basics of Computer Science	Compulsory	71	3.5	64	2.1	English Listening (IV)	Compulsory	64	3	54	1.4
English Pronunciation	Compulsory	94	1	18	4.4	Comprehensive English (IV)	Compulsory	60	6	108	1
Oral English (I)	Compulsory	95	3	54	4.5	English Writing (I)	Compulsory	71	2	36	2.1
English Listening (I)	Compulsory	79	3	54	2.9	Physical Education (IV)	Compulsory	95	1.5	32	4.5
Extensive English Reading (I)	Compulsory	72	3	54	2.2	Contemporary World Economy and Politics	Free Elective	79	2	36	2.9
Comprehensive English (I)	Compulsory	72	6	108	2.2	English for Tourism	Free Elective	77	2	36	2.7
Physical Education (I)	Compulsory	90	1.5	32	4	Pedagogy	Free Elective	83	2	36	3.3
Military Training	Compulsory	A	2	0	4.5	English for Secretaries	Free Elective	93	2	36	4.3
An Outline of Modern & Contemporary History of China	Compulsory	74	2	36	2.4	English Debating	Free Elective	95	2	36	4.5
Basics of Computer Programming	Compulsory	79	3.5	64	2.9	General Psychology	Free Elective	63	1	20	1.3
Oral English (II)	Compulsory	95	3	54	4.5	Translation Theory and Practice	Compulsory	82	3	54	3.2
English Listening (II)	Compulsory	86	3	54	3.6	Second Foreign Language (Germany) (I)	Compulsory	75	3.5	62	2.5
Extensive English Reading (II)	Compulsory	69	3	54	1.9	Advanced English (I)	Compulsory	71	3.5	62	2.1
Comprehensive English (II)	Compulsory	74	6	108	2.4	English Writing (II)	Compulsory	73	2	36	2.3
Physical Education (II)	Compulsory	84	1.5	32	3.4	British and American Literature	Compulsory	80	4	72	3
Psychological Health	Free Elective	80	1	18	3	Community Service	Compulsory	A	2	0	4.5

Public Relations	Free Elective	68	1	18	1.8	International Trade Practices	Distributional Elective	60	2	36	1
Fundamentals of Marxism	Compulsory	72	3	54	2.2	English Correspondence for Foreign Trade	Distributional Elective	72	2	36	2.2
Basics of Computer Application	Compulsory	66	3.5	64	1.6	Introduction to Aesthetics	Free Elective	88	1	20	3.8
English Listening (III)	Compulsory	78	3	54	2.8	Introduction to Metallurgy	Free Elective	99	1	20	4.9
Comprehensive English (III)	Compulsory	68	6	108	1.8	English Linguistics	Compulsory	81	2	36	3.1
British and American Culture	Compulsory	93	3	54	4.3	Second Foreign Language (Germany) (II)	Compulsory	78	3.5	62	2.8
Physical Education (III)	Compulsory	93	1.5	32	4.3	Advanced English (II)	Compulsory	61	3.5	62	1.1
English Grammar	Free Elective	77	2	36	2.7	International Commercial Law	Distributional Elective	83	3	54	3.3
Public Speaking	Free Elective	94	2	36	4.4	International Business Negotiation	Distributional Elective	90	2	36	4
Online Autonomous English Learning	Free Elective	84	2	36	3.4	Graduation Thesis	Compulsory	B	12	0	3.5
Contract Law	Free Elective	90	1	20	4	Pre-graduation Internship	Compulsory	B	6	0	3.5

Total Credits:162.5 Compulsory Credits: 131.5 Distributional Elective Credits: 9 Free Elective Credits:22
Average GPA:3.0

Teaching Affairs Office of xx University (Official Stamp)
Date: ××

（三）推荐信的翻译

国外大多数高校都需要申请者提供两至三封推荐信，这也是申请者能否被录取的重要条件之一。推荐信一般由申请者的老师或院系领导所写，对推荐者在校期间的表现、学业及研究能力、工作能力、性格品德等进行评价，因而大多数推荐信都是赞美的话语。赞美的话语固然对申请者有利，但如果内容空洞，尽是华而不实的辞藻，便会适得其反。因此在翻译推荐信的时候一定要仔细斟酌，要客观、公正、诚恳地表述出推荐人的意图。同时要合理地处理一些形容词，不要过多地使用 wonderful、outstanding、excellent 等词语；注意避免过多和重复地使用形容词，尽量通过转换词性或使用其他表达方式使推荐信更加客观，更加有说服力。

例5

亲爱的女士/先生：

我很高兴向您推荐我的学生××申请××大学。

××于2008年被××大学录取。从那时起，她就在我的班上学习，我们已经成为挚友。××是一位可靠而坚持不懈的好姑娘。平易近人，与同学相处和睦。2008—2009学年度，我教她××和××两门课程。在课堂上，××总是认真听讲，积极参与课堂活动，表现活跃，并能很好地完成老师布置的作业，在她所在的班级成绩名列前茅。2009年9月—2010年6月，她顺利通过了全国计算机等级考试和大学英语六级考试。特别是她所撰写的××论文质量高，体现了较强的理解能力和在专业方面的深厚功底。

除了学术活动，她较强的社会能力也给我留下了深刻的印象。在课外活动中，××充分展现了组织、领导和协调能力。在过去四年里，她成功组织了多项活动，尤其是她诙谐幽默的口才给大家留下了深刻印象。××能在课内课外找到平衡，这在大学生中是不多见的。

因此，我很开心且荣幸地推荐××读贵校的研究生课程。感谢您对她申请所做出的友好/谨慎决定。如果我能提供任何帮助，或其他信息，请随时联系我。

推荐人：×× （签名）

2012年5月25日

May 25th, 2012

To Whom It May Concern:

It is my great pleasure to recommend to you a former student of mine, Miss ××, to be an ideal candidate for ×× University.

Miss ×× was enrolled by ×× University in 2008. Since then she has been in my class, and we have been good friends. Miss ×× is a reliable and persistent girl. She has a pleasing manner and is well liked by her associates. She took two of my courses during the 2008–2009 academic year, as follows: ×× and ××. In my class, Miss ×× always listened attentively, did excellent work and handed in well-written assignment. Compared against other students, I would say that Miss ×× ranks among the top students. She also passed the National Computer Rank Examination and the College English Test Band 6 from September 2009 to June 2010. In particular, her paper on ×× was of exceptionally high quality, and showed that she fully understands and has a strong background in her major field.

Besides her academic activities, I was also impressed by her social activities and capabilities. Miss ×× has a strong ability in organizing, leading and managing extracurricular activities. In the past four years she co-ordinated many activities successfully, and many were impressed by her leadership, humor and eloquence. Miss

×× strikes a delicate balance in academic and extracurricular activities, which is rarely seen in university students.

Therefore, I am happy to highly recommend ×× for admission to your graduate program. Your kind / serious consideration of her application would be most appreciated. If I can be of any further assistance, or provide you with any further information, please do not hesitate to contact me.

Sincerely,

×× (Signature)

Professor, Dean (Title)

×× School, ×× University

（四）个人简历的翻译

英文简历有两种说法：resume 和 curriculum vitae。现在美式英语常用 resume 或 CV，而英式英语常用 curriculum vitae。Curriculum vitae 可简写为 CV，较正式。个人简历的格式多种多样，但其主要内容无外乎个人基本情况、教育背景、工作经历、个人特长、个人业绩以及职位目标等。格式上可采用左顶格式、中间式、混合式（将各项主要标题置于页面中心，而各项中的不同内容采用左顶格式）。简历要求实事求是、简明扼要、语言规范，在翻译时尽量使用简单句或短语，将句子简化为短语结构。

例 6

个人情况

姓　　名：刘崇瑞

性　　别：男

出生日期：1992 年 12 月 5 日

婚姻状况：未婚

健康状况：良好

通讯地址：湖北武汉武汉科技大学黄家湖校区南三楼 401 室

邮　　编：430065

电　　话：027-68895632

电子邮箱地址：liuchongrui@mail.wust.edu.cn

个人爱好：小提琴，足球

学历

2004 年 9 月—2007 年 7 月武汉市第六十四中学（初中）

2007 年 9 月—2010 年 7 月武汉市第二中学（高中）

2010 年 9 月—2014 年 7 月武汉科技大学城建学院土木工程系

获奖情况

全国高中物理联赛二等奖（2008）

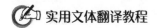

湖北省优秀学生干部（2009）

武汉科技大学学业优秀一等奖学金（2011—2014）

武汉科技大学结构设计大赛三等奖（2012）

武汉市大学生数学建模竞赛二等奖（2013）

证明人

朱真民，武汉市第二中学校长（电话027-82711285）

李宏建，武汉科技大学土木工程系教授（电话027-68895638）

Name: Liu Chongrui

Gender: Male

Date of Birth: December 5, 1992

Marital Status: Single

Health: Excellent

Address: Room401, Dormitory Building South No. 3, Wuhan University of Science and Technology (WUST), Wuhan, Hubei, P. R. China

Postcode: 430065

Telephone: 027-68895632

E-mail: liuchongrui@mail.wust.edu.cn

Hobbies: Violin, football

Education

 September, 2010–July, 2014, Civil Engineering Department of Urban Construction College of WUST, Wuhan, P. R. China

 September, 2007–July, 2010, No. 2 Middle School (Senior high school), Wuhan, P. R. China

 September, 2004–July, 2007, No. 64 Middle School (Junior high school), Wuhan, P. R. China

Prize

 Second prize of the National Physics Contest for senior high school students (2008)

 Outstanding Student Leader of Hubei Province (2009)

 First-grade Scholarship for Excellent Student of WUST (2011–2014)

 Third prize in the Structure Design of WUST (2012)

 Second prize in Mathematical Modeling for university students, Wuhan (2013)

References

 Zhu Zhenmin, principal of No. 2 Middle School, Wuhan, P. R. China, Postcode: 430010, Phone: 027-82711285

Li Hongjian, Professor of Civil Engineering Department, WUST, Wuhan, P. R. China, Postcode: 430065, Phone: 027-68895638

二、证明材料的翻译

除了申请材料外,各种涉外证明材料也必不可少。如去美国自费留学需要办理申请人的毕业公证书(Notarization of Graduation Certificate)、成绩单公证书(Notarization of Academic Transcript)以及美国接受院校发布的留学生签证资格证书,即符合资格认证证明(Certificate of Eligibility for Admission),方能获得美国签证。又如:去日本、德国等国探亲或定居,一般需要办理亲属关系公证书(Notarization of Family Relation);去智利探亲或定居,除了办理亲属关系公证书外,还需要办理出生公证书(Notarization of Birth)和婚姻状况公证书(Notarization of Marital Status)等。

这些证明或公证书一般有固定的格式和术语,具有域外法律效力,因而翻译时应当遵循笃信逼真、严谨得当、格式规范的基本原则。

(一)学历(学位)公证书证词的翻译

例7

兹证明前面的复印件与××大学(学院)于××年××月××日发给××的编号为××的毕业证书(或学位证书、结业证书、肄业证书等)的原件相符。原件上××大学(学院)的钢印、印章和校长××的签名(或签章)均属实。

This is to certify that the photocopy attached hereto conforms to the original of Graduation Certificate (Degree Certificate / Completion Certificate / Attendance Certificate / Incompletion Certificate) with the certificate No. ×× and issued to ×× by ×× University / College on ×× (date), and both the official seals (including embossed steel seal) of ×× University / College and the signature of the President ×× affixed to the said certificate are authentic.

(二)成绩报告单公证书证词的翻译

例8

兹证明前面的复印件与××校于××年××月××日发给××成绩单原件相符。原件上"××学校"的印章及"××学校学籍管理专用章"均属实。

This is to certify that the photocopy attached hereto is in conformity with / conforms to the original of Official Transcripts issued to ×× by ×× University on ×× (date), and that the official seal "×× University" and "special Seal for Students' Status of ×× University" affixed to the original are found to be genuine and authentic.

（三）亲属关系证明书的翻译

例 9

申请人：××（男/女，××年××月××日出生，现住××）
关系人：××（男/女，××年××月××日出生，现住××）
……
兹证明申请人××是关系人××的××（申请人与关系人之间的称谓）
Applicant: ×× (male / female, born on ××, residing in / at ××)
Interested Party / Parties: ×× (male / female, born on ××, residing in / at ××)
…
This is to certify that the applicant, ××, is ×× of the interested party ××.

（四）居民户口本的翻译

例 10

居民户口本
中华人民共和国公安印制

户别	家庭户 / 集体户 / 非农业户	户主姓名	
户号		住址	
省级公安机关户口专用章		户口登记机关户口专用章（××市公安局××派出所）××年××月××日签发	
承办人签章			

常住人口登记卡

姓名		与户主关系	
曾用名		性别	
出生地		民族	
籍贯		出生日期	
本市（县）其他住址		宗教信仰	
公民身份证件编号		身高		血型	
文化程度		婚姻状况		兵役状况	
服务处所		职业	
何时由何地迁来本市（县）			
何时由何地迁来本址			

承办人签章：　　　　　　　　　　　登记日期：　××年××月××日

Household Register Under
the Supervision of the Minister of Public Security of P. R. C

Household Category	Family Household / Collective Household / Non-agricultural Household	Name of Household Head	
Household Number		Domicile	
Seal for Household Registration of ×× Provincial / Municipal Public Security Department (Seal) Signature of Registrar: ×× Seal for Household Registration of ×× Municipal Public Security Bureau ×× Police Station (Seal) Date of Issue: ××			

Registration Card for Permanent Resident

Name		Relationship with Household Head	
Former Name		Gender	
Birthplace / Place of Birth		Nationality	
Native Place		Date of Birth	
Other Address in This City (Country)		Religion	

Citizen ID Card No.		Height		Blood Type	
Education Background / Highest Education Attained		Marital Status		Military Service	

Place of Work		Occupation	
Residence Before Migrating to This City(Country) and Date of Migrating			
Residence Before Migrating to the Present Residence and Date of Migrating to the Present Residence			

Seal of Registrar: Date of Registration:

（五）大学在读证明的翻译

例11

在读证明

兹证明××，男，于2010年9月进入我校学习，现是我校管理学院会计学专业大三在读学生，如一切顺利，将为2014年7月毕业并取得管理学士学位证书。

××大学（公章）

2012年××月××日

Credential

××, male, has been enrolled into our university in September 2010. Now he is a junior student of the Accounting Department, Management School in our University. If everything goes smoothly, he will obtain a graduate certificate and a Bachelor of Management Degree in July 2014.

×× University (Seal)

×× (month) ×× (day), 2012

（六）考试成绩报告单证明的翻译

例12

大学英语四、六级考试成绩报告单

CET

姓名：××
学校：××
院系：××
准考证号：××
身份证号：××
考试时间：××
总分：××

照片

听力 35%	阅读 35%	综合 10%	写作与翻译 20%

成绩单编号：××

教育部高等教育司
委托发布单位：
大学英语四、六级考试委员会（章）
考委会网址：www.cet.edu.cn

College English Test Band 4 / Band 6 Transcript

CET

Photograph

Name: ××

School: ××

Department: ××

Candidate No. / Admission Card for Examination No.: ××

ID No.: ××

Test Time: ××

Aggregate Score: ××

Listening Comprehension 35%	Reading Comprehension 35%	Comprehension Contents 10%	Writing and Translation 20%

Report Card Serial No.: ××

Higher Educational Department of the Ministry of Education Organization for Certificate-Issuing College English Test Band 4 and Band 6 Board of Examination
Website: www.cet.edu.cn

例 13

全国大学英语四、六级口语考试证书

CET

××大学

学生××于××年××月参加全国大学英语四、六级考试口语考试，成绩达到A/B/C/D等。特授予证书。

证书编号：××
填发日期：××

教育部高等教育司
委托发布单位：
大学英语四、六级考试委员会（章）

Certificate of CET Spoken English Test

CET

×× University

This is to certify that the student ××, took the examination of CET Spoken English Test in ×× (month) ×× (year), and has been awarded the Grade A/B/C/D Certificate.

Certificate No. ××
Date of Issue: ××

Higher Educational Department of the Ministry of Education
Entrusted Organization for Certificate-Issuing
College English Test Band 4 and Band 6 Board of Examination
(Official Stamp)

（七）银行存款证明书的翻译

例14

中国银行
存款证明书

号码：××

日期：2012–10–27

兹证明截止到2012年10月27日××先生/女士在我行存款如下：

存款号码	货币	金额	存款起息日
××	人民币	￥50,000.00	2008–05–03
××	人民币	￥50,000.00	2009–03–27
××	人民币	￥200,000.00	2011–04–25
以下空白	以下空白	以下空白	以下空白

中国银行××支行

有权签字人：××（签章）

说明：

1. 本证明书不得用于担保和变相融资，不得用作提取上述存款的凭证；
2. 本证明书为正本，涂改复印无效。

Bank of China
Certificate of Deposit

No.: ××

Date: Oct 27th, 2012

We hereby certify that on Oct 27th, 2012. Mrs. / Mr. x x has a deposit account with this bank as follows:

Deposit Certificate No.	Currency	Amount	Value Date of Deposit
××	CNY	￥50,000.00	2008-05-03
××	CNY	￥50,000.00	2009-03-27
××	CNY	￥200,000.00	2011-04-25
The End	The End	The End	The End

Bank of China ×× Branch (Official Stamp)

Authorized Signature: ××

Note:

1. This certificate of deposit is non-negotiable and cannot be presented to the bank for payment.

2. This certificate of deposit is made out in one original. Change or copy hereof is invalid.

（八）父母双方收入证明书的翻译

例15

工作（在职）收入证明

兹证明××，男/女，系××父亲/母亲，自××年以来一直在我公司××部门工作，担任××，其近三年的收入为：

年份	年薪	奖金	其他	总收入
2011	60000	10000	2000	72000
2012	65000	12000	2500	79500
2013	70000	18000	3500	91500

证明人：××

联系电话：××

×年×月×日

Employment (Income) Certification

This is to certify that Mr. / Mrs. ××, ××'s father / mother, has been working in this company as ×× since ×× (year). His / Her incomes with this company in the past three years are as follows:

Year	Salary (yuan)	Bonus (yuan)	Others (yuan)	Total (yuan)
2011	60,000	10,000	2,000	72,000
2012	65,000	12,000	2,500	79,500
2013	70,000	18,000	3,500	91,500

Approved by:

Telephone:

×× (month) ×× (date), ×× (year)

参考答案

练习一

一、回答下列问题。（略）

二、分析下列两个文本的文体特点。

1. 该文本属于典型的法律文体，其特点突出表现在：（1）较多地使用法律术语（如 pledge、lien、encumbrances 等）、古旧词（herein、hereby、hereof 等）、动词的抽象名词（如 execution、approval、consent、performance 等）、情态动词 shall 等；（2）句子较长，结构复杂；（3）表达规范，逻辑严谨；（4）语言平实，冷静客观，很少使用评价性形容词和副词，鲜少使用修辞手段；等等。

2. 该文本属于便条的一种。读者是熟人，因此语言较口语化，所用词语较常见；句子较短，第一句甚至不是完整句；称呼方式是熟人间的常用方式，直呼其名，不带姓和头衔。

三、通过互联网查找三到五篇下面文本的可比较文本，分析这些可比较文本的文体特点，并在此基础上，将此文本译成英文。

Certificate of Graduation
from Institution of Higher Education

C. No. 201414118023

This is to certify that Wang Dawei, male, born on June 1, 1992, having completed the four-year undergraduate program of English in College of Foreign Languages of this university with satisfactory grades, is hereby awarded this Certificate of Graduation.

Kong Jianyi, President
Wuhan University of Science and Technology
June 30, 2014

练习二

一、将下列句子译成中文。

1. 从临界温度以上的温度快速冷却会形成坚硬的组织结构,而缓慢冷却则产生相反效果。

    (提示:为了使译文通顺,将 from above the critical temperature 译成"从临界温度以上的温度",建议不要直译成"从高于临界温度"。此外,"快速冷却"和"缓慢冷却"形成概念对称,very slow cooling 中的 very 可以省译)

2. 由于这种碳成分的化学分离完全发生在固态中,因此产生的组织结构是铁素体与渗碳体的精密机械混合物。

    (提示:为了避免歧义,建议不要将 a fine mechanical mixture of ferrite and cementite 译成"一种精致的铁素体与渗碳体的机械混合物",这会让读者误以为"是一种精致的铁素体",而原文要表达的意思是"精密机械混合物")

3. 材料被放入加热桶中,混合后压入模腔,冷却硬化成模腔的形状。

    (提示:此句翻译注意语言表达精练简洁。建议不要译为"材料被注入一个被加热的桶,混合(由固态融化成黏稠的液态)后被挤进铸模。材料可以在铸模(型腔)中冷却和凝固成铸模的形状。"这样有违简洁的原则)

4. 电火花加工技术被广泛应用于修复变硬的上、下模具。

    (提示:注意不要将 finds many applications in 中的语法功能词 find 译成"发现")

5. 电火花能量集中在某一部位加工,一段时间后将材料以小切削量的方式逐渐地切除掉。

    (提示:增译"能量集中在某一部位加工")

二、将下列句子译成英文。

1. The three main types of databases are statistical, bibliographic, and full text.

    (提示:原句的宾语"类型"转译成英语句的主语,而原句的主语"数据库"转译成英语句主语的定语)

2. Most metals have relatively high densities, especially compared to polymers.

    (提示:原句的主语"密度"转译成英语句的宾语,而原句的定语"金属"转译成英语句的主语)

3. Metallurgy is the physics, chemistry, and engineering related to metals from ore extraction to the final product.

    (提示:"总称"译成英语时可省译,原句中"涉及……"译成过去分词结构作后置定语)

4. Steel can be hardened to resist cutting action and abrasion, or it can be softened to permit machining.

（提示：原句"通过硬化"和"通过软化"转译成英语句的谓语，"来抵抗"和"以允许"转译成英语句的目的状语）

5. As oil is deep found in the ground, and its presence cannot be determined by a study of the surface.

（提示：主动语态转译成被动语态）

三、将下面的科技短文译成中文。

淬 火

淬火就是把钢件加热至或超过其临界温度范围，后使其快速冷却的过程。如果钢的含碳量已知，合适的加热温度可参考铁碳合金状态图得到。然而，若钢的成分未知，则需做一些预备试验来确定其温度范围。

按如下步骤操作较为合理：将这种钢的一些小试件加热到不同的温度后淬火，再通过硬度试验或显微镜检查观测结果。一旦获得正确的温度，其硬度和其他性能都将有明显的变化。在任何热处理作业中，加热的速率都很重要。热量以一定的速率从钢的外部传导到内部。如果钢被加热得太快，其外部比内部热，就不能得到均匀的组织结构。如果工件形状不规则，为了消除翘曲和开裂，最根本的是加热速率要缓慢。截面越厚，加热的时间越长，这样才能达到均匀的结果。即使在加热到正确的温度后，工件也应在此温度下保持足够长的时间以让其最厚截面达到相同温度。

四、将下面的科技短文译成英文。

Natural Energy

Energy in nature comes in many different forms. Heat is a form of energy. A lot of heat energy comes from the sun. Heat can also come from a forest fire or, in much smaller quantities, from the warm body of a mouse. Light is another form of energy. It also comes from the sun and from the stars. Some animals and even plants produce small amounts of light energy. Radio waves and ultraviolet rays are other forms of energy. Then there is electricity, which is yet another sort of energy.

There are some things about energy that are difficult to understand. The fact that it constantly changes from one form to another makes energy rather like a disguised artist. When you think you know what energy is, suddenly it has changed into a totally different form. But one thing is certain: energy never disappears and, equally, it never appears from nowhere. People used to think that energy and matter were two completely different things. We now know that energy and matter are interchangeable. Tiny amounts of matter convert into unbelievably huge amounts of nuclear energy. The sun produces nuclear energy from hydrogen gas and, day by day, its mass gets less, as matter is converted to energy.

五、翻译下列论文摘要。

1. 英译汉

摘要：泡沫金属是一种用途广泛的工程材料。为了探究相应的多孔构件在弯矩作用下的失效模式，本研究为高孔率网状泡沫金属建立了一种多孔材料的简化结构失效模型，包括孔棱的拉断、剪切和屈曲等。同时确立了由于弯矩载荷作用而导致孔棱失效的系统的数理关系，其中包括孔棱失效时多孔构件所受名义弯矩与孔率的数理关系，以及对应于各种失效形式的条件表征。结果表明：当此类多孔构件承受弯矩载荷时，脆性材质多孔体的孔棱多发生拉断破坏，韧性材质多孔体的孔棱则可能发生剪切断裂。

2. 汉译英

Abstract: The cavitation model significantly influences the calculational results for oil film bearings. Present cavitation models mainly focus on the characteristics of the oil film pressure profile. The oil cavitation mechanism was used here to develop a cavitation model based on the solubility of air in lubricating oil. The model was used in computational fluid dynamics (CFD) simulation of a journal bearing with the calculated results with different eccentricities agreeing well with experimental results, including load capacity, side leakage flow and oil film rupture position. The model is more accurate than the Half-Sommerfeld cavitation model with excellent algorithm stability.

练习三

一、将下列句子译成英文。

1. Seeing the steeply-rising and grotesque peaks, hearing the streams flowing through valleys, walking through the dense forest, one can't help acclaiming the perfect nature of Zhanjiajie National Forest Park.

2. Laoshan Scenic Area is thickly covered with trees of many species, which add credit for its

scenery. Among them over 300 are considered rare and precious, half of which are plants under State-top-level Protection. The most famous species include gingko and cypress.

3. Qingdao is a charming coastal city, whose beauty often appears in poetry. It is not hot in summer or cold in winter. Its 40-kilometer-long scenic line begins from Tuandao at the west to Xiaqing Temple of Laoshan Mountain at the east end.

4. The Imperial Palace, which is the most superb and the best preserved of all ancient architectural complexes, occupies an area of 720,000 square meters. The build-up part, made up of chambers reaching more than 9,000, has a total floor space of some 150,000 square meters.

5. Zhangjiajie National Forest Park is amazing for its peaks and hills, tranquil for its vales and dales, and elegant for its woods and forests. In spring, the mountain flowers are in full blossom with enticing fragrance; in summer, the cool temperature offers an escape from the summer heat; in autumn, the mountains are dyed in diverse colors with ripe fruits, and in winter, the snow-clad peaks are not to be missed.

二、将下列句子译成中文。

1. 巴德兰兹国家公园位于南达科他州西南部，占地224 000英亩，园内冲蚀而成的石丘遍地，尖峰林立，与美国最大的草原保护区融为一体。1939年确定为巴德兰兹国家保护区，1978年更名为"巴德兰兹国家公园"，这里拥有世界上最丰富的化石资源。尽管人类已有11 000多年的历史，但在这些生成于2300—3500万年前的渐新世化石面前，还是要自惭形秽。

2. 夏威夷群岛位于太平洋北部，拥有世界上最迷人的海滩。洁白纯净的沙滩，绿绿的悬崖，夏天，这里是人们冲浪、游泳和潜水的圣地。夏威夷的气候温和宜人，树木葱绿，鲜花绽放，一年四季都令人赏心悦目。

3. 埃菲尔铁塔是19世纪最伟大的工程奇迹，高300米，用7 000吨铁建造而成。许多人认为它是世界上最美的建筑，同时也是巴黎首屈一指的旅游胜地。

4. 弗吉尼亚自然风光多姿多彩。切萨皮克湾是北美渔产最丰富的港湾，而蓝岭则是世界上最古老的山脉。

5. 多元文化之城、花园之城、乐趣之城、艺术之城、通道之城——这些都是人们赋予新加坡的美称。无论是前来度假、想尽享其美的游客们，还是那些希望在新加坡定居的人们，这些美称展示了新加坡城——这个令人兴奋的目的地——能给他们带来什么。

练习四

一、将下列句子译成英文。

1. Our Corporation established on July 1, 1999, is a large state-owned enterprise, and an entity with state authorization for investment and capital management directly under the supervision of Chinese central government.
2. Enclosed please find out one set of the shipping documents covering this consignment.
3. The Certificate is issued in single original (valid with seal), and any duplicate or photocopy of the Certificate bears no validity.
4. Customer should conduct his/her transactions at the counters of the Bank in person. He/She might be required to show his/her identification documents. The Bank may refuse to act on the instruction of such customer if he/she fails to do so.
5. All disputes arising out of this insurance between the Insured and the Company shall be settled through friendly negotiation. Where a settlement fails after negotiation, such dispute shall be submitted to arbitration or to court for legal action.

二、将下列句子译成中文。

1. 诚请贵公司给我方寄来你方最新目录。
2. 请妥善保存本水单,在二十四个月内可凭本人护照和此水单兑回外汇。
3. 本存款证明不具有银行经济担保作用,不得作为质押凭证;本存款证明仅证明存款人在一定期限内在银行有一定存款,且该存款在存款证明有效期内不得办理取现、转账。
4. 自开户成功日起三个月后,不论客户是否确实使用该账户,本行将按月从客户账户内自动扣除账户管理费。
5. 所有装运单据应以航空挂号信的形式分两次直接寄至开证行。

三、将下面的商务信函译成中文。

尊敬的西蒙·史密斯博士:

  3月20日来信收悉。谨致衷心谢意。现已对我校艺术教育部设备更新事宜重新进行了考量。现需要购置几台新的计算机及程序用于图形设计学习。随函附上计算机相关设备清单及新设备安装后的楼层布局草图。

  此致!

简·多伊，
艺术教师
janeannedoe@email.com
附：设备购置计划及楼层布局方案

四、将下面的单据条款译成英文。

A bank assumes no liability or responsibility for the form, sufficiency, accuracy, genuineness, falsification or legal effect of any document, or for the general or particular conditions stipulated in a document or superimposed thereon; nor does it assume any liability or responsibility for the description, quantity, weight, quality, condition, packing, delivery, value or existence of the goods, services or other performance represented by any document, or for the good faith or acts or omissions, solvency, performance or standing of the consignor, the carrier, the forwarder, the consignee or the insurer of the goods or any other person.

练习五

一、将下列句子译成英文。

1. Crimes of embezzlement and bribery, crimes of dereliction of duty committed by State functionaries, and crimes involving violations of a citizen's personal rights such as illegal detention, extortion of confessions by torture, retaliation, frame-up and illegal search and crimes involving infringement of a citizen's democratic rights—committed by State functionaries by taking advantage of their functions and powers—shall be placed on file for investigation by the People's Procuratorates.
2. Defence lawyers may, from the date on which the People's Court accepts a case, consult, extract and duplicate the material of the facts of the crime accused in the current case, and may meet and correspond with the defendant in custody. Other defenders, with permission of the People's Court, may also consult, extract and duplicate the above-mentioned material, and may meet and correspond with the defendant in custody.
3. Article 35 A partnership's debts shall be secured with the partners' property in proportion to their respective contributions to the investment or according to the agreement made. Partners

shall undertake joint liability for their partnership's debts, except as otherwise stipulated by law. Any partner who overpays his share of the partnership's debts shall have the right to claim compensation from the other partners.

4. The people's governments of provinces, autonomous regions and municipalities directly under the Central Government may establish their local standards for the discharge of pollutants for items not specified in the national standards; with regard to items already specified in the national standards, they may set local standards which are more stringent than the national standards and report the same to the competent department of environmental protection administration under the State Council for the record.

5. If the defendant is blind, deaf or mute, or if he is a minor, and thus has not entrusted anyone to be his defender, the People's Court shall designate a lawyer who is obligated to provide legal aid and serve as a defender.

二、将下列句子译成中文。

1. 在本条中，由独立评估师确定的价值为双方认定的合营公司价值。但如果相关法律就国有资产的保全另有规定，双方可同意对上述评估价值在相关法律允许的范围内进行调整。

2. 转让方应承诺如果关联受让方未能履行本合同项下的义务，转让方并不因此解除该义务，仍对本合同条款的全部履行和任何违约所致的损失与关联受让方承担连带责任。

3. 如果合营公司的经营规模比双方原来预期的规模有大幅度缩减，或合营公司持续遭受严重亏损，导致在双方商定的业务计划中所未预期的盈余保留负数，或在任何相关法律允许或双方一致同意的情况下，则双方可以协议按原有出资比例减资。

4. 假如存在一项关于注册资本的所有转让均必须经过原审批机关批准的规定，而且因为该原审批机关要求公司提供经过签署的同意书、优先权放弃书和经过一致通过的董事会决议，则按照条款5.6（b）的规定，对任何此等转让的假定同意就很难实现和生效。

5. 在发生争议，且该争议需要友好协商或仲裁时，各方当事人应当继续履行各自在本合同项下的各项权利和义务，但争议所涉及的各项事项除外。

三、将下面的短文译成英文。

　　The law protects citizens who are wrongfully deprived of their liberty by another. If you have been the subject of an arrest by the police or other state or federal official which took place without probable cause, in bad faith or if someone deprived you of your liberty, you may be able to make a claim and recover damages, including attorney's fees and costs. Your rights are safeguarded by both the United States Constitution and state common law. False imprisonment is frequently alleged by a person who feels that he or she was unlawfully arrested. If the police did not have "probable cause" to arrest you, you can sue for false imprisonment. "False arrest" is really just a type of false imprisonment. The police have probable cause when there are enough facts to lead a reasonable person to conclude that you are committing or have committed a crime. This is a considerably higher standard than the mere "suspicion" an officer needs in order to stop you briefly to investigate possible criminal activity. If you feel that you have been the victim of a false imprisonment or false arrest you may wish to contact an attorney. Time is of the essence in many of these cases. In some instances, claims may be barred if they are not brought within a short time after the date of the occurrence. For more information, talk with an attorney.

四、将下面的短文译成中文。

未成年人（或者十八周岁以下的人）通常因所犯轻罪在少年法庭接受审判。轻罪与谋杀、强奸、殴打相比没那么严重，但理应受到惩罚。犯罪通常分为重罪与轻罪。一般来说，重罪是严重的犯罪行为，在监狱受罚；轻罪是性质不严重的犯罪，受罚方式为罚款或在县级/本地监狱关押。伪造是重罪，但超速驾驶属于轻罪。刑法中的法则定义了什么是重罪、什么是轻罪。有时，根据犯罪情节不同，同样的罪名可能重判也可能轻判。比如说，初犯可能轻判，但重复犯同一轻罪，就会发展为重罪。对未成年人犯罪的惩罚，根据犯罪的严重性以及看是否有前科，可以缓期执行或送到少年管教所。如果未成年人有很长的严重犯罪记录，则可能被视为成年人，在普通法庭接受审判。要了解更多有关未成年人法的信息，请向律师咨询。

练习六

一、请翻译下面的新闻消息。

美国宣布停止遣返年轻非法移民

美国总统奥巴马上周五公布了一项停止遣返年轻非法移民的新政策，大约80万在幼时进入美国的年轻非法移民因此至少受益两年。这项新政策有望在美国总统大选之际为奥巴马赢得拉美裔选民的选票。

奥巴马在白宫告诉记者："这不是大赦，也不是豁免，更不是取得国籍的途径也不是一项长期措施。"奥巴马补充说，有关美国移民政策的长期解决方案应该由国会出台。

民主党人奥巴马颁布此项政策意在讨好美国越来越多的拉美裔民众，争取在今年11月6日的美国总统大选中战胜共和党候选人米特·罗姆尼，成功连任。罗姆尼对非法移民的态度非常强硬。美国大多数非法移民都是拉美裔。

奥巴马政府表示，按照该计划，符合上述条件的非法移民将可以在美国生活工作和生活两年，并有资格继续延期。

奥巴马一直支持允许非法移民的子女在美学习和工作的政策，但由于共和党反对，类似决议一直没能在国会获得通过。

此举绕开了国会，也使共和党面临挑战。据估计，美国目前有1200万非法移民，很多共和党人认为对遣返的宽容就等于对非法移民的大赦。

共和党立法者批评了奥巴马的新政，指责他逐渐渗入了国会立法管理美国国籍的权威。

但奥巴马说："这只是一项临时的消除差距的政策，使我们能够更明智地集中资源，同时让有才能、有动力且爱国的年轻人得到一丝安慰，也让他们看到希望。"

这其中有很多非法居民已经在美国生活了大半生，在美国就读中小学。奥巴马说："他们的心理和思想上都是美国人，除了名义上，他们在所有方面都是美国人。"

在新罕布什尔州进行竞选宣传的罗姆尼说："总统的举动使得达成长期的移民政策更困难了。"

根据移民组织的估计，有多达200万非法移民在幼年时期就来到美国，并一直生活在这里。美国官员表示，新政策将影响到大约80万人。

二、请对下面两例新闻进行编译。

1. 汉译英

Indian PM Vajpayee Concludes China Tour

Indian Prime Minister Atal Bihari Vajpayee left Shanghai for home Friday afternoon, concluding his six-day official visit to China.

Vajpayee arrived in the Chinese capital Sunday evening as guest of Chinese Premier Wen Jiabao. It is the first visit to China by an Indian prime minister in 10 years.

Chinese Premier Wen Jiabao and Vajpayee Monday signed a declaration on principles for bilateral relationship and comprehensive cooperation. The declaration, together with a series of other documents signed between China and India, set out the foals and guiding principles for bilateral relations and outlined cooperation of the two countries in various fields.

Vajpayee visited china in 1979 as Indian foreign minister.

2. 英译汉

新加坡批评美国人权报告双重标准

新华网新加坡8月16日电 新加坡外交部16日发表声明说,美国国务院在2011年度人权报告中再次歪曲关于新加坡政策法规的事实和真相,报告体现出的双重标准令人不安。

声明说,新加坡一直以来施行的《内部安全法案》主要用于应对内部安全威胁,包括威胁公共秩序、威胁社会和谐稳定,以及颠覆和恐怖活动等。

《内部安全法案》允许在特定情况下对特定人员不经审判采取预防性拘留措施。美国国务院5月24日发表的年度"国别人权报告"批评新加坡近年来利用这一措施对付那些"所谓的恐怖分子",指责新加坡对一些罪犯施以鞭刑的行为。

新加坡外交部在声明中回应说:"如果不是使用双重标准,我们很难理解美国在自身仍然保留关塔那摩监狱的前提下,却对(新加坡的)《内部安全条例》无端地指责。"

新加坡外交部说,关塔那摩监狱凌驾于美国法律体系之上,而新加坡《内部安全条例》则对预防性拘留提供了合理的法律框架,制定了规则。

声明同时痛批美国人权报告年复一年地歪曲事实真相。"美国国务院对真相似乎并不感兴趣。并且,依据其意识形态,遵循事实是得不出他们想要的结论的。正因为这样,该报告难言客观。"

声明说:"新加坡政府并未声称其体系是完美的,或者在其他国家同样适用。我国政府通过民主选举和法治对公众负责。并将持续以公民的权益为准绳,以社会权利和义务的平衡发展为目标,改进政策。"

练习七

一、将下列广告文本译成英文。

1. Leader of Range Hood

   Improving human cooking environment

2. Achieve profitable growth

   Emphasize innovation

   Preserve a good name

   Be a good place to work

3. Science and Technology   Creative Home Decoration

4. Mantanghong— sincere corporation
5. The choice of a new generation.
6. We lead, others copy.
7. Fly China South Airlines,
   Discover the Amazing Canton.
   Enjoy your Guangzhou 72-hour Visa-free Transmit.
8. SM Home Appliances are leading the global home appliance market with innovation and top technology. Excellent quality, stylish design and reliable performance build the brand image of SM. The materials used by SM Home appliances must undergo strict screening and rigorous testing. Requirements of consumers are the most important for us.
9. Life can be really hectic in the city. Since we don't eat nor exercise regularly, meeting our daily nutritional needs is almost impossible! To help us lead a healthy life, we'll be sure to take F&H Health Supplements to replenish daily nutritional needs.
   F&H Health Supplements are made from natural food essence concentrations, which are derived from high-tech extraction process. With nearly 100 products to fulfill our specific health needs, staying healthy every day has been made easy.
10. Malt flavor, slim figure,
    And filled with chocolate flavor
    To your heart's content,
    Giving you 100% pure joy and satisfaction.

二、将下列广告文本译成中文。

1. 箭牌瓷砖——高品位生活选择。
2. 利落型变。
3. 卓越创新，商用之本。
4. 让我们共建智慧的地球
5. 更好版型，更好夹克。
6. 客户远近不同，如何转瞬即达？
   联邦快递，优势由人启动。
7. 你比你想象的更强大。
8. 当巧克力味道恋上红酒风味的香醇，
   交织的浓情滋味，
   忘却了时光，融化了心。

9. 机身重量仅 158 克，22.5 毫米的超薄工艺设计，能轻松放入任何大小的口袋或手提包中。采用顶级金属机身，搭配奢华的皮纹处理，使 NX mini 成为品位追求者的不二之选。

10. 1912—2012 年

江诗丹顿酒桶形腕表的百年辉煌历程

马耳他系列四款全新腕表

  1912 年，江诗丹顿的首款酒桶形腕表诞生，自此，成为此系列的经典之作。

  2012 年，江诗丹顿重新设计了马耳他系列，并推出四款秉承经典设计理念和风格却更为现代的新型腕表。表厂同时还借此机会，推出了专为马耳他陀飞轮腕表设计的全新酒桶形机芯：由江诗丹顿自行开发和制作的 2795 型机芯，并镌刻日内瓦印记。

  全新的马耳他系列不仅是江诗丹顿向过去一个世纪酒桶形腕表创作取得的丰硕成果的致敬之作，也宣扬了其追求经典、优雅和精湛技艺的品牌价值观。

练习八

一、将下列句子译成英文。

1. After comprehensive considerations of future development trends and conditions, the plenum proposed the following as the major targets for economic and social development in the next five years: to maintain stable and relatively fast economic growth; to achieve major development in economic restructuring; to universally raise people's incomes at a relatively fast pace; to remarkably enhance social construction; to continuously deepen reform and opening-up; to achieve substantial progress in transforming the economic development pattern; to remarkably strengthen the country's comprehensive national power, international competitiveness and capability in shielding against risks; to make notable progress in meeting people's living and cultural demands; and to further consolidate the foundation for the making of a better-off society in an all-round way.

2. Article 12 The Administrative Center manages the corporate meeting room. Meeting conveners need to apply orally to the director or vice director of the Administrative Center before using the meeting room. Overall considerations should be given to the size and urgency degree of the meetings when more than one meeting has been applied for at the same time.

二、将下面的会议记录译成中文。

森林残留物讨论小组

主持人：王晶鑫

记录人：艾米·韦尔奇

与会者：王晶鑫，艾米·韦尔奇，刘裘德，托尼·尼古特

  森林残留物研讨小组经讨论，认为当前此类原料最好的所在地为美国东北部。这些原料来源可以分为三类：首先是采伐剩余物、燃料处理和修剪树木的废弃物；其次是磨坊废渣和酒类制浆残渣；第三是城市木材剩余物。本组成员一致认为，关于这些原料储存数量的最佳信息来源是主管能源或林业以及设有林学专业或自然资源相关院系高校的国家机关。也有一些州有自己的储备记录。例如，西弗吉尼亚州在县级单位可查寻全州境内伐木和磨坊残渣的详细信息。此外，还可利用丰富的空间分析工具。

三、将下面的祝酒词译成中文。

祝 酒 词

尊敬的女士们、先生们、朋友们：

  晚上好！

  为庆祝上海市政府与联合国区域发展中心联合主办的第二届"城市可持续发展和防灾管理"国际培训研讨班开幕，今晚我们大家欢聚一堂，举行欢迎宴会。首先，请允许我代表上海市政府向远道而来的中外政府官员、专家、学者和朋友们表示热烈的欢迎！向为这次培训研讨班如期举办而付出辛劳的联合国区域发展中心的各位朋友及同行表示衷心的感谢！

  中国有句俗话："有朋自远方来，不亦乐乎？"各位来宾，虽然你们来自不同国家和民族，我们彼此之间不曾相识，但是为了人类可持续发展和防灾减灾事业，今天，我们走到了一起。为此我感到格外荣幸。我相信，这次培训研讨活动必将进一步增进中国与其他亚洲国家的合作与交流。

  最后我提议：为预祝"城市可持续发展和防灾管理"国际研讨班取得圆满成功，为在座的女士们、先生们、朋友们的身体健康、家庭幸福，干杯！

四、将下面的会议通知译成英文。

MEETING NOTICE

Subject: INFORMATION SECURITY COMMITTEE MEETING NOTICE

Dear Committee Member:

  You are cordially invited to participate in a meeting of the Information Security Committee (ISC), Section of Science & Technology, American Bar Association (ABA), on Friday / Saturday, October 18–19, 2006, in Boston. The Committee will advance its development of commercial key escrow guidelines as well as consider digital signature legislative initiatives in the several States and other jurisdictions, and continue its consideration of digital signature evidence and liability. Consistent with Section policy, ISC meeting participants MUST be members of both the ABA and the ABA Section of Science and Technology. Please contact Ann Kowalsky, Manager Section of Science & Technology, at ABA offices in Chicago by phone: +1-312-988-5599, fax: +1-312-988-5628, or e-mail: sciencetech@attmail.com for membership information. It is possible to become a paid member of the ABA and the ISC at the meeting. Dan Greenwood, ISC member, has kindly agreed to host the meeting at the Information Technology Division of the Commonwealth of Massachusetts. Dan can be reached at 617-973-0071 or DGreenwood@state.ma.us for directions & logistical information.

Meeting details appear below. I look forward to seeing you in Boston.

Sincerely,

Michael S. Baum

Chair, Information Security Committee

Section of Science & Technology, ABA

练习九

一、将下列句子译成中文。

1. 祝财运亨通!
2. 愿您健康长寿!
3. 请多保重!
4. 祝您今后获得更大成就。
5. 在这特殊的日子,向您致以新年的祝福,希望不久我们能相聚在一起。
6. 祝新年快乐,并愿你幸福吉祥,前程似锦。
7. 愿新年带给你和你所爱的人许多美好的事物和无尽的祝福!

二、将下面的邀请函译成中文。

亲爱的先生 / 女士:

感谢您 2011 年 1 月 9 日的来信。我很高兴您于下月来武汉。我很荣幸将在商品交易会上与您会面。

我公司将于2011年1月13日晚在假日酒店举办招待会。届时期待您的光临。

此致

CEO 迈克

三、将下面的邀请函译成英文。

Dear Susan,

  I know you are interested in traditional Chinese painting, so I'm sure you'll be interested in Mr. and Mrs. Xie Peng. They are coming here for supper next Sunday, September 12, and we'd like you and Mark to come, too.

  Mr. and Mrs. Xie Peng are very charming couple that we met in London last summer. They have a wonderful collection of traditional Chinese painting of various stages, and I understand that Mr. Xie Peng is quite an authority on traditional Chinese painting. I'm sure you and Mark will thoroughly enjoy the evening in their company.

  We're planning supper at six, and that will give us a nice long evening to talk. If I don't hear from you before then, I'll be expecting you on the 12th!

四、将下面的请柬译成英文。

Dr. and Mrs. Hou Lei

request the pleasure of your company

at a small dance

at ten o'clock

Sunday, the eighth of November

The Culture Square

练习十

一、将下列启事译成中文。

1.

征稿启事

  由中国国家体育总局、第16届亚运会组委会和中国体育科学学会联合主办，广州体育学院承办的"第16届亚洲运动会科学大会"将于2010年10月10至12日在广州召开。本次大会的主题是"亚洲体育：科学与发展"。会议将邀请境内外知名体育科学研究专家发表主旨演讲。大会现向亚洲各国和地区的学者征集论文。

会议内容：体育管理；体育媒体和体育媒体传播；经济学与体育产业；体育史；体育法和体育立法；奥林匹克研究；体育旅游；亚运会的历史、现状与未来。

摘要提交：2010年3月20日至6月30日

通讯地址：中国广州市广州大道中1268号，邮编：510500。

官方网站：http://www.agsc.gz2010.cn

第16届亚运会科学大会秘书处：电话：+86 20 38025032 / 38025033

传真：+86 20 38024567

电子邮件：gztykyc@163.com

中国国家体育总局
广州亚运会组委会
中国体育科学会
广州体育大学

2.

《纽约时报书评》：先读先评为快！

订阅《纽约时报书评》，就可以在周日前收到报纸。

每周只需1.75美元，就可拥有《纽约时报书评》，就可先人一步知晓文学界的新动向和重要事件。

通过最新鲜出炉的书评和《纽约时报》畅销书榜，最炙手可热的书籍和作家一览无余；

儿童书籍专栏，为各个年龄段的孩子找到很棒的书；

暑期阅读专栏：这里有你喜欢在海滩上、飞机上和度假时阅读的书；

假日图书专栏：提供本季最精彩图书最简明扼要的介绍，让你把握阅读时尚；

拥有这一切，每周只要1.75美元。

如需电话联系，请拨打我们的服务中心电话：1-800-698-4637。客户服务工作时间：周一至周五早上五点至夜里十二点，周六周日早五点至下午五点。

3.

招聘行政助理

工作职责：主要是与票据有关的Excel工作表的数据输入；生成发票数据和附件；发送外包产品报价要求；查验项目数量、协助制定销售定价；生成月度报告；确认销售价格和货品计价指令；根据需要协助项目经理工作；其他指派的行政工作。

技能要求：2—3年文书或行政工作经验，票据或金融从业者优先考虑；熟悉计算机操作包括Excel的使用；良好的组织和沟通能力。

招聘公司：当纳利集团
地点：马萨诸塞州海德公园
工作性质：全职员工
工作类别：行政/文书

4.

招领启事

2010年4月6日上午8点左右，我机场工作人员在安检口捡到一个黑色牛皮LV钱包，内有一张从深圳到成都的EU2218航班的机票、一张信用卡、一张身份证和一些港币。请失主与我们联系，电话：0755-23235666，或直接到机场问讯处认领。

深圳国际机场

二、将下列启事译成英文。

1.

Contribution Invited & Subscription Welcomed

Since its launching, our journal has won favor of many an author, to whom we offer our heartfelt gratitude here. Would all the authors please give us your detailed address, email and telephone numbers when submitting your papers so that we could contact you in time?

As we are limited in human resources and email capacity, we kindly ask all our authors to submit your manuscripts in the printed form via the post office, which will prevent any delay in your paper processing. And would all our authors not post us your papers more than once, as this will bring us much inconvenience? Besides, we'd like to ask our authors to keep well your original manuscript since your submissions won't be returned to you.

Subscribe to 2012 *Anhui Sports Science and Technology*, a bi-monthly journal (CN34-1153/N; ISSN1008-7761) available to the general public. For each issue, you will have to pay only 10 yuan, and 6 issues in a year cost only 60 yuan!

Contact Information: Editorial Department of *Anhui Sports Science and Technology*, Anhui Vocational and Technical College of Sports, 1 People's Street, Baohe District, Hefei 230051, China. Tel.: 0551-3686559.

Editorial Department of *Anhui Sports Science and Technology*

2.

School Doctor Recruitment

Charity School of Suzhou Industrial Park is a special education school mainly open to mentally retarded children and teenagers. To further its development, the

School is now recruiting one school doctor.

    1. Application Time: May 15, 2012–June 15, 2012

    2. Requirements:

(1) Good health, observation of laws and regulations, serious attitude towards work, loving heart toward children, and sound professional ethics;

(2) Diploma or degree in medicine or related fields. Outstanding applicants may also be accepted even if they do not meet this requirement. Applicants with experience of working as a school doctor are preferred.

    3. Application Procedures:

Applicants should post their resumes, photocopies of all credentials (including education certificate, certificate of professional titles, qualification certificate, etc.) and a recently two-inch photo to the School. They may also come to the School directly for an interview.

    4. Contact：

(1) Address: 211 Yangdong Road, Suzhou Industrial Park, Suzhou 215021, China.

(2) Tel.: 0512- 86660212 (Please ask for Mr. Gu)

(3) Email: sipras@163.com

(4) School Website: www.sipras.net

3.

Missing

Jan. 10, 2012

    Li Ke, an 11-year-old boy, of medium height, with short black hair, small round face, small eyes and a pair of glasses. He wore white T-shirt, blue jeans and black sneakers when he was lost in Qianmen Street on Jan. 8. Please contact Mr. Li at 010-65885962 if you've ever seen him or have any information about him. Great reward is offered.

Mr. Li

练习十一

一、将下列公示语译成英文。

1. Beef & Pork
2. Escalator
3. Parking by Permit Only

4. No Pets Allowed
5. Tickets from all stations to all stations available
6. Crew Only
7. Secure all loose items
8. Better Living, Better Future
9. For your own safety, please do not sit here. Thank you!
10. Good Luck / Drive Carefully / Safety First in Driving

二、将下列公示语译成中文。

1. 塑料制品
2. 无糖百事可乐
3. 专用停车位
4. 禁用食物饮料
5. 休闲运动服
6. 年度减价促销
7. 天天省钱
8. 团体服务
9. 今年更多新货，价格更加优惠
10. 建设生态型花园式现代化大城市